Increasing Persistence

Increasing Persistence

Research-Based Strategies for College Student Success

Wesley R. Habley
Jennifer L. Bloom
Steve Robbins

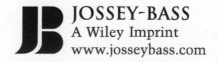

JOSSEY-BASS
A Wiley Imprint
www.josseybass.com

Figures 8.1, 8.2, 8.3, 8.4, 9.1, 9.2, 9.3, 9.4, 9.5, 9.6, 10.1, 10.2, 10.3, 10.4, and 10.5 and Tables 7.5, 7.6,
7.7, 7.8, 7.9, 7.10, 7.11, 8.5, 8.6, 10.1, 10.2, 10. 3, 10.4, 10.5, 10.6, 10.7, 10.8, 11.1, 11.2, 11.3, 11.4,
11.5, 11.6, 11.7, 13.1, 13.2, 14.1, 14.2, 15.1, 15.2, and 15.3 are used by permission of ACT and are
© 2012 by ACT, Inc. All rights reserved. Tables 8.1, 8.2, 8.3, 8.4, 8.7, 8.8, 8.9, and 8.10 Copyright
© by the American Psychological Association. Reproduced with permission. The Official citation
that should be used in referencing this material is Robbins, S., Allen, J., Casillas, A., Peterson,
C. H., & Le, H. (2006). Unraveling the differential effects of motivational and skills, social, and
self-management measures from traditional predictors of college outcomes. Journal of Educational
Psychology, 98(3), 589. The use of this information does not imply endorsement by the publisher.

Library of Congress Cataloging-in-Publication Data

Habley, Wesley R.
     Increasing persistence : research-based strategies for college student success / Wesley R. Habley,
Jennifer L. Bloom, Steve Robbins.—First edition.
        pages cm
     Includes bibliographical references and index.
        ISBN 978-0-470-88843-8 (cloth), ISBN 978-1-118-22108-2 (ebk.),
        ISBN 978-1-118-23484-6 (ebk.), ISBN 978-1-118-25947-4 (ebk.)
        1. College dropouts—United States—Prevention.   I. Bloom, Jennifer L.   II. Robbins,
     Steven B.   III. Title.
     LC148.15.H33   2012
     378.1'69130973—dc23

                                                                                    2012011835

Printed in the United States of America
FIRST EDITION
HB Printing   10 9 8 7 6 5 4 3 2 1

Contents

Preface   xiii

The Authors   xxix

Acknowledgments   xxxiii

Section 1: What Do We Know About Retention and Persistence to Degree?   1

1 Defining, Refining Perspectives on Student Success   3

2 Overview of Theoretical Perspectives on Student Success   19

Section 2: The Case for Intensified Campus Efforts   41

3 The Demographic Challenge   43

4 Public and Private Benefits of College   63

5 Retention or Recruitment: Examining the Return on Investment   79

Section 3: Core Components of Student Success   99

6 Institutional Culture and Student Engagement   101

7 Academic Preparation   117

8 Psychosocial Characteristics   137

9   Career Development   161

10   Assessing the Impact of Academic, Psychosocial, and Career Development Factors on College Student Success   181

Section 4: Proven Student Success Practices   211

11   Historical Perspective on *What Works in Student Retention*   213

12   Assessment and Course Placement   235

13   Development Education Initiatives   255

14   Academic Advising   283

15   First-Year Transition Programs   311

Section 5: Making Student Success a Priority   335

16   Expanding the Retention Framework: Implications for Public and Institutional Policy   337

17   Creating a Student Success Culture   363

18   Leading the Campus to Student Success   383

Appendices

A   What Works in Student Retention, 2004 Survey   397

B   What Works in Student Retention?   411

References   425

Name Index   453

Subject Index   459

Figures and Tables

Figures

Figure 2.1   Habley Retention Model
Figure 8.1   Student A: Low ACT, Low Motivation
Figure 8.2   Student B: Low ACT, High Motivation
Figure 8.3   Student C: High ACT, Low Motivation
Figure 8.4   Student D: High ACT, High Motivation
Figure 9.1   Example Outcomes That Effective Career Planning Can Support at Different Life Stages
Figure 9.2   The World-of-Work Map
Figure 9.3   Percentage of Students Persisting in Their Current Major, by ACT Scores and Interest-Major Fit
Figure 9.4   Percentage of Students Attaining a Timely Postsecondary Degree, by ACT Scores and Interest-Major Fit
Figure 9.5   Example Interest-Major Fit
Figure 9.6   Example of Risk Indices
Figure 9.7   Career Decision Making Model
Figure 9.8   Career Center Resources by Stage
Figure 10.1   Pyramid for Success
Figure 10.2   Expected and Hypothesized Paths to Outcomes
Figure 10.3   Results–Path Model
Figure 10.4   College Developmental Course Best Practices
Figure 10.5   Three Pillars of Success
Figure 12.1   Test Only Placement Model

Figure 12.2   Multiple Conditions Placement Model
Figure 12.3   Multiple Considerations Placement Model
Figure 12.4   Decision Zone Placement Model
Figure 18.1   Considerations in the Change Process
Figure 18.2   Attitudes Toward Change

Tables

Table 3.1   Projected Population Percentage Change
                in Regions by Race and Hispanic Origin:
                1995–2025
Table 3.2   Projected Percentage Change in Public High
                School Graduates from 2008–09 to 2018–19 by
                Region and Race/Ethnicity
Table 3.3   High School to College Pipeline by Race/
                Ethnicity
Table 3.4   Degree Completion Rates at Two- and Four-Year
                Institutions
Table 3.5   Percentages of College Participation/Completion
                of the U.S. Population 18 Years and Over by
                Race and Hispanic Origin: 2009
Table 4.1   The Public and Private Benefits of Higher
                Education
Table 5.1   Cost to Recruit an Undergraduate Student:
                1983–2009
Table 5.2   Cost of Tuition and Fees: 1983–2009
Table 5.3   Impact on Tuition/Fees Revenue: Typical
                University
Table 5.4   Impact of 3% Improvement in Retention
                Rates on Tuition/Fees Revenue:
                Typical University
Table 5.5   Impact on Cost of Recruitment
Table 7.1   NAEP Pipeline—Reading Scores 1984–2008
Table 7.2   NAEP Pipeline—Math Scores: 1986–2008
Table 7.3   NAEP Pipeline—Writing Scores: 1998–2007
Table 7.4   NAEP Pipeline—Science Scores: 1996–2005

Table 7.5   Entering Class Admission Test Pipeline
               to College—2006–2010
Table 7.6   ACT's College Readiness Benchmarks
Table 7.7   Percentage of Students Meeting Benchmarks
               for 8th Graders, 10th Graders, and High School
               Graduates (2010e)
Table 7.8   Percentage of Students Achieving at Least
               a 2.5 GPA by Performance Level
Table 7.9   Percentage of Students Retained from
               Year-to-Year by Performance Level
Table 7.10   Percentage of Students Making Reasonable
               Progress by Performance Level
Table 7.11   Percentage of Students Persisting to Degree by
               Performance Level
Table 8.1   Salient Psychosocial Constructs from
               Educational Persistence Model and Motivational
               Theory Perspectives
Table 8.2   Psychosocial and Study Skill Factor Constructs
               and Their Representative Measures
Table 8.3   Meta-Analysis Results: Predictors of Retention
Table 8.4   Meta-Analysis Results: Predictors of GPA
Table 8.5   SRI Scale Definitions and Sample Items by
               Student Control Factor
Table 8.6   Sample SRI-College Profiles
Table 8.7   Results of Hierarchical Linear Regression Models
               for Predicting GPA at Four-Year Institutions
Table 8.8   Results of Hierarchical Linear Regression Models
               for Predicting GPA at Two-Year Institutions
Table 8.9   Results of Hierarchical Logistic Regression
               Models for Predicting Retention at Four-Year
               Institutions
Table 8.10   Results of Hierarchical Logistic Regression Models
               for Predicting Retention at Two-Year Institutions
Table 10.1   Success Rates Passing Foundational Studies
               Math (Spring 2009), by COMPASS Pretest and
               Behavioral Rating Levels

Table 10.2   Success Rates Passing Elementary (Precredit) Math, by COMPASS Pretest and Behavioral Rating Levels

Table 10.3   Mean Math Gain Scores for Elementary (Precredit) Math, by Math Pretest and Behavioral Rating Levels

Table 10.4   Categorizing College Interventions

Table 10.5   Categorizing Psychosocial Factors (PSFs) & SRI Scales

Table 10.6   One-on-One Meetings in Student Affairs

Table 10.7   2007 Retention in 2008

Table 10.8   Resource and Services Utilization

Table 10.9   Association of Risk Level & Academic Service Use on Retention & First-Year GPA

Table 11.1   2004 Survey Respondents

Table 11.2   2010 Survey Respondents

Table 11.3   Dropout-Prone Characteristics, 1980 and 1987 WWISR Studies

Table 11.4   Practices with the Greatest Mean Contribution to Retention

Table 11.5   Interventions Cited as One of the Top Three Interventions by 9% or More Respondents

Table 11.6   Summary of Retention Rates by Institutional Type: 1983–2011

Table 11.7   Percentage of Respondents Identifying Retention Interventions Among the Top Three

Table 13.1   Five Select Learning Initiatives from the *What Works in Student Retention (WWISR) Survey* (Habley et al., 2010)

Table 13.2   Remaining Thirteen Learning Assistance Initiatives from the *WWISR Survey* (Habley et al., 2010)

Table 14.1   Top Five Advising-Related Practices

Table 14.2   Incidence and Mean Ratings of 10 Remaining Advising Practices

Table 15.1   Ratings and Incidence Rates for First-Year
               Transition Programs by Institutional Type
Table 15.2   Transition Programs Identified Among Top
               Three Interventions ≥ 10% of Respondents
Table 15.3   Percentage of First-Year Seminar Types
Table 16.1   The Expanded Retention Framework
Table 17.1   Prevention, Intervention, and Recovery
               Initiatives Chart

Preface

This is not simply another book on college student retention. In fact, although college student retention may be the most studied and discussed aspect of American higher education, over the last forty years, nearly every empirical study on the causes of attrition and the impact of interventions on retention has yielded only modest results. Some studies yield confounding and even contradictory results. The literature is also replete with "how-to" retention advice on virtually every campus program—advice which is either anecdotal in nature or difficult to adapt to other campus cultures. One would expect that observable strides in college student retention would coincide with the proliferation of retention studies, but this is not the case. Sadly, one out of every three students who enters higher education in a given fall term will not return for a second year (ACT, 2010e) and approximately 40% (Tinto, 1993) of all college students will never earn a degree anywhere, at anytime in their lives. Those percentages have not changed appreciably since the middle of the twentieth century.

Our firm conviction is that because of stagnant college retention and persistence-to-degree rates, this cannot be just another book on student retention. We do highlight the urgency of the retention issue and its impact on individuals and society and we provide brief overviews of retention theory and research. We also document the direct and indirect costs of recruiting versus the return on investment of students who succeed. We respect and believe in the necessity of theoretical perspectives and in the importance of empirical research, but this book does not include a comprehensive review of the retention literature. There are many other places where readers may go to find such reviews. We will, however, focus on research to the extent that it supports our assertions. For example, a thread throughout the book is our use of the results from ACT's *What Works in Student Retention* (WWISR) (Beal & Noel, 1980; Cowart, 1987; Habley & McClanahan, 2004; Habley, McClanahan, Valiga, & Burkum, 2010) surveys because they provide three decades of longitudinal results from institutions of higher education. The consistency of WWISR results on the causes of attrition and on practices that lead to student success are at the core of this book. In addition, authors affiliated with ACT, Inc. have made significant contributions to the literature on student success, particularly on the impact of psychosocial characteristics and career development. Most of the references contributed by ACT researchers are attributed to major juried journals and published books on measurement and on applied research. Those works provide a focal point for our discussion of student success.

If this isn't simply another book on retention, then what is it? First and foremost, this is a book for practitioners and those who are responsible for coordinating and leading retention efforts at both the institutional and the public policy levels. We urge these individuals to focus intensively on those components and interventions that have been consistently tied to student success. Our study of the literature caused us to peel back the layers of theory and identify the core conditions that are necessary for students to succeed in college. We concluded that there are three primary—and, perhaps in the reader's mind, intuitive—conditions necessary for students to be successful in college. The first of these is that students must learn. Although this condition may seem so obvious that it needs no further discussion, the fact is that many students are not academically prepared to learn and thus succeed in college. Many do not demonstrate the academic skills necessary for success in the classroom and, as a result, their ability to learn is compromised. Students will succeed if they learn!

The second condition necessary for success is that students must exhibit behaviors and develop personal characteristics that contribute to persistence. Among those are motivation, commitment, engagement, and self-regulation. The degree to which these characteristics fuel the desire to achieve an educational objective is directly related to the likelihood of success. Students will succeed if they are committed to their academic goals.

The third and final core condition is the ability to identify and commit to a plan of study that is congruent with interests and abilities. The attrition landscape is filled with students who entered academic programs where their choices were based on inaccurate information, inappropriate advice, or simply unrealistic expectations. Students will succeed if they connect to a plan of study that fits with their interests and abilities.

Hand in hand with these core conditions are the retention programs that support them. One of our concerns is that many institutions are using a shotgun approach to retention programming. That is, although we believe that all aspects of campus life contribute to retention, this book will not be a "how-to" compendium of multiple programs and services. There are many far more detailed, indeed book-length, resources on specific campus programs and services aimed at improving retention. This book is focused not on such details but rather on the basic principles that guide retention practices. We believe that institutions must focus on those programs that maximize the possibility that the core conditions above are addressed. In addition, we agree with current critics of retention efforts who suggest that many retention efforts involve simply layering on of additional services when an at-risk population is identified. The result is a hodge-podge of unintegrated programs.

Our focus has been narrowed down to four intervention areas: assessment/course placement, developmental education initiatives, academic advising, and student transition programming.

There are multiple reasons why we focus only on these four intervention areas. First, in over four decades of research, these areas have been consistently cited as the most important retention initiatives in all institutional types. Second, these areas best support the three essential conditions for student success. Third, in an era of finite resources, institutional student success strategies that stress these areas are most likely to maximize the return on the investment of scarce institutional resources, both fiscal and human.

As important as these intervention programs are, we felt that the existing institutionally based retention framework supported only a limited definition of student success. The framework is both linear and temporal. It is predicated on the notion that when students enter specific colleges, they should be retained, they should persist from year to year, and they should earn a degree in a reasonable time frame. If these conditions are met for a significant percentage of the student body, then the institution is successful. Measures of institutional quality and accountability are based on the linear and temporal assumptions. As a result, the outcome metrics are retention and graduation rates. The rates tell a story about institutional success, but not about student success.

We will make the case that the existing retention framework must be expanded to account for additional measures of student success. We will argue that true student success is predicated on student achievement of educational goals regardless of the institution where the goals are achieved and the time it takes a students to achieve them. The expanded framework is not confined to one institution and it is not constrained by time or a narrow definition of student outcome. The outcome measure is the student's attainment of an educational goal even if the achievement of that goal includes enrollment in multiple institutions and ultimate completion over an undefined time period. The framework poses the question: What would we do (or do differently) if the outcome was individual student success?

While many would argue that student success is the underlying goal of all postsecondary institutions, the fact is that success is an institutional metric that discounts the educational achievements of students who pursued and perhaps achieved their educational goals at other institutions.

Finally, everyone associated with higher education has a role to play in improving student success. Those who make policy and allocate resources can have a positive effect by reviewing and revising accountability measures and structuring interinstitutional cooperation. Campus leaders must envision and work at developing a student success culture. In addition, administrators, faculty members, student affairs, and technical and support staff must recognize that the quality of relationships that students have with all members of the campus community are pivotal to student success.

Following are brief introductions to the five sections of this book.

Section 1: What Do We Know About Retention and Persistence to Degree?

We review the evolution of complex student departure terminology in Chapter One, suggesting that the semantics surrounding student departure have evolved considerably over the last sixty years. Early definitions defined departure as a student problem—one of curiosity but limited institutional consequence. Students who departed before earning a degree were dropouts, nonpersisters, or simply leavers. Later definitions (retention, attrition) focused on institutional descriptors. Current thinking acknowledges that the causes of departure are shared by students and institutions. Recognition of this evolution positions institutions and their representatives for a breakthrough to create solutions based on a much broader definition of retention.

In Chapter Two, noting that this book was not intended to provide readers with an exhaustive review of the literature on retention theory, we provide a brief overview of the five major perspectives from which retention theory is drawn: sociological, psychological, organizational, economic, and cultural. We argue for an eclectic, integrative approach to these theoretical perspectives, observing that no single perspective can completely capture the complexity of student retention. In addition to these theoretical perspectives, we describe two models that are useful in conceptualizing factors influencing student retention: Seidman's Retention Formula (2005b) and Habley's Staying Environment Model (1981). This chapter also includes a review of student and institutional characteristics, as well as institutional retention interventions. In simplifying theoretical underpinnings that are varied and intertwined, we assert that educators are now coming to understand that virtually all of what we know about student and institutional characteristics related to retention and about practices that promote retention has not changed appreciably in more than four decades. This chapter opens the door to consider new ways of looking at retention from the broader perspective of student success.

Section 2: The Case for Intensified Campus Efforts

Higher education is changing. Institutions are facing major demographic shifts in their student bodies, new technology influxes, and pressures created by the global economy that have an impact on students, faculty, and staff. It is in this context that institutions must grapple with a decades-old issue: student persistence and retention. In this first section, we offer what we believe to be compelling reasons why increasing the number of students who succeed in college is a national imperative.

In Chapter Three we review the basic demographic changes that are affecting student success, chiefly that by 2050 50% of the United States population will be minorities. The implications of these major demographic shifts are multifold. For example, it is expected that the U.S. Hispanic population will increase dramatically, yet college enrollment and persistence to degree among Hispanic students is significantly lower than that of all other racial/ethnic groups. In addition to the Hispanic population, the college access and completion picture for black and for Native American/Alaskan Native students is also bleak. These demographics provide significant cause for concern when considering the future preparedness of the U.S. workforce in relation to increasing global competition. If the U.S. educational system is not able to ensure that more underrepresented minorities have access to and are able to complete college, the nation will be at a competitive disadvantage with the economies of other developed countries.

In Chapter Four we explore both the public and private benefits of higher education, arguing that the government has long taken an active role in promoting higher education through legislation such the Morrill Acts, National Defense Acts, and through other government funding subsidies. This vested public interest should come as no surprise given the number of public economic and social benefits of higher education. College graduates provide benefits such as increased tax revenue, greater productivity and consumption, decreased reliance on government support, and a positive economic community. As individuals, college graduates earn higher salaries, have greater mobility, have increased personal savings, have access to better health care, have longer life expectancies, provide a better quality of life for their offspring, and enjoy increased personal status, to name only a few benefits. When looked at in their entirety, the benefits of a single college graduate can be quantified at $97,180 (McMahon, 2009), with the public benefits outweighing the private benefits.

Institutional economics of retention are explored in Chapter Five as we discuss the cost of recruitment in relation to the cost of retention. Direct costs of recruitment are relatively simple to calculate. They include personnel, travel, facilities, and supplies. Indirect costs are more difficult to calculate, but they are part of the costs of providing a competitive recruitment process. Indirect costs of competing for students include, but are not limited to, such things as classroom technology, recreation centers, and residence hall renovations.

Retention costs, however, are difficult to calculate and include lost tuition, cost of replacing a lost student, lost student aid, and reduced need for instructional staff. While it would be problematic to produce an exact figure, and it is far easier to measure recruitment costs than it is to calculate retention costs, the authors maintain that it is more cost-effective to retain a student through to degree completion than it is to replace a lost student. In addition, the benefits to the individual student retained are immeasurable.

We build a strong case that because retention and degree completion statistics have been stagnant for nearly a half century, investing in retention programming is not only cost-effective but is also an institutional imperative. Finally, we call for concerted efforts to provide evidence and empirical data on student success beyond anecdotes and heartwarming stories. In an environment of finite resources, it is critical that institutions show that what they do makes a difference in student success.

Section 3: Core Components of Student Success

Building on the previous section's focus on the need to intensify retention efforts, this section addresses what we believe to be the most important components that should guide campus retention programming.

First, in Chapter Six we examine the roles of institutional culture and student engagement in student persistence. The strength of the American higher education system is in its diversity, which creates unique campus cultures, each with its own ethos. This diversity means that there is no such thing as the "right" institutional culture just as there is no such thing as a typical student. Our review includes the results of the Project on Documenting Effective Education Practice (DEEP), which is derived from the National Survey of Student Engagement (NSSE), as well as Kramer's elements that foster student success (2007). Those reports suggest that student success must be woven throughout the culture of an institution. Student success is everyone's responsibility. Finally, we present concrete suggestions for creating a culture that supports and encourages student success.

Chapter Seven includes a brief review of relevant literature that underscores the importance of student academic preparation for college-level coursework and the dramatic impact it has on college success. We describe the level of preparation necessary for college success and the effect of solid preparation on student grade point average, progression, retention, and persistence to degree. Then, we examine the purported key indicators of college readiness, including high school grades, dual enrollment programs, and advanced placement courses. We conclude that grade inflation, dual enrollment, and advanced placement may actually mask the college readiness picture because (1) grade inflation is on the rise and (2) students who participate in dual enrollment and AP programs are those who are already most likely to succeed in college. Such programs focus on the academically talented students, not on average students and certainly not on at-risk students. Despite these initiatives, overall academic preparedness is not improving, and some would suggest it is declining. One certainly is that the global competitiveness of U.S. students is in decline. Finally, we discuss the role that postsecondary institutions can and do play in college academic readiness.

Chapter Eight focuses on the relationship between psychosocial development and student success. Along with other researchers, we contend that to fully understand student persistence one must understand student personality, attitudes, and behavior, and we offer a meta-analysis supporting that position. The meta-analysis pinpoints the relationship between educational persistence and theories of motivation and self-efficacy. We explore nine domains that encompass students' psychosocial development in relation to persistence, including: achievement, goals, commitment to institution, perceived social support, involvement, self-efficacy, self-concept, academic skill, financial support, size of the institution, and institutional selectivity. Of these factors, the academically related ones are the most significantly correlated with student success. Finally, we focus on the use of psychosocial assessment tools to assist colleges in the creation of targeted initiatives to improve retention and academic success in high-risk areas.

Chapter Nine focuses on the role of career development in student success. We present a review of the literature, concluding that career development and direction are a critical component of student persistence. Our belief is that structured career exploration is necessary because students frequently lack the knowledge, confidence, and social support to engage in significant career exploration on their own. For many students college is the first opportunity they have to explore career options in a meaningful way. Our assertions are bolstered by empirical data showing that career planning has a positive impact on student success because it broadens student opportunities, increases a student's sense of purpose, creates academic relevance between coursework and a student's real-life goals, and increases a student's overall engagement with the institution. Career exploration and development also is an element of student-environment fit, drawing attention to students' strengths and encouraging persistence by aligning students' educational goals with their interests and their values. Finally, we offer a number of practical ways for an institution to guide students through the career exploration process.

In Chapter Ten we provide an analysis of the collective impact of academic, psychosocial, and career development initiatives on student persistence and success. All three areas are incorporated into a comprehensive model that informs and supports academic persistence and success. Academic success builds confidence and thus drives all other indicators and success outcomes. Finally, we present a pyramid for success, which depicts a cognitive foundation upon which the psychosocial and career factors rest. Within the pyramid framework, we offer specific intervention strategies to successfully integrate the components of student success outlined in the preceding chapters.

Section 4: Proven Student Success Practices

Guided by the critical components (culture, academic preparation, psychosocial development, and career preparation) discussed in the previous section, the focus of section IV includes the identification and discussion of the practices that provide the best opportunity to successfully address those components. This examination is based on a review of three decades of data derived from ACT's *What Works in Student Retention* Surveys (WWISR).

In Chapter Eleven, we report on the first comprehensive and collective review of all four WWISR studies comparing and contrasting the common themes that run throughout. This comparative view, including all institutions, provides a broad perspective of practices that are particularly successful in student retention. Following our review of the themes, we explore the data patterns from three perspectives: institutional characteristics that contribute to attrition; student characteristics that contribute to attrition; and retention programs, practices, and interventions. In all four WWISR surveys, student characteristics were rated as the single greatest cluster of factors contributing to attrition. Finally, utilizing additional data reports run on WWISR (Habley, McClanahan, Valiga, & Burkum, 2010), we examine high-risk populations and the specific factors that contribute to minority student attrition and retention. We conclude that over the last forty years most of what we know about the causes of attrition and about successful retention initiatives may have varied in semantics but not in substance.

Chapter Twelve provides an overview of the impact of course placement practices on student success. Based on our review of the literature, we contend that only 25% of students entering college are prepared to succeed in the classroom (ACT, 2005), leaving nearly 75% of college students underprepared and at-risk in at least one subject area. One way that institutions can reduce this risk is to place students in the correct courses, where their academic skills are identified and the coursework matches their performance level. Effective course placement minimizes the possibility of frustration, which often leads to failure. The benefits of an effective course placement process include producing data to help with resource allocation decision making, creating proper program enhancements including course revisions and learning support programs, helping design targeted retention initiatives, and assisting in accreditation and securing funding opportunities. We provide several suggestions for assessing student academic readiness and appropriate course placement, including four course placement models: test only placement, multiple conditions placement model, multiple considerations placement model, and the decision zone placement model. Multiple models allow institutions of differing sizes, missions, and student populations to work with a model that best fits their needs, their students' needs, and the institutional culture.

We discuss developmental education initiatives in Chapter Thirteen. Developmental education is a broadly defined term that may include remedial coursework, tutoring, supplemental instruction, and other forms of learning assistance. We point out that President Obama and the Gates Foundation have identified developmental education as the gateway to college degree attainment for at-risk student populations. We explore the role of higher education institutions in remediation, noting that while there is an obvious need for remediation, there is a gap in the literature when it comes to assessing the overall effectiveness of remedial/developmental programs. ACT's WWISR survey (Habley et al., 2010) identified four specific areas in developmental education that can make a significant contribution to student retention and success. They include required remedial coursework, supplemental instruction, tutoring, and early warning systems. These areas are discussed in Chapter Thirteen; in addition we present a brief glimpse of thirteen other areas of developmental education that were not found to be as effective or as widely used, but which may still have a positive effect on student persistence. We conclude the chapter by highlighting several promising programs and innovative ideas both at the institutional and statewide level.

Academic advising is the next student support program covered in this section. In Chapter Fourteen, we note that the history of academic advising spans nearly the length of the history of American higher education, whereas more formal and structured advising programs are a more recent development. Advising offers every student the opportunity for interaction with an institutional representative with whom they can build a relationship and develop an individual plan for academic and cocurricular engagement at the institution. We explore multiple advising theories and delivery models and frameworks for refining the way that academic advising is delivered to students. We also look at best practices in academic advising as well as factors that affect the success of advising programs.

First-Year Transition Programs and the role they play in student success are covered in Chapter Fifteen. First-year transition programs are designed to help students move from existing educational, career, and social environments toward academic and social integration into college life. We delineate first-year transition programs as constituent parts of a broader concept often called the first-year experience and focus on describing the increasingly complex and comprehensive approaches to first-year transition programs. These programs are specifically designed to ease the transition process. Orientation programs, which previously were single events, now serve as the beginning stage of a longer-term transition process that includes practices such as extended orientation, first-year seminar courses, and learning communities. We explore the emergence and effectiveness of learning communities and first-year seminars and conclude by noting that a successful first-year program is not a one-size-fits-all process, but rather a program based on the unique confluence of students' needs with institutional characteristics and culture.

Section 5: Making Student Success a Priority

The final section draws upon all of the information presented throughout the book to offer a comprehensive student success framework for policymakers, institutions, and individuals.

Chapter Sixteen targets institutional and public policymakers and describes the expanded retention framework. This framework suggests there are important roles that policymakers and institutions can and should play to support a more holistic focus on student success. Based on our contention that the responsibility for student success must be shared between institutions and those engaged in public policy, we offer several recommendations as to actions that can be taken. As the foundation of these recommendations, we continued emphasis on building an integrated and holistic P-20 educational system. At the postsecondary level, policymakers should streamline transfer and articulation agreements between institutions to minimize complexity and expand options for students. We encourage the development of common course numbering systems and broader implementation of course applicability systems to help students move seamlessly between and among colleges. In addition, we contend that accountability measures must be redefined from a focus on retention to an overall student success model because it is more important for students to meet their educational objectives (regardless of where they began) than it is for a single institution to take credit for and be held accountable for student success. Finally, we cite a number of institutional policies that may inhibit student transitions, and we advocate for a thorough continuous review of institutional policies and requirements to ease student transition into, out of, and within the institution.

Chapter Seventeen offers practical suggestions for creating a student success culture at an institution. As we consistently contend, there is no cookie-cutter formula for an institution to follow in creating a culture that supports student success. We offer a dynamic approach, Appreciative Inquiry (Cooperrider & Srivastva, 1987), for creating an institutional plan focusing on student success, Appreciative Inquiry shifts the focus away from problem identification to an opportunity creation focus. We recommend that institutions focus on the Appreciative Inquiry Summit phases (Define, Discover, Dream, Design, Deliver) to build their student success interventions. Finally, we state that viewing student success through the Appreciative Inquiry framework allows an institution to meet the unique needs of their students and design a customized approach to student success.

In the final chapter of the book we present a practical plan for all members of the academy to contribute to student success regardless of their position or authority at the institution. The plan focuses on change at the micro level and outlines what an institutional representative can do to instigate the change process. We suggest that three areas of human capacity need to be deployed: cognitive skills, interpersonal skills, and intrapersonal skills (Klemp, 1988). By delving into these three areas, practitioners will be well positioned to cultivate opportunities for student success in their work. Our final charge to practitioners is to take action and to create change that fosters student success.

The Authors

Dr. Wes Habley has held numerous positions at ACT, Inc. and is currently the principal associate and coordinator of ACT's Office of State Organizations. He earned his BS in music education and MEd in student personnel from the University of Illinois-Urbana/Champaign, and his EdD from Illinois State University in educational administration, where he was recently inducted into the College of Education Hall of Fame. Prior to joining ACT, Habley served as an academic adviser and later as director of the Academic Advisement Center at Illinois State. Habley also served as the director of Academic and Career Advising at the University of Wisconsin-Eau Claire.

Habley is coeditor of two editions of *Academic Advising: A Comprehensive Handbook*. Among more than 100 additional publications are ACT's *What Works in Student Retention?* (2004, 2010), monographs on four national surveys of academic advising, and book chapters in *Fostering Student Success, Developmental Academic Advising*, and *Faculty Advising Examined*. Additional work has appeared in the NACADA Journal, *The Journal of College Student Personnel*, *NASPA Journal*, NACADA *Monograph Series*, the Jossey-Bass New Directions Series, and monographs from the First-Year Experience Program at the University of South Carolina.

Habley has delivered more than 400 presentations at meetings of professional associations and has served as a consultant or workshop leader at more than 125 colleges in the United States, the Middle East, and Canada.

Habley has served the National Academic Advising Association (NACADA) as a founding board member, past president and past treasurer of the. He inaugurated the Summer Institute on Academic Advising (1987), and served as its director for 22 years. In 2006, Habley was named director emeritus and in 2007 the Summer Institute Scholarship was named in his honor. He is the recipient of NACADA's awards for Outstanding Contributions to the Field of Academic Advising and Service to NACADA.

Jennifer L. Bloom, EdD, is a clinical professor and director of the master's degree program in the Higher Education & Student Affairs Program housed in the Department of Educational Leadership and Policies at the University of South Carolina. Prior to her appointment at the University of South Carolina in August, 2007, she served as the associate dean for Student Affairs & the Medical Scholars Program at the University of Illinois College of Medicine at Urbana-Champaign. She earned her doctorate in Higher Education Administration from the University of Illinois at Urbana-Champaign in 1995.

Dr. Bloom served as the 2007–08 president of the National Academic Advising Association (NACADA). She received the NACADA Outstanding Advising Administrator Award in 2005 and University of Illinois' Campus Academic Professional Excellence Award in 2007. In 2008, she received the University of South Carolina's Black Graduate Student Association's Faculty Mentor Award as well as the University of Illinois College of Medicine at Urbana-Champaign's Senior Class Special Tribute Award.

Dr. Bloom has coauthored three books, three book chapters, and eleven articles. The first book, *Career Aspirations & Expeditions: Advancing Your Career in Higher Education Administration,* was released in 2003 and coauthored by Nancy Archer-Martin. The second book, *The Appreciative Advising Revolution,* was released in September 2008 and is coauthored by Bryant Hutson and Ye He. The third book is titled *Appreciative College Instruction: Becoming a Positive for Change in the Classroom* and is co-authored by Bryant Hutson, Ye He, and Claire Robinson. In addition, Dr. Bloom has delivered 10 national webinars and over 160 presentations on her work at institutions and conferences across the country.

Steve Robbins is principal research scientist in the Center for Academic and Career Readiness and Success at Educational Testing Service (ETS). He is a nationally recognized social scientist and scholar interested in the interplay of career, personality, and cognitive factors as they affect education and workplace readiness and success. Steve and his coauthors have addressed the evidentiary basis of post-secondary practices on retention, academic mastery, and degree attainment behavior. He has published over 90 research studies and is the author and coauthor of several personality and career-based assessments. These include the Career Factors Inventory (Consulting Psychologist Press) and the Personal Skills Assessment suite in ACT's WorkKeys system. He led the development of ACT's ENGAGE for students and teachers, aimed at measuring academic behavior readiness and risk for college, high school, and middle school students.

Previous to ETS, Steve served as vice president of research at ACT, which supports Education and Workforce business units. He oversaw a complex, highly technical staff organized into several departments, including Validity and Policy Research, Psychometric and Measurement Research, Reporting Services, Survey Services, and Education and Career Transitions Research. As a member of the ACT executive leadership team, he participated in product architecture and delivery, and product innovation and development.

Steve is a former professor and chair of psychology at Virginia Commonwealth University. He helped build a nationally ranked and accredited counseling psychology program and was elected Fellow of the American Psychological Association in 1992. More recently he served as adjunct professor in the Department of Management, Tippie College of Business, at the University of Iowa. He taught strategic employee development in the MBA program.

Steve is a skilled management consultant and adviser to business and industry and to academic and education organizations. He is a highly sought-after public speaker and workshop presenter, and has mentored multiple doctoral candidates and professional-level staff. He is a licensed psychologist in Iowa and Virginia, and a member of the National Register of Health Service Providers.

Acknowledgments

From the initial discussion of this book on student success through final submission and publication, we have been supported and nurtured by professional colleagues and personal cheerleaders who believed in us and believed in the importance of student success.

At the professional level we thank our current and former colleagues at the University of South Carolina, and ACT, Inc. Special thanks go to Jacqueline Snider for locating out-of-the-way and out-of-date resources; to Erin Konkle for a great job in providing the section introductions; and to Katie Pauls for her painstaking preparation of the manuscript. In addition, Jenny thanks Helen Halasz for her assistance and support throughout the writing process. Finally, we each want to thank our coauthors for challenging our ideas, improving our writing, and for fostering a spirit of teamwork without which this project would still be an idea waiting to happen.

At the personal level, we believe that whatever our achievements, they are unquestionably a product of affectionate people who nurture our aspirations and urge us into the future with their expressed faith in our capacities. In that context we thank the following people.

Wes expresses his thanks to his wife, Katherine, who, for more than 35 years, has provided constant support, encouragement, and belief in what he was doing; to children, Brent and Kelly, who have grown into adults who would make any father proud; and to his parents, Gertrude and Florian, who always stressed the value of education even though neither finished high school.

Jenny thanks her husband, Steve Sanderson; her mother, Ada Bloom; step-father, Ed Morrison; brother and sister-in-law, Andrew and Judy Bloom; step-daughter and husband, Kathy and Matt Rassette; Teri Breitenfeldt; Amanda Cuevas; Erin Konkle; Catherine Paulson; and her aunts, uncles, and cousins. Special thanks go out to the prides and joys of Jenny's life, her grandchildren: Cody Breitenfeldt, Kaitlyn Breitenfeldt, Rachel Rassette, and Rian Rassette.

Steve thanks his wife, Anne, who has stood by him through thick and thin, and knows all too well the tension that surrounds the writing process. Steve and Anne's children, Jonathan and Abigail, are unique individuals who navigated college life in their own ways with the same positive outcomes; they are inquisitive, caring about others, and dedicated to lifelong learning. Both have clearly defined career goals, and traveled successfully across the College to Work Bridge. Steve's parents, Marilyn and Lawrence, instilled in him the importance of education and the will to succeed. These values have stood the test of time.

Finally, a project of this scope cannot be completed without guidance and support from members of the editorial team at Jossey-Bass. We thank Erin Null, who guided the process at the beginning and the end, and Alison Knowles and Lisa Coronado-Morse for their support throughout the project.

Increasing Persistence

Section 1

WHAT DO WE KNOW ABOUT RETENTION AND PERSISTENCE TO DEGREE?

1

DEFINING, REFINING PERSPECTIVES ON STUDENT SUCCESS

Defining *retention*, *attrition*, and *persistence* and the constructs related to those terms is fraught with pitfalls and complexity. In the most simplistic form, a student is retained if that student remains in continuous full-time enrollment from the point of matriculation to the completion of a degree. Although this straightforward definition may have been appropriate prior to the last half of the twentieth century, Hagedorn (2005) suggests that defining and measuring student retention is one of the most vexing measurement issues in higher education. This chapter will focus on describing the evolution of various terms that have been used, sometimes interchangeably, to define the outcomes of higher education from the institution's perspective and from the student's perspective. Tracing the use of these terms, we suggest that student failure to succeed in college was once seen as a student shortcoming that eventually shifted to an institutional responsibility. Currently, the terms in vogue are those that delineate the interaction between students and institutions as the nexus of student success. Though we applaud these current approaches to understanding student success in college, we close this chapter by offering a critique of current definitions and accountability measures as too narrow and too institution-centric to bring about dramatic increases in student success.

Terms Associated with Students

Terms defining the behavior of students are in great abundance. These terms can be divided into three viewpoints: students who persist, students who leave but persist elsewhere, and students who leave.

Students Who Persist

A student who persists is one who continues to enroll at the institution after matriculation. Although this seems like a fairly straightforward description of a persister, there are several definitions with not-so-subtle variations. Lenning (1978) suggests that a persister is one who enrolls continuously without interruption. In addition to continuous enrollment, Astin (1975) adds full-time status and pursuit of a degree as qualifiers. And, in identifying a persister as a stayer, Guthrie (2002) adds the expectation of graduation in about four (or two) years. The resulting definition becomes enormously complex: a persister is a student who enrolls full-time, continuously pursues a degree with the expectation of graduation in about four (or two) years. And, as the qualifiers are added, fewer and fewer students can be called persisters. Perhaps the *Merriam-Webster's Third New International Dictionary* (2002) definition of a persister applies here: a person who "goes on resolutely or stubbornly despite opposition, importunity, or warning: to continue firmly or obstinately."

Students Who Leave But (May or May Not) Persist Elsewhere

The literature describes several types of students who progress toward their educational objectives but are not characterized by the one-institution, continuous-progress, and timely graduation constraints of the traditional definition of persistence.

Among the most prominent of these groups is the *part-time student*. The National Center for Educational Statistics

(2002) reports that 38% of undergraduate students are pursuing higher education on a part-time basis. A subcategory of part-time students is the *slowdown*, identified in Guthrie (2002) as a student who remains enrolled but moves from full-time to part-time status.

The term *transfer student* identifies a significant number of undergraduates. The National Center for Educational Statistics (2001) reported that 28.9% of community college students transferred to four-year colleges. Although data on transfers between four-year colleges and transfers from four-year to two-year colleges are limited, Berkner, He, and Cataldi (2002) found that 41% of students in their study attended more than one institution during their college career and 32% had changed colleges at least once.

The *stopout* is the third prominent category of student who does not pursue a traditional path to a degree. Astin (1975) defines a stopout as a student who "interrupts education for a relatively brief period of time and returns to complete a degree" (p. 9).

Lenning (1978) is less restrictive in defining the stopout. He omits the word "brief" from his definition, thus expanding the length of time that a student may be considered a stopout. One might safely assume that the increases in time to degree reported by Adelman (2004) suggest that stopping out is on the increase. Yet, stopout behavior is impossible to measure, for there is no real agreement on the length of time a student can be considered a stopout before becoming a *dropout*.

Over the past few years, the concept of *swirling* has been applied to attendance patterns of college students. In its basic form, swirling is defined as achieving a higher education degree via enrollment at two or more institutions simultaneously. Although swirling is very difficult to measure, Berkner et al. (2002) found that 11% of students in the study were simultaneously enrolled in more than one college. Undoubtedly, these figures would be far higher if these students were asked to identify other ways (including online courses taken from other institutions) in which they earned college credit.

Students Who Leave

Bean (1990) suggests that, far too often, terms describing students who leave an institution have been pejorative in nature and usually focused on student shortcomings. Woodring (1968) suggested that "many of the students now in college have no sound reason for being there, and would not have entered if they had been given valid information" (p. 13). Pervin, Reik, and Dalrymple (1966) focused on educational preparedness as a primary cause of attrition and suggested that the dropout rates would be substantially reduced by raising minimum high school grade point averages and standardized test scores required for admission. Other causes for dropping out include nonacademic reasons: boredom, financial hardship, lack of motivation, and mental and physical health (Cope & Hannah, 1975). Also cited in the early literature were personal and social maladjustment, marriage, job opportunities, and lack of motivation to succeed. Regardless of the multiple causes of departure, nearly one-third of all students who enter higher education each year will not return to the institution for a second year (ACT, 2010e), a statistic that has remained relatively constant over the past five decades.

The operant descriptor of student departure is the term *dropout*, an antonym to persister. A dropout is a student who "is not enrolled, has not earned a degree, and is no longer pursuing a degree" (Astin, 1975, p. 9). Summerskill (1962) states that a dropout is a "student who leaves college before advancing their education to the point of earning a degree" (p. 627). Similar definitions are offered by Pervin et al. (1966), Lenning (1978), Guthrie (2002), and a host of others. Other terms which attribute departure to student shortcomings include *underachievers* (Keniston, 1966), *nonpersisters* (Astin, 1975), *stayouts* (Horn, 1998), and *discontinued students* (Iffert, 1957).

There is one positive description in the literature of a student who leaves the institution with no intention of returning. Lenning (1978) describes an *attainer* as a student who drops out prior to graduation but after attaining a particular goal. Although not using the descriptor attainer, Hossler, Bean, and Associates (1990) describe a group of students who enroll in college, get from it what they want, and go on about their lives.

It should be noted here that in virtually all of the literature prior to 1975, the causality for attrition is attributed to student characteristics with virtually no causality assigned to the institution (ACT, 2010e). Chapter Eleven of this book points to the fact that even today, student characteristics are seen as the primary contributors to attrition, whereas institutional characteristics are believed to make minimal contributions to attrition.

Terms Associated with Institutions

The terms associated with institutions differ markedly in a number of ways from the definitions associated with students. First of all, the institutional terms do not define a behavior or an action. In addition, they are aggregate descriptors of a cohort of students rather than terms applied to individual students. As such they are always expressed as rates or percentages (for example, the retention rate for last fall's first-time, full-time, degree-seeking cohort was 68%). Finally, the terms associated with institutions are value neutral; in and of themselves, the terms are neither positive or negative. It is only when they are compared to external benchmarks or institutional goals that they take on meaning.

Retention

A review of early literature leads to the conclusion that the term *retention* as applied to college student enrollment patterns was not widely used until the 1970s. Prior to 1966, no ERIC documents referred to college student retention. Prominent books in the student development field (Lloyd-Jones & Smith, 1954; Mueller, 1961; Williamson, 1961) contain no references to retention. And early publications that focused on student departure almost universally refer to dropouts, stopouts, and other terms that characterized individual student behavior (and, for the most part, negatively). By 1980, the literature on departure began to feature the term *retention* as an approach to describing departure behavior at the institutional level. *Retention* appeared in the titles of several books and monographs. Among those publications were Lenning, Sauer, and Beal (1980); Beal and Noel (1981); and Noel, Levitz, Saluri, and Associates (1986).

Retention is usually expressed as a rate or percentage of students who return from one enrollment period to another. But, as Lenning et al. (1980) pointed out, retention can have several definitions:

1. Program completion as retention
   a. Graduating in the time designated for the degrees or certificates offered
   b. Graduating after the time designated for the degrees or certificates offered
   c. Graduating (at any time) at the institution of initial entry
   d. Graduating from an institution other than the one in which initially enrolled
   e. Graduating in the curricular program initially entered
   f. Graduating in a curricular program other than the one in which initially enrolled
2. Course or term completion as retention
3. Personal Goal attainment as retention (pp. 6–7)

Although these interpretations captured the nuances of institutional retention, there was (and continues to be) little agreement among institutions as to how retention should be measured: Which students would be included? What about students who fail academically or those who stopout or those who transfer in or out? Hagedorn (2005) believes that higher education researchers may never reach a consensus on the definition and measurement of retention.

In an effort to standardize the collection and reporting of data on all colleges receiving federal student assistance, the federal government established the Integrated Postsecondary Education Data System (IPEDS) in 1993. Among many other data elements, the IPEDS system collects information on enrollment, completion, and graduation rates. In that process, IPEDS has standardized the definition of retention as the percentage of first-time, full-time, degree-seeking students from the previous fall who either reenrolled or successfully completed their program by the current fall. The simplicity of the IPEDS definition, however, reflects Hagedorn's contention. At its best, the definition standardizes the reporting of retention. And at its worst, it reflects a most narrow definition of student success.

As a final commentary on the use of the word *retention*, the dictionary defines retention as holding or continuing to hold in possession or use. *Attrition*, an antonym of retention, is defined as the condition of being worn down or ground down by friction.

Retention, then, is a measure of the rate at which institutions reduce friction that stands in the way of a student's continued enrollment.

Graduation/Completion/Persistence to Degree

There has been only limited debate on the definition of graduation, completion, and persistence to degree. These are interchangeable terms always expressed as the rate or percentage of students who complete a degree within a specified time period. The IPEDS Graduation Rates survey collects information about student graduation rates by gender and race or ethnicity by tracking a cohort of undergraduates and their completion status at 150% of normal time (six years for four-year degrees and three years for two-year degrees). A cohort includes full-time, first-time, degree- or certificate-seeking students who enter college either during the fall term or during the 12-month period between September 1 of one year and August 31 of the next year and are enrolled in courses creditable toward a degree, diploma, certificate, or other award. Like the IPEDS definition of retention, the graduation rate survey standardizes the collection of data, and although it recognizes that college completion does not always take place in two years or four years, it is still a linear definition that fails to account for students who transfer, those who swirl, and those who stop out for prolonged periods of time.

Progression

Often overlooked in discussion of student departure behavior is the concept of progression. It is defined as the percentage of first-time, full-time, and degree-seeking students who reenroll and achieve a class standing commensurate with the number of years they have attended. On the surface, it is a positive that these students are retained at the institution. Yet, students who fail to progress or keep pace with their cohort group are at risk of dropping out of the institution at a later date. Progression may be hindered by academic performance or by injudicious course withdrawals.

Terms Associated with Interaction Between Student and Institution

Since the mid-1970s several theoretical perspectives have been proposed and tested. Each of these theories is included in this chapter because they describe the interface between the student and the institution. The theories are described only briefly here because greater detail is included in Chapter Two.

Involvement

Alexander Astin first articulated the construct of involvement in *Preventing Students from Dropping Out* (1975) and in so doing, hinted at an institutional role in student success. Involvement focuses on the amount of energy a student invests in the academic experience. Involvement is both physical and psychological and emanates from both qualitative and quantitative academic and social experiences. The basic tenet of involvement is that students learn more the more they are involved in both the academic and social aspects of the collegiate experience. Astin defines a highly involved student as one who "devotes considerable energy to studying, spends much time on campus, participates actively in student organizations, and interacts frequently with faculty members and other students" (1999, p. 1). That is, greater participation in meaningful experiences on campus leads to learning and to personal growth. Clearly, the campus plays a role in involvement: the type and structure of learning experiences inside and outside the classroom and campus programs and policies are related to involvement. Because significant learning takes place outside the classroom, the role of extracurricular activities figures prominently in the research on involvement.

Integration

Educational sociologist Vincent Tinto introduced the concepts of social and academic integration. Although Astin's theory of involvement began the dialogue on the relationship between the student and the institution, Tinto believed that institutional factors were pivotal to understanding student departure (1993). His theory of integration posited that student departure is a result of the extent to which students come to share the attitudes and beliefs of their peers and faculty and the extent to which students adhere to the structural rules and requirements of the institution—the institutional culture.

Engagement

George Kuh (2001) advanced Astin's earlier work and incorporated Chickering and Gamson's definition (1987) of best practices in undergraduate education into the concept of student engagement. Student engagement includes two tenets. First, student success is more likely to occur as students increase the time and effort they put into their studies and other activities. Second, student success is more likely to occur when the institution focuses resources on organizing learning opportunities and services and encourages students to participate in and benefit from such activities.

Reflections on the Definitions and Constructs

In reviewing the definitions and constructs related to retention, it becomes clear that our understanding of and response to student departure behavior continue to evolve. Several factors support this assertion. First, there is increasing recognition that the causes of student departure are not confined solely to student shortcomings. Early research on student departure behavior focused almost entirely on student academic preparation, test scores, socioeconomic status, sex, parent level of education, family wealth, attitudes, and commitment to goals. Although these student characteristics, particularly academic preparation, are still critical to the retention equation, it is clear that decisions about departure or continuation reside at the confluence of institutional programs or services and student characteristics.

A second reflection on our understanding of retention is that the perspective and the terminology accompanying it are shifting, albeit slowly, from the pejorative (Bean, 1990) to the affirmative: from the glass is half empty to the glass is half full. Though such a shift may seem inconsequential, the use of terminology illustrates the importance of the shift. The following definitions from the Merriam-Webster Third New International Dictionary (2002) illustrate this point.

Below are terms found in the early literature, with negative connotations.

- **Dropout**: one who leaves school before achieving her or his goal
- **Persister**: a person to goes on resolutely or stubbornly despite opposition, importunity, or warning: one who continues firmly or obstinately
- **Retention**: holding or continuing to hold in one's possession
- **Attrition**: the condition of being worn down or ground down by friction

Even the titles of early publications included such terminology. Among those publications are *Preventing Students from Dropping Out* (Astin, 1975), *Reducing the Dropout Rate* (Noel, 1978), and *Leaving College: The Causes and Cures of Student Attrition* (Tinto, 1993).

Although terms such as *retention* and *attrition* continue in wide use as aggregate descriptors of institutional functioning, these terms are also negative by definition. It seems obvious that institutions would prefer not to be characterized by the rates at which they hold students in their possession (retention) or by the rates at which students depart because they are ground down by the people, policies, and programs of the institution (attrition).

In contrast to these negative definitions, there are several positive terms that underscore the importance of the nexus of student and institutional characteristics. These terms predominate in the current literature. Described briefly earlier in this chapter, those terms and their dictionary definitions are:

- **Integration**: the combination and coordination of separate and diverse elements or units into a more complete or harmonious whole
- **Involvement**: to draw in as a participant
- **Engagement**: to gain over: win and attach

These terms are encompassed in the broader concept of student success. And indeed, the most recent and influential publications in the field include student success in their titles. Those are: *Student Success in College* (Kuh, Kinzie, Schuh, & Whitt, 2005); *Fostering Student Success in the Campus Environment* (Kramer & Associates, 2007); and *College Student Retention: Formula for Student Success* (Seidman, 2005a).

Since the mid-twentieth century, then, the approaches to and understanding of college student retention have continued to evolve in several ways. First, student retention has moved from a somewhat peripheral issue to one of major concern not only to individual institutions but to society as a whole. Second, the underlying causes of student departure are no longer attributed solely to student shortcomings. Underlying causes have evolved to the point where the complex interplay of student characteristics with institutional people, policies, and programs determines students' decisions to stay or to leave. And, as a corollary to this point, the focus has gradually shifted from assigning blame to looking for solutions.

A Broader Perspective on Student Success

In spite of the evolution of terms related to student success in college, the current retention framework is based on two faulty assumptions: simplistic assumptions that confound the definition of student success. First, Habley and Schuh (2007b) and Jones-White, Radcliffe, Huesman, and Kellogg (2009) suggest that the fallacy of the simplistic definition is that it is based on the assumption that the process of achieving an educational objective is both linear and temporal. In reality it is neither. A linear process is one in which the student attends a single institution from matriculation to graduation. A study by Berkner, He, and Cataldi (2002) found that 41% of college students attended more than one institution during their college career, 11% had simultaneously enrolled at more than one college, and 32% had changed colleges at least once. Hagedorn (2005) identifies 10 enrollment scenarios that suggest that linearity is not realistic. And there are probably many more scenarios that could be identified. A temporal process is one in which events occur within a defined time frame. The likelihood of that taking place has moved from probable to possible over the past several decades as students are taking longer and longer to complete degree requirements. ACT data reveal that only 39.6% of four-year college students complete a bachelor's degree in four years and an additional 16% complete the degree in six years (2010e). In addition, 13.6% of two-year college students complete an associate's degree in two years and an additional 10% complete in four years (ACT, 2010e). Though it is convenient to believe that students enroll at only one institution, identify and commit to a program of study, take and succeed in the right combination and number of courses to earn a degree within the appropriate time frame (two years or four years), such an assumption is, indeed, ill-founded.

A second faulty assumption is that all students enter post-secondary education with a desire to complete a college degree or certificate. Although the majority of students enroll full-time with the intent to earn a degree, many undergraduate students attend college part-time, and a number of these students have specific educational objectives that do not include earning a degree. Some students come to upgrade their work skills while others come to completely retrain. Some intend to complete one or two courses that will be transferred to another institution to complete degree requirements. Still others come out of intellectual curiosity, to take a course in an area of personal interest, or to explore the possibilities for additional postsecondary education. Many of these individuals succeed yet none of them fit the linear or temporal definition of retention. In addition, the situation is exacerbated by the fact that institutional effectiveness is often judged by—and institutional reputation is often established by—a crude measure of success based on the simplistic definition of retention as the percentage of the previous year's students who did not graduate and returned to school the following year.

But refuting this simplistic definition of retention does little to aid in the understanding of retention; rather, it only increases the complexity of the discussion. Indeed, some of the terms are conflicting or overlapping. Our review of terminology related to student departure yields no less than 21 different descriptors of student departure. Twelve of the descriptors characterize students, six focus on institutional measures, and three reflect a responsibility shared between student and institution, focusing on student success. For the sake of consistency and the economy of words, *retention* is an umbrella term that refers to the plethora of descriptors that follow. It should not be construed as the author's preferred descriptor.

The stark reality of the retention and persistence-to-degree data is that despite the considerable energy the higher-education community has expended in understanding retention and degree completion, such understanding has not resulted in a concomitant improvement in student success in college. The community can document the personal and societal benefits that accrue from a college degree. The community can identify the student, institutional, and environmental factors contributing to retention. In addition, the higher education community can pinpoint institutional interventions that contribute to retention. Yet, in spite of all that is known, there has been little change in retention and degree completion rates in more than four decades. Nearly one-third of all first-year students do not return for a second year, fewer than half of all students who earn bachelor's degrees do so within five years of high school graduation, and approximately 40% of all students who enter higher education in a given fall will not earn a degree anywhere at any time in their lives. With the additional factors of multiple ways in which students can earn college credit and the phenomena of student swirling and increased time to degree, it is not likely that the future holds a great deal of promise for improvements in retention or degree completion based on the existing retention framework.

Because of the faulty underlying assumptions, the existing retention framework has three major limitations. The first limitation is that institutions are held accountable for retention and degree-completion outcomes over which they have some influence but very little control. Because student success is fraught with complexities, policymakers and resource allocators rely on accountability measures that sink to the lowest common denominators. How many students matriculate? How many students are retained? How many students graduate? How long did it take to earn their degrees?

The second limitation is that the traditional retention framework fails to take into account the significant variety of institutional types that make up the American higher education system. Theoretically, all students who have a high school diploma or have completed the GED have access to postsecondary education. Because this is the case, first- to second-year retention and degree completion rates vary greatly based on mission, selectivity, and the academic ability of students who enroll. Once again, accountability measures undergirding the traditional retention framework fail to take into account this institutional diversity.

The third major limitation is that institutions compare themselves and compete with other institutions. Students are a renewable yet finite commodity. Thus, institutional success is predicated on how well a college attracts and keeps students. Those who matriculate elsewhere or students who leave the college represent loss but evince little concern for their success as students. The traditional retention framework creates three basic comparisons and concomitant mindsets. The first is "we are better than average," which provides little stimulus to change. The second mindset is "we are about average," which may or may not stimulate change. And the third, "we are below average," should stimulate change. Though comparisons with peer group institutions may be useful as broad indicators, such comparisons do little to create a road map that leads to continuous improvement.

Accountability measures based on antiquated and faulty assumptions on how students pursue higher education have done little to advance college success. Retention and persistence-to-degree rates have not changed appreciably in the last five decades. We believe that campus-based retention efforts must focus on programs that support learning, motivation, and career development. Those programs are assessment/course placement, academic advising, learning support, and first-year transition— programs that have stood the test of time and continue to have a significant impact on student success. Finally, we believe that it is time to jettison the notion that student success in college is confined to a single institution of first enrollment. The remainder of this book is organized around these beliefs.

2

OVERVIEW OF THEORETICAL PERSPECTIVES ON STUDENT SUCCESS

The inclusion of retention theory and research in this book is obligatory rather than necessary. It is obligatory because no book on retention would be complete without a consideration of these two topics; it is less than necessary because there are numerous books and documents on these topics that provide for both greater depth and breadth than can be accomplished here in single chapter. Readers interested in a more detailed coverage of retention theory should consult Kuh, Kinzie, Buckley, Bridges, & Hayek (2006); Spradlin, Burroughs, Rutkowski, Lang, and Hardesty (2010); Braxton (2000); Pascarella and Terenzini (2005); or Seidman (2005a). In addition, myriad research studies have examined not only the student and institutional characteristics that individually predict college success but also the relationship(s) between and among those characteristics. Finally, there are numerous studies that purport to measure the impact of selected institutional interventions implemented to improve retention and persistence to degree rates. The purpose of this chapter, then, is neither to provide a comprehensive recapitulation of theoretical perspectives or an exhaustive review of retention research. Rather, this chapter offers an overview of the complexity of theoretical perspectives and summarizes research on the student and institutional factors that contribute to retention.

Theoretical Perspectives

In Chapter One we provided a discussion of the evolution of definitions from *dropout problem* (the 1950s) to current terminology (*persistence and engagement*). Although there were earlier antecedents of theory construction, prior to 1970, the issue of student attrition was seen largely as a phenomenon of student shortcomings, holding little consequence for the institution or society as a whole. Since that time, attempts to explain student departure resulted in multiple theoretical perspectives that were first posited and then studied. These perspectives fall into five primary categories discussed in the following section of the chapter. Those perspectives are sociological, psychological, organizational, economic, and cultural.

Sociological Perspectives

Sociological perspectives have been the dominant retention construct for the last forty years. Spady (1970) was the first to propose a widely recognized model for college student dropout. Drawing from Durkheim's (1951) suicide model, Spady proposed a sociological model of the dropout process. Against a backdrop of family background, he proposed five variables (academic potential, normative congruence, grade performance, intellectual development, and friendship support) that contributed directly to social integration. These five variables were then linked indirectly to the dependent variable, dropout decision, through two intervening variables (satisfaction and institutional commitment). Subsequently, Spady (1971) designed and executed an empirical study, the findings of which resulted in his addition of structural relations to the model. The results of the empirical study indicated, "Over a four-year period . . . formal academic performance is clearly the dominant factor in accounting for attrition among both sexes" (Spady, 1971, p. 38).

The most widely recognized sociological perspective is Tinto's interactionalist theory (1975). Like Spady, Tinto linked this multivariate model to Durkheim's (1951) suicide model. The core of Tinto's original model focused on students' academic integration and social integration, both formal and informal. The degree to which students were successful in their pursuits determined the degree to which they are committed to their career and educational goals as well as to the institution. Pascarella, Terenzini, and Wolfe (1986) referred to "person-environment fit [as] the model's conceptual core" (p. 156).

Tinto's revised theory (1987) and his ultimate model incorporated Van Gennep's rites of passage, "separation, transition, and incorporation" (1960, p. 11), the stages that mark an individual's path in the process of moving from "youthful participation to full adult membership in society" (p. 92). (See Tinto, 1988, for a more detailed examination of the application of Van Gennep's theory to student retention.) Elkins, Braxton, and James (2000) observed that "Tinto extends these stages to the process through which college students establish membership in the communities of a college or university in general, and to the case of early student departure from college in particular" (p. 252). According to Braxton and Mundy (2002), the primary principles of Tinto's model of institutions with effective retention programs are those that committed to the development of supportive social and educational communities in which all students are integrated as competent members.

Further work by Tinto (1993) led to the development of a longitudinal, explanatory model of departure. This expanded work added "adjustment, difficulty, incongruence, isolation, finances, learning, and external obligations or commitments" (p. 112) to his original model. In sum, he proposed that "the stronger the individual's level of social and academic integration, the greater his or her subsequent commitment to the institution and to the goal of college graduation" (Pascarella, Terenzini, & Wolfe, 1986, pp. 155–156).

In this later work, Tinto (1993) recognized that different groups of students (that is, at-risk, adult, honors, and transfer) had distinctly different circumstances requiring group-specific retention policies and programs. In addition, he reasoned that different types of postsecondary institutions (nonresidential, two-year, urban, and large public) also required different types of retention policies and programs.

Psychological Perspectives

Additional perspectives focus on the psychological characteristics and processes that are significant determinants of students who stay and those who leave college. Included among these characteristics and processes are academic aptitude and readiness, motivation, personality, and student development.

The most prominent psychological perspective was proffered by Bean and Eaton (2002). Based on their earlier work focusing on the behavioral concept of approach/avoidance, Bean and Eaton formulated a model that was based on four psychological processes that led to academic and social integration. These processes were: positive self-efficacy, handling stress, increasing efficacy, and internal locus of control. Bean and Eaton suggested that, when applied to entering students, these psychological perspectives shape their perceptions of college and university life. They stressed the importance of institutional provisions for service-learning, freshman interest groups and other learning communities, freshman orientation seminars, and mentoring programs to support student success.

Astin's (1984) theory of student involvement refers to "the amount of physical and psychological energy a students devotes to the academic experience" (p. 397). Astin's theory was constructed as a "link between the variables emphasized in [traditional pedagogical theories] (subject matter, resources, and individualization of approach) and the learning outcomes desired by the student and the professor" (p. 300). This theory was based on the findings of Astin's early work and was designed "to identify factors in the college environment that significantly affect the student's persistence in college" (p. 302).

Astin's later work (1993) was an empirical study of the model. Using longitudinal data collected by the Higher Education Research Institute (HERI) at the University of California, Los Angeles in its annual survey of freshmen, he found that the three most important forms of student involvement were academic involvement, involvement with faculty, and involvement with student peer groups. A comparison of faculty, curriculum, institutional type, and peer group effects led to a primary finding of the study: "the student's peer group is the single most potent source of influence on growth and development during the undergraduate years" (p. 398).

Astin (1993) posited that the implications for practice should be overarching, rather than singular in nature:

> Institutions need not look far afield to find the key to enhanced student retention. It is achievable within the confines of existing institutional resources. It springs from the ongoing commitment of an institution, of its faculty and staff, to the education of its students.
>
> But such commitment requires institutional change. It requires that institutions rethink traditional ways of structuring collegiate learning environments and find new ways of actively involving students, as well as faculty, in their intellectual life. It requires a deeper understanding of the importance of educational community to the goals of higher education. (p. 212)

Organizational Perspectives

Bean (1980) developed the Model of Student Departure to explain the factors contributing to student attrition. The model was an adaptation of Price and Mueller's organizational turnover model (1981) developed to explain employee turnover in work organizations. Bean's causal model (1980) posited:

1. The background characteristics of students must be taken into account in order to understand their interactions within the environment.

2. The student interacts with the institution, perceiving objective measures, such as grade point average or belonging to campus organizations, as well as subjective measures, such as the practical value of the education and the quality of the institution.

3. These variables are in turn expected to influence the degree to which the student is satisfied with the college.

4. The level of satisfaction is expected to increase the level of institutional commitment.

5. Institutional commitment is seen as leading to a decrease in the likelihood that a student will drop out of school. (pp. 158–160)

Findings from an empirical test of the model (Bean, 1980) indicated that institutional quality and opportunity were the two most important variables influencing commitment. When it came to satisfaction, however, "men left the university even though they were satisfied while . . . women who were satisfied were more committed to the institution and were less likely to leave." (p. 178). He proposed further research to determine intervening variables not identified in the model. In a subsequent study, Bean (1985) proposed a revised model and found, in the empirical study of the model, that:

1. A student's peers are more important agents of socialization than is informal faculty contact;

2. Students may play a more active role in their socialization than previously thought; and

3. College grades seem more the product of selection than socialization. (p. 35)

Although Berger and Braxton (1998) and Pike and Kuh (2005) have also studied retention from this perspective, evidence of the relationship between student retention and institutional structures and processes remains inconclusive.

Economic Perspectives

The economic perspective, based in human capital theory (Becker, 1964), suggests that students weigh the costs and the benefits of continuing enrollment. This perspective holds that if a student perceives that the cost of staying in school outweighs the perceived benefits of degree completion, the student will leave college. This perspective may also be applied to student participation in a wide variety of curricular and cocurricular activities. Although monetary considerations (tuition and fees as well as foregone income) are direct costs, the economic perspective also applies to indirect costs, the time and the energy students need to devote to any activity as well as to college itself. Although these indirect costs parallel, to a certain extent, Astin's notion of psychological and physical energy (1984), students weigh the benefits accrued in relation to both the direct and the indirect costs. Multiple studies suggest that student ability to pay for college and student perceptions of the cost of college have an impact on persistence. St. John, Cabrera, Nora, and Asker (2000) provide a thorough review of the influences of economics on student persistence.

Cultural Perspectives

With the dramatic increase in the diversity of those entering college, which we discuss in Chapter Three, there has been increasing interest in and research on the impact of cultural factors on student persistence. This perspective focuses not only on traditionally underrepresented racial/ethnic minorities but also on international students as well as those who are first in their families to attend college. Kuh and Love (2000) shared eight propositions regarding student cultural beliefs that are related to student departure. Those are:

1. The college experience, including a decision to leave college, is mediated through a student's cultural meaning-making process.

2. One's cultures of origin (or cultural backgrounds) mediate the importance attached to attending college and earning a college degree.

3. Knowledge of a student's cultures of origin and the cultures of immersion is needed to understand a student's ability to successfully negotiate the institution's cultural milieu.

4. The probability of persistence is inversely related to the cultural distance between a student's culture(s) of origin and cultures of immersion.

5. Students who traverse a long cultural distance must become acclimated to dominant cultures of immersion or join one or more enclaves.

6. The amount of time a student spends in one's cultures of origin after matriculating is positively related to cultural stress and reduces the chances they will persist.

7. The likelihood a student will persist is related to the extensity and intensity of one's sociological connections to the academic program and to affinity groups.

8. Students who belong to one or more enclaves in the cultures of immersion are more likely to persist, especially if group members value achievement and persistence. (p. 201)

There continues to be debate on the degree to which college success for students from differing cultural backgrounds is predicated on the adoption of prevailing values and conformity to institutional norms and mores.

Integrated Perspectives

Although the sociological, psychological, economic, cultural, and organizational perspectives provide considerable insight into departure behavior, other approaches to explaining persistence behavior have been developed and studied. The term *theory* is difficult to define and the utility of any one retention theory is illusive. The *Merriam-Webster Third New International Dictionary* (2002) provides five main definitions with fourteen applications of the term *theory*. Those applications range from "a hunch or guess" to a scientifically proven set of principles that explain a concept or a phenomenon. It is our notion that retention theories fall somewhere in between these two definitions. Each of the theoretical perspectives previously described is useful in understanding selected elements that contribute to our understanding of student departure, yet no one theoretical perspective is comprehensive enough to encompass all of the factors that contribute to student persistence. Each of the perspectives is a macro in nature—useful in generalizing about a set of phenomena and predicting likely behavior of most individuals within a group. It is less useful when examining individual behavior. In reality, the key to an individual's decision to depart (or to stay) is based not on one of the perspectives, but rather on the blending and temporal shifting of the five perspectives as well as additional and idiosyncratic beliefs, attitudes, or circumstances. Though it is likely that to some degree each of the perspectives plays a role in the decision to remain enrolled or to leave, it is also likely that the dominance of a given perspective varies from student to student and, for individual students, may change over time. For example, the economic perspective may predominate for a student who is of low socioeconomic status. Yet, dominance of that perspective may diminish with the awarding of a scholarship. The psychological perspective may be dominant in the departure decision for a student with a low level of academic confidence. Yet, dominance of that perspective may change if academic success accrues. Finally, despite reams of research establishing the veracity of each of these perspectives, it is the integration of these perspectives into a comprehensive model that challenges researchers and practitioners alike.

Braxton, Hirschy, and McClendon (2004) attempted to do just that by extending the work of Tinto using empirical findings from organizational, psychological, sociological, and economic perspectives. Because they believe that factors influencing student departure differ based on college type, they developed separate models for studying retention in residential colleges and universities and in commuter colleges and universities. The models vary in the influence of student entry characteristics. The residential college model focuses on more traditional college entry attributes: academic achievement and ability, race, gender, parental education, and family SES. Although parental education is included among influential entry characteristics in the commuter model, the model focuses more on psychosocial factors: motivation, control issues, self-efficacy, empathy, affiliation needs, and anticipatory socialization. The models also differ in the role of social integration. The authors posit that in the residential college, social integration is influenced by institutional commitment to student welfare, institutional integrity, communal potential, proactive social adjustment, and psychological engagement. Though social factors contribute to the persistence decision in the commuter model, those influences are seen as products of the external environment: finances, support, work, family, and community.

Earlier on, Pascarella (1985) developed a general causal model. In presenting the model, he noted that "causal modeling is an important methodological approach which should find increased use by those interested in the cognitive and other outcomes of college" (p. 49). He suggested that causal modeling could be used to "understand the pattern of influences involved in the impact of postsecondary education on learning and cognitive development" (p. 49). In this model, student background/precollege traits and structural/organizational characteristics of institutions have a direct impact on the college environment. Quality of student effort, student background/precollege traits, and interactions with agents of socialization directly influence learning and cognitive development. All other variables in the model indirectly affect learning and cognitive development. Findings from the empirical study indicated that residential facilities and the dominant peer group were strong influences on academic achievement. Less strong, but nonetheless noticeable, was the effect of informal student/faculty interaction outside of the classroom.

Additional Perspectives

Two additional perspectives warrant consideration in this chapter. The first is the retention formula articulated by Alan Seidman (2005b). Although conceptual in nature, the formula is intuitive and utilitarian when contrasted with many complex and confusing statistically based studies that validate practice. It holds that retention is a product of early identification plus early, intensive, and continuous intervention. Early identification means the early determination of a student who is potentially at risk academically, socially, or psychologically. The terms *early intervention*, *intensive intervention*, and *continuous intervention* require little further explication. Though actualizing effective identification and intervention is not a trivial matter, the questions it poses should be at the core of identifying and assessing the impact of retention efforts.

The second perspective is that of the staying environment articulated by Habley (1981). In his Retention Model (Figure 2.1), Habley identified eight potential causes of attrition and proposed that the staying environment was one in which educational interventions are most likely to lead to student success.

Figure 2.1 Habley Retention Model

REASONS FOR LEAVING	EDUCATIONAL ENVIRONMENT	REASONS FOR STAYING
Institutional Mismatch		Institutional Match
Irrelevance		Relevance
Boredom		Stimulation
Low Concern for Student		High Concern for Student
Low (E $\times$ A to R) ratio		High (E $\times$ A to R) ratio
Health Concerns		
Personal Problems		
Financial Needs		

The first five variables in the model operate on continua and are dramatically influenced by interventions undertaken in the educational environment. These five continua are affected by institutional interventions that if delivered artfully, produce compelling reasons for staying. The institutional mismatch/ match continuum depicts the extent to which the educational environment provides an academic program that is consistent with students' educational goals and interests. Students who identify and commit to academic programs that are consistent with their educational and career goals are more likely to remain in the environment, whereas students who do not identify appropriate academic programs are candidates for attrition. A more thorough discussion of the relationship between student success and career development is the subject of Chapter Nine.

The second continuum is irrelevance/relevance. This continuum depicts the extent to which selected academic programs provide coursework and other learning experiences that students believe are significantly related to their educational goals. Students who view learning experiences as extraneous to their goals are less likely to be retained whereas those who understand the relevance of curricular requirements and actively participate in learning experiences both inside and outside the classroom are more likely to remain enrolled. We suggest that a critical component of communicating relevance resides in academic advising, which is the subject of Chapter Fourteen.

Academic boredom/academic stimulation is the third continuum. This continuum, related to the irrelevance/relevance continuum, is influenced by a number of factors. One of these factors is the degree to which students are placed into appropriate levels of instruction. An ineffective course placement program may result in student enrollment in courses that are inappropriate to their skills. For students who have previously mastered course content, such courses may result in academic boredom. We provide a thorough consideration of assessment and course placement in Chapter Twelve. The second issue here is, at least for first-year students, the apparent repetition of subject matter taken previously. That is, most first-year program plans focus on completing general education requirements (for example, English, mathematics, social sciences, humanities). Anxious to take courses in their majors, students may see these classes as no more than an extension of high school coursework. The third factor is the degree to which faculty members deliver challenging and engaging instruction. One of the major contentions in this book is that students are more likely to succeed when they are stimulated to learn. Stimulating instruction is essential for student success.

The fourth continuum depicted in Figure 2.1 indicates the level of concern for students. High concern for students is the extent to which the student is viewed as the most important person on campus and is evidenced by the student's interaction with persons, policies, programs, and procedures on the campus. Students who perceive faculty and staff as unconcerned are more likely to drop out. Students will also be more likely to leave the institution if policies and procedures are viewed as roadblocks to, rather than guidelines for, the effective and efficient pursuit of educational goals. The staying environment is characterized by a student-centered ethos.

The final continuum depicts the degree to which students feel that their **E**fforts and **A**bilities are fairly **R**ewarded in the classroom. This variable is expressed on the continuum from low to high ratios of $\underline{E}\text{ffort} \times \underline{A}\text{bilities} = \underline{R}\text{eward}$. In many ways the resulting ratio can be interpreted as a student's return on investment. All students have perceptions of both their intellectual abilities and the amount of effort required to be successful in college. If students achieve at levels substantially above their expectations they have a low reward ratio. The low ratio is a discrepancy between expectation and reality and may lead to academic boredom. A low ratio may also exist for students who perform substantially below their expectations. For them, the dissonance between expectation and reality can lead to frustration, academic failure, and ultimately, to dropping out of college. A high ratio exists when students' expectation of their effort and abilities are commensurate with their classroom achievement. Thus, students who understand both their intellectual talents and the amount of effort required for successful performance in the classroom are more likely to remain in the classroom.

Three of the variables depicted in Figure 2.1 are those most often cited by students as reasons for leaving college: health concerns, personal problems, and financial needs. Though concerns over these variables are often cited as reasons for leaving, the inverse is not necessarily true. That is, just because students are healthy, well adjusted, and can afford to attend, those circumstances do not mean that they will continue to enroll.

Student Characteristics Contributing to Retention

Perhaps no topic has been the focus of more research in higher education in the last five decades than student characteristics that increase (or decrease) the likelihood of persistence to a degree. The authors will not attempt to share a complete summary of the research because it is both voluminous and, more than occasionally, contradictory. Chapters Three and Seven provide detailed information of the impact of student demographics (including race/ethnicity) and academic performance respectively. Other studies focus on gender, family educational background, effort, aspirations, family support, socioeconomic status, financial aid, precollege programs, enrollment patterns, and multiple institutional attendance.

Utilizing data from more than 90,000 students, Astin and Oseguera (2005) conducted a comprehensive study of student characteristics related to retention. They suggest that a significant proportion of existing research has focused on the development and testing of empirical models that either predict a student's likelihood of degree completion or identify the optimal conditions that will yield the best chance of completing a degree. Astin and Oseguera contend that empirical studies of college student retention have two practical applications: prediction and control. *Prediction* focuses on the odds of a student completing a degree within an acceptable time period, and *control* refers to the institution's capacity to enhance students' chances of completing a degree. The findings of the study revealed that the student characteristic that carried the most weight in estimating a student's chance of completing a degree was high school grades. In addition, the number of years of foreign language study showed the strongest positive effect on college completion, whereas smoking cigarettes had the greatest negative effect. Other factors exhibiting a positive relationship to degree completion were father's education level, mother's education level, parents alive and living with each other, parental income, gender (female), Roman Catholic religion, Jewish religion, self-rated emotional health, plan to participate in community service, and time spent in student clubs and groups.

Institutional Conditions Contributing to Retention

Just as the literature is replete with research on student characteristics, it is also clear that there is a relationship between student success and institutional conditions/properties. Though not focused specifically on student retention, practices in teaching that enhance student learning are the paramount contributors to student success. Chickering and Gamson (1987) underscore the importance of improving college teaching and student learning. And in turn, quality teaching and student learning lead to student success and improved persistence. They articulate seven principles for good practice in undergraduate education.

Chickering and Gamson (1987) suggest that effective instruction:

1. Encourages Contact Between Students and Faculty

Frequent student-faculty contact in and out of classes is the most important factor in student motivation and involvement. Faculty concern helps students get through rough times and keep on working. Knowing a few faculty members well enhances students' intellectual commitment and encourages them to think about their own values and future plans.

2. Develops Reciprocity and Cooperation Among Students

Learning is enhanced when it is more like a team effort than a solo race. Good learning, like good work, is collaborative and social, not competitive and isolated. Working with others often increases involvement in learning. Sharing one's own ideas and responding to others' reactions sharpens thinking and deepens understanding.

3. Encourages Active Learning

Learning is not a spectator sport. Students do not learn much just by sitting in classes listening to teachers, memorizing pre-packaged assignments, and spitting out answers. They must talk about what they are learning, write about it, relate it to past experiences, and apply it to their daily lives. They must make what they learn part of themselves.

4. Gives Prompt Feedback

Knowing what you know and don't know focuses learning. Students need appropriate feedback on performance to benefit from courses. When getting started, students need help in assessing existing knowledge and competence. In classes, students need frequent opportunities to perform and receive suggestions for improvement. At various points during college, and at the end, students need chances to reflect on what they have learned, what they still need to know, and how to assess themselves.

5. Emphasizes Time on Task

Time plus energy equals learning. There is no substitute for time on task. Learning to use one's time well is critical for students and professionals alike. Students need help in learning effective time management. Allocating realistic amounts of time means effective learning for students and effective teaching for faculty. How an institution defines time expectations for students, faculty, administrators, and other professional staff can establish the basis of high performance for all.

6. Communicates High Expectations

Expect more and you will get more. High expectations are important for everyone—for the poorly prepared, for those unwilling to exert themselves, and for the bright and well motivated. Expecting students to perform well becomes a self-fulfilling prophecy when teachers and institutions hold high expectations for themselves and make extra efforts.

7. Respects Diverse Talents and Ways of Learning

There are many roads to learning. People bring different talents and styles of learning to college. Brilliant students in the seminar room may be all thumbs in the lab or art studio. Students rich in hands-on experience may not do so well with theory. Students need the opportunity to show their talents and learn in ways that work for them. Then they can be pushed to learn in new ways that do not come so easily. (pp. 3–5).

Chickering and Gamson also suggest that the implementation of the seven principles relies on several institutional qualities. Those are: "a strong sense of shared purposes; concrete support from administrators and faculty leaders for those purposes; adequate funding to achieve the purposes; policies and procedures consistent with the purposes; and continuing examination of how well the purposes are being achieved" (p. 5).

Tinto (1993) identified three basic institutional principles and their application to retention. First, Tinto argued that effective retention programs require an institutional commitment to student welfare ahead of other institutional goals. He believed that successful retention relied less on the formal programs it devised than on the institution's underlying "orientation toward students which directs its activities" (p. 146). Tinto's second principle was that institutions must commit to educating all of the students it admits. He believed that effective retention programs did not leave learning to chance. Finally, Tinto posited that successful institutional retention programs ensured "the development of supportive social and educational communities in which all student are integrated as competent members" (p. 147).

Kuh, Kinzie, Schuh, and Whitt (2005) undertook the two-year Documenting Effective Educational Practice (DEEP) project. They studied 20 colleges with higher-than-predicted graduation rates to identify what those colleges did to promote student success. They discovered that there were six overarching features held in common by the DEEP schools. Those were: a living mission and a lived educational philosophy, an unshakeable focus on student learning, environments adapted for educational enrichment, clear pathways to student success, improvement-oriented ethos, and shared responsibility for educational quality and student success. The authors also described broad categories of effective practices. DEEP colleges, they wrote:

- Provided academic challenge
- Used active and collaborative learning techniques
- Reported higher levels of faculty-student interaction. Provided students with a wide variety of educational experiences
- Featured high-quality student relationships with other students, faculty, and administrative personnel.

Institutional Interventions Contributing to Retention

The literature on institutional interventions is remarkably consistent through more than four decades of research. Although there are minor variations in semantics and emphasis, virtually all major retention sources cite four primary programming clusters that are critical to institutional retention efforts. Those clusters focus on programs that:

- Facilitate a smooth transition into college through pre-enrollment and post-enrollment orientation to college life;
- Provide advice and counsel that helps students identify and commit to a program of study;
- Assess entry level academic skills that result in placement in courses that are consistent with demonstrated academic skills and provide learning support for students who are at risk;
- Focus on student learning as an active, collaborative, and challenging process.

Following is a review of selected research studies that support the four programming clusters as the foundation of a quality retention program.

Early on, Pantages and Creedon (1978) strongly supported the "college fit" theory, which stressed the importance of the interaction between student and institutional characteristics and its effect on persistence. They suggested that admission policies and counseling programs (broadly defined) were key institutional factors contributing to persistence. Noel (1978) agreed that admissions management was critical, but further defined counseling interventions to include both academic advising and career planning as essential retention interventions.

Tinto (1993) suggested there were numerous practices that were critical to student retention. Without additional elaboration, those practices are initial interactions with admissions personnel through the recruiting process, orientation, assessment and placement, first-year transition programs, community building, academic involvement and support, monitoring and early warning, and counseling and advising. Tinto goes on to make the case that the most effective retention program is not necessarily one in which practices are in place, but rather a program that is integrated into a coherent first-year experience for students.

Although the findings from ACT's *What Works in Student Retention* (WWISR) (Habley, McClanahan, Valiga, & Burkum, 2010) surveys are reported in detail in Chapter Eleven, the successful retention interventions are remarkably similar across all four surveys. In the first WWISR survey, conducted by ACT and the National Center for Higher Education Management Systems, Beal and Noel (1980) identified several institutional characteristics and interventions that supported retention efforts. Those were faculty and staff attitude, academic advising, adequate financial aid, curriculum revisions, counseling support, academic support, and career planning. The second WWISR study (Cowart, 1987) affirmed the interventions identified in the Beal-Noel study and expanded the list of characteristics and interventions to include high-quality teaching, student involvement, admissions management, a counseling program, and an early-warning system. The third ACT study (Habley & McClanahan, 2004) identified 82 interventions sorted into 12 clusters. Although many of the interventions had a positive effect on persistence, the clusters of interventions that were seen as having the greatest impact were transition programs, academic advising, learning support, and assessment. In the fourth WWISR study (Habley et al., 2010) those clusters also surfaced as primary contributors to retention.

Additional research efforts corroborate those of the WWISR studies. In its study of four-year public colleges, the American Association of State Colleges and Universities (2005) concluded that the institutional interventions and characteristics having the most positive impact on student success were first-year-experience programs, intentional advising, coordinated and integrated student services, and specific curricular features designed to build greater student identification and engagement. Parallel conclusions were drawn by Hossler and Bean (1990). And finally, along with advising, transition programs, learning support, and assessment/course placement, Tinto (1993) also identified recruitment/admission, community building and monitoring, and early warning as critical to institutional retention efforts.

Conclusion

In this chapter, we set out to provide an overview of the complexity of theoretical perspectives and summarize research on the student and institutional factors that contribute to retention. Over the last forty years, theoretical perspectives have been proposed, tweaked, and, in some cases, at least partially validated. Assertions on the causes of attrition have remained consistent. Transition programs, advising, and learning assistance remain the most prominent interventions, with only shifts in emphases and minor variations in delivery over the years. Yet there have been virtually no changes in rates of retention or persistence to degree. Have theorizing, researching, and experimenting with intervention been for naught? We think not. We prefer to view the last forty years as precursors to a breakthrough in how we support the success of individual students.

Section 2

THE CASE FOR INTENSIFIED CAMPUS EFFORTS

3

THE DEMOGRAPHIC CHALLENGE

In a pattern nearly as predictable as the sun rising in the eastern sky, the fall of each year brings an influx of first-time students to colleges and universities throughout this nation. More than three million students bring their dreams and expectations, their hopes and fears, and their aspirations and goals with them as they enter college. Each person is shaped by a unique combination of life experiences, personal characteristics, attitudes, and values that brought them to college and will play a significant role in their success in college. In addition to uniquely personal factors, the demographics of educational attainment, particularly among underrepresented minorities, has become a critical consideration in this country. On the surface, the story of racial/ethnic demographics can be described in one simple statement. Minorities will constitute nearly 50% of the U.S. population by the year 2050. When combined with the personal characteristics of entering college students, the demographics of race/ethnicity pose complex major challenges in both access to and success in college.

The purpose of this chapter is threefold. First, we will provide a snapshot of selected characteristics of entering college students. In addition, we will examine the critical role that race/ethnicity plays in understanding student movement toward, into, and through college into the world of work. Finally, we will examine the impact that educational attainment has on individuals, society, and U.S. global competitiveness. The chapter will close with persuasive arguments for doubling and redoubling practices and interventions that lead to student success in college. It should be noted that this chapter does not focus on academic preparation and performance of entering college students. That is the subject considered in Chapter Seven.

Characteristics of College Students

As mentioned in the chapter introduction, every student who enters higher education is the product of a unique set of life experiences and characteristics. Although each of the experiences and characteristics is likely to affect access to and success in college, it is not possible within the scope of this chapter to both enumerate and discuss each of these characteristics. Rather, the authors' intent is to paint a broad picture that will stimulate the reader to consider the impact of the characteristics singly or in combination with others. Following are selected characteristics of college students, taken from a wide-ranging variety of sources.

Race/Ethnicity (NCES, 2009a)

- 64% are white
- 13% are black
- 11% are Hispanic
- 7% are Asian/Pacific Islander
- 1% are American Indian/Alaskan Native
- 4% are multicultural
- 3% are international students

College Attendance Patterns (NCES, 2009a)

- 62% attend full-time; 38% are part-time
- 77% attend public institutions; 23% private institutions
- 65% attend four-year colleges; 35% attend two-year colleges
- 70% enrolled within a year of high school graduation; 30% enrolled a year or more after high school graduation

Family Background (U.S. Census Bureau, 2010a)

- 26% have lived in a single-parent household
- 33% have lived in step-families at one time
- 30% have moved primary residence in the previous five years
- 26% come from out of state (ACT, 2010a)

Marital Status (U.S. Census Bureau, 2010a)

- 10% in community colleges; 7% in four-year colleges are married with no dependents
- 15% in community colleges; 6% in four-year colleges are single parents
- 20% in community colleges; 10% in four-year colleges are married parents
- Educational Plans (ACT, 2010a)
- 40% plan to earn a bachelor's degree at time of first enrollment
- 36% plan to earn an associate's degree
- 13% plan to earn a certificate
- 11% have no specific degree plans
- 20% are undecided about a college major

Financial Issues (NCES, 2009a)

- 63% will receive financial aid
- 61% of students in community colleges are financially independent
- 35% of students in four-year colleges are financially independent

Additional Characteristics (NCES, 2009a)

- 57% are female; 43% are male
- 31% are 24 years or older at time of first enrollment

- 11% have a documented disability
- 10% (estimate) are GLBT (personal conversations)

These selected characteristics illustrate that assumptions regarding the background and nature of what was once a typical college student have given way to the reality that there is no such thing as a traditional college student. The exception has become the rule.

The Demographics of the Educational Pipeline

Although these selected characteristics illustrate the fascinating mosaic of factors that shape students' attitudes toward and motivation for enrolling in college, they shed little light on the flow of students through the educational pipeline. In reality, that pipeline begins at birth, but for the purposes of this chapter, a flow model will be constructed that begins with enrollment in the 9th grade and concludes with the adult population's educational attainment levels. There are methodological complexities that result in a flow model that is inexact but nevertheless informative. The flow model is derived from multiple data sources, some with single data points and others with longitudinal databases beginning and ending in different years. Some data sources include historical data only, whereas others include projections for the future. A second complexity is that the data are based on different methodologies for reporting high school completion. As an example, terms representing high school completion come in the form of high school dropout rates, high school graduation rates, and status dropout rates. Each of these terms results in different perspectives on high school completion and yields different results. Finally, different metrics are used to report data. Some reports use numbers, some use percentages, and some report differences in numbers or percentages. Because of these complexities, it is hoped that the explanatory text and the table titles will clearly define the content of the chapter.

The message conveyed in this chapter, however, is not based on the precision of the data. Rather, it is hoped that the data illustrate the cause for concern and provide a sense of urgency for improving the leaking educational pipeline.

A Shifting and Diversifying Population

There is no doubt that the population of the United States is shifting geographically while diversifying significantly by race and ethnicity. Table 3.1 illustrates the fact that between 1995 and 2025, approximately 80% of the 72.3 million growth in the U.S. population will occur in the southern and western states. As reported by the U.S. Census Bureau (2010b), of the 50 fastest-growing metro areas, 27 were in the South and 20 were in the West, topped by Dallas-Fort Worth and Atlanta. Among towns in the Midwest and Northeast, Detroit lost more than three times as many people as any other metro area—its population declined more than 27,300 between 2000 and 2009. Other metro areas in the Midwest and Northeast losing more than 5,000 people were Pittsburgh, Cleveland, Youngstown, and Buffalo.

Table 3.1 Projected Population Percentage Change in Regions by Race and Hispanic Origin: 1995–2025.

Region	Change	White % change	Black % change	Am. Ind. % change	Asian % change	Hispanic orig. % change
United States	72,295	21.6	16.5	1.1	16.6	44.3
Northeast	5,927	–1.9	25.2	5.4	39.1	70.1
Midwest	7,306	25.0	25.4	2.7	15.5	31.5
South	29,558	35.2	25.9	6.7	6.1	32.2
West	29,504	18.4	3.1	1.3	22.8	54.3

Source: Adapted from U.S. Bureau of the Census, Population Division (1996).

The statistics on racial/ethnic composition of the U.S. population also illustrate dramatic growth in racial/ethnic minorities. Table 3.1 indicates that the growth rate for individuals of Hispanic origin far outpaces the growth rates of American Indians, blacks, and Asians in all regions, and outpaces the percentage growth of the white population in all regions but the South. Although recent reports suggest that the economy and stricter immigration laws are slowing population growth among Hispanics, Passel and Cohn (2008) report that by the year 2050, persons of Hispanic origin will account for just fewer than 30% of the U.S. population, whereas the population proportion of whites is expected to decline from 67% in 2005 to 47% in 2050. During that same time period, as a percentage of the U.S. population, black persons will remain steady at about 13% and the Asian population will increase from about 5% to 9%.

Getting to College

Geographic shifts and increasing population diversity in the US are mirrored in the patterns of secondary school enrollment, high school completion, and enrollment in college. Table 3.2 depicts changes in public high school graduates from 2008–09 to 2018–19. The United States is expected to experience only a slight increase in the number of public high school graduates with noticeable losses in the Northeast and Midwest and a significant gain in the South. During the same time period, the number of nonpublic high school graduates is projected to decline by nearly 7%. Most notable among the ten-year changes by race/ethnicity are major increases in Asian/Pacific Islander and Hispanic public high school graduates across all regions. Also noted are declines across all regions in both black non-Hispanic and white non-Hispanic high school graduates. Projections for nonpublic high school graduates are not available by race/ethnicity.

Table 3.2 Projected Percentage Change in Public High School Graduates from 2008-09 to 2018-19 by Region and Race/Ethnicity.

	U.S. (%)	Northeast (%)	Midwest (%)	South (%)	West (%)
Overall Change	+0.5	−9.4	−5.3	+10.9	+1.0
American Indian/ Alaskan Native	+1.5	+25.9	−3.6	+21.8	−8.1
Asian/ Pacific Islander	+36.9	+41.4	+52.3	+80.1	+18.8
Black non-Hispanic	−7.3	−13.4	−12.8	−2.4	−13.3
Hispanic	+46.0	+19.1	+78.7	+80.8	+27.6
White non-Hispanic	−12.6	−17.0	−12.4	−7.8	−16.5

Source: Adapted from Western Interstate Commission for Higher Education (WICHE), (2008).

Moving Toward College

Tracking the pipeline of students from entry into high school to graduation is fraught with complex, conflicting, and confounding approaches. Heckman and LaFontaine (2007) suggest that "depending on the data sources, definitions, and methods used, the U.S. graduation rate is estimated to be anywhere from 66 to 88 percent in recent years—an astonishingly wide range for such a basic statistic. The range of estimated minority rates is even greater—from 50 to 85 percent" (p. 3).

Rather than engage in extensive verbiage defining and discussing the merits and shortcomings of these various approaches, the graduation rates reported in Table 3.3 are the Averaged Freshman Graduation Rates (AFGR) calculated by the National Center for Educational Statistics (NCES). The AFGR is an estimate of the percentage of an entering freshman class graduating from high school on time (in four years).

Table 3.3 High School to College Pipeline by Race/Ethnicity.

	Column 1	Column 2	Column 3
	AFGR[1] (%)	College enrollment rate[2] (%)	Percentage of H.S. freshmen who graduate in 4 years AND enroll in college within one year of graduation
All races	74.9	70.1	52.5
White alone (non-Hispanic)	81.0	69.2	56.1
Black alone	61.5	68.7	42.2
Hispanic (of any race)	63.5	59.3	37.7
Asian/Pacific Islander	91.4	92.2	84.3
American Indian/ Native Alaskan	64.2	N/A	N/A

[1] Stillwell (2010).

[2] U.S. Bureaus of Labor Statistics (2010a).

The percentage reported in the first column of Table 3.3 is derived from the total number of diploma recipients in 2006–07 divided by the average membership of the 8th grade class of 2002–03, the 9th grade class of 2003–04, and the 10th grade class of 2004–05.

The AFGR percentages reported in column 1 of Table 3.3 clearly illustrate the significant gaps in high school completion rates between the Asian (91.4%) and the white (81.0%) cohorts and the black, Hispanic, and American Indian/Native Alaskan cohorts. These gaps become even more pronounced when one reviews the graduation rates in the nation's largest school districts, those most likely to have high concentrations of black and Hispanic students. Indeed, seven of the nation's 50 largest school districts report high school graduation rates below 50%, with Detroit (37.5%), Milwaukee (41.0%), and

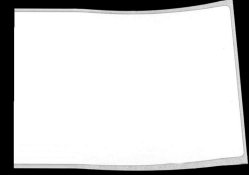

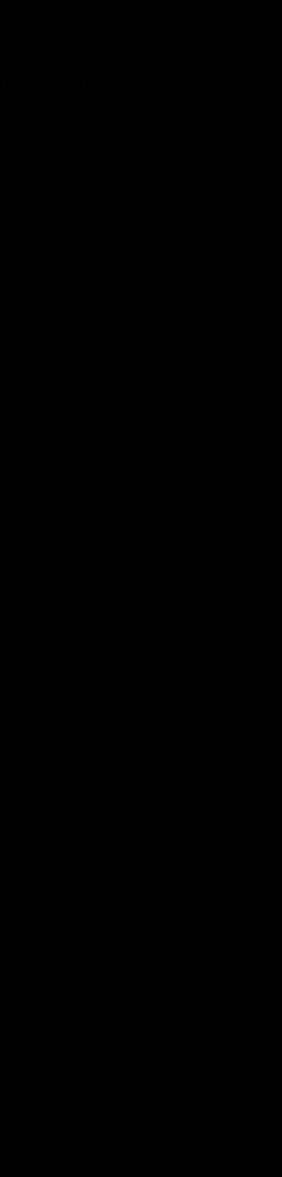

Baltimore (41.5%) at the bottom of the list (EPE, 2008). The nation's three largest school districts—Los Angeles, New York City, and Chicago—report AFGRs of 44.4%, 50.5% and 51.0%, respectively (EPE, 2008).

Although the pipeline to high school graduation narrows considerably for Hispanics, blacks, and American Indian/Native Alaskans, enrollment in college constricts that pipeline even further. Column 2 of Table 3.3 reports on the percentage of students who enroll in college within a year of high school graduation. These data, from the Bureau of Labor Statistics (2010a), report that in 2009 the college enrollment rate reached an all-time high of 70.1%, rising more than 20% since 1959. It is encouraging to note that more than nine of ten Asian high school graduates enroll in college, and more than two-thirds of white and black high school graduates continue on to some form of higher education. Yet, it is discouraging to note that although the on-time high school graduation rate of Hispanic students is 63.5%, only 59.3% of those students enroll in some form of postsecondary education within a year of earning a high school diploma. Although data for American Indian/Alaskan Native students are not available, it is likely that their college enrollment rates are low.

The combined effects of the AFGR and college enrollment rates are reported in Column 3 of Table 3.3. For example, 62.3% of Hispanic students earned a high school diploma on time and 59.3% of those entered college within a year of high school graduation. The net result is that only 37.7% of Hispanic high school freshmen graduate on time and enroll in postsecondary education. Although the college enrollment rates for black students are close to the national average, a low high school completion rate accounts for the fact that only 42.2% of black high school freshmen graduate high school on time and enroll in college within a year of graduation.

Table 3.3 does not, however, provide the most complete picture of educational attainment. The assumptions underpinning the table are narrowly defined. They do not account for individuals who take longer than four years to earn a high school diploma or those who ultimately complete the GED. And the assumptions do not account for students who do not enroll in college immediately after high school, choosing other options before enrolling in college at a later date. While the reader may take issue with the definitions, the sources of data, or the methodology applied to this analysis, debate on such issues obscures the real problem: the educational pipeline from the first year of high school to college completion results in significant attrition of Hispanic and black students. And while college success must be improved among students of all races and ethnicities, improvement of success rates of Hispanics and blacks is imperative.

Moving Through College

Enrolling in college is a significant accomplishment, but data indicate that success in college is far from a foregone conclusion. Success is predicated on academic performance, retention, progress, and persistence. In a comprehensive tracking study, Noble and Radunzel (2007) studied cumulative grade point averages, year-to-year retention, progress to degree, and degree completion rates. While several studies track one or more of these success factors, no single study tracks all of these factors including a large sample of two-year and four-year college students. Data for the study included approximately 200,000 ACT-tested students who enrolled in college as first-time entering students in fall 1998 through 2003. Over a hundred institutions were represented, including all public institutions from three state systems. About 123,000 of the students were enrolled at four-year institutions and just over 73,000 were enrolled in two-year colleges. In this study, underrepresented minority students (black, Hispanic, and American Indian) were aggregated. Underrepresented students constituted 15% of the sample enrolled in four-year colleges and 17% of the sample enrolled in two-year colleges. Data from the Noble-Radunzel study comparing the performance of whites with the performance of underrepresented minorities are summarized below.

Moving Through Four-Year Colleges. Data on the grades earned reveal significant difference in the academic performance of whites and underrepresented minorities. Across all four years, approximately 70% of white students earned cumulative grade point averages of 2.5 or above, whereas rates for underrepresented minority students hovered at or near the 50% mark.

Same institution year-to-year retention rates indicate that white students are only slightly more likely to be retained from the first to second year than underrepresented minorities. For whites, that rate is 71% compared to 69% for minorities. That gap widens to 5% in ensuing years with third- to fourth-year retention rates reported at 48% for whites and 43% for minorities.

Progress to degree in the Noble/Radunzel study was defined using end-of-year thresholds of 24, 48, 72, and 96 earned credit hours for Years 1, 2, 3, and 4, respectively. Gaps between whites and minorities were observed across all four years. The first-year difference of 12% (70% to 58%) narrowed to 9% (48% to 39%) in year 4.

Moving Through Two-Year Colleges. Data on the grades earned reveal significant differences in the academic performance of whites and underrepresented minorities. Across all three years, 63–64% of white students earned cumulative grade point averages of 2.5 or above while rates for underrepresented minority students hovered between 47% and 49%.

Retention rates for the two-year colleges were defined as retention at any college. First- to second-year retention rates for whites and minorities were 67% and 59%, respectively, and rates from the second to the third year were 49% for whites and 39% for underrepresented minorities.

For two-year institutions, end-of-year cumulative hours were defined as 18, 36, and 54 credit hours earned for Years 1, 2, and 3, respectively. Across all three years, the gap between white student progression and minority student progression was approximately 10%. Rates for whites were 65%, 46%, and 35% for years 1, 2, and 3, respectively. And for underrepresented minorities, rates for the same years were 55%, 35%, and 28%.

The Noble/Radunzel study echoes the same theme articulated in previous sections of this chapter. Underrepresented minorities are less likely to complete high school on time; those who do complete are less likely to enroll in college; those who enroll in college are less likely to earn 2.5 grade point averages, less likely to make reasonable academic progress, and finally, less likely to be retained.

Completing College

Ultimately, it is college completion that is an indication of success for students in the educational pipeline. There are two methods for examining that success. The first method is identifying those who complete college in a reasonable time frame from point of first enrollment. ACT (2010b) data indicate that 31% of full-time degree-seeking students in community colleges earn an associate's degree within three years of entry. The six-year degree completion rates for full-time, degree-seeking students at four-year public and four-year private colleges are 49% and 59%, respectively. Table 3.4 is drawn from the Noble and Radunzel (2007) study. It provides an overview of the five-year degree completion rates for whites and for underrepresented minorities at both four-year and two-year colleges. The completion rates for minority students in both four-year and two-year colleges are not very encouraging. Even though white students outperform underrepresented minorities, their completion rates are no cause for celebration.

Table 3.4 Degree Completion Rates at Two- and Four-Year Institutions.

		Four-year institutions		Two-year institutions			
	Variable	Yr. 4	Yr. 5	Yr. 2	Yr. 3	Yr. 4	Yr. 5
Race/ ethnicity	Minority	12%	26%	6%	13%	16%	18%
	White	19%	39%	9%	20%	25%	27%

Six-year college completion rates at four-year institutions are reported by categories of race/ethnicity in the *Condition of Education* (NCES, 2010a). About 57% of first-time students seeking a bachelor's degree and attending a four-year institution full-time in 2001–02 completed a bachelor's degree at that institution within six years. Six-year graduation rates by race/ethnicity were: Asian/Pacific Islanders (67%), whites (60%), Hispanics (48%), blacks (42%), and American Indians/Alaska natives (40%). Applying these six-year completion rates to the data in Column 3 of Table 3.3 leads to a reasonable, but not precise, calculation of the percentage of freshman high school students who complete high school on time, enroll full-time in college within a year of high school graduation, and graduate from a four-year college within six years of first enrollment. To complete such a calculation requires the percentage of college students who enroll at four-year colleges. The *Digest of Educational Statistics* (NCES, 2009a) reports that about 63.5% of postsecondary students are enrolled in a four-year college. For example then, the calculation for all races is 52.5% (college enrollment rate) × .635 (proportion of four-year college students). The resulting outcomes are 33.3% of high school freshmen of all races, 33.1% of white high school freshmen, 26.9% of black high school freshmen, 23.9% of Hispanic high school freshmen, and 53.5% of Asian/pacific Islander freshmen will earn a high school diploma in four years, enroll in a four-year college within one year of high school graduation, and will earn a bachelor's degree within six years of initial college enrollment. Unfortunately, comparable measures of two-year college completion rates by race/ethnicity are difficult to come by, but ACT's *Retention and Persistence to Degree Tables* (2010e) report that 31% of two-year college students seeking an associate's degree complete that degree within three years or less.

The second measure of college success rates is found in Table 3.5, which reports college participation/completion rates of the adult population (18 and over) by race/ethnicity. The table validates the data arrayed earlier in this chapter. Underrepresented minorities lag far behind whites and Asians in the attainment of college degrees. Of the adult population of all races, 35.5% have earned an associate's degree or higher. In comparison, 25.3% of adult blacks (alone) and 17.7% of adult

Table 3.5 Percentages of College Participation/Completion of the U.S. Population 18 Years and Over by Race and Hispanic Origin: 2009.

	Some college (%)	Associate's (%)	Bachelor's degree (%)	Above a bachelor's (%)
All races	19.5	8.5	17.7	9.3
White (non-Hispanic)	20.0	9.2	19.9	10.6
White alone or in combination	19.4	8.6	18.1	9.4
Black alone	22.2	8.1	11.6	5.6
Black alone or in combination	22.5	8.2	11.7	1.1
Hispanic (of any race)	15.6	5.8	8.8	3.1
Asian alone	13.9	6.6	29.8	18.7
Asian alone or in combination	14.6	6.7	29.5	18.2

Source: Adapted from U.S. Census Bureau (2010c).

Hispanics (of any race) have earned an associate's degree or higher. About one of every two Asian adults has earned a bachelor's degree or higher while one of every three whites, and only one of every five blacks, and one of every ten Hispanics have done so.

A review of the data provided in this section of the chapter could lead one to launch a polemic on the imprecision of the data analysis. Some suggest that demography is destiny whereas others strongly resist that assertion. Without engaging in that debate, suffice it to say that Hispanics, the fastest growing ethnic group in this country, will constitute 30% of the population by 2050 (CNN, 2008). Unless dramatic changes take place in access to college and success in college, Hispanics will continue to be the ethnic group far less likely to complete high school, far less likely to enroll in college, and far less likely to earn college degrees than white or Asian students. In addition, although the proportion of blacks in 2050 will increase only slightly to 15% of the U.S. population, their movement through the educational pipeline is only slightly better than that of Hispanics. Finally, American Indians/Alaskan Natives, whose college completion rates are below those of both Hispanics and blacks, will account for about 2% of the U.S. population. Indeed, those least likely to succeed in the K–16 pipeline will, by the year 2050, constitute just under 50% of the U.S. population.

The Impact of Educational Attainment

Although the demographics of the educational pipeline sadly chronicle the waste of human potential, without significant educational interventions, these demographics may lead to profound and debilitating effects on individuals, on the national economy, and on this country's global competitiveness.

At the individual level, postsecondary education has moved from nicety to an economic necessity over the last four decades. According to data provided by the U.S. Bureau of Labor

Statistics (BLS) (2010b), there are significant differences in 2009 unemployment rates by level of educational attainment. The range of these rates is from 14.6% for those with less than a high school diploma to 2.4% for those with doctoral or professional degrees. The difference in unemployment rates between those with only a high school diploma and those with a bachelor's degree is 4.5%, with rates reported at 9.7% and 5.2%, respectively (U.S. Bureau of Labor Statistics, 2010a).

The BLS (2010a) also reports on the differences in 2009 median weekly earnings by level of educational attainment. The range of median weekly earnings is from $1,530 for those with doctoral or professional degrees to $454 for those with less than a high school diploma. The difference in median weekly earnings between those with only a high school diploma and those with a bachelor's degree is $399, with weekly earnings reported at $626 and $1,025, respectively.

In addition to the effects on individual economic well-being, educational attainment is inextricably linked to workforce trends. Carnevale, Smith, and Strohl (2010) suggest that America is on a collision course with the future in that far too few students are enrolling in college and earning college degrees. The authors predict that the percentage of jobs that require at least some college will increase from 28% of the new jobs available in 1973 to 63% of the new jobs that will be available in 2018. During the same time period the authors predict significant decreases in jobs available for high school dropouts (from 32% to 10%) and for high school graduates (40% to 28%). Finally, the authors suggest that between 2008 and 2018, the labor force will require 22 million new college degrees but with current college completion rates there will be a shortfall of 3 million individuals with postsecondary degrees.

These individual and workforce concerns created by current U.S. levels of educational attainment will likely have a major impact on this country's position in the global economy. Joshi (2009) suggests that the global economy is the interdependence of national economies throughout the world in the movement of goods, service, technology, and capital. Because education is critical to national economic well-being, Joshi's definition raises the issue of educational attainment levels in comparison to other countries. Such comparisons have been made by the Organization for Economic Cooperation and Development (OECD). The United States participates in the OECD, a group of countries that are thought of as the major industrialized democracies of the world. OECD routinely conducts comparative studies on the educational attainment levels of its members. The most recent report, *Education at a Glance*, was completed in 2009 and focused on data for 2007. The OECD report included data on secondary school enrollment and graduation rates. In addition, the OECD study provided data on matriculation and completion rates in Tertiary Type-A programs (comparable to U.S. bachelor's degree) and Tertiary Type-B program (comparable to U.S. associate's degree). Mortenson (2010) utilized data from the OECD report to conduct further analyses of the data on the changes that had taken place in OECD data between 2000 and 2007. OECD data (2009) and Mortenson's extended analysis (2010) are reported below.

Secondary school enrollment rates

- In 2007, the United States ranked 23rd of 35 countries on the enrollment rate for 15- to 19-year-olds (79.9%). The mean for reporting countries was 81.5% (OECD, 2009a).

- Between 2000 and 2007, the United States ranked 10th among 23 countries on change in enrollment rate with a 7.1% gain. The mean change for countries reporting was +4.4% (Mortenson, 2010).

Upper secondary (high school) graduation rates

- In 2007, the United States ranked 20th of 28 countries in secondary school completion rates with a rate 77.5%. The mean for reporting countries was 82.1% (OECD, 2009b).

- Between 2000 and 2007, the United States ranked 9th of 22 countries on secondary school completion rate with an increase of 7.7%, ranking 9th of 22 countries. The mean change for reporting countries was +5.9% (Mortenson, 2010).

Tertiary Type-A (bachelor's degree) enrollment rates

- In 2007, the United States reported a bachelor's degree enrollment rate of 64.6%, which ranked 10th of 32 countries reporting. The mean enrollment rate for reporting countries was 56.0% (OECD, 2009b).
- Between 2000 and 2007, the United States ranked 20th of 28 countries on change in bachelor degree enrollment rates with a negligible increase of 1.0%. The mean for all reporting countries was +4.2% (Mortenson, 2010).

Tertiary Type-A (bachelor's degree) and Tertiary Type-B attainment rates

- In 2007 with 36 countries reporting, the United States ranked 12th, with 40.4% of 25- to 34-year-olds having completed an associate's degree or bachelor's degree. The mean for reporting countries was 34.2% (OECD, 2009a).
- Between 2000 and 2007, the United States ranked 29th of 32 countries in tertiary completion rate change for 25- to 34-year-olds. The increase was a modest 1.4%, which was considerably below the mean (+6.4%) for the countries reporting (Mortenson, 2010).

The OECD/Mortenson data can be succinctly summarized. Although the United States is near or above the mean for OECD countries on each of the four indicators and above the mean on positive changes in high school enrollment and high school completion rates, this country is losing ground on both bachelor's degree enrollment rates and on degree completion rates at the two-year and four-year levels. When coupled with future workforce preparation needs, these data support the contention that the United States may be losing ground in the global economy. In fact, in its most recent report on global competitiveness, the World Economic Forum (2010) found that the United States has been replaced by Switzerland as the top country on the global competitiveness index.

Conclusion

Few can argue with the contention that educational attainment is a critical topic on the national agenda. In particular, an educated workforce is absolutely essential to individual well-being, national productivity, and competitiveness in the global economy. The indicators suggest that this country is losing ground in all of these areas. The shifting composition of the U.S. population is immutable. Those who are least likely to succeed in the educational system will account for nearly half of the U.S. population by mid-century.

If this country is to educate all of its children, it will be necessary to implement systemic and systematic reform to slow down and perhaps reverse the leaking educational pipeline.

These concerns do not rest solely on American higher education. The solutions will not only require collaborative efforts across all levels of education, but it will also require significant efforts at each level of education. The imperative for post-secondary educators is to identify and engage in practices and interventions that increase the likelihood of success.

4

PUBLIC AND PRIVATE BENEFITS OF COLLEGE

This chapter addresses why it is important for students to be successful in college. College graduates themselves and society in general reap benefits from persisting to graduation. This chapter will provide a brief history of the benefits of college completion before delving into the specific public and private benefits that accrue when students successfully complete college degrees.

History of Higher Education's Benefits

Higher education has historically played an important role in the growth and development of the United States and its citizens. "Discussion of the benefits of higher education has its roots in the earliest days of American higher education" (The Institute for Higher Education Policy [The Institute], 1998, p. 7). Thomas Jefferson advocated that education was an important means of sustaining the fragile new United States democratic government, advancing society, and preparing its citizens to make substantive innovative discoveries and contributions:

> I know of no safe depository of the ultimate powers of society but the people themselves; and if we think them not enlightened enough to exercise their control with a wholesome discretion, the remedy is not to take it from them, but to inform their discretion by education. (Pine, 2001, p. 8)

One indicator of how well early colonial state governments understood the value of higher education was through their support of the first private and public institutions (The Institute, 1998). The Morrill Act of 1862 created land-grant institutions to equip citizens with the skills (agricultural and industrial) that they needed in the workplace. Abraham Lincoln said, "Upon the subject of education, not presuming to dictate any plan or system respecting it, I can only say that I view it as the most important subject which we as a people can be engaged in" (*Quotations of Abraham Lincoln*, 2003, p. 14). The second Morrill Act of 1890 funneled money that was generated from the sale of federal land to help fund the operation costs involved in running land-grant colleges. This act also designated funding for 17 land-grant institutions to specifically educate African-American students (Rainsford, 1972). The Morrill Acts "exemplified the ideal of the institution of higher learning as a solver of local problems and a servant of the people" (Bloom, Hartley, & Rosovsky, 2006, p. 294).

The role of higher education later expanded in the late 1950s when the country called on colleges and universities to play a high-profile role in developing the nation's defense. In reaction to the Soviet Union's launching of Sputnik, the National Defense Act was passed, creating the first federal student aid program as well as raising Americans' awareness about the importance of educating more citizens in science and math as a way to protect our country from the Soviet threat (The Institute, 1998).

Another role that higher education was called upon to address was poverty. Legislation, including the Higher Education Act of 1965 and the Education Amendments of 1972, created what would later be called the Pell grants and was viewed as an opportunity to "equalize economic and social opportunities" (The Institute, 1998, p. 8).

In the 1980s, however, as the economy began to slow and state budgets needed to be curbed, government officials began to shift the dialogue about higher education benefits from a focus on the public benefits to a focus on the private economic benefits of higher education (The Institute, 1998). This argument essentially stated that given the private economic benefits that college graduates obtain, state and federal governments do not need to invest as much money in higher education. Instead, individuals attending college should pay for this privilege because they are the ones reaping the benefits. However, Bloom, Hartley, and Rosovsky state that "public subsidies of higher education benefit society at large" (2006, p. 295), although they decline to take a position on the debate about whether the societal benefits justify the public expenditure on higher education.

Public and Private Benefits of Higher Education

To provide an accurate overview of the benefits of higher education for both society and individuals who attend college, we will be sharing an in-depth analysis of the public economic, private economic, public social, and private social benefits of higher education. Table 4.1 is an updated and enhanced version of the "Reaping the Benefits" report that was prepared by The Institute for Higher Education Policy in 1998. Specifically, we draw heavily upon Walter McMahon's recent and thorough economic analysis of the benefits that accrue to individuals and societies in his 2009 book, *Higher Learning, Greater Good: The Private and Social Benefits of Higher Education*.

This chart will serve as the outline of how we will present the public economic, private economic, public social, and private social benefits of higher education.

Public Economic Benefits

This section will highlight the many benefits that the public gains from having citizens enrolled in and graduating from higher education institutions. The public economic benefits that will be covered include increased tax revenues, greater

Table 4.1 The Public and Private Benefits of Higher Education.

Type of Benefit	Public	Private
Economic	Increased tax revenues	Higher salaries and benefits
	Greater productivity	
	Increased consumption	Employment
	Increased workforce flexibility	Higher savings levels
	Decreased reliance on government financial support	Improved working conditions
	Economic impact of higher education institutions*	Personal/professional mobility
Social	Reduced crime rates	Improved health/life expectancy
	Increased charitable giving/community service	Improved quality of life for offspring
	Increased quality of civic life	Better consumer decision making
	Social cohesion/appreciation of diversity	
	Improved ability to adapt to and use technology	Increased personal status
	Contributions to democracy*	More hobbies, leisure activities
	Increased environmental awareness*	Smaller families*
		Lifelong learning*

*These are additions made to the original Institute table based on McMahon's 2009 book *Higher Learning, Greater Good*.
Source: The Institute, 1998, p. 20.

productivity, increased consumption, increased workforce flexibility, decreased reliance on government financial support, and the economic impact of higher education institutions.

Increased Tax Revenues. Simply put, people who have attended higher education institutions make more money and thus pay more taxes (Bloom, Hartley, & Rosovsky, 2006). The importance of this is illustrated by the College Board's finding that "The typical college graduate working full-time year-round paid over 100 percent more in federal income taxes and about 82 percent more in total federal, state, and local taxes than the typical high school graduate" (Baum & Payea, 2005b, para. 3). McMahon found that "Taxes give rise to public services that benefit the taxpayer, but these public goods also benefit others" (2009, pp. 206–207) by funding tax-supported public service entities such as national and local defenses (for example, the military, local and state police forces, and so on), scientific bodies (for example, the National Science Foundation and the National Institutes of Health), societal infrastructure (for example, roads and bridges), K–12 education, and even public radio and television.

Greater Productivity. Not only do people who have attended college contribute to the tax base, but "Empirical work in econometrics suggests that after controlling for differences in amenities and individual wages, an increase in the share of college graduates in the labor force leads to significant increases in productivity and wages for all workers" (Hill, Hoffman, & Rex, 2005, p. 2). One report attributed the majority of the growth in U.S. productivity in the 1980s and 1990s to the increased education level of U.S. workers (The Institute, 1998). Greater productivity also increases the country's global economic competitiveness.

Increased Consumption. Given that people who have attended college earn more money (see Private Economic Benefits section below for further information on this), it makes sense that college-educated people spend more money on consumer items (The Institute, 1998). This increased consumption leads to more tax revenues and more jobs. "Studies indicate that the overall growth in consumption in the last four decades is associated with the increasing education levels of society, even after controlling for income" (The Institute, 1998, p. 14).

Increased Workforce Flexibility. Given the frenetic change of pace that accompanies ever-multiplying technological advances, today's workforce needs to be able to adapt more quickly than at any point in our nation's history. Higher education is an important player in preparing the workforce to adapt to changes in the workplace by teaching students essential higher order thinking and communication skills, thus contributing to the country's ability to be an economic and technological leader in the world (The Institute, 1998, p. 14).

Decreased Reliance on Government Financial Support. McMahon (2009) writes:

> With respect to welfare costs to state governments in the United States, only 0.5% of all college graduates ages twenty-five to thirty-four received public assistance or Aid for Dependent Children (AFDC), compared to 5.6% of all high school graduates receiving these welfare payments. This is a 5.1 percent point difference (National Center for Education Statistics, 1992). (McMahon, 2009, p. 220)

McMahon (2009) predicts that two-thirds of state welfare costs could be reduced if white and black students earned their high school diplomas and that number would be reduced another 91% if these high school graduates graduated from college.

The Economic Impact of Higher Education Institutions. Higher education institutions are economic engines for the cities where they are located as well as the regions they surround, although the impact decreases as you move farther away from the school (McMahon, 2009).

> For community colleges the impact has been estimated to be about $1.50 to $1.60 in local income created per dollar spent by the college or its students. This is equivalent to 69 local jobs created for every $1 million of the college's operating budget. For 4-year schools these influences are a bit larger: $2.20 in local income created per dollar spent and 67 jobs created per $1 million in the campus budget. (McMahon, 2009, p. 184)

Private Economic Benefits

As mentioned, people with college degrees earn higher salaries than people who do not, but the private economic benefits are not just limited to increased salaries, as this section will highlight. The specific private economic benefits that will be covered include: higher salaries and benefits, employment, higher savings levels, improved working conditions, and personal/professional mobility.

Higher Salaries and Benefits. McMahon (2009) states that the salaries of college graduates are 70% higher than the salaries of high school graduates, and the gap is even wider for people who have graduated from well-respected private institutions. Further, he notes that the gap between the salaries has "increased dramatically" since 1970 (McMahon, 2009, p. 252). Similarly, McMahon (2009) found that high school graduates' real earnings remained constant from 1980 to 2007 at under $30,000 while college graduates' real income increased from $43,730 to $66,363 during that same time period. Various sources estimate that the difference in lifetime earnings between high school and college graduates ranges from one to two million dollars; McMahon (2009, p. 84) estimates, "The long-term payoff for finishing college is about $1.1 million in future dollars." This figure takes into account the cost of a college education and the forgone income people do not receive while enrolled in college. It is important to note that any increase in education level (some college or a two-year degree) carries with it an increase in salary and that there are career fields that do not require a bachelor's degree that may make more money than bachelor's degree holders, but these are isolated findings. As the U.S. Bureau of Labor Statistics (2011a) labels its median weekly earning chart that clearly demonstrates the positive impact of post-college education on earnings—"Education Pays." Findings also indicate that those who attend college enjoy better benefit packages, including better health benefits and vacation time, than high school graduates (The Institute, 1998).

Employment. High school graduates are over three times more likely to be unemployed than college graduates (U.S. Bureau of Labor Statistics, 2011b). Perhaps more important is the fact that the number of jobs requiring two-year or four-year college degrees has increased, and there has been a subsequent 49.5% and 48% increase, respectively, in the wages these people earn. Given that the number of jobs that do not require a college degree has not risen as quickly and the oversupply of people without college degrees (64% of the U.S. population), the wages for unskilled laborers have not changed much since 1980 (McMahon, 2009).

Higher Savings Levels. Not only do college graduates make and save more money, but they also earn higher savings return rates than nongraduates, partially because they make better savings option choices and because they spend a smaller percentage of their incomes on gambling (McMahon, 2009). Their assets earn more interest and college graduates also contribute more to retirement plans and other long-term savings options (The Institute, 1998).

Improved Working Conditions. College graduates tend to work in white-collar jobs that provide more day-to-day comforts (such as air conditioning and heating) and conveniences (accessible child care, standardized work hours) than blue-collar positions (The Institute, 1998). McMahon (2009) found that college graduates are happier in their positions and spend less time searching for jobs than nongraduates.

Personal/Professional Mobility. People who have attended college tend to have more transferrable skills than those who have graduated from high school, thus leading to more job opportunities in other geographic regions and more types of positions that are available (The Institute, 1998). Thus, if employees are unhappy in their positions, individuals with a college education are less likely to feel stuck in that position because they have more job options.

Public Social Benefits

It is clear from the previous two sections that a college degree has a significant impact on public and private economic benefits, but there are also public and private social benefits associated with earning a bachelor's degree. This section focuses on eight different public social benefits of higher education: reduced crime rates, increased charitable giving/community service, increased quality of civic life, social cohesion/appreciation of diversity, improved ability to adapt to and use technology, contributions to democracy, and increased environmental awareness.

Reduced Crime Rates. Mauer (1994) found that 1993 incarceration rates per 100,000 people were 1,829 for people with one to three years of high school, 290 for high school graduates, and 122 for people who had attended some college. McMahon (2009) thus advocates for state spending on basic and higher education as a means of decreasing costs associated with incarcerating inmates and reducing the crime rate.

Increased Charitable Giving/Community Service. McMahon (2009, p. 206) found that "The college-educated give 3% or more of their income to charity, about twice as much as do high school graduates at the same income level." On the community service side, a study by O'Brien (1997) found more than two-thirds of college grads had participated in community service. "Higher levels of education are correlated with higher levels of civic participation, including volunteer work, voting, and blood donation" (Baum & Payea, 2005a, p. 7).

Increased Quality of Civic Life. College graduates are more likely to serve in leadership roles in civic organizations (for example, city councils, school boards, and so on) and nonprofit boards (such as YMCA, hospitals). College graduates are more likely to fulfill civic obligations (for example, serving on juries) and vote more frequently (McMahon, 2009). Bloom, Hartley, and Rosovsky (2006) found that people who have attended college are 45% more likely to volunteer in their communities. College graduates are more likely to read newspapers, be up to date on current events, and commit to lifelong learning—all of which make them aware of issues facing society (McMahon, 2009) and position them to make educated voting decisions.

Social Cohesion/Appreciation of Diversity. Individuals with a college education have "a massive effect on social connectedness" (The Institute, 1998, p. 17) and appreciation for a diverse society. Those with more than a high school education have significantly more trust in social institutions and participate in civic and community groups at much higher rates than others (The Institute, 1998).

Similarly, McMahon cited studies finding college graduates have "greater racial tolerance, less cynicism and less unquestioned support for authority" (2009, p. 207) than high school graduates.

Improved Ability to Adapt to and Use Technology. McMahon (2009) posited that, "What is probably the largest and most important social benefit of higher education is the benefit to the broader society from the dissemination of new knowledge" (p. 224). The dissemination of knowledge that emanates from colleges and universities spreads to the government and private industry via their graduates, who share what they learned from their professors in classes. The knowledge spreads to community and junior colleges via faculty members who conducted research to earn their advanced degrees and then share the information in the community college classrooms with their students. Graduates are also empowered to continue to learn about new discoveries via their ability to read and understand knowledge that is shared in academic journals and scientific magazines. Plus, college graduates are the only people qualified to conduct research in most private companies or in graduate degree programs (McMahon, 2009).

Contributions to Democracy. McMahon (2009) uses a compilation of many of the above items (increased volunteerism, giving to charity, paying of additional taxes, and so forth) to say that all these things contribute to a stable democracy. A large number of college-educated citizens are needed to sustain and improve democracies. Higher education contributes to the smooth functioning of the democracy by training lawyers and judges to conduct fair trials as well as knowledge workers that contribute to a safe and healthy citizenry. A democracy "also requires politically a large and growing middle class with significant per capita income that wants a say in governance. This increasingly makes authoritarian regimes unsustainable" (McMahon, 2009, p. 203).

Human rights are more likely to be found in democratic countries with informed citizens. "After controlling for all three of these effects, education independently at both the secondary and higher education levels has highly significant positive relationships to increased human rights" (McMahon, 2009, p. 208). Thus, higher education contributes to a stabilized democracy.

Increased Environmental Awareness. College graduates are more aware of environmental issues via their coursework and service experiences. Thus, college graduates are less likely to contribute to polluting the air and water (McMahon, 2009). Also, research institutions are making significant contributions to "green" technological advances to address pressing societal environmental issues such as deforestation and air and water pollution (McMahon, 2009).

Private Social Benefits

The previous section outlined the social benefits that society derives from having college graduates, but now we turn to the private social benefits that college graduates enjoy. The private social benefits include: improved health/life expectancy, improved quality of life for offspring, better consumer decision making, increased personal status, more hobbies/leisure activities, decrease in fertility rates, and lifelong learning skills.

Improved Health/Life Expectancy. Receiving a college degree clearly has a positive impact on health outcomes and life expectancy:

> The evidence is reasonably clear that, in the presence of statistical controls for salient confounding influences, increased educational attainment significantly lowers the probability of mortality at any particular age; specific health problems, such as disability or frailty, mortality from cancer and cardiovascular disease; and having risk factors for cardiovascular and other diseases. (Pascarella & Terenzini, 2005, p. 588)

The main reason for these improved health outcomes is the ability of college graduates to make smarter health and lifestyle choices, including smoking fewer cigarettes, exercising more, drinking less, and eating healthier (Pascarella & Terenzini, 2005; McMahon, 2009). Habley and Schuh (2007a) in fact argue that smoking fewer cigarettes should also be considered a public benefit since this decreases the health care costs to society. Another contributing factor to the positive health outcomes for college graduates is their more regular and better use of the health care system (McMahon, 2009). Grossman (2006) "concludes that the value of education to own health is about 40% of the market value of the benefits from education" (p. 602).

Improved Quality of Life for Offspring. Not only do college graduates accrue benefits from their degrees, but it turns out their children also benefit. "For example, parents' higher levels of formal education are positively associated with good prenatal care, parental involvement in a child's school, reading to a child, helping with homework, and providing access to computer resources" (Pascarella & Terenzini, 2005, p. 589). Educated parents are more likely to read books about parenting newborns, ask questions of physicians, and have other behaviors that decrease infant mortality and positively impact children's overall health (McMahon, 2009).

These benefits to the children of college attendees extend to the academic arena, as these children do better in math, science, and reading comprehension achievement scores. "This effect is likely attributable to the fostering of 'learning capital' in offspring of the college-educated, much of it indirectly through the home environment" (Pascarella & Terenzini, 2005, p. 590). In terms of offspring attending college, the research indicates that the education level of the mother is the most important influence (McMahon, 2009).

Better Consumer Decision Making. More education translates into better decisions on how to run a household in terms of consumer choices, time efficiencies, and financial assets (McMahon, 2009). One study estimated that this increased efficiency contributes $290 in annual household income (Michael, 1982).

Increased Personal Status. College graduates are more likely to be in white-collar positions that have prestige associated with them.

Having a college education has long been associated with increased personal status. Indicators of that status can range from having a more prestigious job—doctor, engineer, or college professor, for example—to being seen as a "leader" within a family. This is especially true for first-generation college attenders. (Terenzini, 1996)

More Hobbies/Leisure Activities. As is the case with college graduates making better decisions about health care, they also make better use of their leisure time.

The evidence is that college graduates tend to be less addicted to television than those with a high school education or less, more selective in the programs they watch, more inclined to read, more prone to engage in adult education, more likely to attend cultural events and participate in the arts, more likely to take part in community affairs, and more likely to take international vacations. (McMahon, 2009)

Smaller Families. College-educated women tend to have smaller families. McMahon (2009) posits that college-educated women intentionally limit their number of children in order to have healthier and better-educated children and because they have work pursuits that limit their time at home raising children.

Lifelong Learning Skills. Undergraduate students learn how to learn. "The undergraduate experience provides information and cognitive skills that increase the capacity for lifelong learning and continuing intellectual development" (Pascarella & Terenzini, 2005, p. 585). McMahon (2009) notes that this lifelong learning capacity helps graduates more readily adapt to changing circumstances.

Conclusion

Higher education has provided numerous benefits to the United States since before our country's inception. A fundamental component of America's flourishing democracy, as this chapter has highlighted, is the economic and social benefits that higher education brings to both society at large as well as to college graduates themselves. McMahon (2009) estimates that the total public and private benefits of earning a bachelor's degree totals $97,180 in 2007 dollars and McMahon (2009) estimates that 52% of the total benefits of higher education are public benefits. He goes on to argue that this is an "estimate of the percent of the total investment in higher education that needs to be publicly financed if economic efficiency is to be achieved" (McMahon, 2009, p. 252). It is clear that both society and individuals have a great stake in funding higher education and that both parties benefit from investing in higher education.

5

RETENTION OR RECRUITMENT: EXAMINING THE RETURN ON INVESTMENT

There is a widely believed postulate in higher education that it costs more to recruit a student than it does to retain one. Although on the surface the aphorism seems logical and intuitive, there have been few, if any, attempts to support or disprove this assertion. The simplistic interpretation is that when a student leaves the institution before completing a degree, new institutional resources must be used to recruit a replacement. Retaining a student requires no additional investment of resources. In reality, however, understanding the economics of recruitment and its relationship to the economics of retention is far from simplistic. Quantifying that relationship is fraught with difficulties. And the critical question is, "Do we have any evidence to suggest that the resources consumed by retention efforts provide a return on investment?"

The recruitment process is delineated by the universally accepted admissions funnel, which begins with identifying prospective students and culminates in enrollment, graduation, and alumni involvement. Because sequential stages in the funnel are clearly defined, it is possible to measure progress from one stage to another, to study the impact of various strategies, and to determine the return on investment of those strategies. The recruitment process is a cyclical one providing a clear beginning and a clear ending; that is, each fall, success is measured by the number and mix of students enrolled and then the process begins anew. The retention process is not as clearly defined, making the measurement of progress, the impact of strategies, and return on investment particularly difficult. Retention is a continuous process. It has no beginning and it has no end. It provides no opportunity to begin anew. Finally, students entering college are an annually renewable resource. With only minor historical glitches, the number of high school graduates and the percentage of those graduates enrolling in college increase each year. The enrolled student population is a finite population. Students who leave can only be replaced by newly recruited students.

These conditions aside, this chapter will provide an analysis of the direct and indirect costs of recruiting students and the institutional costs of student attrition. In addition, models for calculating return on retention investment will be reviewed. Finally, though recruitment and retention are both critical elements in student success, a case for increased investment in retention programs will be presented.

The Costs of Recruitment

The calculation of the costs of the recruitment process is relatively straightforward. The costs of fulfilling the admissions function include both human and material resources; however, indirect costs must also be figured into any assessment of the return on investment.

Direct Costs

Calculating the direct costs of recruiting a student is a relatively straightforward process. Recruiting costs include salaries for admissions personnel as well as travel, telephone, printing, supplies, postage, advertising, and equipment. When these costs are divided by the number of newly enrolled students, a per student recruitment cost can be determined. For example, the enrollment of 1,000 new full-time students at an institution

Table 5.1 Cost to Recruit an Undergraduate Student: 1983–2009.

Institutional Type	1983 Median Cost	2009 Median Cost	% Change
Two-year public	$47	$263	+460
Four-year public	$64	$461	+620
Four-year private	$455	$2,143	+371

Table 5.2 Cost of Tuition and Fees: 1983–2009.

Institutional Type	1983 Tuition/Fees	2009 Tuition/Fees	% Change
Two-year public	$528	$2,137	+305
Four-year public	$1,148	$6,319	+450
Four-year private	$5,093	$24,692	+384

whose recruitment budget is $1 million, results in a recruitment cost of $1,000/student. It is clear that the cost of recruiting has increased rather dramatically in the past twenty-five years. Watkins (1983) reported on a survey conducted by John Minter and Associates which documented the per student cost of recruitment. Although per-student costs vary by institutional type, size, and mission, the median per-student recruitment costs reported in Table 5.1 provide a comparison by institutional type. Included with the Minter data are the results of a recent Noel-Levitz survey (2009) of recruiting costs. A quick scan of Table 5.1 reveals rather dramatic increases in the per-student recruitment cost: more than fivefold in two-year public colleges, more than sevenfold in four-year public colleges, and just under fourfold in four-year private colleges.

By way of comparison, Table 5.2 reports on increases in tuition and fees between 1983 and 2009 (NCES, 2009b). The dramatic increases in tuition and fees parallel the increases in per student recruitment costs. It should be noted here that recruitment costs at two-year and four-year public colleges have risen at far greater rates than tuition and fees.

These percentage increases in tuition and fees take on additional meaning when compared to far lower increases in more recognizable economic indicators. The Consumer Price Index rose only 115% from 99.6 and median household income rose by 95.5% from $32,941 to $64,400 between 1983 and 2010 (U.S. Bureau of the Census, 2010a). Increases in recruitment costs and tuition/fees, then, have far outpaced the increases recorded for these more traditional economic indicators.

Although the causes of increasing costs of college tuition and fees are not the focus of this chapter, the causes of increasing college student recruitment costs do deserve attention. Frank (2001) and others (Winston, 2004; Mause, 2009) strongly suggest that the costs of recruitment have spiraled upward because of competition for students. Mause (2009) believes that colleges and universities "currently invest a vast amount of resources in order to attract well-qualified students" (p. 1107). Frank (2001) calls this the ultimate "winner-take-all" market. In an effort to attract more well-qualified students, colleges increase budgets for staff, consultants, satellite offices, advertising, travel, print and electronic media, and other attempts to impress prospective students. The net result of competition is essentially a zero-sum game. This zero-sum game is a situation in which one institution's gain or loss is balanced by the losses or gains of other institutions. And though the pool of college-eligible students is both renewable and relatively stable each year, an individual college's recruitment success relies on the institution's ability to compete with other colleges for a finite group of qualified students. And such competition drives the escalation of direct costs.

Indirect Costs

The need to compete also drives indirect costs. Whereas direct costs are both identifiable and quantifiable, indirect costs are identifiable but more difficult to quantify. There is little doubt, however, that programs and facilities generating indirect costs support the recruitment process with the intent of providing a competitive edge in attracting students. Examples of indirect costs of competition for students are private rooms in residence hall suites, food courts, state-of the-art recreation facilities, recruitment of star faculty, upgrades in technology, and tuition discounts for certain targeted groups. Frank (2001) suggests that colleges that do not offer these amenities are unable to compete with colleges that do have such enticements. Yet indirect costs are also constrained by the zero-sum game. Efforts to enhance campus attractiveness that result in gains (or losses) in recruitment are balanced by gains or losses of other institutions. The zero-sum game also drives competition and that competition, in turn, drives the escalation of indirect costs.

This overview of recruitment costs is not complete without enumerating several cautions regarding possible misinterpretation. First, a quality recruitment program is essential to institutional success and, indeed, student-institution fit is a critical element in student persistence. The previous section of the chapter is not intended to suggest that institutions downsize fiscal and human resources that support recruitment. It is, however, an exhortation for campus leadership to measure the impact of escalating direct costs created by competition for students to determine the cost-effectiveness of recruitment strategies.

Second, one must concede that there is solid evidence that program and facility enhancements play an important role in attracting students. But there is little if any evidence that such enhancements decrease attrition. Though it is possible that the absence of a private residence hall room or a state-of-the art recreation complex may play a role in a student's departure decision, that role is likely to be a very minor one when compared to other far more pressing causes of attrition. Students do not leave college because their residence hall does not have a food court or because there are too few elliptical trainers in the campus recreation center.

Third, there is a significant difference between the cost of upkeep and the cost of keeping up. Upkeep is the state of being maintained in good condition, and it is incumbent upon campus leaders to maintain functional facilities in a safe and clean environment. Upkeep is a necessary and ongoing process. Keeping up requires upgrading and expanding to be competitive with other institutions in attracting students. Once again, it is incumbent on campus leaders to determine the cost-effectiveness of recruitment strategies.

Finally, both the direct and the indirect costs of recruiting students are a recurring and, as discussed, escalating expense to the institution: an expense that is driven by competition in a zero-sum game. A case will be made later in this chapter that investment in retention interventions that lead to student success is, unlike recruitment, not a zero-sum game.

The Costs of Attrition

When a student leaves college, there are no winners. When a student leaves college before identifying and achieving an educational goal, the economy and the society in general lose. When a student leaves college before identifying and achieving an educational goal, that student loses. The student loses career mobility, the potential for increased income, and other benefits that accrue from holding a certificate or a degree; perhaps more important, the student may lose a dream. The costs of attrition on an individual student are incalculable; some of these losses can be calculated and are reported on in the following chapter.

Finally, when a student leaves college, the college loses. The focus of this section is on the institutional economics of student departure.

Lost Tuition

The first and perhaps greatest cost to an institution is the loss of tuition and fees that would have accrued had students persisted. These losses are also the easiest to calculate. Table 5.3 illustrates

Table 5.3 Impact on Tuition/Fees Revenue: Typical University.

	Attrition	Lost Students	Semesters Remaining	Lost Tuition/ Fees
Year 1–Year 2	26%	520	6	$9,360,000
Year 2–Year 3	16%	237	4	$2,844,000
Year 3–Year 4	10%	124	2	$744,000
Year 4–Year 5	7%	68	2	$468,000
Year 5–Year 6	2%	21	1	$63,000
TOTAL		1020		$13,479,000

the calculation of lost tuition and fees for Typical University based on the following parameters: it is a four-year public university with an entering first-year class of 2,000 students. Tuition and fees are $3,000/semester and the first-to-second-year retention rate (74%) and six-year degree completion rate (49%) are at the national averages for four-year public colleges (ACT, 2010e). Readers can easily substitute institutional data to calculate lost tuition. In all respects, Typical University is not typical at all. Nevertheless, it is a hypothetical model in which the data assumptions may be replaced by specific institutional data to provide a general understanding of the degree to which student attrition affects institutional economic well-being.

The simple calculations in Table 5.3 indicate that nearly $13.5 million in tuition and fees would be realized if all students who entered in a given cohort completed a degree within six years. This scenario might be true in the best of all possible worlds, but it is of course unrealistic. Not all students will be retained. Even the most selective institutions report six-year graduation rate percentages around 85%. Table 5.3 serves merely as a starting point to calculate scenarios based on improved retention rates.

If an institution establishes a goal of improving retention, it is possible to calculate the impact that goal has on revenue generated through tuition and fees. Setting a first-to-second-year retention goal for an institution is fraught with pitfalls. Success or failure often rests on the establishment of realistic short-term and long-term goals. Short-term goals that are set too high often result in frustrated faculty and staff, and goals that are set too low may be achieved but could result in nothing more than blips on the data radar screen. Short-term goals for retention should focus on incremental but meaningful improvement.

Setting long-term goals can be a slippery slope for a number of reasons. First, although the conventional wisdom suggests that about one-third of all first-year students fail to return for a second year, establishing an institutional goal to beat that figure is as inappropriate for an open-admissions community college as it is for a highly selective private college. Second, though it is tempting to establish long-term goals based on national averages, there is a problem with citing national averages when determining goals for retention. On some campuses, being "above average" provides a convenient rationale for maintaining the status quo; on "below average" campuses, getting to "average" may prove unrealistic.

Comparison with peer institutions may provide more realistic benchmarks. Yet these comparisons may not reflect the nexus of student characteristics and institutional characteristics that exist on a specific campus. The goal should not be to be "average," for even if all campuses miraculously improved retention, progression, and degree-completion rates, "below average" campuses would still exist. The goal to stay above average is really not a goal at all. Retention goals should be improvement goals.

Where possible, institutional goals should include target goals for selected programs and student groups. For example, within an overall institutional goal to improve first-to-second-year retention, the planning team might establish subgoals for at-risk students, undecided students, or students who participate in supplemental instruction. Or, as the result of the implementation of a particular program strategy, the planning team might establish a target goal for students who participate in that program strategy.

Table 5.4 Impact of 3% Improvement in Retention Rates on Tuition/Fees Revenue: Typical University.

	Attrition	Lost Students	Semesters Remaining	Lost Tuition/ Fees
Year 1–Year 2	23%	460	6	$8,280,000
Year 2–Year 3	13%	200	4	$2,400,000
Year 3–Year 4	7%	94	2	$564,000
Year 4–Year 5	4%	50	2	$300,000
Year 5–Year 6	1%	12	1	$36,000
TOTAL		816		$11,580,000

And as another example, variable retention improvement goals may be established for individual academic programs.

For illustrative purposes, Table 5.4 details the impact of a 3% increase in retention rates at Typical University. It should be reported here that according to the ACT *What Works in Student Retention* study (Habley, McClanahan, Valiga, & Burkum, 2010), the mean retention goal for the four-year public colleges reporting such a goal was 4.5%, well above the 3% improvement used in the Typical University illustration.

The difference in total tuition revenue based on a 3% improvement is $13.48 million (Table 5.3 TOTAL) minus $11.58 million (Table 5.4 TOTAL). Typical University's class-to-class retention yields a sizable difference in tuition revenue: just under $1.9 million for one cohort of entering students. Just as dramatic is an increase of 204 students who persist to earn degrees within six years of first enrollment. The retention calculator found on the website of the Educational Policy Institute (EPI, n.d.) provides a model that includes additional factors in estimating the lost tuition caused by attrition. Among those factors are the number of out-of-state students and the tuition/fees charged to them, projected percentage increases in tuition/fees, and the average government subsidy (if any) received per student.

Table 5.5 Impact on Cost of Recruitment.

	Current Retention Rate	3% Retention Gain
Number of lost students	1,020	816
Recruitment cost/student	$461	$461
Cost to replace	$470,220	$376,176

Recruitment Costs

If enrollment equilibrium is an institutional goal, a new student must be recruited to replace each student who leaves the campus before earning a degree. That cost is the amount it would take to replace that student: the per student cost of recruitment. According to the Noel-Levitz figure cited earlier in this chapter, that cost would be $461. Utilizing the example outlined in Tables 5.3 and 5.4, the cost of replacement is illustrated in Table 5.5.

The difference in recruitment cost based on a 3% gain is $94,044 annually. This calculation is not reported with the intent of urging cuts in the recruitment budget. Although that is one option, it is possible that at least some of the savings might be reallocated to retention program initiatives.

Financial Aid

Schuh (2005) reports that institutional financial aid is another cost. Institutions invest money through tuition discounts or grants, neither of which has to be repaid. Thus, the investment of institutional funds is lost when students depart before completing a degree. Once a practice found primarily at private institutions, such discounting is being implemented at public institutions as well. In the Typical University example, the current scenario accounts for a loss of 60 more students between the first and second year than the scenario featuring a 3% increase in retention. Assuming that the grants (or discounting) account for 50% of annual tuition and that the percentage of students receiving aid is at the national average (68.6%) for four-year public colleges (Financial Aid Facts, 2011), first-to-second-year lost revenue would be $123,480. This calculation is not reported with the intent of urging cuts in institutional grants or discounting policies. Although that is one option, it is possible that at least some of the savings might be reallocated to retention program initiatives.

Instructional Staff

Calculating the impact of attrition on the need for instructional staff requires the addition of three assumptions about Typical University that were identified earlier. These assumptions are: (1) the typical faculty teaching load is four (three semester hour) undergraduate courses per semester in addition to meeting other institutional expectations; (2) the typical undergraduate course load is five (three-semester hour) classes per term; and (3) the average class size is 25. It should be noted that these assumptions are for illustrative purposes only: they are not recommendations. In reality, these assumptions vary greatly both within and across institutions and these numbers have been chosen solely for the purpose of illustration. Sparing the reader the burden of wearisome calculations, an improvement in Typical University's class-to-class retention requires instruction for an additional 5,880 semester hours which, based on Typical University's teaching load, student course load, and class size assumptions, will require the addition of 59 faculty members. This calculation is not reported with the intent of applying instructional resources generated by increased retention solely toward the addition of new faculty. Although that is one option, it is possible that at least some of the new revenue generated could be reallocated to promising retention program initiatives.

Additional Costs

There are, of course, additional costs of attrition that are predicated on the inability to recruit replacements for students who have departed. Schuh (2005) points out that a student living in a residence hall who leaves campus and is not replaced accounts for a significant loss in revenue. Other losses could be in textbooks and supplies, athletic revenue, state subsidy (in public institutions), and a variety of other income-producing ancillary services.

Contrasting Recruitment and Retention

Contrasting recruitment and retention begins with an apologia. The authors realize that a successful and fully functioning enrollment management program is responsible for enrolling all the students the institution is capable of serving (recruiting) and for serving all the students it is capable of enrolling (retaining). And clearly, the ultimate goal of both recruitment and retention is to produce students who identify and achieve their educational goals. It is necessary, however, to deconstruct the elements of recruitment and retention in order to examine the differences between the two and to support the argument that in an environment of fiscal constraint, institutions should (1) invest in retention programs and (2) strive for a greater balance in the allocation of scarce resources between recruitment and retention strategies.

The first area of contrast between recruitment and retention focuses on maintaining enrollment rather than replacing students who have left the institution. As pointed out earlier in this chapter, recruitment is a zero-sum game, whereas retention is not. During the recruitment process, institutions compete with other institutions for a finite group of prospects and incur both direct and indirect expenses in attempts to attract students. Competition requires the increasing expenditure of resources to keep pace. In addition, resources are utilized to attract students who do not ultimately enroll. Although enrolled students constitute a finite population, retention is not a competitive process. Resources expended on retention interventions can be focused entirely on the success of students currently enrolled. Resources are necessary to launch retention programming, but successful interventions generate cost savings.

A second contrasting element is that unlike recruitment, there is little agreement on the definition of retention. In Chapter One we challenged the simplistic definition of a persister as an individual who enrolls in college and remains enrolled until completing a degree. Habley and Schuh (2007b) suggest that the path to student success is neither linear nor temporal and is not confined to a single institution. In Chapter One we also note that many students enter college with educational goals that do not include the completion of a degree; however, these students are often included in retention calculations. The consequences of the lack of a shared definition of retention is that institutions fall back on a "who is here, who is not" approach.

The absence of a clear definition of retention is the underlying cause of the third contrasting element: the ability to measure outcomes. This means, on the one hand, that it is difficult to make data-driven decisions. On the other hand, measurement of the success of recruitment is possible because the definition of success is "bringing in the first-year class." Recruitment is a defined, cyclical, and annualized process that has a beginning and an end. Recruitment includes data-driven metrics and markers within the process that indicate success or lack thereof. Enrollment officers set yearly goals for overall enrollment, as well as for class mix, including in-state/out-of-state students, underrepresented students, men/women, academic ability, and so forth. On the tenth day of classes, goals are either met or they are not met and new goals are established for the size and mix of next year's entering class. Retention is a cumulative process beginning at the point of first enrollment and continuing until students achieve their educational goals. Though it is possible to measure successful stages in the recruitment process, the only measure of retention is whether the student stayed or left.

Control and accountability for outcomes is the fourth differentiator between recruitment and retention. Although the recruitment process is influenced by intangibles and unintended outcomes, responsibility for the failure to reach recruitment goals rests on the shoulders of the individual who manages and directs the recruitment process: the chief enrollment officer. And, in fact, more than one chief enrollment officer has been terminated for failure to meet recruiting expectations. In the case of retention efforts, campus administrators are quick to pronounce that retention is everyone's responsibility and that just as institutional culture is owned by everyone and controlled by no one, no single individual can be held accountable for retention outcomes. Perhaps an indication of the prevalence of the notion that retention is everyone's responsibility, only about two-thirds of campus respondents to the *What Works in Student Retention* (WWISR) study indicate that an individual has been assigned to coordinate retention programs (Habley et al., 2010). Furthermore, the titles of individuals responsible for coordinating retention programs are widely distributed among position levels (director to provost) and across both academic affairs and student affairs. WWISR data also indicate that the retention component of the admission/recruitment funnel is not generally assigned to the chief enrollment officer. The chief enrollment officer coordinates retention programs at fewer than one in five four-year private colleges and only at about one in ten community colleges and four-year public colleges.

Finally, the return on investment (ROI) in recruiting is obvious. ROI is a measure used to evaluate the efficiency of an investment or to compare the efficiency of a number of different investments. Data drive the ROI for recruiting. The institution expends known resources to enroll a known number of new students. If increasing that investment results in enrolling more new students (and gaining more tuition income), then more will be invested. There is almost no compelling evidence that resources applied to retention interventions yield a comparable return on investment.

Investing in Retention Interventions

The discussion of direct and indirect costs as well as the return on investment of recruitment and retention efforts suggests that although both functions are critical to institutional success, the investment of human and fiscal resources in proven retention strategies can have a dramatic impact on student success.

Retention and Recruitment: Apples and Oranges

In Chapter One, we suggested that the stark reality of the retention and persistence-to-degree data is that despite the considerable energy that the higher education community has expended in understanding retention and degree completion, such understanding has not resulted in a concomitant improvement in student success in college. Retention and degree completion rates have been stagnant for nearly four decades. Simply stated, retention proponents have found it difficult, if not impossible, to prove that retention interventions yield a return on investment. And there is only limited evidence that any specific retention intervention is more likely than another to yield a return on investment. Although investing resources in retention is intuitively reasonable, retention is ill-defined, difficult to measure, and lacks an accountability mechanism.

Yet there are compelling circumstances that are likely to intensify the focus on retention programs. The first circumstance is that there is a diminished supply of qualified prospects. Although the number of high school graduates blips up and down over time, in Chapter Three we noted that the general trend is upward. The concern is, however, that the proportion of qualified and interested students is shrinking and may continue to shrink. The educational pipeline to college will include students less likely to complete high school, less likely to enroll in college, and less like to graduate from college. Although the pipeline to college completion is a systemic educational issue, ensuring that students who do enroll will succeed in college will require campus leaders to redouble efforts to implement interventions that are proven to increase the likelihood of student success.

Earlier in this chapter, we discussed the impact of competition on the recruitment process. Though competition among similar institutions is not likely to decrease in the foreseeable future, traditional higher education institutions are facing additional recruitment challenges. First, advances in technological delivery of learning experiences provide educational options that are attractive to students. The National Center for Educational Statistics (NCES) reported that there were more than 10 million enrollments in undergraduate-level credit-bearing online or hybrid courses in the 2006–07 academic year (2009c). Increases in the demand for online learning will require institutional leaders to make strategic decisions about the role such courses play in attracting and in retaining qualified students.

An additional competitive challenge is the dramatic increase in student enrollment in for-profit colleges. Between the 2004–05 and the 2008–09 academic years, enrollments in for-profit colleges increased by more than 61% (NCES, 2010c) to the point that more than one of every eight postsecondary students is enrolled in a for-profit institution: a figure that constitutes more that 40% of total postsecondary enrollment gains during that four-year period. Although recruitment practices at such institutions have recently come under scrutiny, it is clear that for-profit colleges are a competitive force to be reckoned with.

Finally, colleges are under increasing accountability pressures. Levine (2001) suggests that higher education has transitioned from a growth industry to a mature industry, and concurrently the government has reduced autonomy, increased regulation, and demanded greater accountability. Whether driven by scarce resources, concerns about global competitiveness, or dramatic increases in traditionally underserved populations, there is no doubt that college success rates will need to improve.

The Need for Evidence

Although retention interventions make intuitive sense, much of the evidence in support of retention programs centers on anecdotes and heartwarming stories. There are studies that purport to measure the impact of programs on student success, yet opinions on the quality and interpretation of such research is far from consistent. Kuh, Kinzie, Buckley, Bridges, and Hayek (2006) suggest that academic and social support systems consistent with institutional mission provide clear pathways to succeeding in college. Under that broad umbrella, Kuh and his colleagues identify multiple programs that support college success: orientation, transition courses, tutoring, study groups and summer bridge programs, study skills workshops, mentoring and student support groups, student-faculty research, and senior capstone projects. Patton, Morelon, Whitehead, and Hossler (2006) found far less compelling support for the impact of retention services. They reviewed the empirical evidence and discovered that few programs resulted in improved retention. They found that only 16 methodologically sound studies provided documentation linking a program to increased retention. Their analyses concluded that the evidence in support of counseling programs and mentoring programs was weak. There was a small to moderate level of evidence supporting learning communities and faculty-student interaction, and moderate to strong evidence in support of transition/orientation programs. They concluded that evidence is sparse and inconsistent.

While researchers are engaged in intellectual dialogue about the quality of retention research and the outcomes of that research, institutional leaders cannot wait for the debate to be resolved. They are scrambling for ways to improve student success rates, and they are seeking to validate the return on investment for the resources allocated to enhance student success.

Fortunately, there are two tools available to provide educators with a greater understanding of the return on investment. The first of these is the Noel-Levitz Return on Investment Estimator (n.d.). The Estimator is an online auto-calculating worksheet to estimate institutional return on investment for a single retention initiative or for a combination of retention initiatives. The Estimator can be used for both two-year and four-year colleges. It requires the input of three data elements: the amount that the institution is planning to invest in retention; the number of students in a single incoming cohort who you expect, as a result of the initiative, to be retained from first to second term; and the estimated average net tuition revenue you expect to receive for each incoming full-time student. Typical University data on the 30 additional students retained from first to second term and net tuition income ($3,000) were entered into the Estimator along with a $50,000 investment in retention initiative(s). The calculation resulted in a first-to-second-term return on investment of 80%. Utilizing the same data elements, however, and with the assumption that at least some of the retained students remained enrolled beyond the second term, the Estimator calculated a whopping 797% long-term return on investment.

Though the data elements used for this scenario are hypothetical, institutions can use their own data to illustrate the dramatic revenue impact of increase retention. Institutions can also run multiple scenarios utilizing different first-to-second-year retention rates.

The Return on Investment Estimator is an excellent tool for illustrating the overall revenue impact of retention programs and for influencing decision makers to invest in retention initiatives. The Estimator's shortcoming, however, is that it does not provide guidance in identifying the intervention(s) that are more likely to yield a return on investment. That shortcoming appears to have been addressed through a pilot program developed by Jobs for the Future (2009), working with the Delta Project and funded by the Walmart and the Lumina Foundations: Investing in Student Success. The program focused on exploring whether first-year programs designed to retain students were a cost-effective investment for colleges and universities. The project tied program-level cost data to student outcomes and explored the extent to which the additional revenue generated by retention initiatives offset the costs of those programs. The pilot project focused on student success programs for low-income, first-generation, and at-risk students at 13 campuses. With a focus on data-driven decision making, the project required student retention and comparative group data, information on staffing and spending for the program, and campus-level financial data. Data from a nine-page set of detailed worksheets were entered into the Investing in Student Success Cost-Return Calculator (ISS Calculator). Major findings from the pilot included:

1. On most campuses data about spending in relation to performance outcomes is unavailable.

2. Annual direct program costs varied widely (from $59 to $1,601 per student).

3. Seven of the thirteen campuses showed an increase in retention that could be associated with the student success program.

4. The ISS-Calculator is a viable tool for decision-making.

5. Almost all campuses experienced a change in conversation around first-year programs (p. 3).

The ISS Calculator shows great promise for campuses struggling with retention concerns. It provides a data-driven model for identifying the retention initiatives that increase student persistence and, in turn, return their investment to the institution.

Conclusion

This chapter began with the postulate that it costs more to recruit a student than it does to retain one. The enigma is that although it is relatively easy to calculate the direct and, to some extent, the indirect costs of recruiting a student, the absence of both a definition of retention and the tools to measure retention outcomes results in subjective decisions based on opinions, hunches, and stories of others' successes. It is now very clear that the dartboard approach to retention planning must give way to data-driven decision making. The ISS calculator is a step in the right direction, but it challenges campuses to ramp up the collection of data that inform decisions. Resources cannot, should not, and will not be devoted to initiatives that do not yield a return on investment. It is also very clear that it is time to put the postulate out to pasture, to underscore the contention that recruitment and retention are equal partners in student success. Both have a dramatic influence on institutional effectiveness and fiscal well-being.

Section 3

CORE COMPONENTS OF STUDENT SUCCESS

6

INSTITUTIONAL CULTURE AND STUDENT ENGAGEMENT

The strength of the American higher education system lies in its diversity, encompassing size, mission, location, degrees offered, academic major choices, entering student demographics, and much, much more. This diversity also includes the culture and ethos of the institution. Thus, there is no one "right" culture that supports student success. Although perhaps it would be easier to have one magical "right" answer, the uniqueness and complexity of higher education institutions necessitates a far more nuanced approach. The literature on campus culture tends to be more focused on describing the cultures of particular institutions that have been successful in establishing a student success–focused culture, and using the findings from these institutions to develop broad generalized principles for establishing similarly focused cultures at other institutions. This approach avoids the precarious pitfall of trying to dictate a one-size-fits-all approach to "fixing" the diverse cultures of higher education institutions.

A great deal of attention has been given to the study of institutional culture and its impact on student persistence. Entering student demographics certainly have an impact on student graduation and persistence rates, but institutions themselves also do have the power to have a positive impact on student success rates. This chapter will provide an overview of the literature on how institutions can create a campus culture/ethos to support student success and student engagement in the institution.

Defining Institutional Culture

Before delving into the literature on institutional culture, it is important to first define institutional culture, which has proven to be an elusive and complex term. Schein (2004) defines the culture of a group as:

> A pattern of shared basic assumptions that was learned by a group as it solved its problems of external adaptation and internal integration, that has worked well enough to be considered valid and, therefore, to be taught to new members as the correct way to perceive, think, and feel in relation to those problems. (p. 17)

Schein's work has some application in this context, but a more relevant definition is offered by Kuh and Whitt (1988). Given this book's focus on higher education, we will use their definition of institutional culture in this chapter:

> The collective, mutually shaping patterns of norms, values, practices, beliefs, and assumptions that guide the behavior of individuals and groups in an institute of higher education and provide a frame of reference within which to interpret the meaning of events and actions on and off campus. (Kuh & Whitt, 1988, p. 162)

Kuh and Whitt (1988) further explain, "Although culture is fairly stable, it is always evolving, continually created and recreated by ongoing patterns of interactions between individuals, groups, and an institution's internal and external environments" (p. 163).

Levels of Culture

Schein (2004) proposes analyzing culture at three different levels: "These levels range from the very tangible overt manifestations that one can see and feel to the deeply embedded, unconscious, basic assumptions that I am defining as the essence of culture"

(p. 25). His three levels of culture are: artifacts, espoused beliefs and values, and basic underlying assumptions.

Artifacts. Schein (2004) defines artifacts as "all the phenomena that one sees, hears, and feels when one encounters a new group with an unfamiliar culture" (p. 25). Examples of artifacts include organizational charts, the physical layout of the campus, the mission statement, ceremonies (such as convocation and graduation), rituals, language, signs, symbols, stories, traditions, classroom and office space design, the way people dress, and so forth (Kuh & Whitt, 1988; Schein, 2004). College campuses typically have rich traditions, rituals, symbols, and ceremonies that are handed down through generations of college students. It may be easy to see these artifacts, but Schein (2004) cautions against making quick judgments about what these artifacts mean in the individual culture, because their meaning is often complex and deep.

Espoused Beliefs and Values. Schein (2004) describes these as a group learning "that certain beliefs and values, as initially promulgated by prophets, founders, and leaders, 'work' in the sense of reducing uncertainty in critical areas of the group's functioning" (p. 29). The beliefs become a way for group members to guide their work; formal and informal policies are sometimes put into place to reinforce these beliefs. Strategies and goals are also created to ensure that these beliefs are confirmed.

Basic Underlying Assumptions. Basic underlying assumptions are formed when an approach to an issue is so consistently successful over time that it becomes the way to do something (Schein, 2004). One of the dangers of these underlying assumptions is that if an organization believes so fervently in something, it may seek to reject group members that do not hold the same basic underlying assumptions. Another potential pitfall of these underlying assumptions is that they are difficult to change, and attempts to do so can induce stress among group members (Schein, 2004).

A Cultural Framework

Another way of grasping the concept of culture is to use Tierney's cultural framework of higher education institutions (1988) to analyze the key dimensions of culture. His framework is based on an anthropological approach and includes the following key dimensions: environment, mission, socialization, information, strategy, and leadership. The environmental piece looks at how participants define the environment and their attitude toward the institution's environment. The mission involves examining what the mission statement is, how it is perceived, and how much it is used to make decisions. The socialization aspect focuses on how new people are socialized into the institution and what members need to do to be successful in the institution. Information encompasses who has important information and how information is generated and distributed. The strategy element is concerned with how decisions are made and who makes those decisions. Finally, the leadership dimension looks at formal as well as informal leaders, and what the institution expects from those leaders.

Institutional Culture and Student Engagement Studies

This section will highlight findings on institutional culture from the Project on Documenting Effective Educational Practice (DEEP), Gary Kramer and Associates' book (2007) titled *Fostering Student Success in the Campus Community*, and "Enhancing Campus Climates for Racial/Ethnic Diversity" by Hurtado, Milem, Clayton-Pedersen, and Allen.

DEEP Study Results

Much of the current work on the importance of institutional culture has emerged from the National Survey of Student

Engagement (NSSE). Specifically, Kuh and Associates focused on 20 institutions that did a better-than-expected job of graduating students based on their entering student demographics, and scored higher than predicted on five study benchmarks for good educational practice (Kinzie & Kuh, 2004). A group of researchers on Project DEEP (Documenting Effective Educational Practice) first identified these institutions and then spent over a year at each institution to better understand factors that contributed to each institution's success.

Kinzie and Kuh's (2004) analysis of the 20 institutions that were researched in Project DEEP found four central themes in terms of what these institutions had in common: "leadership, partnerships between academic and student affairs personnel, student agency, and what the team defined as 'the power of one'" (p. 3). First, these institutions had senior campus leaders with a clear and direct sense of purpose. Although their purposes varied, campus leaders at the DEEP institutions were all strong advocates for the establishment of a campus community that valued students and focused on creating conditions where students could be successful. They also found that leadership across the institution shared this commitment.

Another commonality at DEEP institutions was that faculty and student affairs professionals partnered to create vibrant learning experiences for students inside and outside the classroom (Kinzie & Kuh, 2004). Instead of the traditional chasm that has existed between academic affairs and student affairs, on the DEEP campuses there was a great deal of respect and admiration between the parties. A third commonality among the DEEP institutions was that the campuses were intentional about having students take responsibility for their collegiate experiences rather than be spoonfed learning opportunities (Kinzie & Kuh, 2004). Institutions helped students take responsibility by having them serve as peer advisors, teachers, and tutors and by actively inviting students to participate in campus decisions. The final commonality among the DEEP institutions was their recognition and encouragement of individual campus constituents contributing to student success. These campus constituents included faculty, staff, janitors, bookstore cashiers, and coffee shop baristas—highlighting that each person on campus has the potential to have a positive impact on students.

Kezar (2007) used the DEEP study results to consider the role that campus ethos plays in creating a culture focused on student success. Kezar (2007) defines *ethos* as "the fundamental character or spirit of a culture, connects individuals to a group; it expresses a particular group's values and ideology in a way that creates an emotional connection" (p. 13). She describes ethos as a way to engage students' hearts in addition to their minds. A strong campus ethos does not happen by itself; Kezar (2007) posits that the campus ethos should be in alignment with the institutional mission statement and should be actively created and sustained by campus constituents through their policies, traditions, and practices. These strategies for supporting the campus ethos include: shared understanding, cocreation, anticipatory socialization, listening to constituents, and relationship building. The shared understanding component involved institutions intentionally aligning their ethos with the campus mission statement and then providing multiple opportunities to share and imbue the ethos throughout the campus community. The ethos was not just dictated by the administration; instead, there were opportunities for students and other campus constituents to help shape and share the message. Anticipatory socialization at the DEEP schools entailed systematic efforts to teach new faculty, students, and staff about the ethos through orientation sessions, convocations, classes, and staff meetings. The DEEP schools were not content to rest on their laurels, but instead they were constantly assessing their efforts to ensure that they were listening to students and keeping up with new student needs and trends. Finally, Kezar (2007) found DEEP institutions were intentional about providing opportunities for students, faculty, and staff to get to know each other and build relationships.

Fostering Student Success in the Campus Community (Kramer & Associates, 2007)

Gary L. Kramer and Associates (2007) examined the components that constitute a successful campus experience in their book *Fostering Student Success in the Campus Community*. Kramer and Associates (2007) identified common themes that emerged about components of a student success–focused culture as well as specific recommended steps for creating such a culture. The common themes include: a clearly defined mission statement, collaboration among the campus constituents, assessment and keeping the assessment initiatives focused on students, knowledge of who students are, engagement of students, establishment of a friendly environment, development of collaborations between academic and student affairs, cross-training of student affairs personnel, and the use of technology to promote student success (Kramer & Associates, 2007). There are obvious overlaps between the DEEP study results (Kinzie & Kuh, 2004; Kezar, 2007) and Kramer and Associates' findings, including leadership that is committed to student success, increased communication and collaboration across campus, and the establishment of a student-friendly environment. But there are also points in Kramer and Associates' analysis that warrant further discussion.

For example, both Kinzie and Kuh (2004) and Kramer and Associates (2007) highlight the importance of having a living, breathing mission statement that accurately reflects the core mission and values of the institution. Although all institutions have a mission statement, the percentage of campus constituents who can recite it varies greatly by institution. The DEEP schools have had a mission statement that rang true for campus constituents and was common knowledge at those institutions. This helps ensure that large and small decisions on campus are made in such a way that they are in alignment with the mission statement. Kramer and Associates (2007) suggest that the mission statement should be focused on student learning and success.

The importance of assessment is a theme that is covered extensively by both Kramer and Associates (2007) and Kezar (2007). Kramer and Associates (2007) in particular state that decisions about student success initiatives must be data-driven and aligned with established institutional outcomes for students. The assessment must be continuous, include multiple measures, and make students accountable for fulfilling their responsibilities.

All members of the campus community are a focus in all of the student success literature, and the consensus is that this responsibility does not belong solely to the faculty. In fact, all of these studies (Kezar, 2007; Kinzie & Kuh, 2004; Kramer & Associates, 2007; Kuh & Whitt, 1988) celebrate the importance of all campus community participants, including faculty, staff, professionals, students, and building service workers. Each member of the campus community has the potential to make positive contributions to students' collegiate experiences. It can mean the difference between a student staying at an institution or leaving it when someone in a campus office cares enough to greet him or her warmly, or when a residence hall housekeeper asks how a test went earlier that day. In addition, when institutions make services readily accessible they also contribute to student success. Members of the campus community must always remember they are part of a proverbial village and though they need not have all the answers to students' issues and problems, they need to know what resources are available on campus and how to effectively refer students to those resources (Kramer & Associates, 2007). Kramer and Associates (2007) point out how important it is to know who our students are, where they come from, and what their needs are before designing programs to help them accomplish their goals.

"Enhancing Campus Climates for Racial/ Ethnic Diversity" (Hurtado et al., 1998)

Hurtado, Milem, Clayton-Pedersen, and Allen (1998) examined the issues and barriers that underrepresented minority students face in terms of campus climate. The authors examined campus climate through a lens of four equally important dimensions: institutional context, structural diversity, psychological dimension, and behavioral dimension.

Institutional context refers to understanding the influence of institutions' historical decisions related to desegregation and the perceptions of underrepresented students on college campuses. In terms of what institutions (particular predominantly white institutions) can do to deal with the vestiges of these historical issues, Hurtado et al. (1998) encourage institutions to acknowledge the past but also focus on insuring "that diversity becomes a central value of their educational enterprise" (p. 284).

Structural diversity focuses on the lack of underrepresented students on college campuses. This impacts the learning of both white and underrepresented students. To increase structural diversity on campus, Hurtado et al. (1998) propose that colleges de-emphasize standardized test scores in the admissions process and increase financial aid packages.

The psychological context involves how members of the campus community view racial groups' interactions on campus, how much racial conflict occurs on campus, how institutional leaders respond to such conflict, and how different racial groups view each other on campus (Hurtado et al., 1998). Hurtado et al. (1998) offer keys to creating a better campus climate, including having clear policies that deal with discrimination and settling conflicts, providing training for people to learn how to confront racist stereotypes, comments and/or behaviors, and providing specific student organizations and support services for underrepresented students.

In contrast to the perception of group interactions on campus discussed in the psychological context, the behavioral context documents student interaction between and within racial groups and the nature of that interaction (Hurtado et al., 1998). To increase student success for minority and majority students, it is important for institutions to proactively provide opportunities for all students to interact and engage in dialogue inside and outside the classroom.

Suggestions for Next Steps for Institutions Seeking to Foster a Culture of Student Success. There is an abundance of advice from the literature about how to create a culture focused on student success. The advice is specific and based on findings from the research literature, but knowledge in and of itself does not necessarily translate into how to transform an institution's culture. In Chapter Seventeen, we will offer specific suggestions about how to institutions can introduce change to improve student persistence and how to negotiate cultural barriers in opposition to that change.

Student Success in College by Kuh and Associates

Based on the DEEP Project that emerged from the National Survey of Student Engagement results, Kuh, Kinzie, Schuh, and Whitt (2005) wrote a book titled *Student Success in College* highlighting campus programs and initiatives that emerged from the study as having a positive impact on student retention and success. Based on these results, the book concludes with a series of guiding principles divided into three categories: tried-and-true, sleeper, and fresh ideas. This section will highlight the findings from each of these categories.

Tried-and-True Guiding Principles. Kuh et al. (2005) have identified tried-and-true principles that work to enhance student success:

1. The mission of the institution reflects a commitment to "talent development" and then works hard to make that happen. This means that the institution meets students where they are in terms of their academic and social development and then work hard to empower students to achieve without regard to their starting level.

2. The institution has policies and procedures that support student success.

3. Not only must the institution have programs available to support students, employees must go out of their way to ensure that the majority of students use the services and programs.

4. The institution has set high standards for students and provides the infrastructure to ensure that students are able achieve those standards.

5. The leaders of the institution are committed to student success.

6. Financial and other types of resources are in place to support student success initiatives.

7. Institutional leaders display fortitude and commitment when there are pressures to abandon student success initiatives.

8. The bottom line is the culture has to be focused on student success. In particular, the authors identify three common cultural themes among the DEEP schools: a commitment to talent development, high academic performance, and an appreciation for diversity.

Sleeper Principles. These principles were identified by Kuh et al. (2005) as unique aspects of the DEEP institutions' cultures, many of which were born out of challenges the institutions had faced:

1. There is no one right organizational structure. Each of the DEEP institutions has significant differences in its organizational charts.

2. The basis of how many decisions are made at the DEEP institutions is data that have been collected and used in making decisions.

3. Assessment initiatives are used to help all campus constituents (students, faculty, and staff) to become better at what they do.

4. Peer leaders are being used in a variety of offices (advising, tutoring, student engagement, and so on) to help educate students. Benefits of this arrangement accrue both to the peer leaders and the students they are charged with assisting.

5. The DEEP institutions are intentional about providing multiple opportunities for students and faculty to engage outside of the classroom.

6. The mission of the student affairs divisions at the DEEP institutions is consistent with the institution's mission. Thus, collaboration between the academic and student affairs divisions is palpable.

7. DEEP schools are using technology to enhance interactions with and for students.

8. Students at DEEP schools feel a sense of physical and emotional connection with the institution.

Fresh Ideas. Following are new ideas that Kuh et al. (2005) found at DEEP institutions that were not necessarily being duplicated at a large number of other institutions:

1. DEEP institutions tend to employ multiple strategies aimed at increasing student learning. This creates momentum

among the faculty and staff, further solidifying the importance of using cutting-edge practices such as active and service learning strategies.

2. Students bring a wealth of experiences and skills to the
classroom. It appears that at DEEP institutions there is
a commitment among the faculty to assess those experiences and skills and then capitalize on individual students'
strengths to benefit the learning of the entire class.

3. DEEP institutions have an institution-wide and coordinated
commitment to student success. Commitment comes from
student affairs, academic affairs, all the subunits of these
divisions, plus others. Everywhere students turn, programs
have been designed to meet their needs and help them
reach their potential.

4. DEEP institutions celebrate the best of the tradition of
liberal arts with the provision of opportunities to gain experiences that will enable students to secure jobs after they
graduate.

Fostering Student Success

Kramer and Associates (2007) also share specific suggestions for
how to foster student success at colleges and universities. The
first is to gather and analyze data about their students. In order
to know what needs students have, institutions must take the
time to learn more about them. This goes beyond their demographic information, such as ACT scores, high school ranks,
and the like; he also recommends using a cultural lens to inves-
tigate how students learn, what their interests are, how they use
technology, and how they interact with both the academic and
cocurricular aspects of the institution.

Next, Kramer and Associates (2007) advocate that institutions should place students at the heart of the institution. This
means ensuring that instructional techniques and institutional

policies are developed and revised based on the needs of students. This does not mean standards should be lowered; instead, the emphasis should be on articulating clear student learning outcomes and appropriately challenging and supporting students to meet those outcomes. In addition, instructional techniques should facilitate students' abilities to identify and refine their goals and values. Kramer and Associates (2007) also urges institutions to regularly seek input from students to suggest new programming and services.

The third suggestion from Kramer and Associates (2007) is that institutions hold students accountable for their own learning and performance both in and out of the classroom. This can be accomplished by having faculty clearly delineate what the academic and cocurricular expectations are for students and holding students to those standards. Students should be afforded ample opportunities to figure out who they are and what they want to accomplish in their lives through classroom assignments and participation in cocurricular activities.

Kramer and Associates' fourth suggestion (2007) implores institutions to create a student-centered culture where all constituents are working together to make student success a reality. To accomplish this goal, he discusses the importance of providing programming in alignment with curricular and student learning outcomes, having a continuous and comprehensive assessment program, and encouraging productive and stable relationships between academic affairs and student affairs partners. He also mentions the importance of academic advisers in helping students select courses and cocurricular activities in alignment with their personal values and professional goals.

The fifth step is to take advantage of opportunities to instigate cultural change (Kramer & Associates, 2007). This effort involves building effective leadership by hiring good people and clearly communicating the institution's expectations about employees' contributions to foster student success. It also necessitates that organizational structures not obstruct the submission of new ideas and the execution of new plans for meeting student success goals. The organization needs to be aligned for student success. This leads into Kramer and Associates' (2007) sixth recommendation, which states that institutional leaders must have the fortitude to carry out student success plans. Part of this step involves hiring student service professionals who are leaders of change and are not afraid to challenge the status quo. However, the responsibility for creating student-centered change is not just limited to student service leaders. In order to make these change initiatives "stick" institutional leaders at all levels must give a clear and consistent message about the importance of student success initiatives.

The seventh step is a reminder to institutions to be aware of students' expectations of their higher education (Kramer & Associates, 2007). Millennial students expect that a campus community will meet their needs and provide them with the support needed to excel in the classroom. Technologically savvy, today's students expect instant access to the information and resources they need to register for classes, learn about campus resources, and more. Along this same line, Kramer and Associates (2007) advocate in their eighth step that campuses establish one-stop centers for students where all of their student service needs are provided in a central area with hours that are convenient for students. Creating one-stop centers can be a challenging undertaking for higher education institutions due to tight space considerations and the traditional "silos" that keep offices functioning as independent entities instead of as a cohesive whole. There are multiple benefits that accrue to students from this type of setup, but institutions also benefit by saving costs on shared resources, including supplies, labor, and overhead.

Kramer and Associates' (2007) ninth and tenth recommended practices remind institutions of the importance that various services, especially advising, first-year seminars, transition programs, and learning support programs, can play in helping students assimilate their experiences inside and outside the classroom as well as the important roles that all of these services play in student retention.

Conclusion

Much is known about the components of creating a culture focused on enhancing student persistence and graduation rates. The main themes that have emerged from the DEEP study (Kuh et al., 2005) and from Kramer and Associates' findings (2007) seem to be the importance of senior leadership consistently affirming and advocating for a student-centered culture, the importance of committed collaborations between academic and students affairs, the necessity of a student-centered mission statement, and the establishment of a comprehensive assessment program to help drive decisions and new innovations. Hurtado et al. (2008) provide specific suggestions for steps institutions can take to enhance the success of underrepresented minority students. This knowledge, however, does not necessarily translate into establishing a culture focused on student success. After exploring the literature and data concerning specific initiatives that have proven to be either successful or not in terms of their impact on retention rates, the last section of this book will bring forward for consideration a new approach to creating an institutional culture centered on students.

7

ACADEMIC PREPARATION

In Chapter Three we outlined the reasons why shifting demography will pose a significant challenge to those who are intent on improving college access and success rates. In this chapter we turn our attention to the lack of academic preparation for college-level work, a major cause of attrition cited in the *What Works in Student Retention* (WWISR) survey (Habley, McClanahan, Valiga, & Burkum, 2010) by respondents from all institutional types. Using a 5-point scale where a 5 signified a major contributor to attrition, community college and four-year public college respondents rated student preparation for college-level work at the top of a list of 42 student and institutional characteristics contributing to attrition. Mean ratings of student preparation were 4.3 for community colleges and 3.9 for four-year public colleges. The mean student preparation rating for four-year private college respondents was 3.6, ranking third behind adequacy of personal financial resources (3.9) and financial aid available to students (3.7) as a cause of attrition.

Student lack of preparation for college-level work was also a dominant attrition theme in the three previous WWISR surveys. In the 1980 survey, low academic achievement was the top-rated attrition factor for all institutional types, with a 4.5 overall rating on a 5-point scale (Beal & Noel, 1980). And among AASCU colleges responding to the 1987 WWISR survey, low academic achievement was cited as the number one cause of dropout behavior (mean = 4.7) (Cowart, 1987). And, consistent with the earlier survey findings, WWISR 2004 reported that lack of academic preparation was a major contributor to attrition

(Habley & McClanahan, 2004). Mean ratings by institutional type were 3.5 (four-year private colleges), 3.8 (four-year public colleges), and 4.3 (community colleges).

It is clear from the consistent results reported by respondents to the four WWISR studies that academic preparation is believed to be a key to student success in college, and the lack thereof is believed to be the primary cause of student departure. The purpose of this chapter is twofold: to describe the level of academic preparation of prospective college students and to examine the impact of academic preparation on student success in college.

The first purpose can be accomplished by reviewing indicators of college readiness. Historical data on academic performance (grades and test scores), are readily available and can be used in much the same way as demographic data. That is, the indicators of academic performance can be examined both over time and at various points in the educational pipeline to determine college readiness of students in the future first-year class. Among these indicators are trends in dual enrollment, credit through assessment, and historical data on school performance of students in the educational pipeline.

High School Grades on the Rise

High school grades constitute the first indicator of the level of academic preparation of students in the college pipeline. There is absolutely no question that grade point averages of high school students are on the increase. Using a 5-point grade scale, Nord et al. (2011) reported that between 1990 and 2009 grade point averages for women have increased from 2.77 to 3.10 and from 2.59 to 2.9 for men.

Although there are variations in high school grade point averages by gender and race/ethnicity during the same time frame, increases ranging from .21 to .32 were reported for each of these groups. In addition, Woodruff and Ziomek (2004) reported that the mean high school grade point average for ACT-tested students rose from 2.94 in 1991 to 3.20 in 2003. They reported that grades grew by as much as .26 (4-point scale) in that 13-year period. The most recent information from ACT indicates that the mean grade point average for ACT-tested students in the high school graduating class of 2010 reached 3.20 (personal communication from Robert Ziomek, director, ACT Research).

The data from Nord et al. (2011) and from Woodruff and Ziomek (2004) are corroborated by student-reported data from *The American Freshman: Forty Year Trends* (Pryor, Hurtado, Saenz, Santos, & Korn, 2007), which indicate that high school grade point averages have been steadily increasing. Between 1966 and 2005, the percentage of first-year college students reporting high school grade point averages of A+, A, or A– increased from 19.4% to 40.4%. The most recent study (Pryor, Hurtado, DeAngelo, Blake, & Tran, 2009) reported that the percentage had risen to 48.6%.

If one relied on the high school grade point average as an indicator of college preparedness, the obvious conclusion is that first-year students are increasingly well-prepared to meet the academic challenges they confront in college. As comfortable as it might seem to rely on grades as evidence of adequate academic preparation, there are significant reasons to challenge the notion that increasingly high grade point averages are indicative of improved preparation for college. In fact, there is a raft of data that support the contention that grade inflation is rampant at the high school level. Grade inflation is what takes place when grades go up, but the academic achievement they represent remains stable. Zirkel (2007) suggested that grade inflation was a hoax on the American public, which continues to believe that a grade of C is average and a grade of A is outstanding. And, Woodruff and Ziomek (2004) suggested that high school grades inflated by as much as .26 (four-point scale) in the 13-year period between 1991 and 2003. Schmidt (2007) reported similar findings on the performance of high-school seniors on the reading portion of the National Assessment of Educational Progress (NAEP). Reading scores declined from 1992 to 2005, even though high school students were taking more classes in tougher subjects, and their median grade-point averages were rising steadily, from 2.68 in 1990 to 2.98 in 2005.

Dual Enrollment on the Rise

One of the indicators of college preparedness resides in the rapid growth of students participating in dual enrollment programs. Dual enrollment programs provide high school students and, in some cases, students who are not currently enrolled in high school, with the potential to earn college credit prior to high school completion.

Although there are several terms used to describe such programs, in this chapter the general term *dual enrollment* will serve as an umbrella descriptor for dual credit, joint enrollment, concurrent enrollment, and postsecondary opportunity programs. Lerner and Brand (2006) reported that dual enrollment programs exist in all 50 states and at the time of their publication, dual enrollment programs were legislated in 40 states. Lerner and Brand went on to report that dual enrollment programs differ on several significant characteristics. Those are:

- Faculty: high school or postsecondary instructors
- Credit-granting postsecondary institution: public or private, two-year or four-year, academic or technical
- Location: in a high school classroom or on the college campus
- Tuition and fees: paid by student, school district, or postsecondary institution
- Availability of support services: transportation, tutoring, and counseling (p. 19)

An additional difference among dual enrollment programs is the qualification of students who are eligible to take courses. In some programs, high schools establish enrollment requirements, whereas in other programs the postsecondary institutions establish requirements. Among others, such requirements may include minimum high school grade point average, class standing, completion of prerequisites, or satisfactory admission test scores.

These program differences make it difficult to determine both the national scope of such programs and the impact these programs have on college student success. For the year 2002–03, NCES (2005) reported that 57% of all high schools offered dual credit for college courses and 813,000 students earned college credit while still in high school. That data set reported that nearly 680,000 students had taken college courses with a dual enrollment program and an additional 133,000 took college courses outside a formal dual enrollment program. Unfortunately, the data in the 2005 report are the latest national data available, but statistics from the state of Iowa suggest that dual enrollment is a rapidly growing phenomenon. According to the Iowa Department of Education (2010), 29,721 Iowa high school students enrolled in 57,931 concurrent (dual) enrollment courses; 6,707 students took 12,306 courses in Iowa's Postsecondary Educational Opportunity program; and 11,316 high school students enrolled in 17,931 AP courses. By fall 2009, dually enrolled students accounted for 25.9% of community college students statewide. There seems to be little doubt the dual credit phenomenon is increasing dramatically as the second decade of the twenty-first century begins. Many interpret the increasing numbers of students enrolling in and succeeding in dual credit courses as an indication of improved college readiness.

Taken at face value, the dramatic increase in students participating in dual enrollment programs suggests that academic preparation of high school students may very well be improving. Myriad studies report that students who participate in dual enrollment earn higher college grades, are more likely to be retained, and are more likely to graduate than students who have not taken dual enrollment classes. Even with these positive results, two nagging questions remain unanswered. First, do students who take dual enrollment courses already possess the required academic skills and the necessary desire to succeed in those courses? As mentioned earlier, there are selection criteria for dual enrollment which provide some assurances that students are prepared for the courses they will be taking. In other words, students who participate are those who are most likely to succeed in college with or without a dual enrollment program. The second and related question is that if only those most likely to succeed are involved in dual enrollment, then what is the educational system doing to improve the academic preparation and college readiness of those who do not participate in dual enrollment programs? Preparation of all students for college is not likely to occur when only those most likely to succeed in dual enrollment courses are the recipients of accelerated education. And student success rates in college are unlikely to improve unless and until educators begin to focus their energies on all students.

Advanced Placement on the Rise

Although there are several ways in which students may earn college credit through assessment, the primary assessment program that offers the possibility of earning college credit through testing via structured coursework is the College Board's Advanced Placement (AP) program. As with dual enrollment, there has been a surge in the number of students enrolling in AP classes and registering for AP tests. Currently there are 30 tests administered across a variety of subject areas which are designed to measure the content of college courses. The College Board (2010b) reported that more than 18,000 U.S. high schools offered Advanced Placement courses, with 1.8 million students taking 3.2 million AP exams. This represents a dramatic increase from 2002–03, when 1.2 million students took 2.1 million AP exams (NCES, 2005). AP exams are scored on a 1–5 scale, with a score of 5 equivalent to a grade of A in the corresponding college course, a score of 4 equivalent to grades of A–, B+, and B, and a score of 3 equivalent to grades of B–, C+, and C in the course. Equivalencies for scores of 1 or 2 are not provided. Scores of 3, 4, or 5 are often called passing scores (College Board, 2010a).

Many would suggest that the increase in students taking AP courses and registering for AP tests is an indicator of improved preparation for college. And though there is little doubt that a rigorous AP course culminating in a well-structured assessment is an important factor in college success, there is some evidence that "simply taking an AP class isn't enough in itself. Only those who do well on the exam see benefits down the road" (Mollison, 2006, p. 37). Part of the concern here is a combination of the scores that students earn and the level at which colleges actually award credit based on AP scores. Although the College Board indicates that a score of 3 is equivalent to a B–, C+, or C, the number of college courses for which a 3 generates credit is questionable. Though nearly all colleges accept scores of 5 in at least some subjects, many colleges accept scores of 4 in at least some subjects, some colleges accept scores of 3 in at least some subjects, and virtually no colleges accept scores of 2 or 1. An examination of the 2010 grade distribution for all subjects from 1989–2010 (College Board, 2010a) illustrates Mollison's concern. During that time period, while the percentage of students earning scores of 4 and 5 remained stable at about 20% and 15% respectively, the percentage of students receiving scores of 1 or 2 rose from 34.5% to 42.1%. More than 1.2 million test takers were unlikely to earn credit for their AP test scores. And, more than 600,000 earned score of 3, which meant that, depending on institutional policy, college credit was a possibility but not a certainty. Finally, between 1989 and 2010 the mean grade for all tests decreased from 3.06 to 2.89.

As with concerns for dual enrollment, AP testing raises two important questions. First, do the AP test grades simply confirm what we already know? That is, students who "pass" AP tests with a grade of 3 possess the subject matter competence and academic skills necessary to succeed in college. And the second question is what to do with the 1.2 million students who, even after enrolling in an AP course, earn a grade or 1 or 2? It is perhaps these students that WWISR respondents believe are unprepared for college level work.

Students who participate in the dual enrollment and AP programs are those who are most likely to succeed in college. It is perhaps not these students who need attention. Student success rates in college are unlikely to improve by citing accountability measures focusing only on the accomplishments of those students who are most academically capable.

Assessment Results Stagnant (at Best)

This section of the chapter will examine data from a broad cross-section of assessment programs intended to measure academic performance. The data reported here are drawn from the National Assessment of Educational Progress (NAEP), the Programme for International Student Assessment (PISA) of the Organization for Economic Cooperation and Development (OECD), ACT's College Readiness Assessments (EXPLORE, PLAN, and the ACT), and the College Board's Scholastic Assessment Test (SAT) and Advanced Placement (AP) Program. PISA is a system of international assessments that focus on 15-year-olds' capabilities in reading literacy, mathematics literacy, and science literacy. NAEP, often called the "nation's report card," is a nationwide program that includes periodic assessment across grade levels of student progress in the areas of mathematics, reading, writing, and science as well as other subject areas not covered here. The NAEP is administered by the National Center for Education Statistics (NCES), a division of the U.S. Department of Education. Readers are spared more lengthy descriptions of each of these assessment programs. It is not our intent to stir up a debate on the utility, the validity, or the reliability of these measures because such debate might obscure the far more critical fact that each of these assessments shows that academic performance is, at best, stagnant. Nor is it our intention to challenge the research that suggests there is a positive relationship between high school grades and success in college. Rather, results from these assessments are being cited to illustrate that over time the use of the multiple metrics cited here paints a picture of academic performance far different from the one suggested by the use of high school grades.

Table 7.1 traces the reading performance on NAEP (2008a) of 9-year-olds, 13-year-olds, and 17 year-olds between 1984 and 2008. While the scores show some progress over time for 9-year-olds, progress for 13- and 17-year-olds is less pronounced. A less obvious but notable observation on Table 7.1 is that the improvement of scores between the 9- and the 17-year-old groups has declined from a high of 81 points (1990) to a low of 56 points (2008). The most recent PISA reading scores (OECD, 2009) for 15-year-olds corroborate the NAEP findings. U.S. students ranked 18th out of 64 countries participating in the assessment, scoring just above the mean for all countries.

Trends in NAEP (2008b) mathematics scores (Table 7.2) follow the same pattern as those for reading. Between 1986 and 2008, score gains for 9-year-olds were greater than gains for 13-year-olds and 17-year-olds. In addition, Table 7.2

Table 7.1 NAEP Pipeline–Reading Scores 1984-2008.

	1984	1990	1996	2004	2008
9 years old	211	209	212	218	230
13 years old	255	257	258	258	260
17 years old	280	290	288	284	286

Table 7.2 NAEP Pipeline–Math Scores: 1986–2008.

	1986	1990	1996	2004	2008
9 years old	222	230	231	240	243
13 years old	269	270	274	280	281
17 years old	302	305	307	307	306

Table 7.3 NAEP Pipeline–Writing Scores*: 1998–2007.

	1998	2002	2007
8th Graders	150	153	156
12th Graders	150	148	153

*Different scoring rubrics used at each grade level.

shows that the improvement of scores between the 9- and the 17-year-old groups has declined from a high of 80 points (1986) to a low of 63 points (2008). PISA rankings in math literacy (OECD, 2009) reported that the United States ranked 29th of 64 participating countries and scored at the mean for those countries.

Table 7.3 summarizes the NAEP (2008c) writing score pipeline from 1998 to 2007. It should be pointed out that the scores by grade level are not on the same scale so it is not possible to measure improvement across grade levels. It is clear, however, that writing scores have only slightly improved within grade level and that scores of eighth graders improved only slightly more than scores of 12th graders. PISA does not assess writing.

NAEP (2006) science scores between 1996 and 2005 are reported in Table 7.4 for fourth, eighth and 12th graders. Of all the NAEP trend data reported in this chapter, science scores raise the greatest concern. With a slight gain for fourth graders, no gain for eighth graders, and an actual decline for 12th graders, these scores do not bode well for student readiness to succeed in college level science courses.

Table 7.4 NAEP Pipeline—Science Scores*: 1996-2005.

	1996	2000	2005
4th Graders	147	147	151
8th Graders	149	149	149
12th Graders	150	146	147

*Different scoring rubrics were used at each grade level.

PISA scores and rankings in science literacy (OECD, 2009) are an additional cause for concern. On the PISA science scale U.S. 15-year-old students ranked 23rd of the 64 participating countries. Finally, U.S. 15-year-olds were outscored in the over-all science rating by 20 OECD countries and eight non-OECD jurisdictions.

National assessment data (NAEP) and international assessment data (PISA) present an academic performance picture which contradicts the positive picture portrayed by the increase in high school grade point averages and high school student enroll-ment in college-level courses. Even cast in the most optimistic light, NAEP data suggest little growth by age cohorts over the last two decades. And, PISA data suggest that U.S. students are about average when compared to the 64 countries participating in the PISA program.

Although NAEP and PISA draw their samples from all stu-dents enrolled at various grade levels, students who are assessed through one of ACT's assessments or through the College Board's SAT are secondary school students who are most likely to be college bound. As a result, a review of trend data for those assessment programs adds an additional dimension to an under-standing of academic performance.

Table 7.5 provides a five-year overview of mean composite scores for ACT's EXPLORE, PLAN, and ACT programs as well as the combined SAT Score for 12th grade test takers. EXPLORE, PLAN, and the ACT are components in ACT's College Readiness System. The assessments share the same content areas

Table 7.5 Entering Class Admission Test Pipeline to College—2006–2010.

Entering Class of. . .	EXPLORE Composite 8th grade[1]	PLAN Composite 10th grade[1]	ACT Composite 12th grade[1]	Combined SAT Math/ Critical Reading 12th grade[2]
2006	17.8	18.8	21.1	1021
2007	17.9	18.9	21.2	1017
2008	17.8	18.8	21.1	1017
2009	17.8	18.8	21.1	1016
2010	17.7	18.7	21.0	1017

[1]Personal communication with ACT research staff.
[2]College Board (2009).

(English, Math, Reading, and Science), similar item construction, and a common score scale. It is clear: These scores have remained flat.

Longitudinal assessment data are unanimous and foreboding. While one may discount the veracity of such assessments taken individually, the collective consistency is telling. PISA, NAEP, EXPLORE, PLAN, ACT, SAT, and AP scores have been and are indeed stagnant (at best).

Underpreparedness and College Success

An additional way to use assessment data to understand the level of student preparation for college is to examine the way in which preparation (or lack thereof) contributes to (or detracts from) various indicators of student success in college. ACT (2010e) has developed a series of College Readiness Benchmarks. The benchmarks were empirically derived and are based on the performance of more than 90,000 students in 98 colleges. Earned grades of these individuals were matched with ACT scores in English, Mathematics, Reading, and Sciences in the development of a college readiness benchmark, a criterion-referenced metric, the score needed on an ACT subject-area test to indicate a 50% chance of obtaining a B or higher or about a 75% chance of obtaining a C or higher in the corresponding first-year credit-bearing college course. These college courses include English Composition, College Algebra, an introductory social science course (for example, History, Psychology, Sociology, Political Science, and Economics), and Biology.

Because ACT's assessments are constructed on the same score scale (1–36), it is possible to identify benchmark scores at the 11th and 12th grade level (ACT), the eighth grade level (EXPLORE), and the 10th grade (PLAN) level. That is, if students who meet a benchmark on the EXPLORE or PLAN level continue to make reasonable academic progress they would be expected to meet the benchmark at the 11th or 12th grade level. Benchmarks are also available for COMPASS scores, ACT's computer adaptive assessment system which is currently used primarily in two-year college settings. Table 7.6 (ACT, 2010e) summarizes the benchmark scores in each subject area of the assessments. The scores are not described in detail here, but readers who are interested in the academic skills represented at each of the score levels should consult ACT's college readiness standards available at ACT's website.

The established benchmark scores can then be utilized to examine the percentage of EXPLORE, PLAN, and ACT-tested students who achieve scores at or above the benchmark. Those percentages are reported in Table 7.7.

Table 7.6 ACT's College Readiness Benchmarks.

College Course or Course Area	Test	EXPLORE 8th grade	PLAN 10th grade	ACT HS Graduates
English Composition	English	13	15	18
Social Sciences	Reading	15	17	21
College Algebra	Mathematics	17	19	22
Biology	Science	20	21	24

Table 7.7 Percentage of Students Meeting Benchmarks for 8th Graders, 10th Graders, and High School Graduates (2010e).

Benchmark Test Area	2009 EXPLORE-tested 8th graders	2009 PLAN-tested 10th graders	2010 ACT-tested Graduates
English	62%	71%	66%
Reading	43	48	52
Mathematics	37	36	43
Science	16	23	29
All four benchmarks	13	17	24

Both the weight of the evidence and the consistency of the messages generated through various assessment metrics are firmly undergirded by the percentage of students meeting the college readiness benchmarks. Mincing few words, the academic preparation of students in the pipeline to college is dismal. Although dual enrollment and the AP program provide a growing number of students with an opportunity for rigor and challenge, those programs appear to have a limited effect on overall college readiness. In reality they provide opportunities for those who need them least: students who would likely succeed in college with or without accelerated academic experiences.

The Impact of Preparation on College Success

As we begin to look at academic preparation as a precursor of college success, the authors will readily concede that which has been documented multiple times. Students with higher high school grade point averages, higher class ranks, higher admission test scores, higher numbers of honors, AP, and advanced classes, and those who have earned more dual enrollment credits succeed in college at greater rates than those who are lower in any or all of these categories. The successful students are likely to attend highly selective or selective colleges and are far more likely to succeed if we do no harm. Putting those intuitive but not very useful findings aside, this section of the chapter will focus on the broader context—the impact of core course–taking and benchmark achievement on four measures of college success. In the comprehensive tracking study that included approximately 200,000 ACT-tested students (and which was described in greater detail in Chapter Three), Noble and Radunzel (2007) examined the relationships between benchmark achievement and college grade point average (GPA), year-to-year retention, progress to degree, and degree completion rates. The data in Tables 7.8–7.11 display information on the performance of students who reported to ACT that they had taken the college preparatory core (four years of English and three years each of mathematics, science, and social science) and those who had not taken the college preparatory core (non-core). In addition, these tables include data on the performance of ACT-tested first-year college students who met none of the benchmarks, those who met between one and three of the benchmarks, and those who met all of the benchmarks.

The following tables have been adapted from Noble and Radunzel (2007). They provide a longitudinal cohort summary

Table 7.8 Percentage of Students Achieving at Least a 2.5 GPA by Performance Level.

Performance Level	Four-Year Colleges				Two-Year Colleges		
	1st year	2nd year	3rd year	4th year	1st year	2nd year	3rd year
Non-Core	58%	58%	59%	59%	57%	56%	55%
Core	69	69	70	70	67	67	65
No Benchmarks	42	42	43	45	49	46	45
1–3 Benchmarks	64	65	66	67	68	68	68
All Benchmarks	82	83	83	83	80	81	79

of the percentage of students achieving at least a 2.5 GPA (Table 7.8), the percentage of students retained from year to year (Table 7.9), the percentage of students making reasonable progress from year-to-year (Table 7.10), and the percentage of student persisting to degree completion (Table 7.11).

Table 7.9 Percentage of Students Retained from Year-to-Year by Performance Level.

Performance Level	Four-Year Colleges			Two-Year Colleges	
	2nd year	3rd year	4th year	2nd year	3rd year
Non-Core	66%	50%	42%	62%	43%
Core	73	58	51	69	52
No Benchmarks	63	45	36	61	41
1–3 Benchmarks	70	54	47	68	51
All Benchmarks	79	66	59	72	58

Table 7.10 Percentage of Students Making Reasonable Progress by Performance Level.

Performance Level	Four-Year Colleges				Two-Year Colleges		
	1st year (24 hrs)	2nd year (48 hrs)	3rd year (72 hrs)	4th year (96 hrs)	1st year (18 hrs)	2nd year (36 hrs)	3rd year (54 hrs)
Non-Core	59%	47%	41%	39%	58%	38%	30%
Core	72	60	54	51	69	50	43
No Benchmarks	47	38	33	32	53	34	27
1–3 Benchmarks	68	55	50	46	69	49	41
All Benchmarks	84	72	66	62	78	61	54

**Table 7.11 Percentage of Students Persisting to Degree
by Performance Level.**

Performance Level	Four-Year Colleges		Two-Year Colleges			
	4th year	5th year	2nd year	3rd year	4th year	5th year
Non-Core	14%	30%	7%	16%	19%	21%
Core	20	40	10	23	28	30
No Bench-marks	8	19	6	13	16	16
1–3 Bench-marks	17	36	10	22	27	29
All Bench-marks	27	52	14	29	36	39

The data included in Tables 7.8–7.11 are consistent and clear. Across all institutional types, across all years, and for all four variables:

- Students who completed core college preparatory courses performed/succeeded at higher levels than students who did not complete core preparatory courses.
- Students who met all four ACT college readiness benchmarks performed/succeeded at higher levels than students who did not meet all four benchmarks.
- Students who met all four ACT college readiness benchmarks performed/succeeded at higher levels than students completed core college preparatory courses.

Academic Preparation and College Success: Now What?

The purposes of this chapter were twofold: to describe the level of academic preparation of prospective college students and to examine the impact of academic preparation on student success in college. Intuitively and unfortunately, the preparation levels are dismal. Those who are less academically prepared are far less likely to succeed in college. By all indications those who believe that the lack of academic preparation is a major cause of college student attrition are right. But being right is not enough. Being right informs a solution, it is not the solution. It is indeed relatively easy for postsecondary educators to lay the blame at the feet of K–12 educators. Yet, one is reminded of an oft-shared adage: you are either part of the solution or you are part of the problem. And indeed, that educators are not immune to the blame game is illustrated by the following verse:

> **College Professor**
> High schools don't stress the skills and knowledge
> For students to succeed in college.
> **High School Teacher**
> Lack of preparation is a shame
> The middle school is really to blame
> **Middle School Teacher**
> From such performance I should be spared
> They sent him to me unprepared
> **Elementary School Teacher**
> Not ready to learn, it's plain to see
> What kind of parents must they be?
> **Parents**
> We sent him to school to learn and grow
> What happened there we do not know

Academic performance is everyone's problem. And, though all the constituencies have a significant role to play in a systemic and systematic approach to improving the academic performance of American youth, those in postsecondary education must make at least three major contributions to the effort. The first of these is to take the lead promoting a dialogue on the disconnect between what students are taught and how they are taught in high school, and the level of preparation necessary to be successful in college. In its recent National Curriculum Survey, ACT (2009c) reported that 91% of high school teachers felt that students in their subject area were prepared for college. In that same survey, only 26% of college faculty felt that students were prepared in their subject areas. In addition, 71% of high school teachers reported that their state's standards prepare students "well" or "very well" for college, whereas only 28% of college instructors felt that state standards led to adequate preparation for college. Both high school teachers and college instructors felt strongly about curriculum depth while suggesting that state standards focused on breadth. Finally, both high school teachers and college instructors believe that less emphasis should be placed on skills such as financial literacy, health literacy, and media literacy than on skills directly related to the content areas of English, mathematics, reading, or science. Advocates suggest that high school academic standards and expectations should be a mile deep and an inch wide rather than a mile wide and an inch deep. If these gaps are to be closed, college personnel must take an assertive role in reaching out to K–12 teachers to close the gap between what is taught in high school classes and what is necessary to succeed in college. The results of these dialogues will be improved high school instruction and better-prepared students who ultimately reach the goal of college success.

The second major postsecondary contribution to improved academic preparation resides in a critical review of teacher preparation programs. Levine (2006a) reported that 62% of teachers surveyed believed that they were not prepared to cope with the realities of today's classrooms. Levine goes on to suggest that teacher education programs, as they currently exist, are increasingly irrelevant in meeting the needs of today's educational system. And, as a further indicator of the need for revision in approaches to teacher education, the policy implications summary from the most recent ACT National Curriculum Study

(2009b) indicates that one of its primary findings was that high school learning standards are not sufficiently aligned with post-secondary expectations. The report goes on to state that:

> Compared to high school teachers, college instructors continue to rate fewer content and skills as being of higher importance, and more skills as being of little or no importance, in the courses they teach and too many of the skills rated as important by high school teachers are not the fundamentals of each discipline that college instructors insist their students must have mastered by the time they enter credit-bearing college courses. (ACT, 2009b, p. 8)

The third and final postsecondary contribution is the focal point of Chapter Twelve on course placement practices. The success rates of students meeting all four performance benchmarks were far higher than students who met none of the benchmarks. And even if there are improvements in the overall academic performance of entering college students, there will be students on every campus who are less likely to succeed than others. Although few educators would argue that all students are capable of succeeding in college, nearly 60% of the students in the study had met between one and three of the benchmarks. It is these students who will most likely benefit from well-designed learning support interventions. Learning support programs were seen by WWISR (Habley et al., 2010) respondents as the most significant contributor to student success.

8

PSYCHOSOCIAL CHARACTERISTICS

Arguing for a new student success paradigm focuses our attention beyond first-year retention outcomes. These outcomes include managing educational and career goals and juggling competing task demands associated with college success, whether choosing a major, passing classes, or engaging in university life. The components of student success, then, must encompass a theoretically rich view of the student that helps explain how students manage these multiple outcomes. In Chapter Six we discussed the importance of institutional culture and student engagement, and the importance of feeling connected to people and place. In Chapter Seven, we highlighted the importance of academic preparation, implicitly suggesting that students must know how to learn and how to master academic coursework. In this chapter, we present a comprehensive model for understanding how student personality characteristics and traits, attitudes, and behaviors differentially influence a range of student success outcomes. We call this constellation of attributes *psychosocial factors*, and their evolution and change *psychosocial development*.

We have organized this chapter into three basic sections. The first identifies and details key psychosocial domains that span K–12 and postsecondary education, using educational persistence and motivational theory perspectives. These sometimes

---

NOTE: The Student Readiness Inventory (SRI) which was the instrument cited in much of the research in this chapter, is now known as ENGAGE.

disparate literatures are integrated using a systematic analysis called meta-analysis and validity generalization (Hunter & Schmidt, 2004). This approach allows us to best capture the critical psychosocial domains related to the student success factors of retention and academic performance. In the second section, we present a conceptual model based on three student control factors associated with motivation, self-regulation, and social engagement. We introduce an assessment system to detail specific facet-level measurement of key psychosocial attributes organized within these three student control domains. These factors were chosen as they are amenable to change, predictive of academic performance or persistence behavior, and, when combined, create a highly robust measure of student risk. We provide specific case examples of students entering college at both high and low levels of academic and psychosocial risk to further illuminate this assessment system. In the third section, we present longitudinal research on the relationship of these psychosocial factors and college success when controlling for traditional predictors such as student demographics and academic achievement and performance as highlighted in Chapters Three and Seven.

Psychosocial Constructs from Educational Persistence Model and Motivational Theory Perspectives

There are no unifying theories that account for the type of student attitudes and behaviors associated with success outcomes and, as Pascarella and Terenzini (1991) point out, there are thousands of studies that address the college change process. The lack of theoretically coherent and empirically based research has resulted in conflicting findings, competing psychosocial theories, and general confusion about what are the key determinants of college success.

At the same time, during the last twenty years we have witnessed considerable research associated with two theoretical

Table 8.1 Salient Psychosocial Constructs from Educational Persistence Model and Motivational Theory Perspectives.

Educational Persistence Models	Motivational Theories
Contextual influences	**Motives as drives**
Financial support	Achievement motivation
Size of institutions	Need to belong
Institutional selectivity	**Motives as goals**
Social influence	Academic goals
Perceived social support	Performance and mastery goals
Social engagement	**Motives as expectancies**
Social involvement(social integration, social belonging)	Self-efficacy and outcome expectations
Academic engagement	**Self-worth**
Commitment to degree	Self-concept
Commitment to institution	

approaches. The first relates to motivational theories of educational performance and the second relates to educational persistence theories. Highlighted in Table 8.1 are examples of the constructs typically discussed from both educational persistence and motivational theory perspectives.

As can be seen, educational persistence models include contextual influences, social influences, social engagement factors, and academic engagement factors. Excellent research syntheses of models of educational persistence can be found in Tinto (1975, 1993) and Bean (1980, 1985). Motivational theories, however, target motives which are broken down into drives, goals, and expectancies to understand academic achievement and success. These theories also tend to include self-worth and self-concept constructs. Reviews by Covington (2000) and Eccles and Wigfield (2002) do an excellent job of capturing motivational theories and academic achievement. Interestingly, along the social dimension, educational persistence models describe social involvement, whereas motivational models describe need to belong. These constructs appear highly similar even though the terms used originate from different literatures. Another area of clear overlap is around the educational persistence notion of academic engagement, represented by the commitment to college construct, and the motivational theory notion of motives as goal, represented by the academic goal construct. Regardless, as you crosswalk the columns in Table 8.1, neither educational nor motivational theories account for the range of psychosocial factors that may be associated with college success.

To try to bridge these two theoretical traditions, and systematically understand the key determinants of academic performance and retention behavior, Robbins, Lauver, Le, Davis, and Langley (2004) undertook a comprehensive meta-analytic inquiry to categorize and test the effects of psychosocial study skill factors and college outcomes. They began by distinguishing between academic achievement and academic persistence outcomes. They identified all empirically based studies within a twenty-year period which included measures of both psychosocial factors and academic achievement or persistence (or both). The inclusion of these studies in the meta-analysis constituted a comprehensive literature review.

In examining the literature, Robbins et al. (2004) organized psychosocial and study skill factor constructs along nine dimensions ranging from achievement motivation and institutional commitment to perceived social support to academic self-efficacy and academic-related skills. They also highlighted three types of contextual influencers: financial support, institutional size, and institutional selectivity. Not surprisingly, these nine domains tie directly back to either educational persistence or motivational theories highlighted in Table 8.1. These nine dimensions and their construct definition and measurement example are summarized in Table 8.2. Selected references, also provided, highlighted these constructs, their definitions, and their measurements.

Table 8.2 Psychosocial and Study Skill Factor Constructs and Their Representative Measures.

Psychosocial and Study Skill Factor Construct	Definition and Measures
Achievement motivation	*Construct definition*: Students' motivation to achieve success; enjoyment of surmounting obstacles and completing tasks undertaken; the drive to strive for success and excellence.
	Representative measures: Achievement Scale (Personality Research Form [Jackson, 1984], used in Paunonen & Ashton, 2001); Achievement Needs Scale (Pascarella & Chapman, 1983; derived from Stern's Activities Index, 1970) need for achievement (Ashbaugh, Levin, & Zaccaria, 1973); Achievement Scale (College Adjustment Inventory [Osher, Ward, Tross, & Flanagan, 1995], used in Tross, Harper, Osher, & Kneidinger, 2000).
Academic goals	*Construct definition*: Students' persistence with and commitment to action, including general and specific goal-directed behavior, in particular, commitment to attaining the college degree; one's appreciation of the value of college education.
	Representative measures: Goal commitment (Pascarella & Chapman, 1983; Pavel & Padilla, 1993; Williamson & Creamer, 1988); commitment to the goal of graduation (Pascarella & Chapman, 1983); preference for long-term goals (Non-Cognitive Questionnaire [NCQ; Tracey & Sedlacek, 1984]); degree expectation (Braxton & Brier, 1989; Grosset, 1991); desire to finish college (Allen, 1999); valuing of education (Brown & Robinson Kurpius, 1997).
Institutional commitment	*Construct definition*: Students' confidence of and satisfaction with their institutional choice; the extent that students feel committed to the college they are currently enrolled in; their overall attachment to college.
	Representative measures: Institutional commitment (e.g., Berger & Milem, 1999; Pike, Schroeder, & Berry, 1997); institutional attachment (Student Adaptation to College Questionnaire [Krosteng, 1992]).

(*continued*)

Table 8.2 (*Continued*)

Psychosocial and Study Skill Factor Construct	Definition and Measures
Perceived social support	**Construct definition:** Students' perception of the availability of the social networks that support them in college.
	Representative measures: Family emotional support (College Student Inventory; Allen, 1999); social support (Coping Resources Inventory for Stress; Ryland, Riordan, & Brack, 1994); social stress (Solberg et al., 1998); family support (Solberg et al., 1998); Perceived Social Support Inventory (Gloria, Kurpius, Hamilton, & Wilson, 1999); Mentoring Scale (Gloria et al., 1999).
Social involvement	**Construct definition:** The extent that students feel connected to the college environment; the quality of students' relationships with peers, faculty, and others in college; the extent that students are involved in campus activities.
	Representative measures: Social Alienation from Classmates Scale (Daugherty & Lane, 1999); social integration (Ethington & Smart, 1986); University Alienation Scale (Suen, 1983); Personal Contact Scale and Campus Involvement Scale (Mohr, Eiche, & Sedlacek 1998); Class Involvement Scale (Grosset, 1991); Student–Faculty Interaction Scale (Pascarella & Terenzini, 1977).
Academic self-efficacy	**Construct definition:** Self-evaluation of one's ability and/or chances for success in the academic environment.
	Representative measures: Academic self-efficacy (Chemers, Hu, & Garcia, 2001); academic self-worth (Simons & Van Rheenen, 2000); academic self-confidence (Ethington & Smart, 1986); course self-efficacy (Solberg et al., 1998); degree task and college self-efficacy (Gloria et al., 1999).
General self-concept	**Construct definition:** A student's general beliefs and perceptions about him- or herself that influence his or her actions and environmental responses.

Psychosocial and Study Skill Factor Construct	Definition and Measures
	Representative measures: Rosenberg self-esteem (White, 1988); NCQ general self-concept and realistic self-appraisal (Young & Sowa, 1992; Fuertes & Sedlacek, 1995); self-confidence (Allen, 1985); self-concept (Williamson & Creamer, 1988).
Academic-related skills	*Construct definition*: Cognitive, behavioral, and affective tools and abilities necessary to successfully complete task, achieve goals, and manage academic demands.
	Representative measures: Time-management skills, study skills and habits, leadership skills, problem-solving and coping strategies, and communication skills.
Contextual influences	*General definition*: The favorability of the environment; the extent that supporting resources are available to students, including (1) availability of financial supports, (2) institution size, and (3) institution selectivity. The three subconstructs are operationally distinct and are therefore treated separately in our analyses. Their specific definitions are further provided below.
Financial support	*Construct definition*: The extent to which students are supported financially by an institution.
	Representative measures: Participation in financial aid program (McGrath & Braunstein, 1997); adequacy of financial aid (Oliver, Rodriguez, & Mickelson, 1985).
Size of institutions	*Construct definition*: Number of students enrolled at an institution.
	Representative measures: Total institutional enrollment (Ethington & Smart, 1986).
Institutional selectivity	*Construct definition*: The extent that an institution sets high standards for selecting new students.
	Representative measures: Institutional selectivity or prestige (Stoecker, Pascarella, & Wolfe, 1988), mean SAT/ACT score of admitted students (Ethington & Smart, 1986).

Robbins et al. (2004) used meta-analysis to understand the impact that each dimension had on either retention or GPA. Summarizing across multiple studies results in more stable and reliable findings than any individual study can reflect. Table 8.3 reports the number of subjects in the studies and the number of studies included in the meta-analysis. The studies are aggregated and the correlation between each psychosocial and study skill factor and retention was calculated. The correlation is in essence an effect size where a small but significant size is .10 to .29, moderate is .30 to .49, and large is .50 and higher (see Cohen, 1988, pp. 79–80, for discussion).

The highest correlations were with academic goals, academic-related skills, academic self-efficacy, social support, financial support, and institutional commitment. The relationships between most other psychosocial factors and retention are moderately positive but at a lower level. Table 8.3 also provides the estimated relationship between traditional predictors, including SES, high school GPA, and ACT test score, and the retention criterion. These validities are relatively lower than the psychosocial factors.

What was surprising about these findings is the importance of academic-related factors (effects bolded in Table 8.3) on retention. This runs somewhat counter to educational persistence models and highlights the importance of these factors in understanding student success.

In Table 8.4 we present the correlation between psychosocial factors and college GPA. The table includes the same information as listed for Table 8.3 except the outcome here is GPA. As you see, results strongly support the relationships between achievement motivation, academic self-efficacy, high school GPA, standardized achievement (ACT score), and college GPA. Not surprisingly, the traditional performance predictors of standardized achievement and high school performance are highly predictive of college academic performance. On top of this, measures of motivation and academic self-efficacy also are predictive. Overall effect sizes are also slightly larger, perhaps

Table 8.3 Meta-Analysis Results: Predictors of Retention.

Predictor	Subjects	Studies	Correlation with Retention	Effect
Psychosocial and study skill factors				
Achievement motivation	3,208	7	.105	Small
Academic goals	20,010	33	.210	**Moderate**
Institutional commitment	20,741	28	.204	Small
Social support	11,624	26	.199	Small
Social involvement	26,263	36	.166	Small
Academic self-efficacy	6,930	6	.257	**Moderate**
General self-concept	4,240	6	.059	Not significant
Academic-related skills	1,627	8	.298	**Moderate**
Financial support	7,800	6	.182	Small
Institutional size	11,482	6	−.010	−.010
Institutional selectivity	11,482	6	.197	Small
Traditional predictors				
SES	7,704	6	.212	Small
High school GPA	5,551	12	.239	Small
ACT/SAT scores	3,053	11	.121	Small

reflecting the difference in variability and sensitivity to change between GPA and retention criteria.

Our findings help clarify the relative importance of different psychosocial factors derived from educational persistence and motivation theory perspectives when predicting differential college outcomes, retention, and GPA, respectively. We see patterns of differential effects depending on the outcomes; in particular, achievement motivation is the most relevant psychosocial factor, along with traditional achievement predictors, when predicting academic performance. Clearly, a range of psychosocial and skill factors are predictive of college retention.

Table 8.4 Meta-Analysis Results: Predictors of GPA.

Predictor	Subjects	Studies	Correlation with GPA	Effect
Psychosocial and study skill factors				
Achievement motivation	9,330	17	.257	**Moderate**
Academic goals	17,575	34	.155	Small
Institutional commitment	5,775	11	.108	Small
Social support	12,366	33	.096	Small
Social involvement	15,955	33	.124	Small
Academic self-efficacy	9,598	18	.378	**Large**
General self-concept	9,621	21	.037	Not significant
Academic-related skills	16,282	33	.129	Small
Financial support	6,849	5	.195	Small
Traditional predictors				
SES	12,081	13	.155	Small
High school GPA	17,196	30	.413	**Moderate**
ACT/SAT scores	16,648	31	.368	**Moderate**

In total, these findings point to the importance of integrating across literatures to create linkages between motivational, social, and regulatory constructs to understand two key student success factors: academic performance and retention or persistence behavior. Although there are several reliable and valid measures of individual psychosocial attributes, there is no comprehensive instrument that brings them together.

Toward a Comprehensive Model for Understanding Psychosocial Development and Risk Behaviors

Historically, prediction of student success has centered on standardized achievement and high school GPA, which are important predictors of college readiness. There is growing evidence that success should be modeled with additional data such as psycho-social and behavioral factors. Because cognitive and psychosocial data are independent, using them in combination improves our predictive models and intervention strategies. The challenge is to create a comprehensive assessment system that predicts education success, is tailored to critical transition points (for example, entry into college), and measures characteristics amenable to change.

As a consequence of the meta-analytic research detailed above, Robbins and his colleagues (Huy, Casillas, Robbins, & Langley, 2005) proposed a comprehensive assessment strategy based on a model of key psychosocial factors. These psychoso-cial factors in combination could be used for two different pur-poses. The first is for risk assessment, by calculating a probability of either academic failure or drop-out behavior. These absolute risk values allow institutions to flag students for intervention based on level of risk. The second purpose is to inform inter-vention strategies aimed at promoting academic performance in classes or increasing persistence and retention behavior. To recap, the goal of this research was to integrate the relevant educational persistence and motivation theory constructs into a coherent model, and apply this model to critical educational transition points such as entering into and out of college.

The resulting assessment is called the **Student Readiness Inventory (SRI)** (ACT, 2008), which is a Likert-scaled self-report personality test that contains 10 scales and 108 items. Table 8.5 shows the scale names and definitions categorized within motivational and skill, social engagement, and self-management categories. As can be seen, there is a heavy emphasis on motiva-tion and skill scales because of the central and driving force of motivation in understanding task performance and academic suc-cess. We know that first-year academic performance is **the** driver of retention and degree attainment. As Allen and Robbins (2010) demonstrated, traditional high school predictors of academic achievement (such as ACT) and performance (such as high school GPA) are critical in understanding likely first-year suc-cess, but once first-year academic success is known, it becomes the

Table 8.5 SRI Scale Definitions and Sample Items by Student Control Factor.

Control Factor	SRI Scale	Definition	Sample Item
Motivation and Skills	Commitment to College	One's commitment to staying in college and getting a degree.	A college education will help me achieve my goals.
	Goal Striving	The strength of one's efforts to achieve objectives and end goals.	I bounce back after facing disappointment or failure.
	Academic Discipline	The amount of effort a student puts into schoolwork and the degree to which a student is hardworking and conscientious.	I consistently do my school work well.
	General Determination	The extent to which a student strives to follow through on commitments and obligations.	It is important for me to finish what I start.
	Study Skills	The extent to which students believe they know how to assess an academic problem, organize a solution, and successfully complete academic assignments.	I summarize important information in diagrams, tables, or lists.
	Communication Skills	Attentiveness to others' feelings and flexibility in resolving conflicts with others.	I'm willing to compromise when resolving a conflict.
Social Engagement	Social Activity	Students' comfort in meeting and interacting with other people.	I avoid activities that require meeting new people.
	Social Connection	Students' feelings of connection and involvement with the college community.	I feel part of this college.
Self-Management	Academic Self-Confidence	The student's belief in his or her ability to perform well in school.	I achieve little for the amount of time I spend studying.
	Emotional Control	Students' responses to and management of strong feelings.	I have a bad temper.

primary predictor of long-term success. The goal, then, is to target those factors mostly likely to ensure first-year academic success, which the Student Readiness Inventory accomplishes by targeting multiple facets of motivation and skill development.

We also see that social engagement is represented through social activity and social connection in addition to different facets of student participation in and connection to a social world. These scales are important in understanding retention behavior as they directly affect likely transfer behavior in community college students (Porchea, Allen, Robbins, & Phelps, 2010) and in third-year retention in four-year college students (Allen & Robbins, 2008). Finally, we also know that self-management is important in understanding student ability to manage daily hassles and to maintain a level of confidence in mastering college-level academic work. These scales are predictive of academic performance behavior and reflect areas that university support services frequently target when students are having difficulties.

As discussed earlier, a psychosocial assessment like the SRI has two purposes: to serve as a measure of risk identification and to provide important information about where and how to target interventions for developmental purposes. From a risk perspective, you can take a weighted composite of scales combined with entering ACT/SAT and/or HSGPA scores to create probabilities of both retention and academic performance success. These probabilities of success can be normed across a national sample, and the relative risk reported. We do this within the SRI for both retention and academic success outcomes. By combining the psychosocial and high school achievement (such as ACT) and performance (such as HSGPA) factors, we have great confidence in the accuracy of these predictions of success. An SRI-college retention index reports the likelihood of returning in the second year, and an SRI-college academic success index reports the likelihood of GPA 2.0 or higher.

These indices allow institutions to target at-risk students and make informed decisions about who they want to help.

By sorting students on relative risk estimates you can strengthen enrollment management planning, inform appropriate central and college-level services, and actively seek to help those deemed most in need. At the same time, you can use individual scale scores from both strength and weakness perspectives to provide feedback to students and to target potential interventions. Each scale reports a percentile score (range 1 to 99); therefore it is easy to create a normative snapshot of students against a national sample. The academic advisor profile report includes the probability indices, but not the individual student. In a sense, you can paint a narrative picture or portrait of a student based on relative strengths and weaknesses using the overall profile. This lets a student and university staff member reach a common understanding and language to talk about those factors directly tied to likely college success.

To highlight use of the SRI, we present four cases of students who entered college during the fall of 2003 and who we tracked as part of an extensive longitudinal research tracking over 14,400 students from 48 two- and four-year institutions (Robbins, Allen, Casillas, Petersen, & Le, 2006). In essence, we pulled four individual student profiles to contrast academic preparation and motivation issues. Two students entered college with low ability (ACT composite of 14 out of 36) and two of high ability (ACT composite of 27). For both Low and High Able students, we also found students who were considered at "low risk" and at "high risk" due to their psychosocial profile. Thus we created a 2 × 2 matrix as represented in Table 8.6.

Table 8.6 Sample SRI-College Profiles.

		Motivation	
		Low	High
ACT score	Low	Student A	Student B
	High	Student C	Student D

Turning to the Low Able students first, we see that both Student A (Figure 8.1) and B (Figure 8.2) have low potential for success in academic and retention behavior because of the criticality of academic preparation (that is, ACT college readiness composite score of 14). But student B comes with certain "strengths" in his or her self-rating of academic discipline, general determination, communication skills, and steadiness. After four years, student B remained in school, managing a cumulative GPA of 2.22. On the other hand, student A has very low motivational scale scores, is unsteady with little academic self-confidence, and not socially active. This student dropped out after the first year with a GPA of 1.5.

Turning to the High Able students, we see that Student C (Figure 8.3) has a highly variable SRI profile; extremely low academic discipline and goal striving scores coupled with a surprisingly lower (35th percentile) academic self-confidence score for someone with an ACT composite of 27. These indicators

Figure 8.1 Student A: Low ACT, Low Motivation

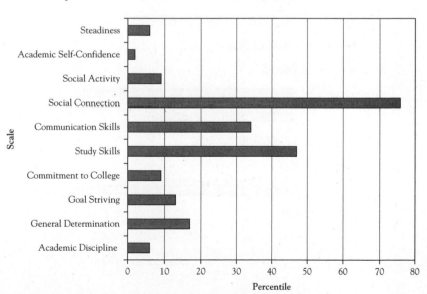

Figure 8.2 Student B: Low ACT, High Motivation

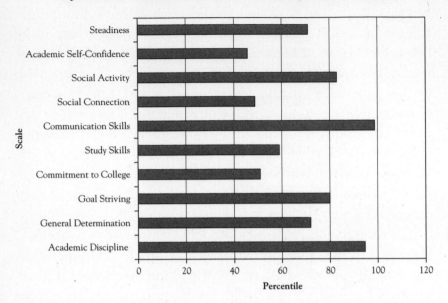

Figure 8.3 Student C: High ACT, Low Motivation

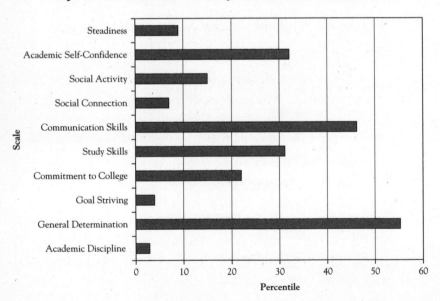

Figure 8.4 Student D: High ACT, High Motivation

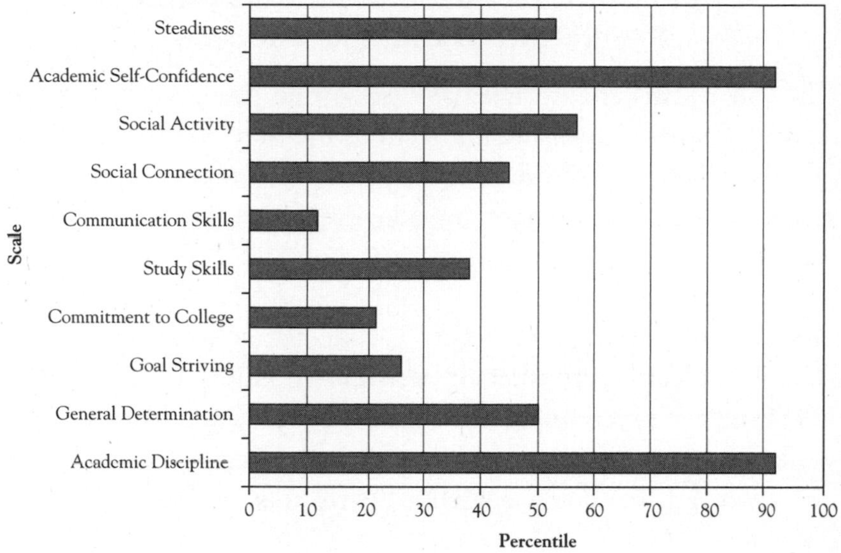

suggest someone not used to disciplined and focused studying and academic performance. In turn, Student C has low social connection and social activity scores, suggesting a lack of socialization and comfort with college. And finally, he or she has limited commitment to college and is unable to manage daily hassles. Not surprisingly, this person dropped out of school during the first year. We know that the student hasn't returned to any postsecondary institution because we tracked all students nationally through the National Student Clearinghouse (http://www.studentclearinghouse.org/default.asp). And what is stunning is that the student departed with a 3.7 grade point average. Finally, we see student D (Figure 8.4), a highly motivated and confident student who graduated in four years with a GPA of 4.0. Yet from a psychosocial development perspective, this student showed surprisingly low communication skills, which raise the question of how he or she will work within teams and within a social milieu upon entering the world of work.

Unraveling the Differential
Effects of Psychosocial and Traditional
Predictors of College Success

Thus far in this chapter we have presented the development of a comprehensive assessment system to measure the psychosocial factors related to college success. As part of the programmatic research and development agenda ACT set when constructing the Student Readiness Inventory, we determined a critical need for longitudinal research that helps unravel the differential effects of traditional predictors (academic achievement, high school academic performance, social economic status, and gender) from the psychosocial factors discussed earlier. In particular, we know that commitment to college and academic discipline are essential to both academic performance and retention behaviors.

We have reported on a large-scale study based on 14,000 students entering 25 four-year and 23 two-year postsecondary institutions in fall 2003. These students had either ACT or Compass (ACT, 2006) scores associated with their student readiness inventory results. Using our relationship with the National Student Clearinghouse, an organization that tracks over 92% of all admitted postsecondary students in the United States, we were able to track the academic performance, retention, transfer, and degree attainment rates of these students over six years.

We could then examine the relative effects of blocks of variables, starting with demographic factors, high school academic achievement factors, and selected scales from the Student Readiness Inventory. We tested these blocks using hierarchical multiple regression models. We used first-year cumulative GPA and year-two retention as the outcomes or criteria for these models, which were built separately for four-year and two-year institutions. Tables 8.7 and 8.8 show the results for these models at four-year institutions. Tables 8.9 and 8.10 show the results for

Table 8.7 Results of Hierarchical Linear Regression Models for Predicting GPA at Four-Year Institutions.

Effect	1st-semester GPA (n = 7,135)				1st-year cumulative GPA (n = 6,744)			
	Estimate	SE	P	R2/R	Estimate	SE	P	R2/R
Institutional				.088/.29				.103/.321
Admissions policy	−.023	.047	.618		.000	.043	.993	
Enrollment	−.144	.048	.003		−.114	.043	.008	
Percentage of minority students	.046	.043	.276		.028	.038	.468	
Control	−.006	.044	.897		−.004	.039	.917	
Variance	.028	.010	.003		.021	.008	.006	
Demographic				.127/.357				.153/.391
Race (four categories)			<.001				<.001	
Gender (male)	−.111	.021	<.001		−.123	.021	<.001	
SES index	.067	.011	<.001		.080	.011	<.001	
Academic achievement				.301/.549				.356/.596
ACT Composite score	.279	.013	<.001		.300	.013	<.001	
High School GPA	.248	.012	<.001		.280	.012	<.001	
SRI score				.336/.580				.390/.625
Academic Discipline	.211	.012	<.001		.207	.011	<.001	
Social Activity (linear)	−.062	.011	<.001		−.068	.011	<.001	
Social Activity (quadratic)	−.028	.008	<.001		−.032	.008	<.001	
Emotional Control (linear)	−.014	.011	.183		−.007	.011	.513	
Emotional Control (quadratic)	−.025	.007	.001		−.016	.007	.027	

Note: GPA = grade point average; SES = socioeconomic status; SRI = Student Readiness Inventory.

Table 8.8 Results of Hierarchical Linear Regression Models for Predicting GPA at Two-Year Institutions.

Effect	1st-semester GPA (n = 7,135)				1st-year cumulative GPA (n = 6,744)			
	Estimate	SE	P	R2/R	Estimate	SE	P	R2/R
Institutional				.043/.206				.032/.178
Enrollment	−.175	.059	.003		−.186	.047	<.001	
Percentage of minority students	.177	.057	.002		.236	.045	<.001	
Variance	.029	.014	.020		.011	.008	.081	
Demographic				.069/.264				.067/.259
Race (four categories)			<.001				<.001	
Gender (male)	−.093	.037	.011		−.074	.041	.071	
Academic achievement				.158/.397				.187/.432
ACT Composite score	.122	.020	<.001		.176	.022	<.001	
High School GPA	.208	.020	<.001		.235	.022	<.001	
SRI score				.191/.437				.214/.463
Academic Discipline	.185	.021	<.001		.157	.023	<.001	
Social Activity (linear)	−.066	.019	<.001		−.064	.022	.003	
Social Activity (quadratic)	−.034	.014	.019		−.001	.016	.947	
Emotional Control (linear)	.003	.021	.889		.040	.023	.089	
Emotional Control (quadratic)	−.044	.014	.001		−.035	.016	.024	

Note: GPA = grade point average; SRI = Student Readiness Inventory.

Table 8.9 Results of Hierarchical Logistic Regression Models for Predicting Retention at Four-Year Institutions.

Effect	1st-semester GPA (n = 7,135)				1st-semester GPA (n = 7,135)			
	OR	95% CI	P	R2a/OORb	OR	95% CI	P	R2a/OORb
Institutional				.024/1.62				.044/1.65
Admissions policy	0.88	0.66-1.17	.356		0.90	0.71-1.14	.378	
Enrollment	0.84	0.62-1.13	.228		1.12	0.88-1.43	.345	
Percentage of minority students	1.08	0.85-1.38	.504		1.04	0.85-1.27	.676	
Control	1.14	0.86-1.52	.329		1.13	0.91-1.41	.250	
Variance	.187	.031-.342	.021		.153	.034-.272	.014	
Demographic				.025/1.63				.047/1.68
SES index	1.08	0.98-1.19	.118		1.12	1.05-1.20	.001	
Academic achievement				.039/1.88				.075/1.92
ACT Composite score	1.31	1.17-1.47	<.001		1.28	1.19-1.39	<.001	
High School GPA	1.22	1.11-1.35	<.001		1.25	1.17-1.34	<.001	
SRI score				.057/2.11				.090/2.06
Academic Discipline	1.13	1.02-1.25	.026		1.14	1.06-1.22	.001	
Commitment to College	1.25	1.14-1.38	<.001		1.19	1.11-1.27	<.001	
Social Connection	1.20	1.08-1.33	.001		1.13	1.05-1.21	.002	
Social Activity	0.89	0.80-0.99	.028		0.89	0.83-0.96	.002	

Note: OR = odds ratio; CI = confidence interval; GPA = grade point average; SES = socioeconomic status; SRI = Student Readiness Inventory.
a. The Estimated variance at the institution level, not transformed to an odds ratio.
b. The model's overall odds ratio (Allen & Le, 2005).

Table 8.10 Results of Hierarchical Logistic Regression Models for Predicting Retention at Two-Year Institutions.

Effect	1st-semester GPA (n = 7,135)				1st-year cumulative GPA (n = 6,744)			
	OR	95% CI	P	R2a/OORb	OR	95% CI	P	R2a/OORb
Institutional				.020/1.30				.016/1.19
Enrollment	1.03	0.78-1.34	.845		0.92	0.77-1.10	.322	
Percentage of minority students	0.92	0.71-1.20	.523		0.95	0.80-1.12	.513	
Variance	.064	0-.169	.215		.040	0-.099	.165	
Academic achievement				.039/1.54				.033/1.40
ACT Composite score	1.62	1.26-2.09	.001		1.24	1.02-1.50	.032	
High School GPA	1.27	1.14-1.42	<.001		1.24	1.14-1.35	<.001	
SRI score				.050/1.66				.049/1.54
Academic Discipline	1.10	0.97-1.25	.128		1.14	1.03-1.25	.013	
Commitment to College	1.14	1.01-1.29	.030		1.11	1.01-1.22	.026	
Social Activity	0.88	0.78-0.98	.022		0.92	0.85-1.00	.054	
Emotional Control (linear)	1.08	0.96-1.22	.181		1.09	0.99-1.19	.074	
Emotional Control (quadratic)	0.96	0.89-1.04	.293		0.93	0.87-0.99	.020	

Note: OR = odds ratio; CI = confidence interval; GPA = grade-point average; SES = socioeconomic status; SRI = Student Readiness Inventory.

a. The Estimated variance at the institution level, not transformed to an odds ratio.

b. The model's overall odds ratio (Allen & Le, 2005).

these models at two-year institutions. In all models, after considering the individual effects of all SRI scales, we built simplified models by selecting only those scales that provided unique and significant variance. We **bold** those variables that significantly predict either GPA or retention outcomes. In all cases, the traditional standardized achievement and high school performance (GPA) predictors were significant. In many cases so was SES. None of this is a surprise. The real question, then, is, after controlling for these traditional performance and demographic factors, what role do psychosocial factors play in understanding retention and/or performance outcomes?

As expected, general motivational measures were predictive of academic performance (as measured by college GPA). In particular, academic discipline was highly predictive of college GPA. Also, general determination, commitment to college, and study skills were predictive of college GPA after controlling for institutional effects and traditional predictors. Surprisingly, motivational factors rather than social engagement factors are better predictors of retention. In many ways, these findings support students C and D as highlighted above. Academic discipline and commitment to college were the top predictors of retention. At four-year institutions, social connection was also predictive of retention. Contrary to our expectations, academic self-confidence, once controlling for traditional predictors, was not correlated with either outcome.

When examining the joint effects of all SRI scales after considering traditional institutional factors, **academic discipline** and **commitment to college** were the strongest predictors of retention outcomes. Academic discipline refers to students' ability to do homework, attend classes, ask questions, and take responsibility for their course performance. In a sense, this is the behavioral compliance component of motivation. Commitment to college refers to a clear and understood belief that college is important and finishing college essential. This commitment to an end goal or target is another component of motivation.

These results help highlight the relative independence of key motivational factors from standardized achievement test scores, and help focus where institutional activity should occur to increase the likelihood of both academic success and retention behavior. Academic discipline is an intriguing motivational facet, as it reflects the amount of effort that students put into schoolwork and the degree to which they see themselves as willing to work hard to complete homework and other academic assignments. It makes sense that the degree to which students follow through on their work expectations will strongly influence their class-based academic performance, which in turn drives retention. Finally, an overall commitment to school is critical regardless of entering ability level. We know that students who feel conflicted or forced into a school environment are less likely to succeed. These longitudinal findings help clarify and support the importance of psychosocial factors, and their relative effects related to the traditional demographic and achievement factors that bring focus to the student success paradigm.

9

CAREER DEVELOPMENT

In this chapter we highlight how student career development is a critical component to college and career readiness and success. Our premise is that student-informed career decision making is critical to student college major stability, time to degree attainment, and ultimately career readiness and search. The primary focus, then, is on how we can enhance career-related services to individuals within postsecondary institutions. To provide a framework for understanding the scope and effectiveness of college-based career and educational planning solutions, we:

- Provide background concerning the importance of structured career exploration and planning and the ways in which it can enhance career readiness and success;
- Explain how person-environment fit is at the foundation of structured career and educational planning and can provide significant benefits to students; and
- Describe the ways institutions can enhance the career and educational planning services we provide to students.

Some Context: Structured Career Exploration and Planning

Career development happens. As emphasized in many of the major career theories, career development is an evolving process that continues throughout life (Osipow, 1990). Even without structured career planning activities, people wade through the complexities of career possibilities and manage the transition into the workforce. Given this, what is so important about the activities that are typically part of structured career planning (providing world-of-work information, job shadowing, career assessment, and so forth)?

Why Is Structured Career Exploration and Planning Important?

During the Industrial Revolution many Americans experienced, for the first time, an open road to a variety of different career futures and real career choices to make. Career planning services began early in the twentieth century in response to the rapid growth in occupational options. As the economy expanded and diversified throughout the twentieth century, the occupational options available to Americans continued to grow.

Fast-forward to the present. The number of occupational options available to current and future workers is immense, and most of these jobs are not well known or understood by the general public. This lack of knowledge about possible career options has two major downsides. First, people can be simply unaware of opportunities. Second, even if a person knows that an occupation exists, a lack of information about that occupation may still make it difficult—if not impossible—to make informed decisions about it. Further, changes in this "invisible" workforce now happen rapidly and globally. Deciding how one fits into a world of copious, unknown, and changing opportunities is daunting at best. For most people, simply "figuring it out as you go" is unlikely to be the best strategy.

Although career exploration and planning are important life tasks, they can be hindered by many factors, such as lack of knowledge (self-knowledge, occupational knowledge, and knowledge of labor market trends), lack of confidence, and lack of social supports. Many students and job seekers do not have the skills, knowledge, and preparation needed to set informed goals and achieve their career aspirations. Assessment of vocational interests, and the exploration it engenders, can have a positive impact on student and job seeker motivation, aspirations, and competency development. Interests play a role in sustaining behavior (Silvia, 2006), and career exploration can encourage a focused range of occupational possibilities. Because the relationship between interests and competencies is reciprocal, feedback on vocational interests and exposure to new career possibilities can motivate people to expand and strengthen their related competencies (Tracey, 2002).

Structured career exploration and planning activities impart knowledge and skills that people need to more effectively meet the career development challenges we all face and to assist in the lifelong process of making informed career decisions and plans. Career planning starts as early as the middle school years, as students begin to develop realistic career plans and start thinking about postsecondary options (Noeth & Wimberley, 2002). Just as important, college plays a central role as students choose college majors and begin realistically planning careers. College major choice is essential, but so is leaving college with a realistic career plan that is congruent with student interests, values, and abilities, and reflects the job or professional training market.

Which Structured Career Planning Interventions are Effective?

Interventions to help with these career-related tasks take many forms. For example, they may (a) be unstructured or structured, (b) involve primarily counseling or primarily teaching, (c) be delivered to individuals or groups, and (d) stand alone or be embedded in a broader guidance program. Regardless of form, the empirical evidence indicates that career interventions are effective and that the effect sizes are, on average, moderate (Brown et al., 2003; Oliver & Spokane, 1988; Ryan, 1999). Positive results are found across the age span from middle school to college (Whiston, Sexton, & Lasoff, 1998). This research also sheds light on what makes these interventions effective. The Brown et al. (2003) meta-analysis found that interventions are more effective if they include:

- Written exercises focused on comparing occupations and on future planning
- Individualized interpretations and feedback
- World-of-work information
- Providing methods and models for exploring occupations and making decisions
- Activities designed to increase understanding of and build support for career choices and plans

This list of effective intervention ingredients aligns well with the typical goals and career exploration and planning activities used with middle and high school students (Whiston, Brecheisen, & Stephens, 2003). The ACT Career Planning Program (ACT, 2007) is a structured set of instructional units designed to build career-related knowledge and skills in middle and high school in order to improve student readiness for success in high school, college, and work. It emphasizes all five of the effective ingredients of career interventions included by Brown, et al. (2003).

What Are the Outcomes of Structured Career Planning?

Career interventions affect both career and academic outcomes. Among career outcomes, moderate to large effect sizes have been found for increasing the following outcomes:

- Accuracy of self-knowledge
- Career-related knowledge

Figure 9.1 Example Outcomes That Effective Career Planning Can Support at Different Life Stages

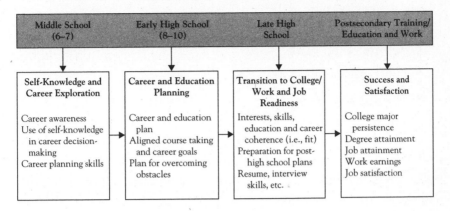

- Career exploration activities/behaviors
- Decision-making skills
- Miscellaneous career skills (problem solving, interviewing, résumé writing, and so on)
- Attitudes toward choice (certainty, satisfaction, and so on)
- Confidence in implementing career plans

The career-related tasks facing middle and high school and college students change over time and in generally predictable ways. Figure 9.1 shows some of the primary outcomes that effective career planning can support at different life stages.

The empirical evidence indicates that structured career interventions also have a significant impact on academic outcomes (Evans & Burck, 1992; Lapan, Gysbers, & Sun, 1997; Visher, Bhandari, & Medrich, 2004). For example, Lapan et al. (1997) reported on the impact of a statewide guidance system that focused on career planning, self-knowledge, and educational/career development. Students attending schools that more fully implemented the system reported earning higher grades and being better prepared for the future. Among academic outcomes, career interventions have been found to have a significant impact on

- Self-reported grades
- High school graduation
- Enrollment in college

These results are consistent with a recent meta-analysis, which found that mental health counseling services benefited student academics (Baskin, Slaten, Sorenson, Glover-Russell, & Merson, 2010). Taken as a whole, these results show that structured career planning (and interventions to improve or increase this planning) has a variety of positive career and educational outcomes. More generally, career planning is intended to promote readiness to achieve and succeed in a changing world by:

- Expanding the range of career aspirations;
- Increasing a sense of direction and purpose;
- Increasing understanding of the relevance of academic content to the real world; and
- Increasing a sense of engagement in school and the opportunities offered.

A Foundation of Career Planning: Person-Environment Fit

Many career theories assert, and seventy years of vocational research has consistently shown, that people gravitate toward occupations that permit them to engage in activities that are congruent with their personal attributes (Dawis & Lofquist, 1984; Holland, 1997; Osipow, 1990). People with excellent leadership skills tend to gravitate toward occupations that permit them to lead others. People who strongly value adventure tend to gravitate toward occupations that involve some level of novelty and danger. People who enjoy asking questions and solving problems tend to gravitate to occupations that permit them to engage in those activities (the sciences, for example). The outcomes of this process can be seen in the measured interests of people in varying occupations. Occupational incumbents and those going into an occupation typically score as one would expect: scientists score highest on a science interest scale, artists score highest on an arts interest scale, and so forth (see, for example, ACT, 1995; Donnay, Morris, Schaubhut, & Thompson, 2005). Birds of a feather tend to flock together.

John Holland's seminal work (1997) on creating a typology of career interests tied to the World of Work, the notion of Person-Environment Fit, and criticality of informed career decision making provides clear guidance on how we should approach student decisions about college major and career search. Seeking college majors and occupations that are rewarding—that provide opportunities to do preferred activities, to use abilities, and to express our attitudes and values—is an example of person-environment fit (hereafter called *career fit*, or simply *fit*). The concept of career fit is often used in vocational behavior research, as well as organizational psychology, and is at the foundation of career planning and many of its assessments.

In vocational research and organizational psychology, measures of fit are often used to predict behavior (for example, to predict persistence in an academic or work setting). In career planning, fit is frequently used as a basis for identifying career possibilities for counselees to consider. Suggesting good-fit possibilities helps counselees focus their career exploration process on a manageable set of options that can be refined, over time, through knowledge and experience.

Effective interpretation of career assessment results moves the career exploration process forward by making person-occupation similarities and differences explicit—that is, by transforming measured self-attributes into work-relevant information (Prediger, 1995). Vocational interests play a large role in career planning and are particularly useful for creating measures of fit because interests tend to be stable and the dimensions underlying interests also underlie basic occupational work tasks (ACT, 2009a). In sum, fit contributes to both the prediction of outcomes and the identification of personally relevant occupational options. It is not surprising that the concept is prevalent in both career research and counseling.

The World of Work Map

Contained in Figure 9.2 is the World-of-Work Map created by ACT. The World-of-Work Map draws upon and extends Holland's (1997) work. It helps people translate their interests into personally relevant career possibilities. The map provides a visual overview of 26 occupational groups (career areas) on two work task dimensions: working with data versus ideas, and people versus things. These compass points underlie basic work tasks and basic interests, permitting both occupational groups and measured interests to be located on the map. Users quickly grasp the basic similarities and differences among career areas, and see where their measured interests locate in the work world. Thus the World-of-Work Map serves as a visual bridge from measured interests to career options.

How Is Career Fit Measured?

A measure of fit can be obtained whenever comparable information about a person and the environment is available. Fit can be represented visually or numerically, and can range from low to high, depending on the degree of similarity between the person and the environment. Although several statistical approaches can be used to measure similarity, researchers at ACT have found that the correlation between person and environment profiles is a consistently useful measure (see Allen & Robbins, 2010).

Figure 9.2 The World-of-Work Map

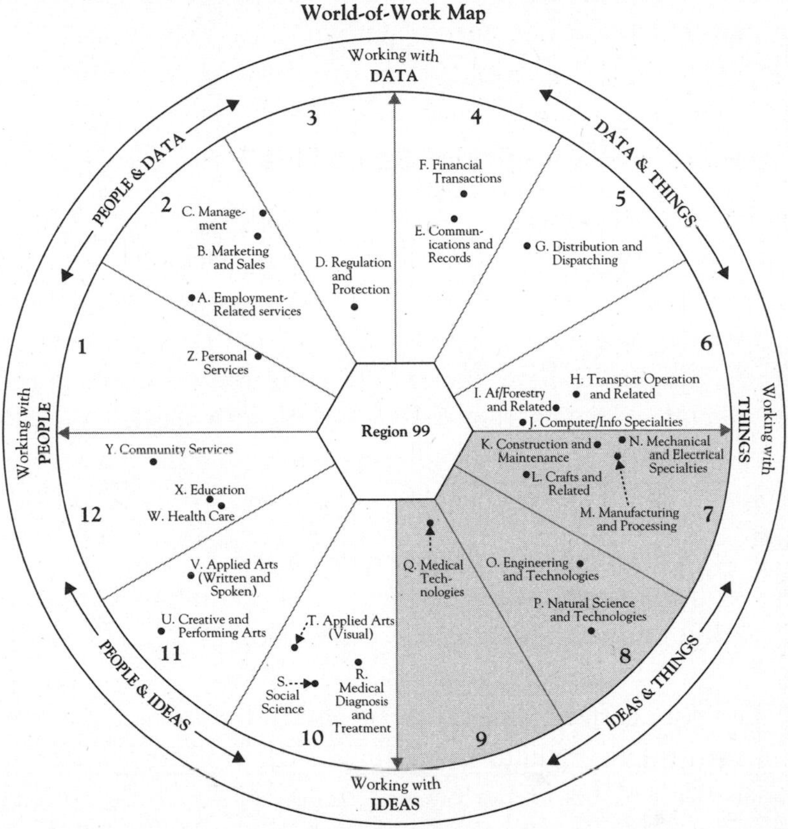

World-of-Work Map

Note: The shaded sections of the map highlight the career areas that involve the kinds of work that best fit the student's interests. The example shows student-reported preferences for working with ideas and things. Shaded career areas (*Natural Sciences & Technologies, Medical Technologies,* and so on) contain occupations that primarily involve working with ideas and things. In EPAS student websites, each career area of the map is clickable, permitting students to view lists of occupations and descriptive occupational information in each career area.

For example, an index of fit can involve the correlation between a high school senior's vocational interest score profile and scores on the same set of interests for a sample of college seniors majoring in biology. Higher correlations indicate higher levels of interest-major fit (with the biology major, in this example). This "profile similarity" measure of fit can be used to identify majors that best fit a student's interests, or to examine the fit between a student's interests and his or her current major.

What Are the Benefits of Career Fit?

Evidence is accumulating on the relationship between interest-based fit and success outcomes (see Van Iddekinge, Putka, & Campbell, 2011). Research at ACT and elsewhere suggests that if students' measured interests (that is, patterns of scores on interest inventories) are similar to the interests of people in their chosen college majors, they will be significantly more likely to:

- Remain in those majors;
- Persist in college (versus dropping out); and
- Complete their college degrees in a timely manner (that is, within four years for a bachelor's degree).

Fit with current major can be used alone or in combination with other predictors to estimate the student's probability of persisting in his or her current major, or attaining a college degree in a timely manner. Figure 9.3 shows the probability of persisting in a current major for students with different levels of academic preparation (measured by ACT scores) and different levels of interest-major fit (Allen & Robbins, 2010). As can be seen, those students with high academic preparedness demonstration retention rates ranging from 49% to 72% depending on Fit level. Interestingly, Low Able students (bottom 25th percentile) with High Fit have surprisingly high persistence rates, comparable to the High Able group (71%).

Figure 9.4 shows the probability of attaining a college degree within four years for students with different levels of academic preparation (measured by ACT scores) and different levels of

Figure 9.3 Percentage of Students Persisting in Their Current Major, by ACT Scores and Interest-Major Fit

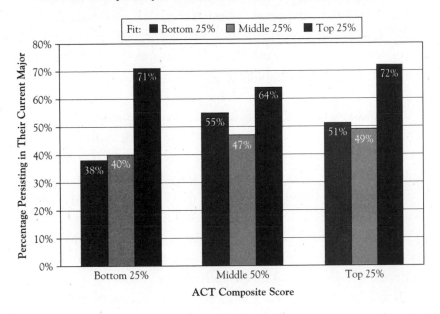

Figure 9.4 Percentage of Students Attaining a Timely Postsecondary Degree, by ACT Scores and Interest-Major Fit

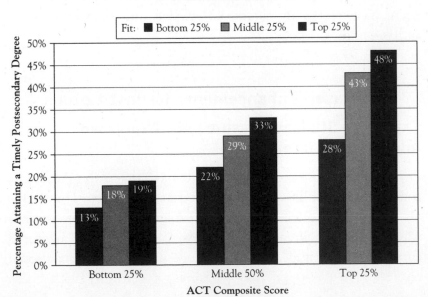

interest-major fit (Allen & Robbins, 2010). These figures show that both academic preparation and interest-major fit contribute to academic outcomes. High Able/High Fit students have 48% timely degree attainment (traditional four-year graduation window). High Able/Low Fit drop to 28%. In the Low Able group, Low Fit students graduate on time only 13% of the time!

Students with better interest-major fit also, on average, tend to have higher college GPAs (Tracey & Robbins, 2006) and earn more money after graduation (Neumann, Olitsky, & Robbins, 2009). It is worth noting that students, on average, prefer and select those majors for which they have good interest-major fit (Porter & Umbach, 2006). Thus, with a higher level of fit, a student is more likely to (a) select a particular major, (b) stay in college and in his or her chosen major (see also Allen & Robbins, 2008), and (c) finish within four years.

While there is growing evidence that fit contributes to success outcomes, fit itself is rarely used as an outcome. Though it is reasonable to expect that career interventions will contribute, in the long term, to increases in the fit between the person and educational/career choices, in the short term other changes—such as increases in career knowledge and decision-making skills—are more likely.

Fit-Based Enhancements for Institutions

Examining Student Measured and Expressed Interests, and Their "Fit"

A majority of postsecondary students have taken the ACT, and therefore the UNIACT career interest inventory. They have also expressed college major and career choices. Put another way, institutions already have access to both student-measured career interests, and *expressed* college major and occupational choices. They also provide measures of certainty with these

Figure 9.5 Example Interest-Major Fit

Intended Coll Maj	Physical Sciences, General
Interest-Maj Fit	82
Certainty of Maj	Fairly sure
Voc Choice 1	Biology, General
Certainty Voc Choice	Not sure
Degree Objective	Prof Level
Hours to Work College	1–10

choices. Educational institutions can benefit from knowing student measured and expressed career choices, and the "fit" between them by taking advantage of easily administered and located information (for example, in the ACT College/High School Reports). The goal here is to identify and target students with poor interest-major fit for additional advising and other interventions to increase retention. Institutions can create guidance on the interpretation and use of these results once this information is disseminated to the appropriate post-admissions unit(s).

The example in Figure 9.5 involves reporting simple descriptive information about intended college major and vocational choice, and their certainty. We also provide a Fit score for a planned major reported by the student on the ACT. The Fit score is a numeric index based on the Euclidean distance between the student's college major (or occupational) choice on the World-of-Work Map, and its distance to the chosen or expressed College Major or Career Choice located on the same map.

Risk Indices. In addition to interest-based Fit scores, you can develop "risk" or "flagging" rules depending on the degree of Fit. We highlight this example in Figure 9.6. We simply report Fit indices across a range of College Major and Career areas, which can be derived from the ACT College Report.

Figure 9.6 Example of Risk Indices

Risk Indices

Timely Degree Attainment
Risk Score: 7

Students scoring at this level have an above-average risk of not graduating in a timely fashion. Such students are among the least likely to be successful in graduating within four years.

College Major Persistence
Risk Score: 9

Scores on both risk indices can vary from 1 (lowest risk) to 9 (highest risk), with 5 representing average risk. Risk is based on ACT Composite score, self-reported high school grades, level of fit between measured interests and planned major, and, in the case of College Major Persistence, certainty of planned major. Refer to the ACT *User Handbook* for additional information.

Curriculum-Based Enhancements as Part of First-Year College Experience

Most colleges and universities offer or require a first-year experience seminar. Institutions understand that such efforts pay dividends by increasing first-to-second year retention rates and, in turn, graduation rates. Topics in these seminars vary, ranging from academic survival, to academic planning, to relationships and personal development. According to the most recent (2006) national survey of first-year seminars, about 50% of colleges and universities included educational or career planning activities in such seminars (Tobolowsky & Associates, 2008). This same survey found that over 50% of institutions offered at least some online seminar components—a percentage that is undoubtedly higher today.

- Materials and activities designed to enhance the educational and career planning activities are available for use in first-year experience seminars. These materials could be made available online as PDFs and activities (such as searching for information about majors) could be done online via a web application. Topics covered in these materials include:

- Choosing a major
- Choosing an occupation
- Making connections between majors and careers
- Successful test taking
- Steps to getting a job (résumés, interviews, portfolios, and so on)

There are several reasons to believe that such materials would be welcomed by institutions. First, many first-year seminars are a hodgepodge of instruction and activities with rotating instructors. Quality support materials can bring structure and add continuity to seminars. Second, with the growing recognition that education and career planning contribute to student motivation and success, institutions are likely to see value in a fully articulated set of materials on this topic.

First-year experience courses often cover psychosocial topics such as self-management skills and social engagement experiences. In Chapter Eight we saw how the Student Readiness Inventory (SRI) can support and enhance these efforts. The SRI can be used to identify students who are at risk for academic failure or attrition and provide targeted intervention based on students' patterns of psychosocial strengths and weakness. In combination with the types of first-year supports provided to all students, this would provide a more comprehensive approach to student success and retention.

Career Guidance and Coaching

Another intervention strategy is to develop a structured career guidance or coaching system that helps prepare students for career search and employment. A range of materials will be needed for such a system, such as career coach guides and training

Figure 9.7 Career Decision Making Model

The Career Decision Making Model

Look at the following diagram and the questions below. Place a check mark in the blank
next to the phase that best describes your present concerns.

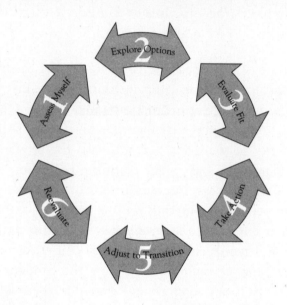

1. **Assess Myself**
   - Who am I?
   - What am I interested in?
   - What do I have to offer?

2. **Explore Options**
   - What is out there for me?
   - How do I find an Internship?

3. **Evaluate Fit**
   - What's important to me?

4. **Take Action**
   - How do I get there?
   - Resume, cover letter, interview skills
   - Informational Interviewing

5. **Adjust to Transition**
   - How do I make the transition from
     student to professional?

6. **Reevaluate**
   - What's next?

Source: Johns Hopkins Career Center http://www.jhu.edu/careers/students/
ExploreyourOptions/careerdecisionmakingmodel.html

materials, participant manuals, evaluation surveys, and so forth.
Career coaches would guide and follow participants through a
comprehensive set of assessment, planning, certification, and
portfolio activities designed to lead to sustained employment in
a good-fitting occupation. The system would also provide career

coaching, training materials, and feedback mechanisms for system evaluation and improvement. A challenge in building such a system will be to make it highly structured to assure that processes are followed, yet sufficiently flexible to make it applicable to a range of locations, partnerships, and stakeholders.

We present the Career Decision Making Model and Career Center Resources by Stage as developed by the John Hopkins Career Center. As you can see in Figure 9.7 there is a six-step process by which students take and evaluate their actions. A premium is put on self-assessment and exploration of options,

Figure 9.8 Career Center Resources by Stage

> ## Carreer Center Resources by Stage

1. Assess Myself
- **Individual Appointments** with a career counselor. To schedule an appointment call 410-516-8056. With the assistance of your career counselor, you can determine the appropriateness of the following assessment inventories:
- **Strong Interest Inventory** – an instrument designed to assist you in clarifying your work related interests.
- **Myers Briggs Type Indicator** – an instrument designed to identify your personal preferences. Interpretation by a career counselor links that information to the world of work.
- **The Career Center Library** has an assessment section containing books that can assist you with the assessment process.

2. Explore Options
Learning About Careers
- **This Fall/Spring in the Career Center** – A listing of career education workshops and events (available in the Career Center and your J-connect account).
- **Best Career Links** – a collection of websites indentified as having high value in the career decision making process.
- **The Career Resource Library** has multiple sections with career related resources.
- **Individual Appointments**
- **This Week in the Career Center** is a weekly email newsletter developed by the Career Center to keep you informed of opportunities, programs, and events on and off campus that will benefit your career development. Sign up for this feature within your J-Connect Account.

Experiences Careers
- **Internships** – the Career Center has a wealth of resources to assist you with your internship search. Start with an Internship Handout or attend one of our Internship workshops. You can also schedule an individual appointment with a career counselor.
- **Field Trips** – Intersession courses and trips on Financial Literacy, Media & Public Relations and Globalization. For more information check the workshop schedule, visit the Career Center website and check with the Registrar's Office in late fall.

Source: Johns Hopkins Career Center, http://www.jhu.edu/careers/students/Explore yourOptions/careercounseling.html

Figure 9.8 *(Continued)*

Reevaluate 3. Evaluate Fit
Evaluate Fit of Career Fields and Majors
To evaluate the fit of a career field or major you must consider what you have learned about yourself and information about the field or major. Identifying how this information relates to you can give you valuable information to make a decision.
• **Individual Appointments**
• **Arts and Sciences Academic Advising 410-516-8216**
• **Engineering Academic Advising 410-516-7395**

Evaluate the Fit of Industries, Employers, and Positions
To find out information on specific employers, fields, or positions, the following resources will be useful.
• **JHU InCircle** (www.alumni.jhu.edu) The JHU alumni database.
• **Career Center Library** has information on specific employers, directories, and online resources to assist you in your research.
• **MSE Library** has a wealth of information in the reference area to assist you with finding valuable information about employers and industries.

4. Take Action
Preparing for the Job or Internship Search
At this stage, you should begin to prepare your resumes and cover letters, polish and practice interview skills, and tap into your career network. These are the tools you need for a successful search.
• **This Fall/Spring in the Career Center**
• **Career Handouts**
• **Individual Appointments**
• **Career Resource Library**

Executing Your Job or Internship Search
Put your tools to work while engaging employers.
• **On-Campus Recruiting**
• **Career and Internship Fairs (both on-campus and off-campus)**
• **Dossier Service (Ph.D. Only)**
• **This Week in the Career Center (e-newsletter)**
• **Individual Appointments**

5. Adjust to Transition
• **Career Center Website (www.jhu.edu/careers)**
• **JHU InCircle (www.alumni.jhy.edu)**
• **Best Career Links**
• **Individual Appointments**
• **Counseling Center**

evaluating fit, and on action planning. Interestingly, there is also an emphasis on anticipating the transition from student to professional, and on evaluating the consequences of career decisions. From a resourcing perspective, John Hopkins deploys a range of activities and assessments that parallel their action agenda highlighted in Figure 9.8. Some of these activities are self-directed, some are presented in psycho-educational groups, and some are connected to practical experiences such as internships, field trips, and employer interviews.

Final Thoughts

In this chapter we have highlighted the importance of career development, both at the onset of college and at the exit of college. We have highlighted the importance of informed career decision making on college major stability, academic performance, and timely degree attainment. We provide examples of interventions tied to the FYE and to advising that focus on career-related issues. At the same time, we argue for the role that postsecondary institutions should play in preparing students for an active and successful job search and career planning. Using a career coaching metaphor, we highlight the range of services that exemplary career centers, such as those found at John Hopkins, use to engage and inform their students. Using Holland and Dawes's theories of person-environment fit and work adjustment, respectively, we detail the criticality of matching interests, values, and abilities to job market opportunities in order to maximize long-term earnings and satisfaction. Perhaps it is crass to say, but successful and satisfied alums are an important resource to any university or college as they contribute in direct and indirect ways to the well-being of the institution and its students.

10

ASSESSING THE IMPACT OF ACADEMIC, PSYCHOSOCIAL, AND CAREER DEVELOPMENT FACTORS ON COLLEGE STUDENT SUCCESS

We have seen in the preceding chapters how academic achievement, psychosocial development, and career development each individually contribute to our understanding of student persistence and performance behavior. Our first goal in this chapter is to examine the interrelationship of these factors by proposing and testing a comprehensive model for understanding student success. In this model, we begin by stating that student cognitive development (achievement level) and acquisition of foundational skills are the cornerstone of college success. A student's ability to do the tasks necessary for academic success (that is, coursework) is dependent on these skills. And we believe that academic success drives all other outcomes. Layered on top of these cognitive foundational skills are psychosocial development and career development factors. We call this stacked set of skills the "Pyramid for Success," which is shown in Figure 10.1. The pyramid exists in the broader context of school and student social capital effects. In other words, all students must be understood within the unique institutional and personal circumstances that define who they are.

NOTE: The Student Readiness Inventory (SRI) which was the instrument cited in much of the research in this chapter, is now known as ENGAGE.

The second major goal of this chapter is to connect our Pyramid for Success to institution intervention strategies as a robust way of understanding what factors promote or impede college student success. We provide two very different examples. The first is a specific institution demonstration project looking at student achievement and behavior on developmental class outcomes. The second is using meta-analytic techniques detailed in Chapter Eight to test the overall effects of different institution intervention strategies on student retention and performance behaviors. We also test how well interventions "work through" psychosocial factors to facilitate positive change and outcomes.

We believe academic achievement and college readiness are essential drivers to first-year academic performance (Allen & Robbins, 2010; Allen, Robbins, Casillas, & Oh, 2008). In turn, we have shown that first-year academic performance is the strongest predictor of retention and degree attainment. In Chapter Seven, we detailed academic achievement factors for college readiness by describing the importance of meeting benchmarks in Mathematics, Science, English, and Reading that correspond

Figure 10.1 Pyramid for Success

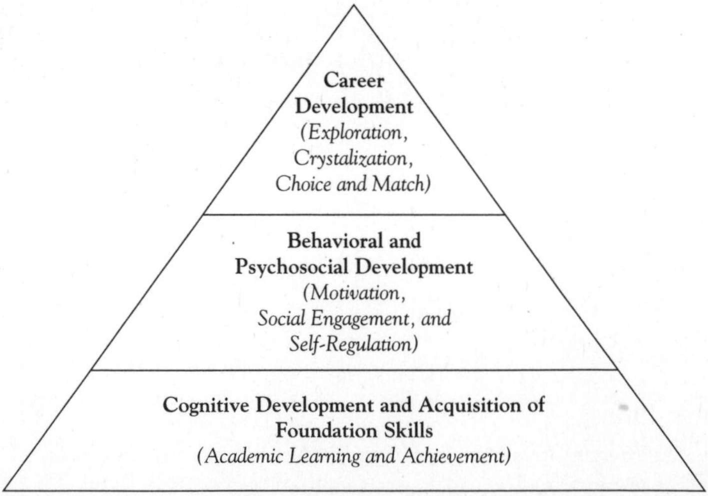

Career
Development
(*Exploration,
Crystalization,
Choice and Match*)

Behavioral and
Psychosocial Development
(*Motivation,
Social Engagement, and
Self-Regulation*)

Cognitive Development and Acquisition of
Foundation Skills
(*Academic Learning and Achievement*)

to the likelihood of obtaining a "B" or better in general education courses required to succeed in both two-year and four-year colleges. Put another way, the ability to master academic coursework is the foundation of all student success, including persistence behavior.

We also know that student academic readiness includes psychosocial attributes or behaviors as categorized through the motivation, social engagement, and self-regulation control factors we discussed in Chapter Eight. These factors are essential for student success. We believe behavioral and psychosocial development influence both persistence and performance behavior. For example, students who do not comply with their homework and other course demands are less likely to succeed. And those students who do not feel connected are less likely to persist or to transfer from a two-year to a four-year college institution. And finally, those students who are not able to manage daily hassles and support a sense of academic self-confidence are less likely to succeed in their courses and to persist into their second year.

We also believe that informed career decision making that allows students to match their interests, values, and abilities to college major and career choices result in greater congruence or career fit. As we have highlighted in Chapter Nine from both Theory of Work Adjustment (Dawis, Fruehling, Oldham, & Laird, 1989; Lofquist & Dawis, 1991) and Person-Environment (PE) fit models (Holland, 1997), the greater degree to which career fit occurs, the more likely it is we will see increased college grade point averages, retention rates, and graduation rates (Tracey & Robbins, 2006). In fact, we know that those students entering college with higher degrees of career fit are more likely to earn greater income 10 years after college graduation than those who demonstrate lower career fit (Neumann, Olitskey, & Robbins, 2009).

But we know that students do not operate in a vacuum. They exist in a real world where they have varying access to social support and to financial and other resources. We call this social capital (Wimberly, 2000). In many ways socioeconomic status (SES) is an important proxy of social capital because it reflects the financial resources available to a student. But beyond financial resources, social capital refers to a student's exposure to and work with significant others who can model what college degree attainment and career success look like. Maintaining these goals are key determinants to building a commitment to college success and to sustaining a meaningful career path. Another demographic predictor, gender, may reflect another source of social capital given that women and men are differentially exposed to role models and other reinforcements that help them internalize and act on a broad range of measured interests and values when making college major and career choices. Social capital is not the only contextual factor. The postsecondary institution itself serves as a key variable in understanding student experiences, whether relating to the rigor of the courses, a sense of connection and belonging, or access to financial and other resources necessary for college success. Interestingly, drawing from recent research on student learning outcomes (Blaich & Wise, 2011), we know that student individual differences and variations in learning are as great within institutions as they are across institutions. In other words, institutional differences in learning are less critical than student Pyramid for Success factors. Nonetheless, we want to better understand individual student factors within the context of social capital and institutional features.

Testing the "Pyramid for Success" Model on Academic Performance and Timely Degree Attainment

Allen and Robbins (2010) tested the Pyramid for Success model using a longitudinal database including 3,072 entering four-year college students in one of 15 institutions and 788 entering two-year college students in one of 13 institutions.

The authors tested the direct effects of interest-major congruence, motivation, ACT score, high school GPA, gender, and SES on first-year academic performance. They then tested the direct and indirect effects of these predictors as they worked through first-year academic performance to predict timely degree attainment. They also controlled for institutional differences or institutional variation without necessarily understanding the reasons for this variation. We present this theoretical model in Figure 10.2, using solid lines for paths based on previous research that showed significant effects, and dashed lines for paths based on hypothesized relationships between antecedent factors and persistence or time to degree attainment.

In Figure 10.3, we present the result of these path analytic models, presenting the four-year and the two-year results side by side for each path. Turning to the four-year students, we see that interest-major congruence directly predicts time to

Figure 10.2 Expected and Hypothesized Paths to Outcomes

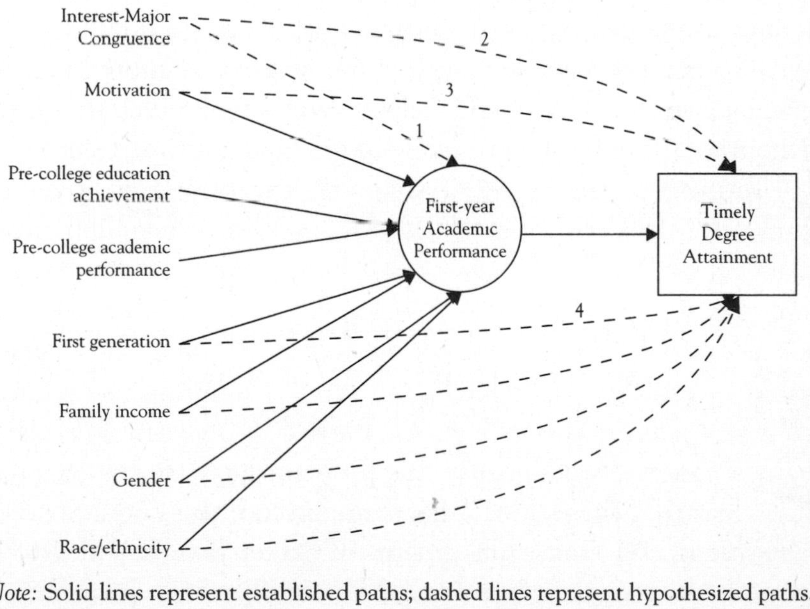

Note: Solid lines represent established paths; dashed lines represent hypothesized paths.

Figure 10.3 Results-Path Model

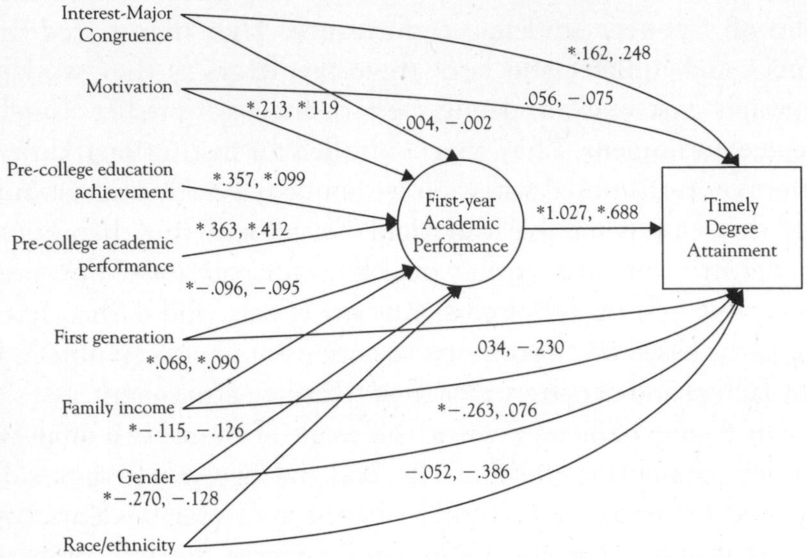

Note: Weights for estimated paths: four-year, two-year. Significant paths are marked with an asterisk (*).

degree attainment (.162). We also see a strong effect for first-year academic performance on timely degree attainment (1.027). We also observe a gender effect where women are more likely to graduate on time than men (−.270). We also observed that first-generation students are less likely to graduate on time (.068).

Turning to the two-year students, the only key driver of graduation from two-year colleges is first-year academic performance (.688). That is, given the many possible outcomes for two-year students (drop-out, transfer, complete), the one central success factor for persistence is mastery of the first-year coursework. Given the high remediation rates of entering community college students, this is a major barrier to success. We highlight a case study addressing this problem later in this chapter. It is clear that these direct effects underscore the importance of assessment and course placement (Chapter Twelve), developmental education and learning assistance (Chapter Thirteen).

We also observe the **indirect effects** of traditional predictors and student motivation as they work through first-year academic performance to influence timely degree attainment. Specifically, in both four- and two-year colleges student motivation (.213 and .119, respectively), student pre-college education achievement level (.357 and .099), and pre-college academic performance (that is, HSGPA at .363 and .412) are all critical determinants of first-year academic success. Within the four-year sample, we also see that first-generation status (.068), family income (−.115), gender (−.270), and African-American status (−.270) are predictive of first-year academic success.

To summarize, the research of Allen and Robbins (2010) tests the simultaneous effects of academic preparation and motivation and career interest-major congruence on first-year academic performance and timely degree attainment. They find that first-year academic performance is critical for long-term college success. They also find that academic preparation, motivation, and career interest–major congruence are all essential. Moreover, student demographic factors, including whether you are first-generation student, a man or woman, and black, are likely to affect first-year academic performance and whether you graduate on time. This research highlights the range of student individual difference factors we addressed in Chapters Seven through Nine; they are all important in understanding student academic performance, persistence, and timely degree attainment. Some factors work indirectly through academic performance, whereas other factors, such as career interest–major congruence, work directly to affect timely degree attainment behavior (and therefore persistence). These research findings are consistent with prior research on long-term college success and the need for students to be prepared for first-year college coursework. Allen and Robbins (2008) demonstrated the direct effects of career fit and college major stability and the centrality of first-year academic performance on time to degree attainment. Allen, Robbins, Casillas, & Oh (2008) modeled third-year retention and transfer behavior using academic performance and psychosocial predictors.

There are several implications of this research. Retention efforts must incorporate approaches that promote academic success through both academic and motivational strategies. Academic skills are critical, and we know that psychosocial factors such as motivation are key to identifying at-risk students unable to engage successively in coursework or to persist into their second year. Academic discipline targets behavioral compliance and course persistence behavior. It is a critical focal area that postsecondary institutions should address to maximize likely student success.

Programs geared toward first-generation students are likely to help support these students and these programs should continue after their first year. More controversial is whether to target men, who are at greater risk than women for sustaining conscientious and dedicated academic behaviors. We already know that there are a diminishing number of men seeking and finishing postsecondary education (ACT, 2010a). We also see that African American students are less likely to succeed than other groups, which is in part because on average they are less academically prepared (ACT, 2010d). Postsecondary institutions need to ensure that culturally sensitive and effective interventions tied to academic success are made available to at-risk students. We will talk more about what these interventions should focus on later in the chapter.

Effective career and educational planning for entering first-year and undecided students also offer an important means of improving student persistence and timely degree attainment. We know that career fit is related to college major stability (Allen & Robbins, 2008). The ACT, for example, includes a career assessment that helps plot an individual's measured interest profile on a World-of-Work Map, which locates within a quadrant system tied to Data-Ideas and People-Things, the location of occupations and college majors. Postsecondary institutions can use individual student results from the ACT record to help map to their potential college and career choices to inform decisions, and to maximize career fit from the perspectives of cognitive ability and career interest.

The challenge, then, is to create multifaceted intervention programs that target key student factors highlighted in the Pyramid for Success and that promote both academic success and persistence behavior. For example, getting students into the "right" general education courses is only one step. Programs are also needed to help students overcome boredom and frustration, comply with demanding homework and class schedules, and manage multiple deadlines.

In the next section, we detail an institutional use case that highlights how to embed student interventions within an academic course context while seeking broad university ownership and resources. In this example, we target remedial education and student academic behavior.

Success in College Developmental Courses

It is a long-standing problem that students entering community college and other postsecondary education are not academically prepared for college-level coursework (Porchea, Allen, Robbins, & Phelps, 2010). Without the necessary prerequisite skills and knowledge, underprepared students are less likely to succeed in college courses or to return for a second year (ACT, 2005). The primary method for helping underprepared students to degree attainment is developmental instruction (see Attewell, Lavin, Domina, & Levey, 2006 for review), a topic we cover in detail in Chapter Thirteen. Due to their open enrollment policies, much of the remediation burden has fallen on two-year colleges. Between 2000 and 2008 the percentage of two-year college students taking at least one developmental course has risen from 39% to 44% (NCES, 2010d). In a study by the Community College Research Center at Columbia University (Biswas, 2007), the estimated percentage of students needing remediation was greater in math (70%) than in English (34%).

Clearly, math instruction should be an area of concern at all levels of education.

As Adelman (1999) pointed out, mathematics preparation is the key to eventual postsecondary success. And we know that initial course placement is essential to putting students into classes where they are able to master the material aligned with eventual successful completion of college algebra. The dilemma of setting rigorous course placement standards was highlighted by Jacobson (2006), who pointed out that placing entering student in noncredit-bearing developmental mathematics courses increased their likely mastery of foundational skills needed for college algebra, but also resulted in reduced program completion due to high attrition rates. Bahr (2010) makes a similar point about student compliance and motivational behavior when highlighting the disparities in completion rates and differing levels of initial math ability. In other words, student persistence behavior was as critical in understanding course completion and success as the math "skill gaps" themselves.

Clearly, we want to place students into courses for which they are likely to succeed, but student attrition is a reality that must be also be addressed. Best practices for learning gap assessment and course placement are discussed in Chapter Twelve. The effectiveness of remedial math courses has been a topic for research for two decades. Golfin, Jordan, Hull, & Ruffin (2005) tried to answer the question of what approaches and strategies work best to strengthen adult students' math skills to help them progress into college-level courses. They highlighted the importance of accurately placing students into the appropriate level math course. They further called for tailored instruction based on effective diagnostics.

The goal, then, is to combine effective course placement, diagnostic testing used to target curricular instruction, and student motivation and behavioral compliance factors to ensure effective completion of developmental mathematics instruction. In essence, we want to combine best practices in the individualized delivery of math developmental education with our knowledge of student motivation and academic behavior (Robbins et al., 2004; Robbins, Oh, Button, & Le, 2009).

Wilbur Wright College created such a model, as shown in Figure 10.4, where they used both cognitive and psychosocial

Figure 10.4 College Developmental Course Best Practices

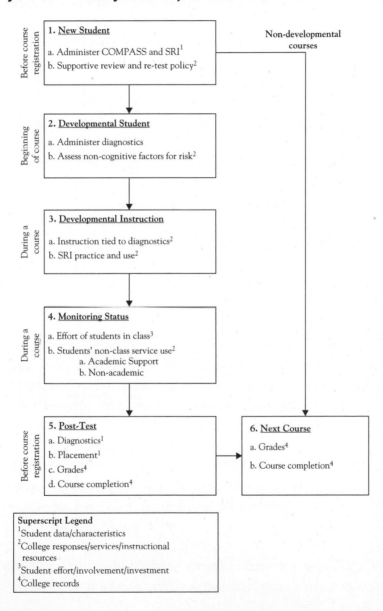

Superscript Legend
[1] Student data/characteristics
[2] College responses/services/instructional resources
[3] Student effort/involvement/investment
[4] College records

assessments to help place, diagnose, and intervene across academic and behavioral domains. They expected that entering student motivation would affect compliance behaviors during the course and that these behaviors would moderate post-course knowledge and course completion. This model allowed them to examine the extent that pre-course academic skills and course behaviors, separately and together, influence course success. Further, they expected that those students with high behavioral compliance will have much higher completion rates and knowledge gain than those students with low behavioral compliance, regardless of entering cognitive ability level.

Not surprisingly, Wilbur Wright observed that entering students, on average, have large discrepancies in their skills across math content domains. For students across intermediate and precollege math course placement ranges there was a broad difference in mathematics proficiency. And just as important, the variability within key content areas within intermediate or precollege mathematics suggests that the typical student's diagnostic score profile features at least one area of weakness and one area of strength (relative to other areas).

Student Effort Ratings

Faculty were asked to rate students on four behaviors, including homework compliance, attending class, class participation, and working with peers. These ratings were strongly related to one another (mean *correlation* = .75). A composite of the four ratings was highly reliable. Further, the average of the four individual ratings was moderately correlated with average post-test results across both math courses (mean *correlation* = .31), as well as average gain in pre- and post-test scores (mean *correlation* = .33).

Combining Compass Scores and Student Effort Ratings
Analyses were conducted using a combination of COMPASS

mathematics diagnostic scores and student behavior ratings to predict achievement-based outcomes:

1. We used average diagnostic pretest score and average student effort rating to predict survival in the course (defined as staying enrolled *and* passing the course) in a logistic regression model.
2. We used average diagnostic pretest score and average student effort rating to predict average *diagnostic* posttest score.

As highlighted in Tables 10.1 and 10.2, student effort rating levels were associated with whether students passed the class. In other words, our findings show that regardless of pretest mathematics knowledge, behavioral compliance was associated with

Table 10.1 Success Rates Passing Foundational Studies Math (Spring 2009), by COMPASS Pretest and Behavioral Rating Levels.

Math Pretest Scores	Behavioral Rating Level		
	High	Medium	Low
High	68%	53%	60%
Medium	71%	49%	29%
Low	74%	54%	10%

Table 10.2 Success Rates Passing Elementary (Precredit) Math, by COMPASS Pretest and Behavioral Rating Levels.

Math Pretest Scores	Behavioral Rating Level		
	High	Medium	Low
High	92%	77%	59%
Medium	91%	62%	17%
Low	69%	44%	6%

Table 10.3 Mean Math Gain Scores for Elementary (Precredit) Math, by Math Pretest and Behavioral Rating Levels.

| | Behavioral Rating Level | | |
Math Pretest Scores	High	Medium	Low
High	19.5%	8.9%	8.7%
Medium	15.7%	11.4%	6.2%
Low	19.7%	14.0%	12.0%

success. This held for both foundational and elementary remedial mathematics classes.

In fact, the moderation of behavior on outcomes is striking. Turning to Table 10.1, we see that those students with high behavioral compliance were likely to graduate at 68% to 74% whereas those with low behavioral compliance dropped down to 10% graduation! We see a similar pattern in Table 10.2. These findings suggest that behavior ratings can serve as a reliable and valid measure of student effort, as well as a useful predictor of student achievement in a course.

As can be seen in Table 10.3, there are dramatic differences in knowledge gains and in course completion rates depending on student effort or behavior compliance. Those students with higher entering knowledge are more likely to do well if they engage in appropriate classroom and homework activities while those students who do not comply have much lower probabilities of success. Conversely, those students at the lower end of the knowledge spectrum and who demonstrate low compliance behaviors are at high risk for failure.

Results from this study reinforce the importance of understanding student motivation and behavior on developmental course success. Higher student effort ratings are associated with increased achievement at the end of a course (that is, higher posttest scores). And higher student effort ratings are associated with a much greater likelihood of persisting *and* passing the course. In other words, as important as effective course placement and diagnostic assessment and instruction are to knowledge gain and academic mastery, a student's willingness to do the work is absolutely essential for course completion and success. Though an intuitive finding, it is not clear that institutions address student behavior as part of the core mission of classroom instruction. Within key gateway courses, our findings suggest this is imperative.

We highlighted the use of COMPASS diagnostic score profiles to show at least one area of weakness and one area of strength (relative to other areas) for most students. This profile of strengths and weaknesses can be used to more effectively target instruction/intervention. Not all students require remediation in all content areas, and helping instructors and students target class modal and individual profiles, respectively, may improve not only student learning but also student engagement in that learning.

And as we demonstrated with our contingency tables, it is the combination of cognitive ability and behavior that is associated with high rates of mastery and persistence outcomes. Students with high behavior rating levels and medium to high knowledge given the course placement band have on average a 70% chance of success. Conversely, those students with low behavioral compliance rapidly drop off, regardless of knowledge mastery (10% to 60% across knowledge pretest score, and 10% to 74% across behavior rating level).

Our findings lend credence to the *Strategic Intervention Model for Developmental Math Education* highlighted in Figure 10.3. In this model, each new student is assessed for both psychosocial risk and effective course placement. Based on extensive research (Robbins et al., 2004, 2009), we know that motivational components, including academic discipline and commitment to school, and self-regulatory components, including academic self-confidence and emotional stability, are critical to academic mastery and persistence behavior. Concurrently, effective course placement

Figure 10.5 Three Pillars of Success

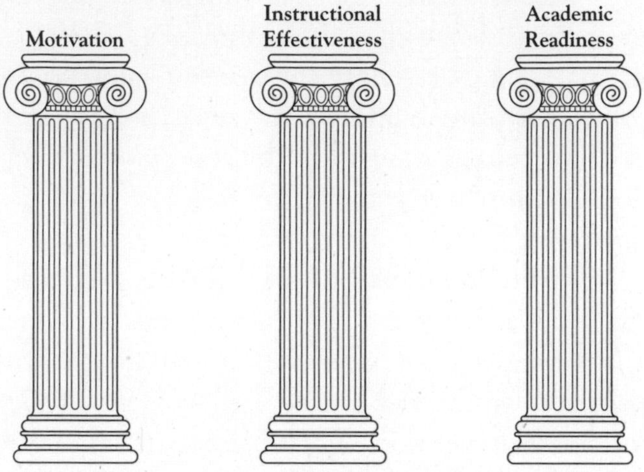

Motivation | Instructional Effectiveness | Academic Readiness

is used to ensure that students are placed in the appropriate band of coursework to move them toward fulfilling their college algebra requirement. Further, teachers are asked to use diagnostic testing to profile the class strengths and weaknesses and to target and monitor instructional gains accordingly. Finally, we promote a sense of shared responsibility by asking students to meet with an advisor to discuss their academic goals, review psychosocial and knowledge profiles, and match student needs to campus resources. Faculties are encouraged to refer students whose classroom behaviors are in the low to medium compliance range and who do not appear able to improve them.

To summarize, we believe that institutions must rely on three pillars for success: Student Academic Behavior and Motivation, Instructional Effectiveness, and Academic Readiness. These pillars are illustrated in Figure 10.5.

Given the variation in student academic readiness and behavior, we must be prepared to:

- Appropriately place in courses and diagnose
- Address motivational skill and engagement behaviors within and outside the classroom

- Connect instruction to the diagnostic and curriculum targets essential to academic achievement (such as Math and English GED) domain

An Evidentiary Based Approach to Institutional Intervention Strategies

As we highlighted at the beginning of this chapter, it is the "Pyramid for Success," or the role of entering academic achievement, career fit, informed decision making, and motivation to succeed in college classes that drive academic performance, college major stability, and timely degree attainment (see, for example, Allen & Robbins, 2008, 2010; Allen et al., 2008). So what does this mean for postsecondary institutions? As we have asserted in several places, early risk assessment and targeting of interventions aimed first at academic success and then at informed career decision making optimize first-year academic success, college major stability, and timely degree attainment. This requires institutional coordination so that course placement, developmental education, academic advising, and first year transition programs complement each other by identifying, targeting and intervening with students who need help. It also increases the need for a comprehensive approach to student success that considers the full array of academic, psychosocial, and career factors that underlie student success.

In this section we highlight the results of a major meta-analytic study (Robbins, Oh, Button, & Le, 2009) of the effects of varying college interventions on both college performance and persistence outcomes as mediated by student psychosocial factors as described in Chapter Eight. Our focus is to highlight what research tells us about what works to affect college student academic success and retention behavior. Further, it is to better understand how student differences in motivation, social, and emotion control factors influence interventions.

In Chapter Eight, we discussed the use of meta-analysis and validity generalization as a standard practice to interpret the aggregation of multiple individual studies that allow for clear and interpretable findings leading to evidence-based practices. By correcting for measurement error and range restriction and by weighting multiple studies based on their sample size, we are able to calculate treatment effect sizes that are much more reliable and generalizable than would otherwise be found in any individual study (Hunter and Schmidt, 2004). In Robbins et al. (2009), prototypic college intervention strategies were sorted into four broad categories: academic skill, self-management, orientation, and First-Year Experience (FYE). These categories, as well as one representing a hybrid of academic and self-management characteristics, are listed in Table 10.4. The academic skill interventions were typically eight hours long, and reflected those programs geared toward improving skills and knowledge deemed critical for successful academic performance. These programs included study skill programs, learning strategy programs, and academically targeted time management programs. Self-management skill programs (typically six hours long) targeted emotional and self-regulatory behaviors including anxiety reduction, stress management and prevention, and self-control and self-acceptance

Table 10.4 Categorizing College Interventions.

Orientation (21 hours)—summer, early fall, time-limited

Freshman Year Experience (45 hours)

Academic (8 hours)

1. Study skills

2. Learning strategies

3. Note-taking

Self-Management (6 hours)

1. Stress management

2. Self-control

3. Anxiety management

Hybrid of Academic & Self Management (12 hours)

interventions. The third type of intervention program, freshman orientation, which typically ranges over three days or 21 hours, was a short-term, intensive socialization approach to help students learn more about college and college life. The fourth intervention category, FYE, was distinguished from orientation programs in that such programs tend to occur after the school year began, lasted a minimum of eight weeks, and were frequently tied to formal classroom schedules whether credit-bearing or not. FYE programs typically covered 45 hours of face-to-face contact. And finally, hybrid programs combined academic skill and self-management activities and were 12 hours in modal length.

As highlighted in Chapter Eight, Robbins et al. (2004, 2006) also categorized individual difference mediators by showing that student educational success was associated with motivation, emotional, and social control factors. Emotional control refers to a student's ability to manage the anxieties and stresses associated with daily college life. Motivational control refers to a student's ability to stay goal-directed, act on the tasks and demands of academic coursework, and sustain energy to successfully fulfill these academic task demands. Social control refers to the feelings of being connected to others and to feeling actively engaged and participating in college life.

Robbins et al. (2004, 2006) constructed the Student Readiness Inventory (SRI) to measure facets of these three domains. These categories as well as the related SRI scales are shown in Table 10.5.

Table 10.5 Categorizing Psychosocial Factors (PSFs) & SRI Scales.

Categories	SRI Scales
Motivational Control	Academic Discipline
	Commitment to College
Emotional Control	Emotional Control
	Academic Self-Confidence
Social Control	Social Connection
	Social Activity

Academic discipline and commitment to college were salient for motivation, emotional control, and academic self-confidence in the emotional control domain. In addition, social connection and social activity were salient in the social control domain. The researchers tested longitudinal prediction and intervention efficacy models using these facets to understand GPA and retention outcomes.

As highlighted in Figure 10.1, Robbins et al. (2009) hypothesized that different intervention strategies would be mediated by different control factors to understand academic performance and academic retention behavior. More specifically, they proposed that academic skill interventions would work through emotional and motivational control to affect academic performance and that academic performance would directly affect retention behavior. They also proposed that self-management interventions would work through motivational control factors to affect both academic performance and academic retention. And finally they believe that FYE and orientation would work through social control and motivational control to affect academic retention behavior.

By testing the model hypothesized in Figure 10.1, we can fully understand several critical questions: first, which intervention strategies have direct and indirect effects on both performance and persistence behavior? Second, which of these interventions are improved by working through mediation of control factors to increase student persistence and performance outcome behaviors? And third, how central are academic mastery and performance to academic retention behavior? Answering these questions is quite important to illuminating which key institutional intervention strategies will have positive student outcomes.

Robbins et al. (2009) found that academic skill–based interventions have the strongest effects on academic performance and success. These interventions work directly to predict performance, but they also work through motivational control factors. Motivational control, in turn, is predictive of both performance and retention behavior. We highlight these findings in the meta-analytic path models found in Figure 10.2. Put another way, the combination of academic skill interventions and motivational control optimize the likely positive influences on student performance and student retention. We see this by observing a direct effect between ASI and academic performance (path = .13), and also that ASI works "through" motivational control (path = .27) when affecting academic performance (path = .14).

We also see that academic skill interventions work through emotional control factors to understand academic performance. This last finding suggests that increasing students' emotional control, such as their internal regulation of academic self-confidence or reduced anxiety around academic tasks, will improve academic performance outcomes. This is highlighted by the significant paths between academic skills intervention on emotional control (.34) and EC on academic performance (.20).

Self-management interventions also play a positive role in understanding academic performance and retention behavior, as illustrated in the path meta-analytic models shown in Figure 10.3. These interventions directly affect emotional, motivational, and social control factors, and work through them to affect either academic performance (see motivational and emotional control) or academic retention (see social control) factors. These robust findings were somewhat surprising and point to the importance of targeting student self-management when trying to improve performance and retention behaviors. Those intervention strategies directed towards a student's sense of motivation and social engagement are likely to optimize performance and retention. These findings highlight the potential payoff that self-management interventions have in increasing student motivation and on improving retention.

A surprising finding from this exhaustive meta-analytic study was the limited influence that first-year experience (FYE) interventions have on academic performance and retention behaviors. In fact, Robbins et al. (2009) found no direct effects of FYE on these outcomes. Rather, they found that FYEs only indirectly work through motivational and social control to influence performance and retention behavior, respectively. These findings are illustrated in Figure 10.4. The authors did not test specific orientation interventions because there were not enough studies to derive or test these meta-analytic path models, but they did have similar weak bivariate effects on student outcomes. Given how FYE strategies are so common and are embedded in a significant portion of institutional practices, these findings suggest that postsecondary institutions need to seriously rethink how to focus resources directly tied to improving academic performance and retention. These findings are also an interesting comparison to institution perceptions of important retention practices.

To summarize, academic skill interventions have the strongest effects on academic performance. Self-management interventions have the strongest effects on academic and retention outcomes, whereas socialization interventions directly affect retention. These findings make sense given that academic skill interventions directly attack those skills necessary to be successful in first-year academic performance. And it is critical to understand that academic success is the driving engine of long-term retention behavior. To a lesser degree, self-management interventions directly affected performance and retention. In retrospect this is not a surprising finding given that focusing on academic performance is tied to improving emotional control functions.

It is surprising how many comprehensive FYE programs are listed as critical to institutional practices influencing student success—and yet, we found weak to negligible effects on student outcomes. There is a significant disconnect between institutional practice and evidence of success. It may be that FYE programs are too broad-based. They neither target specific at-risk students or critical academic performance or psychosocial dimensions. And they may be tailored to affect student satisfaction and knowledge dimensions rather than targeted toward the critical academic skill and performance behaviors that we have found are essential for long-term retention.

Surprisingly, we found academic skill interventions work through both motivational and emotional control factors. This suggests that those students who feel better equipped to handle academic coursework are likely to succeed. That is, these two control factors play important mediating roles between academic skill and motivational-based interventions to optimize student success. The goal, then, is to promote interventions that boost motivational and emotional control factors to directly and indirectly improve academic performance

The disconnect between evidenced-based practices and outcomes suggests the criticality of evaluating institutional practices and of relying on evidence based models to promote theories of action. It is clear that colleges and universities must evaluate the cost-effectiveness of commonly held practices and must emphasize and prioritize those interventions that are most likely to promote positive outcomes given the central role that academic mastery plays on retention.

Institutional Research and Evaluation Informing Best Practices

We have presented an exhaustive research study to highlight which interventions are most effective and how they work through student control factors. Certainly, we have called into question the efficacy of the FYE model if the goal is to improve student academic performance and retention behavior, and we have argued that those strategies driving first-year academic success are most beneficial. We now turn to the importance of determining whether the benefits of institutional practices outweigh the costs. We believe institutions should be engaging in ongoing evaluation of their strategies and monitoring outcomes to design the most cost-effective interventions possible and to ensure that improvements are made to optimize student success across multiple stakeholder groups.

To accomplish what we propose, institutions must integrate three essential strategies: adopt informatics technology (Educause for information, at http://www.educause.edu/) to capture student service use, systematically assess student risk and assign services based on particular needs, and create a feedback and evaluation system that evaluates the relationship between service use and risk on student academic and retention outcomes.

Every institution is unique, but it is also true that effective institutional retention practices require buy-in from multiple stakeholder groups, including faculty, central administration, academic and support services, advising at both central and college level, information technology, and management information units. A change management process is required that effectively articulates institutional goals to adopt evidence-based practices driving clear student success outcomes. This process requires collaboration across units, the willingness to decentralize resources the adoption of a common language, and a basic understanding of student risk and student success.

An Institution-Wide Retention Initiative Using Informatics.

We present a use case of how one four-year college went about a systemwide change management process to affect student academic performance and retention behavior. This study is highlighted in Robbins et al. (2006), which details the innovative approach taken to assess student risk, resource and service use, and monitor student outcomes.

Northern Arizona University is a public comprehensive four-year institution with approximately 800 faculty serving 22,000 students. They historically witnessed 30% dropout rates after the first year. Through institutional leadership, they committed to a broadscale change-management process, including the implementation of a card swiping system to monitor resource use, the systematic use of a student risk assessment for all entering first-year students (the SRI), and the coordination and implementation of strategic intervention model based on student risk models derived from the SRI.

Institutional goals included early identification of and contact with at-risk students, the collaboration but not duplication of services, a systematic model that addressed the whole student, and the reliance on the framework theory of action based on research. The creation of a network of academic and social resources is a major undertaking. A vice president identified a group of staff to spearhead this effort. The working team identified target populations at risk, services linked to student needs, campus collaborators including FYE and first-year advising center, and a process for sending students to the most appropriate office based on risk assessment. This process is outlined in Table 10.6.

Assigning students required early administration of the Student Readiness Inventory (ACT, 2008) and an agreement that any student identified as at risk would be required to come in for an initial appointment at an appropriate location before being allowed to sign up for classes. In essence, this intrusive advising approach was adopted by all stakeholder groups based on a belief that many of the most needy and at-risk students would be least likely to seek services. A waterfall approach was used where summer programs targeted disadvantaged students first, but student academic advising staffs were made available for all other students. One-on-one meetings reviewed results of the Student Readiness Inventory, acknowledging student strengths and challenges, and students

Table 10.6 One-on-One Meetings in Student Affairs.

Assign students to programs/office according to service populations

Look up student schedules and set appointment times

Send postcard home with appointment time

Send postcard to campus address with appointment time

Personal e-mail with appointment time

Appointment time/date placed on student's web calendar

Reminder phone call 1–2 days before appointment

Facebook contacts and text reminders

If miss scheduled meeting, protocol for rescheduling at least two more times.

Table 10.7 2007 Retention in 2008.

	Group Total	Not Retained	Retained	% Retained
Targeted and Met	652	208	444	68%
Targeted and Not Met	427	163	264	62%

were referred to campus activities and resources. A student portal was built that allowed students to follow up in understanding their assessment results and also in pursuing campus resources.

After a year of tracking entering students, an evaluation of these intervention efforts was conducted by the multiple stakeholder groups. From an outcome perspective they saw that the number of students on academic probation dropped from 32% to 18% for those students who met an initial counselor or advisor. Not surprisingly, nontargeted students did about the same as previous years, with over 74% retaining one year later. These percentages as well as the percentage of the targeted students retaining one year later are reported in Table 10.7. Targeted students who had a meeting with a counselor or advisor were more likely to return the following year. Targeted students also fared better than in past years both in terms of cumulative GPA and academic probation and second-year retention.

As interesting as these overall findings are, perhaps more important was an analysis of the relationship between student service use by risk level and outcome. As highlighted in Table 10.8, we summarize different service use categories ranging from academic services to recreational services, the level of use of each service, and average retention and GPA rates within each cell. As can be seen, students in the **moderate use** category had the best overall outcomes. This was not true for those students seeking advising and career sessions where average outcomes for retention were greater in high use categories than moderate use.

Focusing specifically on academic service use and psychosocial risk level, we present in Table 10.9 a breakdown of service

Table 10.8 Resource and Services Utilization.

Resource/Service Category	Level of Utilization					
	High		Moderate		Low	
	Ret.	GPA	Ret.	GPA	Ret.	GPA
Academic Services	.75	2.75	.79	2.92	.70	2.63
Recreational Resources	.77	2.87	.77	2.76	.71	2.67
Social Resources	.72	2.83	.85	2.91	.69	2.63
Academic Referrals	—	—	.88	2.95	.60	2.53
Advisory/Career Sessions	.84	2.67	.79	2.83	.57	2.68

Note: Ret. = Retention Level

Table 10.9 Association of Risk Level & Academic Service Use on Retention & First-Year GPA.

Academic Service Use	Risk Level					
	High		Moderate		Low	
	Ret.	GPA	Ret.	GPA	Ret.	GPA
0 use	.61	2.11	.72	2.58	.77	3.14
1–3 Sessions	.72	2.41	.77	2.81	.84	3.38
4+ Sessions	.62	2.35	.81	2.81	.85	3.22

Note: Ret. = Retention Level.

use based on number of sessions and risk level. You can see in this table that those students at highest risk were most likely to benefit with proportionate improvements in both retention and GPA *greater* than those students least at risk. This does not mean that those students least at risk did not have higher GPA and retention rates, but the proportional changes were greatest for the higher students. This finding emphasizes the benefits of targeting resources to those most at risk, especially given that they are the least likely to seek them out!

Another interesting finding observed in the Table 10.9 is that those students who use services for four or more sessions saw a **drop** in their cumulative GPA and the overall rate of retention. This finding suggests that there is an optimal threshold of service use and that once it's crossed, outcomes diminish. Without understanding fully the reasons for this, NAU put in a flagging system so that when students reached a four-session threshold, service providers were asked to evaluate student status and to consider alternative actions to ensure student needs were being met.

We believe this is an exciting demonstration of the integration of informatics to evaluate the impact of a wide-scale retention initiative; the critical ingredients included the systematic use of a risk assessment, institution-wide leadership and coordination of change management, and effective evaluation or monitoring of student outcomes (Robbins et al., 2006). To summarize several of the key findings, we offer the following:

- Intervene early and strategically;
- Designate a visible individual to coordinate;
- Collaborate and use natural fits with existing resources;
- Conduct systematic analysis of outcomes;
- Use data to provide feedback and to improve the process; and
- Adopt an institution-wide holistic assessment solution to measure student risk.

NAU is putting into place many of the practices that Robbins et al. (2009) highlighted in their integrated meta-analytic path analysis. They are treating academic preparation and performance as the hub of student success. They are clear on their learning goals. They are strategic in the use of resources. And they're not afraid to reach out to those students least motivated and in greatest need of service.

Conclusions

We end this chapter by emphasizing that those practices focused on academic success, and which take advantage of student strengths in motivation, social, and emotional control domains, are most likely to result in increased academic mastery and retention behavior. Our focus was primarily on four-year institutions, but we believe the same determinants of student success (for example, readiness to master college-level material, psychosocial risk, and effective institutional practices) apply to two-year-institutions (see Porchea, Allen, Robbins, & Phelps, 2010, for research on the key predictors of community college success). In essence, our Pyramid for Success model is a robust organizer for creating comprehensive and strategic intervention strategies that affect multiple student success outcomes. Although individual institutions, and students, each have unique characteristics, we believe that rational risk assessment tied to optimal interventions across the array of institutional central and college-level resources will increase retention behaviors and academic success. And ultimately, these practices will increase the likelihood students will achieve their postsecondary goals consistent with career aspirations.

Section 4

PROVEN STUDENT SUCCESS PRACTICES

11

HISTORICAL PERSPECTIVE ON *WHAT WORKS IN STUDENT RETENTION*

For more than three decades, ACT has conducted and reported on four periodic surveys collecting information on aspects of college student retention. The focus, although varied from study to study, included the organization and coordination of retention programs as well as factors related to student attrition. But the primary emphasis of the studies has been on discovering effective retention practices. Hence, the titles for the four surveys became *What Works in Student Retention* (WWISR). Each of these studies has guided postsecondary educators in identifying and adapting retention strategies to better serve students and to fit the needs of their campuses. The findings have also served to support funding requests to pilot or implement program enhancements.

As useful as each study has been in its own right, a collective review of the four studies has never been undertaken. The purpose of this chapter, then, is to compare and contrast the themes across all four of the studies, providing observations on the common threads that run throughout the studies. This approach leads to interesting and, in some cases, disturbing observations. Comparing and contrasting these four studies requires the acknowledgment of several concerns that serve as caveats for the generalizations that will be shared. First, the data reported in these surveys are based on the perspectives of the individuals who responded to the survey. Those perspectives are shaped by position and function in the hierarchy of the institution as well as the respondent's personal experiences and opinions. In that vein, it is not clear the degree to which the responses were informed by solid evidence collected at the respondent's institution. Although satisfaction data and anecdotal information probably informed some of the responses, they do not provide quantitative evidence of the effectiveness of any particular retention intervention. A third caveat is that during the thirty-plus years since the first survey, the number of retention interventions has expanded dramatically, and the terms defining those interventions have grown significantly and increased in specificity. Fourth, institutions responding vary both in number and in name from one survey to the next. The survey response rates range from 31.4% in 2004 (Habley & McClanahan, 2004) to over 50% in 1987 (Cowart, 1987). These response rates are excellent for national surveys, and although they provide a clear reflection of practices, it is not appropriate to suggest that the observations that follow are statistically significant either within a study or across studies. Finally, the summaries provided below represent *all* colleges in each of the studies. As a result, the data represent the broadest perspective possible and should not be viewed as data through which a single institution could be compared.

These caveats notwithstanding, the themes and threads gleaned from the four surveys provide important insights into coordination, organization, attrition factors, and successful campus retention practices. Following a brief description of each of the surveys, these themes and threads will be discussed.

Overview of the Four Studies

What Works in Student Retention (Beal & Noel, 1980)

The first *What Works in Student Retention* study (Beal & Noel, 1980) was a joint project of ACT and the National Center for Higher Education Management Systems (NCHEMS). Staff of NCHEMS and ACT developed and piloted the survey. In the complete study, surveys were sent to 2,459 two-year and four-year colleges with a response rate of 40.2%. As a part of this study, the authors collected information about 17 negative campus characteristics (contributors to attrition), 10 positive campus characteristics (contributors to retention), and 7 characteristics of dropout-prone students. In addition, respondents were asked to rate a list of 20 action programs in terms of both satisfaction and impact on retention. The final report, no longer in print, included a section providing descriptions of selected successful retention programs.

What Works in Student Retention (Cowart, 1987)

In what was essentially a content replication of the earlier survey, ACT collaborated with the American Association of State Colleges and Universities (AASCU) to produce the monograph *What Works in Student Retention in State Colleges and Universities* (Cowart, 1987). The authors collected information about the same attrition, retention, and dropout characteristics that were included in the 1980 study. In addition, respondents were asked to select from the same list of 20 action programs that had been implemented to improve retention. The 370 members of AASCU were included in the survey population, and responses from 190 (51.7%) were included in the analyses. The final report, no longer in print, included descriptions of more than fifty retention programs submitted by respondents. It should be noted that this study was the only one of the four WWISR studies that focused on a single institutional type: a subset of four-year public colleges. In addition, respondents to this survey were asked to base their responses only on activities that had taken place since the 1980 WWISR study.

What Works in Student Retention
(Habley & McClanahan, 2004)—See Appendix A

Seventeen years passed between the 1987 study and the next *What Works in Student Retention* study (Habley & McClanahan,

2004). When ACT study design staff began meeting in the summer of 2003, the intention was to replicate the surveys conducted in 1980 and 1987. That intention was soon abandoned for several reasons. First, it was clear that the retention literature had grown exponentially since the earlier surveys and that much more now was known about student and institutional characteristics that contributed to attrition. Also, far more institutional interventions were cited as contributing to student retention and degree completion. In view of this changed landscape, the design team conducted thorough analyses of the retention literature and, as a result, expanded the original list of institutional characteristics from 10 to 24 and the list of student (dropout-prone) characteristics from 7 to 20. But it was in the area of institutional interventions that the most significant expansion in number of items took place. Whereas the 1980 and 1987 surveys identified only 20 action programs (interventions, practices) as contributing to retention, after first brainstorming and then refining a list that included more than 100 interventions, the design team settled on 82 interventions and practices that became the basis for Section D of the survey.

The design team also concluded that it was important to assess not only the prevalence of particular practices at colleges and universities but also the impact of those programs. Hence, Section D was constructed to include both of these measures. Finally, a Section E was added. In that section, respondents were asked to select three interventions from the list of 82 that appeared in Section D that they believed had the greatest impact on retention. Table 11.1 provides an overview of the responses to the survey.

A report for all colleges on the 2004 survey as well as reports for two-year public colleges, four-year public colleges, and four-year private colleges can be found at: http://www.act.org/research/policymakers/reports/retain.html

Table 11.1 2004 Survey Respondents.

Colleges	Surveys Mailed	Surveys Returned	Return Rate (%)
All	2,995	1,061	35.4
Two-year public	991	386	39.0
Two-year private*	197	46	23.4
Four-year public	536	228	42.5
Four-year private	1,271	401	31.5

*Note: Several responding institutions in this group could not be categorized as both two-year and private colleges. This factor, combined with a low response rate, precluded meaningful analysis of data. As a result, no additional analyses were conducted.

What Works in Student Retention (Habley, McClanahan, Valiga, & Burkum, 2010)—See Appendix B

Data collected through the spring and summer of 2009 are reported in ACT's most recent *What Works in Student Retention* study (Habley, McClanahan, Valiga, & Burkum, 2010). The final reports generated from this survey may also be found at the same web page cited in the previous section. While not a replication of the 2004 survey, this study made only minor modifications in the format and content. Among these were changes in the first section, which collected information on retention and degree completion goals, coordination of retention services and two new areas: the degree of on-line coursework and the extent of collaboration and articulation with other institutions. The section on institutional and student characteristics decreased from 44 to 42 characteristics and was combined in one section (rather than two sections in the 2004 survey). Student and institutional characteristics were randomized in this section to counter the possibility of positive or negative response set. The practices/intervention set was also revised and resulted in an increase from 82 interventions in the 2004 survey to 92 in this survey. Survey mailings and responses are found in Table 11.2 below.

Table 11.2 2010 Survey Respondents.

Type of College/ University	Number of Surveys Mailed	Number of Surveys Returned Completed	Percent of Completed Surveys
Technical	240	70	29.17
Community College	949	305	32.14
Private 2-Year*	97	31	31.96
Private 4-Year	1318	440	33.38
Public 4-Year	598	258	43.14
Total	3202	1104	34.48

*Note: Several responding institutions in this group could not be categorized as both two-year and private colleges. This factor, combined with a low response rate, precluded meaningful analysis of data. As a result, no additional analyses were conducted.

A report for all colleges on the 2010 survey as well as reports for community colleges, four-year public colleges, and four-year private colleges can be found at: http://www.act.org/research/policymakers/reports/retain.html

Comparing WWISR Findings

Although the four WWISR surveys are not exact replications, all four share common topics and in some cases common data elements. Those topics include the institutional characteristics that are viewed as causes of attrition; student characteristics that are viewed as causes of attrition; and the programs, interventions, strategies, or practices that institutions have implemented and the degree to which those programs contribute to the retention effort.

Institutional Characteristics Contributing of Attrition/Retention

The 1980 and 1987 WWISR reports approached this topic by asking respondents to respond to two item sets: negative campus characteristics (17 items) and positive campus characteristics

(10 items). The negative characteristics can be viewed as institutional characteristics related to attrition, while the positive characteristics can be viewed as related to retention. Each of these studies asked respondents to rate the importance of each characteristic on a scale from 1 (low importance) to 5 (high importance). The results of the ratings of negative campus characteristics were both similar and revealing.

Respondents to the 1980 WWISR rated only one negative characteristic—inadequate academic advising—above the midpoint (3) on the importance scale. The importance rating for inadequate academic advising edged only slightly above the midpoint at 3.03. The remaining 16 characteristics, all rated below the midpoint of the scale, ranged from inadequate curricular offerings (2.8) to restrictive rules and regulations (1.8). These responses seemed to convey the message that institutional characteristics did not play a major role in student attrition.

Findings from 1987 WWISR study were similar to those of 1980. Three negative characteristics exceeded the midpoint of the importance scale. Inadequate academic advising (3.4) and conflict between class schedule and job (3.4) led the list. Inadequate financial aid (3.25) was also rated above the midpoint. Fourteen negative campus characteristics rated below the midpoint of the scale, ranging from inadequate counseling support system (2.8) to restrictive rules and regulations (1.4).

When 1980 and 1987 WWISR respondents were asked to rate the importance of positive campus characteristics, most of the ten characteristics were rated above the midpoint on the importance scale. In 1980, WWISR respondents rated eight of the ten characteristics above the midpoint of the scale. Three of those positive campus characteristics were rated above a 3.5 on the importance scale. Those items were caring attitude of faculty and staff (4.3), high quality of teaching (3.9), and adequate financial aid (3.7). The only characteristic rated below 3.0 was early alert system (2.7). The 1987 responses were parallel to those of 1980. The 1987 WWISR respondents rated nine of the ten characteristics above the scale midpoint and four positive characteristics were rated at 3.5 or above. Those were caring attitude of faculty and staff (4.3), consistent high quality of teaching (4.0), adequate financial aid programs (3.5), and consistent high quality of advising (3.5). Only one of ten positive characteristics was rated below the midpoint of the importance scale: system of identifying potential dropouts (early alert system), with a mean rating of 2.9.

The construct for collecting responses on the causes of attrition/retention shifted in the 2004 and 2010 surveys. In 2004, respondents were provided with a list of 24 institutional characteristics and asked to rate those characteristics on a scale ranging from 1 (not a factor contributing to attrition) to 5 (a major factor contributing to attrition). Thus, high ratings would indicate attrition whereas low ratings were viewed as having little impact on attrition.

Of the 24 institutional characteristics contributing to attrition that were included in the 2004 study, only two were rated above the midpoint (3.0) of the rating scale: amount of financial aid available to students (3.5) and student-institution fit (3.1). Those rated the lowest on the 5-point scale could be interpreted as those least likely to contribute to attrition. Among those characteristics were: quality of teaching (2.3), intellectual stimulation or challenge in the classroom (2.5), personal contact between students and faculty (2.5), faculty attitude toward students (2.5), and staff attitude toward students (2.4).

In the 2010 survey, 22 institutional characteristics contributing to attrition were commingled with 20 student characteristics. Respondents were asked to rate the degree to which the characteristics contributed to attrition at their institution on a 5-point scale where 5 = major effect, 3 = moderate effect, and 1 = little or no effect. Only four of the 22 institutional characteristics were rated at or above the midpoint (3.0) of the rating scale: amount of financial aid available to students (3.7), quality of interaction between faculty and students (3.1), student engagement opportunities in the classroom and active learning (3.1), and ratio of loans to other forms of financial aid (3.0). Institutional characteristics rated the lowest on the 5-point scale could be interpreted as those least likely to contribute to attrition. Notable characteristics rated below the midpoint included: out of class interaction between students and faculty (2.7), level of intellectual stimulation or challenge for students (2.7), relevancy of the curriculum (2.6), student access to needed courses in the appropriate sequence (2.5), and campus safety and security (1.9).

Student Characteristics Contributing to Attrition/Retention

Although there were significant differences between the 1980–1987 and 2004–2010 studies, in many respects the results are parallel. The 1980 and 1987 studies focused on the characteristics of dropout-prone students. Thus, respondents were asked to rate only seven items in terms of the relationship each played in dropout behavior. On a 5-point scale, a rating of 1 indicated low potential for dropping out and a 5 indicated a high potential for dropping out. Table 11.3 includes the seven items and the respondent ratings of those items in both the 1980 and 1987 surveys. Readers should recall that the 1980 study included several institutional types while the 1987 study focused only on four-year public colleges who were members of the American Association of State Colleges and Universities. In spite of the difference in the respondent pool, the results of the survey are consistent.

In the 2004 study, the construct of items and the response set were modified in the section focused on student characteristics. The characteristic set no longer asked respondents to rate dropout-prone characteristics. Rather, the item set was

Table 11.3 Dropout-Prone Characteristics, 1980 and 1987 WWISR Studies.

Characteristic	1980 Rating	1987 Rating
Low academic achievement	4.45	4.69
Limited educational aspirations	4.09	4.12
Indecision about a major/career goal	3.93	3.75
Inadequate financial resources	3.65	3.96
Economically disadvantaged	3.21	3.48
First-generation student	2.55	2.86
Commuter	2.41	2.67

expanded from seven to 20 student characteristics that contributed to attrition. The response set also changed with a rating scale ranging from 1 = little or no contribution to attrition to 5 = major contribution to attrition.

The 2004 findings were remarkably similar to the items cited in the early surveys. All five of the dropout-prone characteristics rated above 3.0 in the earlier surveys also appeared among the 13 student characteristics contributing to attrition rated at or above the midpoint of the 2004 survey. In addition to these five student characteristics, other notable student characteristics above the scale midpoint were poor study skills (3.7), lack of motivation to succeed (4.2), and weak commitment to earning a degree (3.2). Items rated by respondents as considerably less likely to contribute to attrition were distance from home (2.2), physical health problems (2.3), and mental or emotional health problems (2.5).

As mentioned earlier, student characteristics and institutional characteristics were commingled in the 2010 study. Again the results on student characteristics contributing to attrition were similar to the findings of the first three WWISR studies. Academic achievement (preparation), financial resources, indecision about a career/major goal, limited educational aspirations, and low socioeconomic status were seen as significant student characteristics contributing to attrition. Fourteen of the 15 highest rated contributors to attrition were student characteristics. Other notable student characteristics above the scale midpoint were poor study skills (3.7), lack of motivation to succeed (3.7), and weak commitment to earning a degree (3.6). It is also interesting to note that mental and emotional health issues rose from a rating of 2.5 in 2004 to 3.0 in 2010. Among the lowest rated student characteristics contributing to attrition were physical health issues (2.2), distance from permanent home (2.4), and commuting (2.4).

A summary of the themes and threads in respondent ratings of student and institutional characteristics reveals remarkable consistency in response patterns. In all four WWISR studies, survey respondents clearly indicate that institutional characteristics are far less responsible for attrition than are student characteristics. The consistency of responses seems to suggest that institutions are not major contributors to student attrition. Although there is room for improvement, consistent ratings below the scale midpoint indicate that important institutional characteristics are satisfactorily achieved. Ratings on quality of instruction, classroom stimulation, relevance of the curriculum, positive attitude of faculty and staff, and access to courses support that contention.

Conversely, consistent findings across all four studies strongly suggest that student characteristics are major contributors to attrition. At the risk of over-simplification, if students were better prepared academically, if students had better study skills, if students were more decisive in choosing a program of study and a career, if students were more committed to earning a degree, and if students had sufficient financial resources, there would be little concern about student attrition. Of course, this conclusion may be overdrawn, but when John Gardner reviewed the results of the 2004 study he commented, "It is disturbing to note that in spite of all we know about student retention that institutions are still inclined to *hold students responsible* for their retention/attrition while dramatically *minimizing the institutional role* in student retention" (personal communication from John Gardner). Placing blame provides for convenient excuses and stymies finding solutions!

Retention Programs, Practices, Interventions

The core of all four *What Works in Student Retention* studies has been the identification of actions (strategies, programs, policies, practices, interventions) that institutional respondents believe had a positive impact on student retention. With the exception of the 1987 study, published survey results included the percentage (incidence rate) of campuses implementing particular practices and an assessment of the degree to which each practice had an impact on student retention.

WWISR 1980 identified 19 action programs believed to contribute to campus retention efforts. Only five of these programs had incidence rates ≥ 33%. Those programs were improvement of academic advising (53%), special orientation activities (49%), exit interviews (40%), special counseling programs (36%), and early warning system (33%). Beal and Noel devised two indices reflecting the impact of the action programs. The general impact index reflected how the campus responded to an action program. Because the general index was not featured in any of the ensuing studies, results are not reported here. The second index was the retention index, which measured improvement in first-to-second-year retention on a 5-point scale. Among the programs rated ≥ 3.3 were new policies, structures (3.6), learning/academic support (3.5), orientation (3.4), early warning system (3.4), curricular enhancements (3.3), advising (3.3), and career assistance (3.3). Only two programs had a retention index below 3.0: cocurricular activities (2.8) and exit interviews (2.7). Unfortunately, these program descriptions were very broad and, as a result, did not provide the specificity necessary to pinpoint successful strategies. For instance, there are a number of possible strategies that might be implemented to improve academic advising, but the study did not delineate those strategies.

Recognizing that specificity of intervention was lacking in the 1980 study, Cowart (1987) utilized the same major program areas as the 1980 study, but she identified 39 specific strategies, many of which fell within the program areas identified in WWISR 1980. Cowart also added several strategies that were not included in the 1980 study. Below is a list of strategies with the highest incidence rates.

- Formal remedial coursework (55.7%)
- Use of students as peer advisors or counselors (52.5%)
- Expanded or continuing orientation program (47.5%)
- Expanded academic support/enrichment/learning services (41.0%)
- Placement testing on entering students (39.9%)
- Training for academic advisors (37.2%)
- Special and significant services designed to retain minority students (36.6%)
- Exit interview conducted (35.0%)
- Advisor manual (34.4%)

Assessing the impact of program strategies was more complex in the 1987 study than the retention index used in the 1980 study. Cowart divided the responding institutions into four categories based on first-to-second-year attrition rates. The attrition rate categories were 0–25%, 26–35%, 36–50%, and ≥ 51%. Although not a precise measure of impact, examining the incidence rates of strategies in institutions with the lowest attrition rates appears to be a reasonable proxy for assessing impact. Strategies identified with the highest incidence rates were special orientation activities (75.5%), improvement or redevelopment of the academic advising program (79.6%), early warning system (75.0%), curricular innovations in credit programs and use of students as peer advisors and counselors (both at 63.6%), and formal remedial courses (59.1%).

The pool of retention strategies/interventions expanded dramatically between the 1987 and 2004 WWISR surveys. The 2004 survey included 82 interventions divided into 11 broad clusters. Respondents were first asked if each retention intervention was offered on their campus. As testimony to increasing interest in retention, incidence rates ≥80% were reported for six interventions: tutoring program, academic clubs, instructional use of technology, individual career counseling services, internships, and pre-enrollment orientation. Incidence rates for 15 of the strategies were at or above 70% and reported incidence rates for 30 interventions were at or above 56%, the highest incidence rate in the 1987 study.

The retention intervention item pool in WWISR 2010 was expanded to include 94 strategies. Incidence rates for nine interventions were ≥ 80%. Among those were four strategies with high incidence rates on the 2004 study (faculty use of technology in teaching, tutoring, internships, and career counseling). In addition to those strategies, incidence rates exceeding 80% were recorded for college social activities, faculty use of technology to communicate with students, pre-enrollment financial aid advising, and student leadership program.

In both the 2004 and 2010 studies, respondents who indicated that a retention strategy existed on their campus were then asked to rate the intervention according to a scale where 5 = a major contribution to retention and 1 = little or no contribution to retention. Table 11.4 reports on interventions that were rated ≥ 3.7 in either of the surveys.

An additional section was added to the 2004 and 2010 surveys which provided additional insights into the perceived impact of retention interventions. After completing the rating of individual retention interventions and practices, respondents

Table 11.4 Practices with the Greatest Mean Contribution to Retention.

Programs, Services, Curricular Offerings, Interventions	2004 Mean	2010 Mean
Comprehensive learning assistance center/lab	3.9	4.0
Freshman seminar/University 101 (credit)	3.8	3.7
Advising interventions with selected populations	3.8	3.9
Increased advising staff	3.8	4.0
Integration of advising with first-year programs	**3.8**	**3.8**
Academic advising center	3.8	3.9
Reading center/lab	3.8	4.0
Center that combines advisement and counseling with career planning and placement	3.7	3.7
Learning communities	3.7	3.5
Supplemental instruction	3.7	3.7
Remedial/developmental coursework (required)	**3.7**	**3.7**
Program for honors students	3.7	3.7
Mandated placement in courses based on test scores	3.6	3.7
Writing center/lab	3.6	3.7
Summer bridge program	3.6	3.7
Training for non-faculty advisors	N/A	3.7
Extended freshman orientation (credit)	3.6	3.7

were asked to review the entire intervention set and identify the three practices they believe made the greatest contribution to retention. Table 11.5 summarizes the responses from both surveys, reporting the percentage of respondents that identified a particular retention practice as one of the top three.

The detail provided in Tables 11.4 and 11.5 underscores the themes that were identified in the first two WWISR studies. Over three decades of WWISR studies, respondents are remarkably consistent in the identification of retention programs/interventions

Table 11.5 Interventions Cited as One of the Top Three Interventions by 9% or More Respondents.

Intervention/Practice	2004 (%)	2010 (%)
Freshman seminar/University 101 (credit)	13	17
Mandated placement in courses based on test scores	11	17
Tutoring program	13	16
Advising interventions with selected student populations	13	12
Comprehensive learning assistance center/lab	10	11
Early warning system	12	16
Remedial/development coursework required	10	10
Academic advising center	9	9
Pre-enrollment orientation	9	6
Summer orientation	5	10

that they believe are closely associated with improved retention. Furthermore, and almost without exception, all successful retention programs/interventions fall into three clusters. In no particular order, those clusters are first-year transition programs, academic advising, and learning support informed by assessment. Although strategies in each of these clusters have evolved and expanded since the first WWISR study, it is clear that survey respondents believe that successful retention requires programs that support adjustment to the campus (transition), guidance in the identification and pursuit of educational objectives (advising) and increase the likelihood of academic success (learning support/assessment).

Retention and Degree Completion Rates

With such consistent and persistent identification of successful retention interventions, one would think it logical that the success of college students would improve as more and more institutions focused on transition programs, academic advising, and learning support. Unfortunately, a review of first-to-second-year retention data for the period from 1975 through 2010 indicates that there have been no appreciable gains in retention and completion rates. Cope and Hannah (1975) reported that the first-to-second-year retention rate was 69.4% at four-year public colleges and 73.2% at four-year private colleges. Since 1983, ACT has reported institutional retention rates calculated from the annual collection of data through its Institutional Data Questionnaire (IDQ). A summary of those data is found in Table 11.6, which includes the highest and lowest first-to-second-year retention rates and the year in which they were reported for institutional types.

A review of these rates invites three significant observations. First, these figures do not vary substantially from those reported by Cope and Hannah (1975). Second, the reported rates are relatively stagnant between 1983 and 2010. Finally, the high-low retention ranges for each of the institutional types are remarkably narrow over time. With the exception of the two-year private college cohort, the spread between highest

Table 11.6 Summary of Retention Rates by Institutional Type: 1983–2011.

	Highest %	Lowest %	Current %
Two-Year Public	55.7 ('10)	51.3 ('04)	55.4
BA/BS Public	70.0 ('04)	66.4 ('96, '05)	65.6
MA/MS Public	71.6 ('06)	68.1 ('89)	71.2
PhD Public	78.6 ('10)	72.9 ('08)	77.9
Two-year Private	72.6 ('92)	55.5 ('08)	57.8
BA/BS Private	74.0 ('89)	68.7 ('10)	69.0
MA/MS Private	78.0 ('85)	71.4 ('10)	71.9
PhD Private	85.0 ('85)	80.3 ('10,'11)	80.3
ALL			66.7

and lowest retention rates is less than 5% for all institutional types. Finally, the stability of these rates over time continues to support the oft-heard orientation exhortation: "Look to your left and look to your right. One of you won't be here a year from now."

ACT (2010e) has also collected and reported data on degree-completion rates between 1983 and 2011. Those rates are also relatively stagnant. A review of those data prompts two important observations. First, the lowest completion rates for all colleges have been reported since the turn of the millennium. In addition, the highest rates for all institutional types (with the exception of four-year private BA/BS-degree-granting institutions) were recorded in 1990 or before. These findings corroborate the statistics cited by Cope and Hannah (1975) that 40% of all students who enter higher education will not earn a baccalaureate degree. Although degree-completion rates have improved slightly in the past thirty years, a significant number of students do not complete degrees. The Education Trust (2010) reported that the six-year graduation rate for four-year colleges was 54%. And Adelman (2004) suggested that there had been virtually no significant change in the eight-year graduation rates for students entering college in 1972 (66%), 1982 (66%), and 1992 (67%).

The stark reality of three decades of WWISR studies is that despite the considerable energy the higher-education community has expended in understanding retention and degree completion, such understanding has not resulted in a concomitant improvement in student success in college. The community can document the personal and societal benefits that accrue from a college degree. The community can identify the student and institutional characteristics that inhibit retention. And the higher education community can identify the institutional interventions that are most likely to contribute to retention. Yet, in spite of all that is known, there have been no appreciable gains in retention and degree completion in more than three decades. Nearly one-third of all first-year students do not return for a second year, fewer than half of all students who earn bachelor's degrees do so within six years of high school graduation, and approximately 40% of all students who enter higher education in a given fall will not earn any degree anywhere at any time in their life. And the implications of the demographics shared in Chapter Three suggest that the road to increased student success will be "heavy lifting" in the years ahead.

Minority Student Attrition and Retention

In Chapters Three and Seven of this book, respectively, we reported on the demographic characteristics and the academic performance of students in the educational pipeline to college. Demographically, those who are least likely to succeed in the educational system will account for nearly half of the U.S. population by mid-century. In its report *Minorities in Higher Education* (Ryu, 2010), the American Council on Education (ACE) cited stagnant postsecondary attainment rates in the United States across virtually all races. And the two largest minority groups, Hispanics and African Americans, have made no appreciable progress in educational attainment rates. In the 20-year period (1988–2008) covered by the ACE study, the high school completion rate for African American students increased only 2% (from 76% to 78%). And while the college enrollment rate increased from 22% to 34%, the percentage of associate's and bachelor's degrees awarded to African American students increased a paltry 1% (from 11% to 12%) between 1997 and 2007. Though movement of Hispanic students through the educational pipeline is slightly different, ultimate educational attainment levels are not encouraging. Hispanic students recorded a 12% increase (from 58% to 70%) in high school completion rates and an 11% increase (17% to 28%) in college enrollment rates. However, these results did not lead to concomitant growth in degree completion. The percentage of associate's and bachelor's degrees awarded to Hispanic students increased from 10% to 11.6% between 1997 and 2007. As a further indication of stagnation in the educational attainment of African American and Hispanic students, Ryu (2010) reports that the percentage of degree holders in the two groups is relatively flat across all age cohorts.

In addition to studying attrition factors and retention practices by institutional type, the fourth WWISR study (Habley et al., 2010) examined four subsets of data drawn from more than 1,100 colleges and universities that responded to the survey. Those subsets were two-year colleges with 20% or more Hispanic students enrolled (N = 37); two-year colleges with 20% or more black students enrolled (N = 83); four-year colleges with 20% or more Hispanic students enrolled (N = 33); and four-year colleges with 20% or more African American students enrolled (N = 95). To compare and contrast attrition characteristics and retention interventions, these subsets were compared to the remaining two-year and four-year institutions in the respondent pool. For the sake of expository simplicity, these subsets are referred to as either colleges with high black (or Hispanic) enrollment, or other colleges.

For the most part, the rankings of the comparisons on the causes of attrition varied little when comparing high minority enrollment colleges with the other colleges. The five highest-rated causes of attrition in both two- and four-year colleges (in order of ratings) were adequacy of personal financial resources, student preparation for college level work, study skills, low socioeconomic status, and amount of financial aid available for students. Although the ranking of attrition causes did not vary, there were obvious differences in the mean ratings of the attrition factors. Specifically, even though the causes of attrition were virtually the same for colleges with high minority enrollments as they were for other colleges, the ratings of the causes of attrition were consistently .2 to .5 higher (on a 5-point scale) for colleges with high minority enrollment. This holds true for all two-year and four-year institutions for both minority groups. One set of differences stands out, however. Respondents from two-year and four-year colleges with high Hispanic enrollments consistently rate their level of job demands, student family responsibilities, and lack of support from significant others well above the respondents from other colleges. This suggests that respondents believe that external and cultural factors contribute to the attrition of Hispanic students. In four-year colleges, there is one additional stark comparison on the causes of attrition. The mean rating for "quality of interaction between faculty and students" was rated 3.47 by respondents from campuses with high Hispanic enrollments while it was rated 2.93 by respondents from other colleges. Across all comparisons, this is the greatest differential in the attrition ratings and, because interaction with faculty is a most important component of student success, warrants further exploration and intervention.

Comparison of the ratings of retention interventions/practices also yields a fairly consistent picture. Table 11.7 reports on

Table 11.7 Percentage of Respondents Identifying Retention Interventions Among the Top Three.

Item	Black Two-Year (%)	Black Four-Year (%)	Hispanic Two-Year (%)	Hispanic Four-Year (%)
Mandated placement of student in courses based on test scores	40	16	32	11
Remedial/developmental coursework required	27	10	18	10
Tutoring	17	16	29	10
Early warning system	13	17	18	22
Academic advising center	10	12	11	19
Freshman seminar/University 101 (for credit)	10	27	11	26

the percentage of respondents at institutions with high Hispanic and black enrollments who rated practices as one of the top three (out of 94) interventions.

Of note in Table 11.7 is that there are differences between two-year and four-year college responses, with two-year college more likely to identify mandated placement, required remediation, and tutoring, whereas four-year colleges are more likely to cite an early warning system, academic advising center, and freshman seminar among the top three retention interventions. Additional interventions that were cited by at least 10% of the high minority (both black and Hispanic) two-year college respondents were training of faculty advisors and a comprehensive learning assistance center. And for four-year high enrollment minority colleges, supplemental instruction and nonresidential learning communities were identified by 10% or more of the survey respondents.

Conclusion

Over the past four decades, there has been a proliferation of programs and services focusing on student retention. Yet, in spite of these efforts, retention and degree completion rates have not improved. In addition, there is evidence that the cohorts of those least likely to succeed in college will be expanding rapidly in the next several decades. We believe that colleges must extend the retention paradigm to ensure student success. And we believe that the core conditions—learning, motivation, career development—discussed in the previous section of the book are the drivers of student success. Finally, we believe that intra-institutional student success should not focus on the layering on of fringe programs and services. Rather, we call upon campuses to intensify efforts to extend and expand programs and services that have stood the test of time. Those services—assessment and developmental education, academic advising, and student transition programs—are at the heart of student success.

12

ASSESSMENT AND COURSE PLACEMENT

Chapter Seven delineated the clear and direct relationship between academic preparation and success in college. Excellent high school grades and test scores as well as rigorous course-taking patterns are indicators of likely success in college. Students who demonstrate academic skills through grades and test scores are ready for college and few could offer defensible arguments to the contrary. Yet, data from ACT suggest that those who are prepared to succeed in college constitute only about one-fourth of the high school graduates who intend to go to college. That group of students is predicted to earn grades of C or above in college algebra, biology, English, and a first-year social science course (for example, history, psychology, or sociology). It is the remaining three-quarters of first-year students who pose a retention challenge for colleges. That challenge requires serving students who may not succeed in one or more college courses without undertaking interventions to address the gap between students' existing academic skills and the skills needed to succeed in college classes. To do this effectively requires that campuses develop a valid and reliable approach to assessing those gaps and placing students in appropriate courses where instruction and learning support can focus on the reduction of those gaps. This chapter focuses on best practices in support of placement decisions; Chapter Thirteen will describe best practices in developmental education and learning support.

Colleges are indeed aware of challenges created by the gap between demonstrated academic skills and skills needed to be successful in college. Respondents to the 2010 *What Works in Student Retention* study (Habley, McClanahan, Valiga, & Burkum, 2010) consistently identified academic preparation for college as the leading cause of student attrition. And they rated placement tests and mandatory placement of students into developmental/remedial courses in the top five interventions contributing to retention. When asked to rate 94 retention interventions on a 5-point scale (5 being high), Community college respondents rated mandated course placement based on test scores at 4.11, and 36% of the campuses indicating that intervention was one of the top three retention interventions. Figures for four-year public colleges and four-year private colleges are 3.7/14% and 3.6/7%, respectively.

This chapter will focus on understanding the course placement process with an emphasis on defining course placement, identifying the benefits of an effective placement program, understanding the sources of data which inform the placement decision, and sharing a model for effective placement practices.

Defining Course Placement

In its most elementary definition, course placement matches students with coursework that is appropriate to their academic preparation and interests. Whitney (1989) suggests that "optimal placement results when students begin with the courses for which all important prior learning outcomes have been satisfied and few important course outcomes have been mastered" (p. 521). Course placement is similar in some ways to admissions in that it is viewed as a selection decision. At two-year institutions, course placement usually involves the decision of whether a student should enroll in a standard college-level credit-bearing course or in a developmental course which may not yield graduation credit. Because of the varying degrees of entry-level academic skills, some two-year colleges have more than one level of developmental course offerings. Many four-year colleges also assess students for placement into developmental courses, although some states prevent public four-year colleges from teaching developmental courses. In reality, an effective course placement program is a dynamic and complex process derived from the use of multiple sources of information, the involvement of many campus departments and units, a wide variety of decision rules, continuous change, and thorough research. Although course placement models may also be applied to more advanced courses through awarding AP, CLEP, International Baccalaureate, or dual enrollment credit, for the purposes of this chapter, course placement will be viewed as the means through which entry-level students are placed in developmental or any one of an array of standard college-level courses.

Benefits of an Effective Placement Program

An effective course placement program provides significant benefits to both the student and the institution. Correct placement in initial basic skills coursework begins a sequential process which, if effective, results in student academic success. The pivotal step in that sequential process is that accurate placement provides challenges commensurate with student academic abilities. Failure to assign students to appropriate levels of instruction portends an outcome which may be irreversible. Placement in a course for which most of the prior learning outcomes have been mastered can lead to academic boredom, a possible antecedent to the decision to drop out of college. And placement in a course for which few of the prior learning outcomes have been mastered is a recipe for frustration and failure and also an antecedent of dropout behavior. If students are accurately placed in an entry-level course, the likelihood of achieving the learning outcomes for the course is dramatically increased. A successful outcome in the original course increases self-confidence, reinforces the commitment to achieve an educational objective, and promotes satisfaction with the college. Accurate course placement is indeed the first and critical step on the road to success.

A well-designed and competently administered course placement system also yields significant benefits to the institution in four areas. The first area of benefits is in providing data for resource allocation decisions. All colleges are faced with the allocation of increasingly scarce and finite instructional resources. Data collected through the course placement program can inform institutional decisions on the allocation of faculty/staff positions as well as the number of sections needed to meet the developmental skill needs of the entering student cohort.

The second area of benefit is that effective course placement programs provide data that guide a wide variety of program enhancements. On the instructional side, such enhancements might include support for course or curricular revisions, or might identify targets for faculty development programs. In addition, course placement data can drive the definition and depth of learning support programs as well as build the case for more intrusive strategies for delivering services to targeted students. Because an effective course placement program increases the likelihood of student success, a third benefit accrues to the institution. The data derived supports collaborative outreach programs with secondary schools and serves as an important marketing and recruitment tool for admissions personnel to share in conversations with prospective students and their parents.

The final area of institutional benefit is that course placement program data can be used to meet external expectations or mandates. These data can be used as baseline data for later documentation of learning outcomes, and they can be used to meet requirements of disciplinary and regional accreditation bodies, supplementing the documentation required for external funding proposals.

Sources of Information Supporting Placement Decisions

Because initial placement in college-level courses lays a strong foundation for future success, institutions must design a placement program that takes advantage of all applicable data sources to inform placement decisions. At the core of most placement programs is the use of academic assessment data, but unfortunately many campuses rely solely on the use of such data to assign students to levels of instruction. Using multiple measures to determine students' academic preparation for college significantly improves the accuracy of a placement program. (ACT, 2010b; Roueche & Roueche, 1999). Although placement testing data are an essential component of placement effectiveness, decisions made on the basis of assessment data alone fail to take into account the nuances created by individual student skills, abilities, needs, and goals. Additional sources of information include previous academic performance (such as high school grades), noncognitive data gleaned from the assessment of psychosocial characteristics and interest inventories, as well as student-identified needs and coursework required by the student's program of study. Each of these areas is discussed in the following section of this chapter.

Assessment of Academic Skills

The accurate assessment of academic skills is the foundation of an effective course placement system. The process is dynamic and complex. This section of the chapter provides a discussion of three critical elements in that process: test selection, establishing cutoff scores, and conducting research to ensure that the placement of students is accurate.

Test Selection. The choice of a quality assessment is a primary consideration. Unfortunately, it is likely that many of the tests used as course placement assessments are not intended for that purpose. Though placements resulting from the use of such tests may appear to inform reasonable placement decision, it is not likely that those decisions are optimal. McDivitt and Gibson (2004) identify 11 elements in identifying a quality test. These elements, based on the Joint Committee on Testing Practices' *Code of Fair Testing Practices in Education* (2002) and *Responsibilities of Users of Standardized Tests* (American Counseling Association, 1987), are:

- *Purpose:* The purpose and recommended use of the test must reflect the goal of the institution's placement program.
- *Validity:* A valid test is one in which the test score results in placement in a course where most, if not all, of the prerequisite academic skills have been met while few of the skills required in the higher-level course are in evidence.
- *Reliability:* A reliable test is one that consistently measures academic skills. That is, students would be likely to earn similar scores if they took the test at two different times without learning interventions.
- *Alignment with the curriculum:* The test must measure the learning outcomes specified for the course.
- *Equity and fairness:* The test should be fair and equitable for all the students being tested.
- *Technical standards:* The norming procedures must be appropriate for and relevant to the population of students being tested.
- *Costs and feasibility:* Are the results of significant quality to justify the direct and indirect costs of program implementation?
- *Consequences:* Before testing, students should be made aware that the test will determine initial placement in courses.
- *Timeliness of score reports:* Test results must be available for placement decisions before classes begin.
- *Motivation:* Before testing, students should be encouraged to take the test seriously.
- *Quality of administrative, interpretative, and technical manuals:* Readily available, high-quality, and user-friendly support materials should be provided.

Noble, Schiel, and Sawyer (2004) provide an overview of widely used and commercially available tests for the course placement process. Though these tests will not be discussed in detail here, they can be organized into three groups. The first of these groups includes tests that may award credit based on scores achieved. These include the College Board's Advanced Placement Program (AP) and College Level Examination Program (CLEP) as well as the Excelsior College Examinations (formerly Regents College Examinations). As discussed in Chapter Seven, the College Board reported (2010b) that more than 18,000 U.S. high schools offered Advanced Placement courses, with 1.8 million students taking 3.2 million AP exams. And more than 2,900 colleges award some form of CLEP credit for students. Institutions vary in their policies on the AP and CLEP scores necessary to earn course credit.

Although these tests generate course credit and are widely utilized, their purpose is to determine whether students have met the specific learning outcomes of a college-level course. Such tests, however, may or may not lead to enrollment in a course at the next level. For example, Advanced Placement in American History may satisfy a course requirement but does not necessarily lead to a more advanced course; as such, an AP test can be differentiated from tests used specifically for placement. Whereas the AP, CLEP, and the Excelsior College Examinations gauge whether students are qualified to exit (earn credit in) a standard college-level course, the placement tests discussed in this chapter examine whether students are qualified to enter a standard college-level course.

The second group of tests is college admissions tests: the ACT and SAT I and II. Although the primary purpose of the ACT and the SAT is to inform the admission process, their use is widely accepted as part of a course placement program. Noble and Camara (2004) provide an excellent summary of each of these assessments and the technical manual for the

ACT (2010b) details the effective use of the assessments in the course placement process.

The third group includes commercially available tests that are designed specifically for the course placement function. The College Board's Accuplacer test is an Internet-delivered computer-adaptive placement test that assesses reading, writing, and math skills. The Accuplacer test includes reading comprehension, sentence skills, arithmetic, elementary algebra, college-level mathematics and the writing test, Writeplacer (http://professionals.collegeboard.com/higher-ed/placement/accuplacer). COMPASS (http://www.act.org/compass/advant/placement.html), a computer-adaptive Internet assessment, and ASSET, (http://www.act.org/asset/) its paper/pencil predecessor, are placement tests developed by ACT. Computer-adaptive tests (CAT) are tailored to the test taker's level of ability. As a student correctly answers a question, the level of difficulty increases and, conversely, the level of difficulty decreases when a student answers a question incorrectly. CAT tests are advantageous in that testing time is shortened and results are immediately available for placement decisions. Regardless of these conveniences, however, placement decisions derived from CAT must be based in research that assures validity and reliability.

For students whose placement test scores are marginal, both COMPASS and ACCUPLACER include diagnostic components which enable educators to structure individualized interventions based on more specific information on academic skill deficiencies. COMPASS includes diagnostic tests in the following skill areas: reading (3 tests), writing (7), and mathematics (14). ACCUPLACER offers five diagnostic tests in each of four skill areas: reading comprehension, sentence skills, arithmetic, and elementary algebra. Succinctly, a placement test identifies content areas of academic skills weaknesses and a diagnostic tests drills down into the content areas to identify the specific skills that contribute to students' low scores. A further discussion of diagnostics tests is included in Chapter Thirteen. And for a more detailed overview of commercially available placement and diagnostic tests, see Noble and Sawyer (2004).

Although the tests described above are the most widely used instruments for placing students in courses, many colleges have developed their own placement tests for one or more academic skill areas. In addition to adhering to McDivitt and Gibson's 11 elements of a quality test (2004), the effectiveness of local placement tests depends on two additional factors. The first is cost benefit. Do the direct costs (printing, proctoring, scoring, and reporting) and the indirect costs (development and research) constitute a wise use of fiscal and human resources? That is, are other equally effective measures available at a lower cost to the institution? The second factor to consider is the research that supports placement decisions. Are placement decisions the result of research that is both well designed and regularly conducted? Many placement decisions are based on hunch, by guess, or through intuition. And still others are based on the application of normative standards developed from an inappropriate reference group. The importance of continuous research on placement effectiveness is discussed in the following section of this chapter.

As this chapter is being written, the Common Core Standards are being considered by many states as a method for identifying what high school graduates should know and be able to do to demonstrate college and career readiness. The criteria, developed by The Council of Chief State School Officers (CCSSO) and the National Governors Association Center for Best Practices (NGA Center), used to identify the standards state that high school curriculum should be:

- Aligned with college and work expectations;
- Rigorous in content *and* include the application of knowledge through high-order skills;
- Built upon strengths and lessons of current state standards;

- Informed by top-performing countries, so that all students are prepared to succeed in our global economy and society; and,

- Evidence- and/or research-based. (2010, p.1)

Based on the standards, efforts are under way to develop common assessment(s). Should these efforts be productive, it is possible that such assessments may be added to those already used for course placement decisions.

Establishing Cutoff Scores. The next critical consideration involves identifying the score points utilized to determine placement. Often called *cut scores*, these score points can be derived through several methods. The first involves the judgment of the faculty who specify the minimum skills and knowledge needed to master the course material and review the placement test to determine the score which corresponds to the minimum level of preparation needed to succeed. The placement literature describes several subjective approaches that rely on the judgment of faculty members. Readers interested in a detailed and technical discussion of these procedures should consult Wall and Walz (2004).

The second method for determining cut scores involves using local or national normative data. Normative data identify the percentage of students who score at or below specific score levels. Institutions in the process of starting a course placement program may initially rely on the recommendations of test publishers to identify cut scores based on national norms. In many cases, students' entering academic skills are studied in relation to performance history in the course in question. The results of such a study serve as a guide to identifying the appropriate percentage of students to be placed in the lower-level course. Unfortunately, some institutions use normative data to set cut scores based on the availability of instructional resources. That is, if the institution can only afford to assign 20% of its instructional resources to developmental education, only those students scoring at or below the 20th percentile will be placed in the lower-level course. Though finite resources are a continuous problem, such an approach is ill-advised because it places some students in courses without the prerequisite academic skills and knowledge needed to succeed. Using this example, if developmental coursework can be offered to only 20% of students but 30% of the tested students score at a level indicating the need for the developmental course, then one-third of the students of the low-scoring students would be in jeopardy through placement in the upper-level course.

The most precise method for determining cut scores and the overall effectiveness of the course placement program is to analyze the statistical relationship between test scores and outcomes of the placement process. A statistical model can be developed to predict a student's chance of success at any point on the score scale. Such a model would identify the percentages of students placed in the lower-level and in the upper-level course, the probability of success in the upper-level course, and the proportion of students correctly placed—in essence, placing students in the courses in which they should be placed. Currently, logistic regression is seen as the utility-based methodology that meets these three criteria. Because a complete discussion of logistic regression is a complex matter, individuals interested in a more thorough consideration of the methodology should consult Hilbe (2009) or Hosmer and Lemeshow (2000). And, for an application of the methodology using ACT scores, individuals should review the ACT Technical Manual (2010b).

Successful placement programs are not, however, limited to predicting success in the initial course. The placement model is complete only when growth in the initial course is measured and a determination is made as to whether that level of growth is sufficient for the student to be successful in a course at the next level. The most logical approach to ascertaining the degree of growth is to readminister the original placement test to see if the student has achieved a level of performance that would predict likely success in the next course in the sequence. If research determining appropriate cut scores is accurate, than posttest scores can be used as predictors of success in the next level course; however, the real issue here is the degree to which the learning intervention (in this case, a developmental course) leads to success in the higher-level course.

Critics of developmental/remedial education are quick to point out that without evidence of future success, resources allocated to developmental education are misdirected. That issue was explored by Sawyer and Schiel (2000), who conducted a study to determine whether taking a remedial course increased the cognitive skills that students needed to succeed in a standard course. The paper describes some indicators based on data from posttesting students after they have completed a remedial course. The authors concluded that the results suggested that students completing remedial mathematics and writing courses had a relatively high probability of scoring at or above the posttest cutoffs and, therefore, of being permitted to enroll in the corresponding standard-level courses. An additional study by Perkhounkova, Noble, and Sawyer (2005) investigated a method of documenting the benefits of developmental courses that involved using placement test scores to predict college outcomes separately for students who took a developmental course before taking standard courses and for those who enrolled in a standard course directly. They discovered that simply taking a developmental course did not usually result in successful outcomes, but students who earned at least a B in developmental courses were more likely than other students to succeed in standard courses or to persist in college.

High School Academic Performance

Critics of the use of college admission tests suggest that high school grades and course-taking patterns are better predictors of student performance in college than test scores. Validity studies suggest that although high school grades typically are slightly better individual predictors of achievement in college, test scores add significantly to the prediction (ACT, 2010; Camara & Echternacht, 2000). These findings tend to hold for all subgroups of students and for all types of measures: freshman grades, course grades, and cumulative grades. Noble and Sawyer (2004) found that high school grade point average (GPA) is more effective than ACT scores in accurately identifying successful students when success is defined as completing the first year of college with a 2.0 (C) or higher GPA. When predicting a high level of success (such as a 3.5 or higher GPA), high school grades are much less accurate than ACT scores.

Though high school grades and course-taking patterns are useful in making college-level course placement decisions, grades include a degree of subjectivity in that curricular frameworks, grading practices, course quality, and content may vary among high schools. Earning a high grade in a high school course does not guarantee that important prior learning outcomes for entry into a standard college course have been satisfied. This supports the contention that multiple measures of academic performance should be used in placement decisions. Neither test scores nor high school grades should be use as stand-alone determinants of college course placement.

Additional Course Placement Considerations

While tests scores and high school grades represent the core of a course placement program, there are several additional sources of information which may be factored into a course placement decision. These include psychosocial factors and career/educational interests.

In regards to psychosocial factors, Tinto's theory of attrition (1993) suggested that there are five such factors that predict a student's decision to drop out of an institution: goals, commitments, institutional experiences, integration, and high school outcome. Robbins et al. (2004) conclude that some psychological factors have predictive strength to that of traditional academic performance factors. The role of psychosocial development is discussed in detail in Chapter Eight.

There is also a developing body of evidence that ties student success in college to the congruence between program of study and interest patterns. Several researchers studied the relationship between Holland's theory of person-environment fit and persistence in college. Allen and Robbins (2008) suggest that academic performance and interest-major fit are key constructs for understanding major persistence behavior. The findings of a study by Leuwerke, Robbins, Sawyer, & Hovland (2004) reinforced the importance of examining both achievement and interest congruence factors in understanding the retention of engineering majors. A more thorough consideration of this topic is the focus of Chapter Nine.

Course Placement Models

Several models, from simple to complex, depict the application of course placement information.

Although placement models can be extremely complex, four basic models illustrate the manner in which placement decisions are derived. In order to simplify the discussion of these models, standardized generic terminology is used for each model. Courses A and B represent two levels of difficulty in course content, with Course A at the lower level and Course B at the higher level. The most common visualization of the courses would be to view Course A as a remedial/developmental course and Course B as the standard first college course. This model may also be extended to include multiple remedial/developmental courses. It is also possible that the course designations could be applied to a sequence of nonremedial, college-level courses. Using Mathematics as an example, Course A could represent College Algebra, while Course B would be precalculus, and

Figure 12.1 Test Only Placement Model

COURSE	A	B
TEST SCORE	0–50	50–100

Course C (not depicted in the model) would be calculus with analytic geometry.

Score scales for commonly used assessments such as ACT, SAT, COMPASS, and ACCUPLACER as well as those for local placement tests vary greatly. As a result, the score ranges used in the flow models are also generic in nature. Numerical values representing test scores in each of the flow models, for purposes of simplicity, range from 0 to 100.

The Test Only Placement Model depicted in Figure 12.1 is an apparently efficient model that leaves little room for interpretation. It employs the use of a single test score as the sole determinant of course placement. The model is clear, but its use raises several concerns. The most critical of these is the degree to which it adheres to McDivitt and Gibson's 11 elements of a quality test (2004). Specifically, the test used must be both valid and reliable, backed by substantial research which supports the accuracy of placement decisions not only in terms of success in the initial course but also in preparation for success in the course which follows in the sequence. Even if the test is valid and reliable, a second issue with this model is the degree to which exceptions may be made and who has the authority to grant those exceptions. A third concern is that although a well-designed placement test may be both valid and reliable, neither psychometricians nor test publishers suggest that a single test should be utilized to make a "high stakes" decision such as college admission or course placement. These concerns might be mediated somewhat if students who challenge the results of the test or present extenuating circumstances that may have adversely affected their test scores are given the opportunity to retest.

Figure 12.2 Multiple Conditions Placement Model

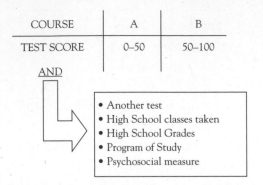

COURSE	A	B
TEST SCORE	0–50	50–100

AND

- Another test
- High School classes taken
- High School Grades
- Program of Study
- Psychosocial measure

The Multiple Conditions Model requires that more than one condition be met to place a student in a course. That is, this model employs multiple measures in determining appropriate placement. An appropriate test score AND additional thresholds/conditions must be met. The model includes several of the more common thresholds/conditions which augment the placement test score. As a hypothetical, albeit extended illustration of the Multiple Conditions Placement Model (Figure 12.2), placement in Course B (College Algebra) requires a minimum placement test score of 50 *and* a minimum score on a local mathematics test *and* four years of high school mathematics with a grade of B or better. The Multiple Conditions Model is likely to improve the course placement decision over the Test Only Model only if the additional conditions are verified through research to increase the accuracy of the decision. This model also raises a concern similar to the Test Only Placement Model. That is, as the number of conditions increase, the issue of exceptions also increases and the need to clarify who has the authority to grant those exceptions becomes more critical.

The Multiple Considerations Placement Model substitutes alternatives to meeting specific conditions (see Figure 12.3). The most common example of this is the substitution of a different test score. As one illustration, a student may be placed

Figure 12.3 Multiple Considerations Placement Model

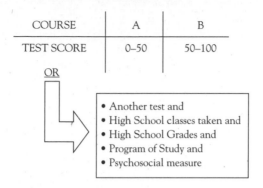

in college algebra with a minimum ACT Mathematics score *or* a minimum SAT Mathematics score *or* a minimum score on a local mathematics placement test. As a second example, a student may be placed in college algebra with a minimum test score *or* grades of B or better in at least three years of high school courses in mathematics. Though this model provides flexibility in the determination of course placement, such flexibility raises significant questions about the comparability of measures. No two tests are alike and the content and rigor of coursework as well as grading practices vary greatly among high schools. Nevertheless, the Multiple Considerations Placement model can be effective if research shows that the accuracy of placement decisions based on one consideration is comparable to the accuracy of decisions based on the test score.

Because of its complexity and the number of possible combinations, an additional placement model—a hybrid of the Multiple Conditions and Multiple Considerations Models—is not depicted here. Specifically, the hybrid model combines "*and*" statements and "*or*" statements in arriving at a placement decision. As an illustration, a student is placed in calculus with a test score of 200+ *and* an additional corroborating test score *or* four years of high school mathematics including precalculus. Concerns with the hybrid model parallel those of the conditions and considerations models.

Figure 12.4 Decision Zone Placement Model

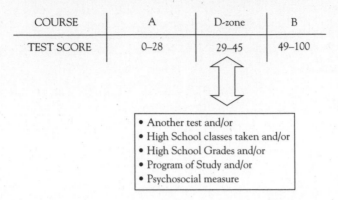

COURSE	A	D-zone	B
TEST SCORE	0–28	29–45	49–100

- Another test and/or
- High School classes taken and/or
- High School Grades and/or
- Program of Study and/or
- Psychosocial measure

The final model, the Decision Zone Placement Model, is depicted in Figure 12.4. The model includes Courses A and B and retains the score scale of 0–100, but this model identifies score scale points at which discretion may be exercised. In the decision zone (D-zone) below students scoring between 29 and 45 may be placed in either Course A or Course B. The conditions and considerations identified in previous models provide the focus for discussion with an academic advisor. And it is in the decision zones that that true art of academic advising is revealed. A decision zone score in mathematics opens the door to a number of questions the answers to which would help determine a decision to enroll in Course A or in Course B.

Those questions would include, but may not be limited to, the number of high school math courses, topics covered and grades in those courses, comfort with math, level of mathematics required (or useful) in the student's program of study, and academic self-confidence.

Conclusion

As we asserted in Chapter Seven, efforts to enhance college preparation (dual enrollment and advanced placement) at the secondary level focus on the students who are most likely to succeed in college level courses and, in turn, persist to degree completion. Left out of the preparation equation are students who enroll in college with marginal academic credentials. According to McCabe (2000), 41% of community college enrollees and 29% of four-year college enrollees were inadequately prepared in at least one of the basic skills areas (that is, writing, reading, and mathematics). By 2007–08 those figures had nudged upward to a point that more than 36% of college students enrolled in at least one remedial course (National Center for Education Statistics, 2009d). In 2001–02, developmental instruction was provided by nearly all public two-year postsecondary schools, 80% of public four-year institutions, and approximately 65% of private four-year institutions (NCES, 2003). By 2008, those figures had risen to 99%, 88%, and 68%, respectively (NCES, 2009d).

Although we accept the explanation that the primary burden for the lack of academic preparation rests with K–12 education, we also believe that colleges and universities who admit students with marginal academic skills are ethically bound to assist those students in the acquisition of the skills necessary to succeed; that is, to deliver effective developmental education and learning support, which we discuss in the following chapter. The foundation of that skill building rests on the ability to implement an accurate course placement system. Students who are misplaced are candidates for attrition. Those who are placed in courses below their skill level may become bored and ultimately leave college, while those who are placed in courses for which they are not prepared are likely to first become frustrated, then to fail and ultimately leave. Success in reaching goals for the dramatic improvement in college completion rates rests in our ability to assess entry-level academic ability and to design learning interventions for student with marginal academic skills.

13

DEVELOPMENTAL EDUCATION INITIATIVES

A crucial component of many institutions' student success efforts is developmental education initiatives. Arendale et al. (2007) define developmental education as "a field of practices and research within higher education with a theoretical foundation in developmental psychology and learning theory. It promotes the cognitive and affective growth of all postsecondary learners, at all levels of the learning continuum" (p. 18). It is conservatively estimated that public higher education institutions spend between one and two billion dollars annually on developmental education (Breneman & Haarlow, 1998; Merisotis & Phipps, 2000; Schmidt, 2008; Strong American Schools, 2008). The organization Strong American Schools estimates that students and their families pay upwards of $708 to $886 million each year in tuition and fees for developmental coursework (2008). Yet, despite the heavy investment in developmental education, there is a lack of high-quality research on the impact and effectiveness of such initiatives. Recent public efforts to "fix" developmental education have been called for by high profile public (President Obama) and private (Bill & Melinda Gates Foundation) entities (Gonzalez, 2010; Killough, 2009). This chapter will provide a definition of developmental education, an overview of hot issues within the field, highlights from large-scale studies of remedial college courses as well as direct student learning assistance initiatives, and discuss best practices for improving developmental education.

Defining Developmental Education

Although the terms *developmental education* and *remedial education* are often used interchangeably, professionals within the field today prefer the former term (Kozeracki, 2002). Other terms that have been used include *preparatory studies, academic support programs, compensatory education, learning assistance,* and *basic skills* (Payne & Lyman, 1996). For purposes of this chapter, we will mainly use the term *developmental education*, although *remedial education* will also be used only sparingly when quoting the work of others.

Historically, *remedial education* has had a negative connotation, and some feel the term implies there is something wrong that needs to be cured through enrollment in remedial programs (Kozeracki, 2002). Arendale (2005) reports that "remedial education was the term used by most in the field from the 1860s through the early 1960s. Remedial education often focused on specific skill deficits of students and educational approaches that addressed these identified needs" (p. 68). The term *developmental education* did not appear until the 1970s and was borrowed from student development theory that college student affairs staff were using at that time; by the 1990s, developmental education acquired a more negative connotation and students in these courses felt stigmatized (Arendale, 2005).

Today there is renewed interest in developmental education, much of it focused on how best to improve student outcomes. As President Obama seeks to significantly increase the number of college graduates in order for the United States to be a more competitive nation in today's global economy, he and others have identified developmental education as "one of the main barriers between millions of students and college degrees" (Killough, 2009, para. 1). Even the most powerful nonprofit foundation, the Bill & Melinda Gates Foundation, has pledged $110 million dollars to assist two-year colleges in improving their developmental education programs. Cochairperson of the Foundation, Melinda Gates, advocated replacing weak

developmental education programs with innovative practices as a strategy for increasing graduation rates at the annual
meeting of the American Association of Community Colleges
(Gonzalez, 2010). Gates said, "Our research indicates that
improving remediation is the single most important thing community colleges can do to increase the number of students who
graduate" (Gonzalez, 2010, para. 4). Clearly, this is an important
time in the history of developmental education. The nation's
spotlight is on the field and there are significant monetary
resources available to higher education institutions that create
and sustain effective developmental programs.

Though much of the research is focused on remedial coursework, professionals in developmental education prefer to think
of the field in much broader terms. Remedial coursework is an
important component of developmental education, as are other
services both inside and outside the classroom. These include
learning assistance initiatives with individual students (tutoring,
learning assistance centers), as well as in-class (Supplemental
Instruction, linked courses, and freshmen seminars) (Kozeracki,
2002). McCabe and Day (1998) write, "Most successful developmental programs offer a wide variety of comprehensive
instructional support services, including assessment, placement,
orientation, tutoring, advising, counseling, peer support, early
alert programs, study skills training, and support groups" (p. 21).
Thus, the focus of this chapter is on developmental education
in its broadest sense, meaning that it includes an overview of
remedial education as well as many learning support practices.

Issues in Developmental Education

This section will highlight some of the hot issues in developmental education, including whether higher education should
even offer developmental courses, who is responsible for the
large number of students who need developmental education
services, the role that diagnostic exams play in developmental

education, and the lack of depth in the developmental education literature.

Should Higher Education Institutions Offer Developmental Courses and/or Programs?

The most enduring issue in developmental education centers on
whether institutions of higher education, particularly four-year
institutions, should offer and fund developmental courses and
programs for students. Those opposed to offering remedial courses
cite a number of reasons for their disdain for the programs: tax-
payers have to pay twice for students to take courses they should
have mastered in high school, there is no clear evidence remedial
programs are effective, institutions have to lower their standards
to meet the needs of students who are not prepared for college,
students enrolled in these courses are negatively stigmatized, and
resources could be better spent on other initiatives (Kozeracki,
2002). Advocates of developmental education programs cite the
economic and social benefits to society that college-educated people contribute (see Chapter Four), the importance of all Americans
having access to the personal benefits a college education affords
college graduates, the inequities that currently exist in the funding of K–12 education, and the need to have a well-educated work
force in today's knowledge economy (Kozeracki, 2002).

Who Should Be Held Responsible for the Demands on Developmental Programs?

Another contentious issue is who should be held responsible
for the large number of students who are under-prepared to be
successful in college. Some college administrators point to the
K–12 education system. K–12 educators acknowledge this by
noting, "Tired of struggling with students who need remediation
and policy makers who don't want to pay for it, they're looking for some relief—and they're turning to those of us who work
in K–12" (Haycock, 2006). Haycock (2006) also argues that

there is no national criterion for declaring students competent to meet college-level standards, and instead these standards are set by each institution. The finger-pointing is a waste of time and energy. The clear message is that both higher education institutions and K–12 schools need to partner together to devise creative solutions to decrease the number of incoming college students who need remedial coursework. It is in both parties' best interest to have these discussions begin sooner rather than later. At least one nonprofit organization, the America Diploma Project, is bringing together politicians, K–12 administrators, college officials, and business executives to ensure that high school graduates are prepared for college work (Killough, 2009).

Clearly, there is a need to develop guidelines and standards that address exactly what it means for a student to be college-ready upon graduating from high school. Even within higher education institutions, individual colleges have different cut-off scores on placement exams that assign students to remedial course sections. "Consequently, there is no objective or generally agreed upon cut-off below which college students require remediation" (Attewell, Lavin, Domina, & Levey, 2006, p. 887). Merisotis & Phipps (2000) argue, "remedial education, more often than not, is determined by the admissions requirements of the particular institution" (p. 72). Bettinger and Long (2008) assert that because 80% of students attend open admissions institutions, the "key academic gate-keeper" is the college placement exams that incoming students are required to take after enrolling in college (see Chapter Twelve for more details). Further, Merisotis & Phipps (2000) point out that cut-off scores at community colleges are going to be different than at highly selective Research I institutions. Because many students attend college close to home, one way to begin to address this issue is to set statewide college readiness standards. For example,

> The 23-campus California State system tackled the issue on a large scale by working with the California Department of Education and State Board of Education to create the Early Assessment

Program. That testing program, which is embedded within the 11th-grade California Standards Test, measures college prepared-ness in English and mathematics. The program gives students an early signal of their college readiness, then helps them adjust senior-year course work to get ready for college-level courses. (Haycock, 2006, p. B38)

This type of communication and collaboration between high schools and postsecondary institutions is essential to developing standards and preparing students to meet the academic demands of college.

Diagnostics

Building on the course placement discussion, another hot topic in developmental education involves the use of diagnostic tests to help educators to identify the most appropriate entry-level courses for students. The use of additional assessments can help to pinpoint the skill sets within the content domain, particu-larly in mathematics and English, that provide a specific focus for intervention. Such is the function of diagnostic tests: they help faculty and students to better understand areas of strength and needs within content areas.

A placement test in mathematics may yield a reasonably accurate assessment of a student's need for developmental math-ematics, but an additional diagnostic test in pre-algebra would help educators identify specific skill sets which would benefit from focused interventions. A pre-algebra diagnostic assessment might include integers, decimals, exponents, square roots, sci-entific notation, fractions, percentages, and averages (mean, median, mode). And for students whose tests indicate place-ment in intermediate algebra, the mathematics diagnostic test might include items on substituting values, setting up equations, factoring polynomials, exponents and radicals, basic operations/ polynomials, linear equations (one or two variables), and rational expressions. Students who place into college algebra may not need, but might benefit from, diagnostic assessment.

The same process applies to the placement of students into developmental English or first-year English. For students placing into developmental English, diagnostic assessment would help educators identify specific skill sets which would benefit from focused interventions. English diagnostics might include the assessment of punctuation, spelling, capitalization, usage, verb formation/agreement, relationships of clauses, shifts in construction, and organization. Students who place into first-year English may not need, but might benefit from, diagnostic assessment.

The connection between diagnostic assessment and learning interventions is apparent. Diagnostic score profiles for students enrolled in developmental courses provide instructors with a means to effectively target classroom instruction to those areas of greatest need. Information gleaned from diagnostic assessment could result in differentiated instruction within developmental classes. An additional benefit of diagnostic testing in developmental instruction is that using diagnostic data is likely to improve student learning, as well as student motivation and engagement in that learning. Timely information may make the course seem more approachable, thus increasing students' sense of mastery, which is in turn related to increased motivation and engagement (see, for example, Hsieh, Sullivan, & Guerra, 2007; Rosenbaum, Redline, & Stephan, 2007; Senko, Hulleman, & Harackiewicz, 2011).

In addition, diagnostic assessment could inform group intervention strategies other than those that take place in the classroom. Examples of such group interventions would be a workshop on fractions, percentages, and averages or mediated instructional modules on organizing a writing assignment. Finally, diagnostic assessment provides a focus for faculty, staff, and/or peer tutoring.

Lack of Depth in Literature on Developmental Education

A challenge facing the field of developmental education is the lack of depth in the scholarly literature (Boylan & Saxon, 2005;

Calcagno & Long, 2008; Grubb, 2001; O'Hear & MacDonald, 1995). Merisotis & Phipps (2000) found that, "Research about the effectiveness of remedial education programs has typically been sporadic, underfunded, and inconclusive" (p. 75). Similarly, Grubb (2001) found there is little research to answer the question of whether or not remedial education is effective, "No one knows much about what works and what does not—or why. . . Too many dimensions of remedial education are poorly understood" (p. 7).

Results from the 2010 *What Works in Student Retention* Survey

Both required and recommended remedial coursework were included in the ACT's *What Works in Student Retention (WWISR) Survey* (Habley, McClanahan, Valiga, & Burkum, 2010) that asked senior campus administrators about the availability of 18 different Learning Assistance/Academic Support programs and perceived contribution to retention at the respective institutions (Habley et al., 2010). Practices incorporated into this section of the survey include: supplemental instruction, summer bridge program, learning assistance center/lab (comprehensive, mathematics, writing, reading, and/or foreign languages), tutoring, study skills course, program, or center, early warning system, midterm progress reports, performance contracts for students in academic difficulty, organized student study groups, service learning programs, English as a Second Language (ESL) programs, online learning support, and a library orientation workshop.

Top Four Learning Assistance Initiatives

In Table 13.1, data for the top four learning support interventions are presented in the left-hand column: remedial coursework (required), Supplemental Instruction (SI), Tutoring, and Early Warning Systems. Note that recommended remedial coursework

Table 13.1 Five Select Learning Initiatives from the *What Works in Student Retention* (WWISR) Survey (Habley et al., 2010).

Learning Assistance Initiative	Four-Year Public			Four-Year Private			Community Colleges		
	Incidence Rate	Mean	% Selected as Among Top 3	Incidence Rate	Mean	% Selected as Among Top 3	Incidence Rate	Mean	% Selected as Among Top 3
Remedial Coursework (required)	76%	3.49		58%	3.55		88%	4.08	Yes (20%)
(recommended)	46%	3.36		38%	3.40		45%	3.82	
SI	72%	3.91	Yes (16%)	54%	3.51		62%	3.84	
Tutoring	97%	3.84	Yes (15%)	90%	3.75	Yes (13%)			
	95%	4.11	Yes (22%)						
Early Warning System	74%	3.53		78%	3.77	Yes (21%)	68%	3.59	Yes (12%)

is also on this table because the literature does not distinguish between required and recommended remedial coursework; thus the discussion of both required and remedial will be handled together in the description of the research on remedial classes. For each topic, results from the *WWISR Survey* (Habley et al., 2010) are shared for four-year public, four-year private, and community colleges. Institution-specific information is shared about the percentage of survey respondents (incidence rate) who indicated that their institution provided each type of support. The survey was designed to measure survey respondents' perceptions about how much the support activity contributed to campus retention (5 = a major contribution and 1 = little or no contribution). Given the results indicating a high incidence rate and high perceived level of contribution to retention across institution types, these interventions will be discussed in detail followed by a brief overview of the remaining 13 learning practices.

Based on these results, we have selected the five most popular learning support/developmental education activities and/or those perceived to be the most effective contributors to campus retention to explore in depth. These include remedial college courses (required/recommended), supplemental instruction, tutoring, and early warning systems. For each of these, an overview of the topic and research about the effectiveness of each learning support activity will be provided.

Remedial College Course (Required and Recommended). Sixty percent of community college students and 25% of four-year students enroll in one or more required or recommended remedial/developmental courses (Kuh, 2007). The *WWISR Survey* (Habley et al., 2010) found that required remedial coursework is more frequently utilized and perceived to be more impactful than recommended coursework across institution types. Community colleges were the most likely to require remedial coursework (80%) and to rate that coursework as more effective in contributing to student retention than either four-year public or private institutions. Combining the required and recommended remedial college course options together is appropriate because the literature does not typically differentiate between the two.

Although the research on developmental education has been rather sparse in the past, the good news is there are at least three recent national studies focusing on the topic. The bad news is that the results of these studies have been mixed and do not definitively answer the question of whether developmental courses are effective. Bridget T. Long, a coauthor of two of the studies, told *The Chronicle of Higher Education* that when comparing the studies, the impact of developmental courses "is either slightly positive, slightly negative or zero" (Schmidt, 2008, para. 4).

The first study, conducted by Calcagno and Long (2008), focused on the detailed academic records of 100,000 community college students in the state of Florida who were just above or below the cutoff score on placement exams. They compared the long-term outcomes of students assigned to developmental courses and those who were placed in regular courses, based on their cutoff scores. Their results "suggest math and reading remedial courses have mixed benefits" (Calcagno & Long, 2008, p. i). The advantages of being assigned to developmental courses included increased student persistence to the second year as well as higher total earned credits. Disadvantages included a decreased likelihood of graduation and fewer credits taken that count towards a degree. They also found that students in developmental math courses were more likely to persist, but performed about the same in further math classes as those who were not assigned to developmental sections. "Taken together, the results suggest that remediation might improve early persistence in college, but it does not necessarily help students on the margin of passing the placement cutoff make long-term progress toward earning a degree" (Calcagno & Long, 2008, p. i). Martorell and McFarlin (2007) pointed out one weakness of the Calcagno and Long (2008) study is they only looked at students' initial placement score instead of taking into consideration retest scores.

The state of Texas was the subject of Martorell and McFarlin's 2007 study of the performance of 255,000 students who started at community colleges and 197,000 students who matriculated at four-year public institutions. Similar to Calcagno and Long's 2008 study, the students selected for this study were those on the cusp of passing or not passing developmental placement exams. "Aside from weak evidence that students in remediation have better grades in first college-level math courses, we find little indication that students benefit from remediation" (Martorell & McFarlin, 2007, p. 26). Further, they found that students enrolled in developmental courses were less likely to finish the first year of college and remediation had no impact on the likelihood of completing a degree.

However, Bettinger and Long's (2008) study of 28,000 students in the state of Ohio who indicated their intention to pursue four-year degrees at four-year public institutions and community colleges found that remediation had a positive impact on student persistence, transfer rates to more selective colleges, and completion rates of four-year degrees. A limitation of this study is that it only looked at traditional-aged, full-time college students who had taken the ACT (Schmidt, 2008, para. 18).

The authors of these three studies acknowledge their findings are limited to the states that they studied and that they only examined students who either barely failed or passed college placement exams (Bettinger & Long, 2008; Calcagno & Long, 2008; Martorell & McFarlin, 2007; Schmidt, 2008). These studies do not address the outcomes of the large number of students who performed poorly on placement exams. It would seem that developmental education courses would be especially important to these students in terms of their future academic performance, persistence rates, and graduation rates. The bottom line is that the findings to date are mixed and inconclusive. It is obvious that there is still a lot of research to be done on the effectiveness of remedial education for students at the margins of passing or failing college placement exams and students who score well below the cut-off scores. However, the lack of consistent evidence about the value of developmental education highlights the discrepancy between perception and proof. The *WWISR Survey* (Habley et al., 2010) indicates the majority of institutions have developmental courses and institutional representatives perceive that developmental coursework makes moderate contributions to retention. As further studies are conducted and shared with college administrators, this information may help institutions make decisions about the level of resources devoted to developmental coursework.

Three papers summarize the literature on what components make specific developmental education programs successful. Below is a condensed version of suggested best practices from these three reviews of the developmental education literature (Achieving the Dream, n.d.; Boylan & Saxon, 2005; Kozeracki, 2002):

a. Classes should be structured and have clearly defined goals.

b. Classes should be driven by adult learning, active learning, and cognitive theories, and be accommodating of different student learning styles and developmental needs.

c. Other services should be incorporated into the course, including counseling and learning assistance programs (such as tutoring, Supplemental Instruction (SI), learning communities).

d. Classes should be regularly evaluated.

e. Instructors and support staff for these courses should be selected and trained carefully.

f. There should be mandatory assessment and placement in courses.

g. The exit standards for remedial courses should be congruent with the entry level standards for regular courses.

h. The curriculum should include study skills, strategic thinking, literacy, and motivation components.

Including these components in developmental education courses have been deemed by developmental education experts in the field to contribute to student success (Achieving the Dream, n.d.; Boylan & Saxon, 2005; Kozeracki, 2002).

Supplemental Instruction. We now shift our attention to looking at specific strategies being used within a classroom setting, both with underprepared students and all students. Arendale (2004) looked at a subset of peer cooperative learning strategies that have been shown to have a positive impact on student persistence. Supplemental Instruction is one of six such programs he highlights, including: Accelerated Learning Groups (ALGs), Emerging Scholars Program (ESP), Peer-Led Team Learning (PLTL), Structured Learning Assistance (SLA), Supplemental Instruction (SI), and Video-Based Supplemental Instruction (VSI). Each program that Arendale (2004) selected met rigorous criteria, including that the approach increased students' content knowledge and persistence, and the program must have been successfully replicated at other institutions.

Supplemental Instruction (SI) is a peer-assisted learning program or strategy that is employed by institutions to help any and all students be successful in traditionally tough "drop out" courses. These courses are most commonly introductory chemistry and biology courses in the natural sciences (46%), as well as courses in the social sciences (20%), math (15%), and humanities (7%) (Arendale, 2004, p. 30). The goals of SI include, "1. To increase retention within targeted historically difficult courses, 2. To improve student grades in targeted historically difficult courses, and 3. To increase the graduation rates of students" (UMKC, 2010, para. 2). The birthplace of SI was the

University of Missouri at Kansas City (UMKC, 2010), where it began in 1973 as a faculty-delivered system to help students enrolled in challenging classes in medicine, dentistry and pharmacy (Ogden, Thompson, Russell, & Simons, 2003). In Habley et al.'s *WWISR Survey* (2010), Supplemental Instruction programs were found at 72% of public institutions, 54% of private institutions, and 62% of two-year colleges. The perceived contribution of SI programs to student retention ranged from a mean of 3.51 at private institutions to 3.91 at public institutions. Only officials at public institutions listed SI among the top three initiatives contributing to student retention (Habley et al., 2010).

SI offerings are typically free and available to all students on a voluntary basis (UMKC, 2010). SI sections are usually led by upper-level undergraduate or graduate students who have previous experience in the course and performed well. SI leaders attend class each week, take notes, and offer multiple SI sessions each week, beginning with the first week of classes, where they facilitate peer-to-peer interaction by providing collaborative learning experiences (Arendale, 2004).

The research literature on the effectiveness of Supplemental Instruction indicates that it has a positive impact on short-term (Arendale, 2004; Doty, 2003) and long-term (Ogden, Thompson, Russell, & Simons, 2003) student success. Doty's (2003) compilation of national data from colleges with SI programs for the International Center for Supplemental Instruction at UMKC from 1998 to 2003 indicates that "the D, F, and W rates of those that attend SI are significantly lower than those that do not attend SI. We also find that SI participants can experience improved grades on average of 0.45 grade points higher than non-SI participants" (p. 8). Arendale (2004) notes that hundreds of studies have been completed on SI and many of them are available at the National Center for SI and other websites.

Tidewater Community College in Norfolk, Virginia, is an example of an institution that adopted the SI model after administrators found students were not taking advantage of the institution's extensive tutoring program or were waiting too long before seeking help (Ashburn, 2006). Results indicated that students who attended five or more SI sessions had a 93% chance of passing the course. In the entry-level math course they found a 65% pass rate for sections with an SI instructor attending class versus 53% for sections without an SI instructor (Ashburn, 2006).

Tutoring. In the *WWISR Survey* (Habley et al., 2010), tutoring was the only learning assistance program with incidence rates of 90% or more across institutional types (public, private, and two-year) and was the only learning assistance program listed in the top three in terms of perceived effectiveness across institutional types. The survey did not specify whether the tutors were faculty, professional staff, or peers, but for the purpose of this section we will focus on peer tutoring. A broad definition of peer tutoring is "people from similar social groupings, who are not professional teachers, helping each other to learn and learning themselves by teaching" (Topping, 1996, p. 322). This definition points out one of the key benefits of tutoring, that both the tutor and the tutee benefit from participating in a tutoring relationship. The tutor learns just by preparing to tutor students, experiences enhanced cognitive processing, and has increased depth of knowledge on the topic being taught (Topping, 1996; Robinson, Schofield, & Steers-Wentzell, 2005).

Tutoring differs across formats, demographics, and domains (Roscoe & Chi, 2007). Differences in formats include cross-age tutoring or same-age tutoring. Topping (1996) suggests a typology that includes 10 different dimensions such as tutor and tutee characteristics, ability, place, and time (in class and/or out of class). In terms of demographics, tutoring has been shown to be effective at all age ranges from elementary school through college and for students with a wide range of academic and cognitive abilities. In addition, tutoring has increased student achievement across all subject areas, including reading, math, and science (Roscoe & Chi, 2007).

Research indicates that learning for both tutors and tutees happens across formats, demographics, and domains (Roscoe & Chi, 2007). However, the research on tutoring is relatively weak (Maxwell, 1990; Roscoe & Chi, 2007). Maxwell (1990) argues the literature is inconclusive in terms of the impact tutoring has on the success of the weakest students. Yet, Maxwell (1990) also notes that students who are tutored remain enrolled in college longer.

One consistent theme in the literature is the importance of high-quality training of peer tutors (Boylan & Saxon, 2005; Kozeracki, 2002; Maxwell, 1990). Robinson et al. (2005) suggest from their review of the literature that the pool of tutors should not be limited to high-ability students because of the benefits tutors themselves receive. Another study found the ability level of the tutor did not affect their tutees' average academic outcomes (Cohen, Kulik, & Kulik, 1982). Cohen et al. (1982) also suggest creating opportunities for students to serve in both the tutor and tutee roles. Gattis (2003) stresses the importance of the tutor creating a relaxed atmosphere during the tutoring session and encourages tutors to provide students with positive feedback. Tutors also need to be evaluated regularly by students and program administrators (Maxwell, 1990).

Early Warning Systems. The WWISR Survey (Habley et al., 2010) results indicate early warning systems are found at 74% of public, 78% of private, and 68% of two-year institutions. The mean of institutional officials' ratings of early warning systems' contributions to student retention by institution type were: public (3.53), private (3.77), and two-year institutions (3.59). These systems were selected in the top three learning assistance practices for their effectiveness in retaining students by the four-year private and community college institutions. Early warning systems seek to identify students at-risk for dropping out or for poor academic performance early in the term so that appropriate interventions can help the student recover early enough to raise their grades. Once students in academic jeopardy have been identified, a variety of institutional responses occur, yet these interventions vary by institution and program. In some programs, academic advisors, student affairs administrators, or even residence life/housing administrators are charged with following up individually with students. The general goal is to raise their awareness of and participation in campus resources such as tutoring, Supplemental Instruction, and so forth. For example, at Hanover College in Indiana, an early-alert team works together to help students stay "engaged and enrolled" (Wasley, 2007). Members of the early alert team include the registrar, associate dean of students, dean of admissions, director of the learning center, and a faculty member. The team works behind the scenes to encourage advisors, faculty, and staff members to reach out to students who have been identified as struggling personally or academically (Wasley, 2007).

"The challenge in establishing any early warning system is to discover a reliable set of predictors" (Beck & Davidson, 2001, p. 710). Beck and Davidson (2001) note a variety of predictors have been utilized by colleges, including measures of intellectual skills or aptitudes (GPA, class rank, ACT or SAT scores), nonintellectual factors (for example, personality constructs and demographic indexes), and specialized early warning indexes, such as the Survey of Academic Orientations (Davidson, Beck, & Silver, 1999). Cuseo (n.d.2) listed the following factors as indicators a student may be at risk for failure or withdrawal:

> (a) poor academic performance in more than one class, (b) delay or failure to pre-register for next-term classes; (c) delay or failure to renew housing agreements; (d) delay or failure to reapply for financial aid or work-study, (e) failure to declare a major by the end of their sophomore year, or (f) request for copies of transcripts before eligibility to graduate. (p. 1)

Early warning systems typically have online or other reporting systems allowing faculty members and other campus community members to submit names of students they are concerned about, usually targeting the first six weeks of class. Poor grades on midterm grade reports are another mechanism that colleges use to compile lists of students in academic jeopardy (Cuseo, n.d.2). There does not appear to be much research on the effectiveness of early alert programs, although it would be difficult to measure the effectiveness of such programs given the diversity of the interventions and the responses to students identified as being in academic jeopardy.

Remaining Thirteen Learning Assistance Initiatives

Because the next set of Learning Assistance Practices were either not as frequently found at survey institutions or were not perceived to be as effective, this section will first present the data in Table 13.2 and then provide a brief overview of the practice. Note that although comprehensive learning assistance labs had incidence rates and perceived levels of effectiveness similar to the top four learning initiatives, the authors decided that, because of the lack of clarity about the differences between comprehensive, math, writing, reading, and foreign language labs, the discussion about these labs would be combined in this section.

Summer Bridge. Summer bridge programs are designed to help at-risk students make smooth transitions from high school to college by acclimating students to campus life and equipping them with study skills. Pascarella and Terenzini (2005) note that "these programs have somewhat different goals than conventional summer orientation programs and are usually longer (a week or more versus a day or two) and more programmatically focused" (p. 404). Summer bridge programs were most frequently found at public institutions (60%) and least likely to be utilized at private institutions (24%) (Habley et al., 2010).

Table 13.2 Remaining Thirteen Learning Assistance Initiatives from the *WWISR* Survey (Habley et al., 2010).

Learning Assistance Initiative	Four-Year Public			Four-Year Private			Community Colleges		
	Incidence Rate	Mean	% Selected as Among Top 3	Incidence Rate	Mean	% Selected as Among Top 3	Incidence Rate	Mean	% Selected as Among Top 3
Summer Bridge	60%	3.83		24%	3.58		37%	3.66	
Comprehensive learning assistance lab	66%	3.92		58%	3.84		73%	4.12	Yes (14%)
Math lab	78%	3.76		49%	3.55		70%	3.99	
Writing lab	90%	3.72		73%	3.54		70%	4.00	
Reading lab	28%	3.86		23%	3.86		50%	4.14	
Foreign language lab	50%	3.19		26%	2.95		24%	3.68	
Study skills, course, program or center	79%	3.73		65%	3.53		80%	3.75	
Midterm progress reports	63%	3.38		81%	3.60		48%	3.43	
Performance contracts	55%	3.53		54%	3.43		35%	3.54	
Organized study groups	45%	3.52		36%	3.40		28%	3.79	
Service-learning programs	59%	3.14		54%	3.23		45%	3.05	
ESL program	59%	3.11		30%	3.01		63%	3.45	
Online student learning	45%	3.19		25%	3.07		66%	3.43	
Library orientation, workshop, or course	84%	2.92		81%	2.74		81%	3.19	

Pascarella and Terenzini's (2005) review of the research literature indicates that research "findings are generally consistent in suggesting that bridge program participants are more likely than nonparticipants to persist into their second year" (p. 404).

Learning Labs (Comprehensive, Math, Writing, Reading, Foreign Language). The *WWISR Survey* (Habley et al., 2010) included these five different types of learning assistance labs, designed to help students improve their skills in the respective fields. According to the *WWISR Survey* (Habley et al., 2010) survey data, the top three types of labs offered at institutions are writing, math, and comprehensive learning. Arendale et al. (2007) defines learning assistance centers as "a centralized location wherein tutorial and study skills assistance is provided most commonly. The center generally provides support to a wide array of academic disciplines. It may sometimes be focused in one academic area (e.g., mathematics, writing)" (p. 22). However, it is not clear how *WWISR Survey* respondents were defining "learning labs" or how they distinguished between the five different types of labs included in this collapsed grouping of learning labs.

Study Skills Course, Program, or Center. These types of study skills interventions can be found in independent centers or embedded within academic units. The broad nature of this category makes it difficult to draw many conclusions from the *WWISR Survey*, but institutional officials did indicate that at least one of these was present at 80% of two-year, 79% of public, and 65% of private colleges (Habley et al., 2010).

Midterm Progress Reports. In the *WWISR Survey* (Habley et al., 2010), private four-year institutions (81%) were found to use midterm progress reports as a retention tool more often than public four-year institutions (63%) or community college institutions (48%). Midterm progress reports are used to give students feedback on how they are performing in classes. In addition, as noted earlier, early warning systems sometimes use midterm progress reports to help identify students who are experiencing academic difficulty. Cuseo (n.d.2) found potential problems with midterm progress reports, such as faculty who do not calculate or report grades and the fact that lower grades themselves do not help administrators identify causes of poor academic performance.

Performance Contracts. Performance contracts were used by a little over half of the public (55%) and private (54%) institutions, but only 35% of community colleges participating in the *WWISR Survey* (Habley et al., 2010). Some performance contracts are being utilized in classroom settings, but outside of the classroom, institutions generally use them with students in academic peril, such as students readmitted to the institution or those on probation as a condition of their continued enrollment.

Organized Study Groups. Study groups developed in class by faculty members or via outside student service units or learning centers are being used by less than half of the *WWISR Survey* (Habley et al., 2010) institutions: 45% at public institutions, 36% at private institutions, and 28% at community colleges.

Service-Learning Programs. Service-learning programs were established at over half of the public (59%) and private institutions (54%) in the *WWISR Survey* (Habley et al., 2010), while only 45% of community college institutions had them. The perceived effectiveness for these programs was low, ranging from a mean of 3.01 at private institutions to 3.45 at community college institutions. Service-learning programs, however, have many beneficial outcomes beyond retention, as widely discussed in the related scholarly literature.

ESL Programs. Community colleges in the *WWISR Survey* (Habley et al., 2010) rated English as a Second Language (ESL) programs as moderately impactful (3.45). Community colleges (63%) were also more likely to have ESL programs than the four-year public (59%) and private (30%) institutions. The public and private institutions ranked this second to last on ratings of perceived effectiveness of the learning assistance initiatives.

Online Student Learning. In the *WWISR Survey* (Habley et al., 2010), private institutions were the least likely to have online student learning programs (25%), whereas community college institutions were the most likely (66%) to host such programs. This may be an indicator of the multiple time demands that community college students have and thus institutions provide more online course options. It will be interesting to monitor this category as more and more for-profit and nonprofit institutions increase the number of online courses they offer.

Library Orientation, Workshop, or Course. Although approximately 80% of the institutions indicated on the *WWISR Survey* (Habley et al., 2010) that they had library orientations, workshops, or courses, institutional leaders at all levels ranked this as the lowest or second to lowest in contributing to student retention.

Promising New Models for Innovation in Developmental Education

In the previous section we covered the different types of learning support programs and perceived effectiveness. The focus of this section is on specific programs and practices that seem to be leading the pack in terms of innovation and effectiveness. Below we will highlight El Paso Community College and the University of Texas at El Paso's partnership with local high schools, the I-Best program in the state of Washington, and a developmental math program at City Tech in New York City.

El Paso Community College and the University of Texas at El Paso

As mentioned earlier, one of the keys to improving the effectiveness of developmental education efforts requires that colleges and high schools partner together to determine how to ensure that more high school graduates are prepared to meet the demands of college coursework (see Chapter Seven for additional information on preparing students for college). For example, Greene and Foster (2003) found that only about one-third of high school graduates are prepared for college-level work. Knowing that partnerships between high schools and colleges must be established is one thing, but actually creating effective partnerships is a whole different ball game.

El Paso Community College and the University of Texas at El Paso (UTEP) have set up a creative partnership with 12 local school districts to increase the number of high school graduates prepared for college-level work.

> Using the College Board's Accuplacer test, the colleges evaluate high-school students for college readiness in their junior and senior years. Those with low scores can take short intervention tutorials, offered jointly by the high schools and colleges, in reading, writing, and mathematics. (Killough, 2009, para. 9)

Students planning to enroll at El Paso Community College are able to take the institution's placement exams while in high school, and those that do not pass the standards can enroll in a summer class before they matriculate (Gonzalez, 2010).

UTEP is also working on changes to the design of their developmental education courses and first-year experience programs. Given the data indicating that students in developmental education courses are less likely to graduate, UTEP is taking steps to decrease the number of students enrolled in developmental education courses. For example, students who do not pass the math placement exam get a chance to be reexamined after taking a six-hour refresher course during orientation; UTEP found that 56% of such students moved up one class level (Redden, 2008). Students also have the chance to spend time in the computer lab learning math via a free computer program. Those who barely miss the cut-off to take regular English courses are given the option to take the nonremedial English if they agree to take an additional course that uses both in-person and online components.

The state of Texas sees these types of programs as ways to help "fix" developmental education, but the state is also looking at other initiatives, including "providing better curricular training, and hiring more permanent faculty members, rather than adjuncts, to teach remedial courses" (Killough, 2009, para. 15). These institutions are choosing to do something positive instead of wasting time blaming each other for the large number of students who place into developmental education classes. This is a valuable lesson for other colleges and school districts!

The I-BEST Program in the State of Washington

In response to the increasing number of students for whom English is not the primary language at home, the state of Washington's State Board for Community and Technical Colleges created a demo project called Integrated Basic Education Skills Training (I-BEST) (Washington State Board for Community and Technical Colleges [WSBCTC], 2005). This innovative program "pairs English as a second language (ESL)/adult basic education instructors and professional-technical instructors in the classroom to concurrently provide students with literacy education and workforce skills" (WSBCTC, 2005, p. 1). What was different about this approach is that it did not force students to pass ESL courses before they could take workforce training classes. It gave students the opportunity to see from the beginning of their studies the relevance of what they were learning and how they might be able to apply their newly acquired knowledge in the work place. The results of this program are indeed impressive with I-BEST students being "five times more likely to earn college credits and 15 times more likely to complete workforce training than were traditional ESL students during the same amount of time" (WSBCTC, 2005, p. 4).

Developmental Math Program at City Tech in New York

A program at City Tech in New York called self-regulated learning has proven in a randomized controlled trial that students enrolled in a developmental math section using the technique were more likely to pass the entrance exam than students in sections that did not use the self-regulating technique (Glenn, 2010). This technique was developed by Barry J. Zimmerman in response to research focusing on what can go wrong when people try to learn new facts and skills. Among the missteps are that students tend to be overconfident about what they know and fail to take responsibility for their academic performance, instead choosing to blame others or circumstances (Glenn, 2010). A key to the self-regulated learning technique is helping students identify their mistakes by providing frequent quizzes, requiring students to rework at least some of the problems they missed and write down where their thinking strategy went astray soon after the exam so that they do not continue to make the same mistakes in the future (Glenn, 2010). Zimmerman's two main principles are that students need to receive fast and accurate feedback about their performance, and that students must then show that they understand the feedback (Glenn, 2010). Given the success in developmental math, City Tech is now experimenting using this with their developmental reading program and has found "students in developmental-writing sections that used self-regulated learning passed CUNY's writing exam at a rate that was 18 percentage points higher than the rate for City Tech students in the normal sections of the course"

(Glenn, 2010, para. 23). In addition, other institutions in New Jersey, Ohio, and New York have adopted the approach.

Conclusion

Developmental education is a broad field that encompasses both courses for underprepared students and other learning assistance practices that assist all students. In its purest sense, developmental education seeks to promote "the cognitive and affective growth of all postsecondary learners, at all levels of the learning continuum" (Arendale et al., 2007, p. 18). The research on developmental education is mixed as to the impact it has on student persistence and success (Calcagno & Long, 2008); therefore, the opportunities for researchers to further delve into this topic are enormous. Some intriguing programmatic interventions were highlighted that help instill confidence that the field of developmental education will continue to innovate and reinvent itself.

14

ACADEMIC ADVISING

Habley (1992) has described academic advising as the "hub of the wheel" in higher education, meaning that advisors are ideally positioned as a central home on campus where students can learn about, and be referred to, the many resources available on campus. Academic advising involves an institutional representative (faculty or non-faculty) who builds relationships with students to help them interpret their educational experiences, become engaged at the institution through involvement in curricular and cocurricular opportunities, and devise an individualized plan for fulfilling their life and career goals. This chapter will provide a brief overview of the history of academic advising before delving into the definitions, theories, and organizational models of advising. We will also be examining the link between academic advising and student retention from the literature, discuss best practices in academic advising, as well as providing an overview of 15 academic advising interventions that were included in the ACT's *What Works in Student Retention* (WWISR) Survey (Habley, McClanahan, Valiga, & Burkum, 2010).

History of Academic Advising

Looking at the historical roots of academic advising is important because "an appreciation of the past is an important key to moving academic advising through the next millennium" (Gillispie, 2003, para. 8). There is much to be learned from the past. Frost (2000) divides the history of academic advising into three distinct eras: advising before it was a defined activity (1636 to 1869), advising when it was a defined activity but not well examined (1870 to 1970), and advising when it was a defined and examined activity (1970 to present). Early colonial colleges had fairly straightforward and structured curricula. "The president of the college, and later the faculty, were responsible for advising students regarding their extracurricular activities, their moral life, and intellectual habits. They acted in loco parentis" (Cook, 1999). In the late 1820s, Kenyon College was the first institution to have a formal advising program where faculty members served as student advisors (Cook, 1999).

During the second era of advising (1870 to 1970), as the number of students and amount of knowledge increased, schools began allowing students to take elective courses, which necessitated a way for students to make knowledgeable choices about the most appropriate elective courses (Frost, 2000). Key events during the time period included appointment of the first dean charged with taking care of student discipline issues in 1870, establishment of the first system of faculty advising established at Johns Hopkins in 1876/1877, the first appointment of a chief of faculty advisors at Johns Hopkins in 1889, and the first dean of women being appointed at the University of Chicago in 1892 (Cook, 1999). The twentieth century saw campus psychologists, chaplains, and even upper-division students taking on the role of advisor. The end of World War II marked the return of thousands of veterans, many of whom took advantage of the opportunity to have their college degrees paid for via the G.I. Bill (Frost, 2000). This influx of students into the system meant institutions had to increase student services, including academic advising, to meet the needs of an increasingly diverse student population both inside and outside the classroom.

The third era of advising began in the 1970s and the beginning of this era was marked by three major events. The first event was the Carnegie Commission on Higher Education's recommendation that "increased emphasis should be placed on advising as an important aspect of higher education" (Cook, 1999). The second was a massive surge in enrollment at community colleges and of new student populations, such as first-generation and low-income students entering higher education. These students needed advisors to help them adjust to college and complete their degrees. Third, two seminal articles penned by Crookston (1972) and O'Banion (1972) appeared in the scholarly literature on the topic of academic advising. In 1986, the first Council for the Advancement Standards (CAS) were established for academic advising. The first conference on academic advising was held in 1977 which eventually led to the establishment of the National Academic Advising Association (NACADA) in 1979 (Cook, 1999).

Defining Academic Advising

As mentioned, in 1972 two separate articles by Crookston and O'Banion discussed the importance of a holistic approach to academic advising. The Crookston (1972) article was the first to make the connection between similarities in functions between advising and teaching. As with teaching, Crookston (1972) points out both the student and the advisor learn and develop in advising sessions. Crookston (1972) also was the first to differentiate between prescriptive and developmental advising relationships. He said prescriptive relationships are similar to a doctor and patient where the patient presents an issue and the doctor makes the diagnosis and prescribes a treatment that the patient must follow. He was quick to point out there are many downfalls to this approach, including that the student is uninvolved in the process and thus not likely to follow through on the advice given; in addition the approach provides the student with a scapegoat, the advisor, if things do not turn out as planned. In contrast to prescriptive advising, developmental advising requires both the advisor and student to actively participate in the conversation and the design of a plan the student will ultimately undertake. O'Banion's article (1972) focused on the five different dimensions of advising he also purported to be a five-step process of academic advising: "(1) exploration of life goals, (2) exploration of vocational goals, (3) program choice, (4) course choice, and (5) scheduling courses" (p. 10). These two articles represent the beginning of redefining academic advising and offer a critical examination of how best to advise students.

The term *developmental advising,* to which Crookston (1972) referred in his article, has been defined and interpreted in multiple ways. Winston, Ender, and Miller (1982) defined developmental academic advising as "a systematic process based on close student-advisor relationship intended to aid students in achieving educational, career, and personal goals through the utilization of the full range of institutional community resources" (p. 8). Chickering (1994) said:

> The fundamental purpose of academic advising is to help students become effective agents for their own lifelong learning and personal development. Our relationships with students, the questions we raise, the perspectives we share, the resources we suggest, the short-term decisions and long-range plans we help them think through all should aim to increase their capacity to take charge of their own existence. (p. 50)

These are just two of more than two dozen or more definitions of academic and/or developmental advising. Even the National Academic Advising Association (NACADA) has struggled with how best to define academic advising. Instead of attempting to define academic advising in one sentence, NACADA's website refers to three documents "that champion the educational role of academic advising in a diverse world": NACADA's Concept of Academic Advising, NACADA's Statement of Core Values, and the Council for the Advancement of Standards (CAS) in Higher Education: Standards and Guidelines for Academic Advising (NACADA, 2006, para. 1). The NACADA Concept of Academic Advising document states there are three components of academic advising: "curriculum (what advising deals with), pedagogy (how advising does what it does), and student learning outcomes (the result of academic advising)" (para. 7).

There are pros and cons to not having an official definition of academic advising. One of the advantages of not having an agreed-upon, clear definition of academic advising is that it allows institutions to define academic advising for themselves within the culture of their respective institutions. However, the major disadvantage is there is not a definition that advisors can utilize when they are explaining their work to students, faculty, administrators, and the public. In the absence of an agreed-upon definition, people create their own definitions. Unfortunately, many faculty, students, and even professional advisors primarily define academic advising as a registration process. Harkening back to O'Banion's definition (1972), advising does involve registering for students for class, but it also involves so much more, including helping students articulate their life and career goals, and selecting a major and courses that will help them achieve those goals.

Major Advising Theories

Since 1999, there have been a number of articles that have sought to move advising theory beyond the developmental advising approach. Hemwall and Trachte (1999) wrote an article that expressed concerns about the diverse meanings of the phrase "developmental academic advising." They were concerned that misunderstandings could occur in the field when people were using the term to mean one thing when their colleagues were interpreting the term quite differently. They advocated in that article the idea of "praxis" might be a better way to think about advising. On a simple level, praxis involves "critical self-reflection" to help students become "citizens of the world" (Hemwall & Trachte, 1999, p. 8). Advisors using a praxis approach would "engage their advisees in dialogue about the purpose and meaning of course requirements. They should talk with advisees about the educational goals, and related values, of the curriculum" (Hemwall & Trachte, 1999, p. 8). In a subsequent article, Hemwall and Trachte (2003) slightly refocus their thoughts on advising by advocating advisors adopt a "learning paradigm" where the focus is on creating conditions to magnify student learning. They recommend that advisors help students develop an understanding of the mission of the college in addition to developing lower-level and higher-level thinking skills. Similarly, advisors need to understand how people learn and how to help students build on their past knowledge to actively incorporate and process new knowledge. In a later article, Hemwall and Trachte (2005) further fleshed out the ideas about what information both students and faculty need to learn in order to create learning partnerships.

Subsequent to Hemwall and Trachte's 1999 article, there have been a number of other articles proposing alternative theoretical frameworks beyond developmental academic advising (Hagen & Jordan, 2008). Lowenstein (2000, 2005) has argued for a shift from the counselor-based traditions of developmental advising to a learning-centered paradigm that more closely models teaching/learning frameworks. Christman (2005) and Hagen (1994) have put forward the concept of narrative advising where the focus is on encouraging students to create new stories about themselves and their futures. Other theories or metaphors that have been published include strengths-based advising (Schreiner & Anderson, 2005), academic advising as friendship (Rawlins & Rawlins, 2005), Socratic advising (Hagen, 1994; Kuhtmann, 2005); and advising as educating (Melander, 2005).

Another advising delivery framework that has become increasing popular is Appreciative Advising (Bloom, Hutson, & He, 2008). Originating out of the organizational development theory of Appreciative Inquiry (Bloom & Martin, 2002), this framework also draws upon brief therapy counseling theory, positive psychology constructs, and motivation theory, to help guide advisors through six phases (disarm, discover, dream, design, deliver, and don't settle) to optimize their interactions with students. "Appreciative Advising is the intentional collaborative practice of asking positive, open-ended questions that help students optimize their educational experiences and achieve their dreams, goals, and potentials" (Bloom, Hutson, & He, 2010, para. 2).

In summary, the past twelve years have seen the introduction of a number of advising-related theories, sparking much discussion in the field of advising. Given the diversity of higher education institutions, students, and advisors, having a smorgasbord of advising theories to select from is a good thing for the profession at this point. Further research will need to be conducted to see which of these approaches are most effective in terms of student retention and satisfaction.

Organizational Delivery Models

Moving beyond advising theories, the focus of this section is on the seven organizational models of academic advising: faculty-only (faculty members do all the advising); satellite (advising is handled by different academic units); self-contained (advising is done within an advising center); supplementary (an advising office supports the work of faculty advisors); split (students move from professional to faculty advisors after selecting a major); dual (students have two advisors); and total intake (all initial advising for new students is handled through a central office and later students are assigned to an academic unit) (Habley, 1983, 2004b; King, M. C., 2008). Later, Pardee (2000) classified the models into three categories: decentralized, centralized, and shared models. As the name indicates, decentralized models are spread across campus in individual departments and advising is conducted by faculty or non-faculty advisors. The two models in this category are the faculty-only model (25% of institutions use this model) and the satellite model (7%). Centralized systems typically have a central advising office that all students come to for advising services. The Self-Contained model is the lone centralized system and it is used at 14% of institutions, according to the latest ACT survey on advising (Habley, 2004b, p. 25). There are four shared models: Supplementary (17%), Split (27%), Dual (5%), and Total Intake (6%) (King, M. C., 2008). In shared models, advising is split between centralized and decentralized advising systems.

Academic advising is "performed by many individuals in various roles at institutions of higher education" (Self, 2008, p. 267). Faculty members were the original advisors in higher education in the United States, but now a number of non-faculty staff also perform this function. There are pros and cons of using faculty versus non-faculty advisors, but both have the potential to positively affect the students they interact with on a daily basis. Non-faculty advisors are often referred to as professional advisors. Self (2008) defines professional advisors as "individuals who have been hired to focus primarily on academic advising activities that promote the academic success of students, with additional attention to general student development at the institution" (pp. 267–268). Community colleges often have professional counselors deliver advising as well as other counseling services such as mental health and career counseling (Self, 2008). Some institutions hire graduate students and peer undergraduate students to deliver specific or overall advising services. Other members of advising delivery teams are support staff members, including office managers, receptionists, secretaries, clerical staff, and technical staff (Self, 2008). Each member of the advising team has the potential to play an important role in the lives of the students the office serves.

Link Between Academic Advising and Retention

McGillin (2010) states, "The field of academic advising has long been searching for an intellectual voice" (p. 3). Although this section makes it clear that there is research available that demonstrates the impact that academic advising has on retention and other outcomes, there is ample room for scholarly inquiry into the effectiveness and outcomes of academic advising efforts. According to Pascarella and Terenzini (2005), "Research consistently indicates that academic advising can play a role in students' decisions to persist and in their chances of graduating" (p. 404). As evidence to that claim, Pascarella and Terenzini (2005) cite a number of single-institution studies that found that students who had been advised were retained at a higher rate than those in control groups (Seidman, 1991; Beil & Shope, 1990; Elliott & Healy, 2001; Metzner, 1989; Peterson, Wagner, & Lamb, 2001; B. L. Smith, 1993; Steele, Kennedy, & Gordon, 1993; Trippi & Cheatham, 1991; Young, Backer, & Rogers, 1989). However, Pascarella and Terenzini (2005) also note that it is unclear in the research whether advising has a direct or indirect impact on students.

Similarly, Cuseo (n.d.1) found that although there is little evidence to show that advising directly affects student persistence, there are findings to indicate it has a positive impact on several variables. Those variables are "strongly correlated with student persistence, namely: (1) student satisfaction with the college experience, (2) effective educational and career and decision making, (3) student utilization of campus support services, (4) student-faculty contact outside the classroom, and (5) student mentoring" (Cuseo, p. 1). In addition, it is intuitive that advising has an indirect effect based on the fact that student interaction with a concerned representative of the institution is a primary indicator of student retention (Pascarella & Terenzini, 2005).

The 2005 annual National Survey of Student Engagement (NSSE) found 88% of freshmen utilized advising services (Kuh, 2008). Based on NSSE data, Kuh (2008) concluded, "Students who met with their advisor more frequently were more satisfied with advising and also were generally more satisfied with their institution" (p. 71). In addition, students who rated their advising experiences at the level of good or better were also more likely to: interact with faculty, have a positive perception of the overall support level at the institution, and get more out of college in most areas (Kuh, 2008). Yet, results of the 2007 NSSE survey found that although 80% of students were happy with the accuracy of the information they received from advisors, 40% indicated that their advisor had not told them about support services available to them on campus (Kuh, 2008). It is clear that good academic advising has the potential to help students make the most of their experiences both inside and outside the classroom, but that potential is not consistently met.

Results from the WWISR Survey

Because academic advising consistently surfaces as a major factor in student success, ACT's *What Works in Student Retention* (WWISR) Survey (Habley et al., 2010) asked senior campus administrators about the availability of 15 different academic advising–related topics and their perceived contribution to retention at their respective institutions.

Top Five Advising Related Topics

In Table 14.1, data for the top five advising-related interventions are presented in the left-hand column. For each topic, results from the *2010 WWISR Survey* (Habley et al., 2010) are shared for four-year public, four-year private, and community colleges. Specifically, for each type of institution, information is shared about what percentage (incidence rate) of survey respondents mentioned their institution provided this type of support, the mean score in terms of survey respondents' perception of the level of contribution the support activity made to campus retention (5 = a major contribution and 1 = little or no contribution). Given the combination of the incidence rate and the high perceived level of contribution to retention across

Table 14.1 Top Five Advising-Related Practices.

Advising-Related Topics	Four-Year Public			Four-Year Private			Community Colleges		
	Incidence Rate	Mean	% Among Top 3	Incidence Rate	Mean	% Among Top 3	Incidence Rate	Mean	% Among Top 3
Training for faculty advisors	74%	3.46		74%	3.15		70%	3.62	Yes (10%)
Training for non-faculty	74%	3.70		46%	3.64		66%	3.76	
Advising interventions with selected student populations	88%	3.93	Yes (14%)	70%	3.93	Yes (13%)	73%	3.91	
Increased number of advisors	38%	3.98		31%	3.87		36%	4.01	
Academic advising center	74%	3.80	Yes (11%)	39%	3.93		64%	3.87	Yes (12%)

institution types, these interventions will be discussed in detail before later presenting a brief overview of the remaining 10 advising practices.

Training for Faculty and Non-Faculty Advisors

We have collapsed together the training for faculty and non-faculty advisors due to the overlap in terms of the best practices we will present later in this section. ACT's Sixth National Survey of Academic Advising (Habley, 2004b) provides important insights into what and how faculty and professional staff advisors are being trained. Across institutional types, only 32% of all academic units mandated that faculty advisors be trained, whereas 60% offered some type of training. This leaves over a quarter of institutions not offering or mandating any type of advisor training for faculty. Similar data were not collected for professional staff advisors. Since graduate-level classes on academic advising are scarce, many faculty members are receiving little to no training on how to be effective advisors.

When faculty advisors do receive training on academic advising, it is most frequently delivered as individualized training (46%), single workshop (38%), or a series of short workshops throughout the year (30%) (Habley, 2004b). In terms of training professional advisors who work in advising centers, Habley's report on the *Sixth Survey of Academic Advising* (2004b) found that across institution types the most frequent type is individualized training (52%), series of short workshops throughout the year (35%), and a single workshop of one day or less (15%). As for the content of training, Habley (1992) first identified the three elements that should constitute good academic advising training: conceptual, informational, and relational. Conceptual components include defining academic advising, theories of academic advising, and student development theories. Informational items include specific information about institutional degree and policy requirements, resources, and procedures (Brown, 2008). Relational training involves teaching people sound communication and interpersonal skills and behaviors that advisors can adopt to help increase the effectiveness of advising appointments with students. Habley (2004b) found that relational topics are the least likely component to be included in training for both faculty and professional advisors.

Best practices in advisor training from Brown (2008) and Davis (2003) include:

1. Form a coordinating committee with appropriate representation of key constituents

2. Do a needs assessment to determine the needs of advisors that will be attending

3. Gather key data about students on your campus and advising assessment results to help guide decisions about what topics will be covered in the training

4. Be sure to include conceptual, informational, and relational components in the training

5. Proactively secure the support of key administrators, faculty, and staff for the training

6. Publicize the event in a variety of ways

7. When training faculty advisors, be sure to highlight the congruencies between their work as teachers and their work as advisors

8. Incorporate active learning exercises and techniques into the training

9. Take a positive approach to the training and those being trained

10. Provide participants the opportunity to assess the effectiveness of the training

11. Follow up with participants afterwards, letting them know about new policies and other items that will impact their advising of students

What is missing from the research literature are any studies that directly link the training of faculty or professional advisors to increased student retention.

Advising Interventions with Selected Student Populations

The increased diversity of today's college students has prompted the establishment of specific advising interventions to meet the perceived unique needs of each population. Harding (2008) and Clark and Kalionzes (2008) identify a variety of student groups that have had advising interventions designed to meet their needs: students with disabilities; adult learners; student athletes; first-generation students; high-ability students; lesbian, gay, bisexual, and transgender (LGBT) students; international students; and students of color (including, but not limited to, black, Hispanic, Asian/Pacific Islander, Native American, biracial, and multiracial).

Because the advising interventions designed for these diverse student populations are multifaceted and extensive, space limitations make discussing these initiatives in detail difficult. However, Clark and Kalionzes' (2008) work offers best practices that can help guide advisors working with members of these specific subpopulations:

1. Understand that students have experienced a wide range of life events that have shaped who they are
2. Learn about students' family and the role family plays in their lives
3. Encourage students to participate in mentoring programs
4. Quickly build trust with students
5. Educate themselves about various student populations and different cultures
6. Develop their multicultural competencies

7. Try to meet students on their own "turf" by informally inter-
acting with them at campus events, club meetings, and coffee shops

Increased Number of Advisors

Between 1998 and 2003, for all institutional types, the mean
number of advisees assigned to individual faculty advisors
increased from 26.4 to 29.2, and the mean number of contacts
between faculty advisors and advisees decreased from 4.0 to 2.7
(Habley, 2004b, p. 35). With advising loads increasing for faculty
advisors, it is not surprising that a concomitant decrease in the
number of interactions would occur. Habley (2004b) also found
that students at four-year public institutions had less frequent
interactions with their faculty advisor than at four-year private
and two-year public schools. Similarly, mean advising loads were
highest at four-year public institutions (38.2) and two-year public institutions (27.3), and lowest at four-year privates (20.2). In
advising centers, full-time advisors had average assigned advising loads of 281.7 students at all institution types, representing a
14.6 average student load increase from 1998. The mean number
of contacts between advisors and advisees each academic term
has remained constant at 2.7 (Habley, 2004b).

Habley (2004a) found that there is no research available
to confirm what an ideal advising load is nor are many in the
advising profession willing to publicly state a definitive ideal
load, but he did assert that "off the record" advising experts generally feel that a 300:1 load for full-time advisors and 20:1 load
for faculty advisors is a worthy target.

Academic Advising Center

According to ACT's *Sixth Survey of Academic Advising* (Habley,
2004b), the number of academic advising centers has increased
dramatically in the past thirty years. The percentage of institutions that reported having an academic advising center increased

from 14% in 1979 to 73% in 2003 (Habley, 2004b). Public two-year (82%) and four-year institutions (86%) are more likely than private two-year (55%) and four-year (58%) institutions to host advising centers. Advising centers are most likely to be staffed by full-time professional advisors (64%) with faculty advisors (20%) a distant second (Habley, 2004). Table 14.2 reports on the remaining 10 advising practices from the *What Works in Student Retention (WWISR) 2010 Survey* (Habley et al., 2010) data on incidence rate and mean rating of effectiveness by survey respondents.

Advising Centers Integrated with Career Planning

Community colleges (49%) appear to be at the forefront of combining career and advising services, ahead of four-year public institutions (34%) and four-year private institutions (29%) (Habley et al., 2010). Community colleges are likely leading the way because these institutions typically have self-contained advising centers that are often staffed with counselors who have the skills to deliver both academic and career advice. Survey respondents felt the integration of academic and career advising produced better than moderate contributions to retention (average mean of 3.6 across institution types). This integration seems to be a logical one because students do not typically make decisions about their majors and their careers in isolation.

Gordon (2006) points out, "The proliferation of academic disciplines, the complexity of the work world, and the unfailing perception on the part of students that college is preparation for a career, require new thinking about how academic and career advising are intertwined" (p. 3). Although a NACADA Survey (2007) found that 74% of advisors agreed or strongly agreed that career advising was an important part of their role as advisors, these results are tempered by the fact that the survey had a 22% response rate. "When advisors have a clear definition of career advising, understand the similarities and differences between

Table 14.2 Incidence and Mean Ratings of 10 Remaining Advising Practices.

Advising Practices	Four-Year Public		Four-Year Private		Community Colleges	
	Incidence Rate	Mean	Incidence Rate	Mean	Incidence Rate	Mean
Center(s) that integrate advising with career planning	34%	3.56	29%	2.6	49%	3.63
Integration of advising with first-year transition programs	60%	3.98	51%	3.83	36%	3.87
Assessment of faculty advisors	26%	2.93	33%	2.91	26%	3.01
Assessment of non-faculty advisors	49%	3.16	23%	3.13	37%	3.13
Application of technology to advising	72%	3.30	57%	2.99	71%	3.29
Recognition/rewards for faculty advisors	38%	2.78	17%	2.72	13%	2.65
Recognition/reward for non-faculty	34%	2.85	12%	2.88	12%	2.61
Specified student learning outcomes (syllabus) for advising	31%	3.09	26%	3.22	32%	3.29
Online advising system	34%	3.39	28%	3.03	41%	3.22
Campuswide assessment of advising	33%	3.08	24%	3.03	25%	3.15

academic and career advising, obtain additional resources and competencies, and work collaboratively with others on campus, they can move toward this integration with confidence" (McCalla-Wriggins, 2009, para. 22). As many institutions establish "one-stop shopping" centers for student services on their campuses that conveniently place all such services under one roof or in one area, career and academic advising centers are often physically located near each other or combined together in an academic/career advising center.

Integration of Advising with First-Year Programs

The WWISR (Habley et al., 2010) Survey found that over half of four-year public (60%) and private (51%) institutions integrate advising into first-year transition programs, whereas only 36% of community colleges use this strategy. The survey results show institutions perceive this strategy to be an effective one (averaging 3.9 on a 5.0 scale of perceived effectiveness). Because of the impact of advising on student retention and the importance of first-year programs, academic advisors have the potential to play an important role in first-year programs. Given that 88% of first-year students meet with their advisors (Kuh, 2008), these interactions are good opportunities for advisors to encourage students to engage in programs and activities aimed at helping first-year students successfully transition to college. In addition, academic advisors sometimes teach or coteach first-year seminar classes or are invited to present on advising-related topics. Some advisors teaching these courses are sometimes officially assigned their students in the course as advisees for the first year, and others serve as informal advisors (King, N. S., 2008). See Chapter Fifteen for more details on first-year transition programs.

Assessment of Faculty and Non-Faculty Advisors

The WWISR Survey (Habley et al., 2010) indicates that four-year public institutions (49%) are most likely to assess their non-faculty advisors than four-year private (33%) and community colleges (26%). Institutions tend to assess their faculty advisors at about the same rate (26–33%) across institution types. Institutions feel these assessment efforts make a moderate contribution to retention efforts.

Cuseo (2008) stated that "Effective assessment serves multiple purposes, measures multiple outcomes, draws from multiple data sources, and uses multiple methods of measurement" (p. 370). Because these multiple assessment measures are typically used with both faculty and non-faculty advisors, we have collapsed these two separate measures from the WWISR Survey (Habley et al., 2010) into one category. Cuseo (2008) described methods for assessing the effectiveness of advisors: student evaluations, pre- and post-assessment tactics, analysis of student behavioral records, and self, peer, and supervisor assessment.

Application of Technology to Advising

Institutions are increasingly trying to leverage technology to enhance the effectiveness of advising services delivery to take care of some of the more mundane, scheduling aspects of advising, so that advisors have more time to spend getting to know and inspire their students (Kramer & Childs, 1996). Technology being utilized at various institutions includes: degree audit software; electronic educational records; course registration systems; websites to recruit and retain students and share policy/programmatic information; and e-mail, listservs, cell phone texting, video calls, and instant messaging to communicate with students (Leonard, 2008). Given the rapid pace with which technology changes, the successful utilization of technology is potentially an expensive proposition and a moving target. Yet, more than half of the WWISR 2010 Survey institutions are utilizing technology to enhance advising, with four-year public institutions (72%) and community colleges (71%) using it more frequently than four-year private institutions (57%). Institutions participating in the 2010 WWISR Survey (Habley, et al.) found that technology use moderately contributed to student retention.

With increasing numbers of students taking online classes that do not require them to set foot on campus, many advising offices are offering a variety of online advising options. This can entail conducting advising sessions over e-mail, instant messaging, video call systems like Skype, or via class management systems like Blackboard. In addition, some advisors are using Web 2.0 technologies such as blogs, social networking sites such as Facebook, Wikis, and podcasts/webcasts to communicate important information to students.

Recognition/Rewards for Faculty and Non-Faculty Advisors

Recognition and reward programs for faculty advisors are most frequently found at four-year public institutions (38%), whereas only 17% of four-year private and 13% of community colleges offer such programs. Similarly, non-faculty advisors are rewarded and recognized at 34% of four-year public institutions and at only 12% of private four-year and community colleges. The paucity of reward and recognition programs for both faculty and non-faculty advisors may be because senior administrators at WWISR survey institutions feel that these efforts make less than a moderate contribution to student retention.

Drake (2008) cites the results of a survey on rewards and recognition of advising that was distributed to 8,769 NACADA members and had 1,969 respondents. Survey results found that the most frequent reward/recognition strategies for professional advisors were: professional support (40%), none (29%), merit (24%), an annual awards event (24%), and cash awards (20%) (p. 404). Professional advisors ranked the following reward/recognition strategies as most important to them personally: professional support, merit, cash award, secretarial support, and thank-you letters. The strategies being most often utilized to reward/recognize faculty advisors include: none (30%), considerations for promotion and tenure (24%), thank-you letters

(21%), cash awards (20%), annual awards event (19%), and a plaque or trophy (18%) (Drake, 2008, p. 405). Faculty advisors ranked the following rewards/recognition strategies as most important to them personally: professional support, consideration for promotion and tenure, merit, cash award, secretarial support, and thank-you letters.

When NACADA survey respondents were asked what change they would make to the reward and recognition program at their respective institutions, the themes that emerged included funding for professional development opportunities, constructing a career ladder for professional advisors, having administrators value and appreciate the work of advisors, and garnering increased respect from advisees (Drake, 2008). The survey also asked which reward/recognition strategies worked well at their place of employment. Select responses included: vacation, flex time, comp time, recognizing advisors at graduation, gift certificates, and positive reinforcement (Drake, 2008).

The Advising Syllabus—Specifying Student Learning Outcomes

The National Academic Advising Association's (NACADA) guiding slogan is "Advising Is Teaching" (Appleby, 2008). One way that both advisors and students can understand there is indeed a link between advising and teaching is for advisors to give students an advising syllabus. "In essence, an advising syllabus is a tool which allows individual advisors or offices to outline the advising relationship and experience for their advisees" (Trabant, 2006, para. 2). As with course syllabi, advising syllabi typically include: advisor contact information, the unit's definition of advising and the advising mission statement, expectations of advisors and students, outcomes of advising, advising resources, and a list of important dates (Trabant, 2006; Appleby, 2008). Sample academic advising syllabi are available online at the NACADA's Academic Advising Clearinghouse: http://www.nacada.ksu.edu/Clearinghouse/Links/syllabi.htm. WWISR Survey data indicates that 26–31% of institutions are utilizing advising syllabi and they are perceived as making a moderate contribution to retention (Habley et al., 2010).

Online Advising System

Online advising systems are typically focused on giving students an online method for registering for classes. These systems are either "home grown" by IT professionals at individual institutions or they are commercially available products such as Banner or Peoplesoft. Although well over half of institutions (ranging from 57% to 72%) indicated they were actively trying to use technology to deliver advising services, only about half as many institutions indicated that they were using an online advising system (ranging from 28% to 41%). Part of the reason for this may be survey responders were uncertain about what was meant by "online advising systems."

Campuswide Assessment of Advising

Similar to the percentage of institutions that assessed faculty advisors on the WWISR Survey (Habley et al., 2010), between 24 and 33% of institutions indicate that they perform campuswide assessments of advising. The contribution of these efforts is perceived by survey recipients as making moderate contributions to student retention.

The Council for the Advancement of Standards has developed Guidelines for Academic Advising which can be used to assess the effectiveness of advising efforts across campus. The guidelines provide a set of outcomes that institutions can use to self-assess or pass on to outside consultants to use to determine the strengths and areas for improvement needed in advising-related services. Other campuswide assessment efforts include student and graduate satisfaction surveys that often include items related to academic advising. As with the assessment of faculty and non-faculty advisors, the key to effective institution-wide assessment efforts is to use multiple assessment methodologies. Troxel (2008) states, "Program assessment is not optional. . . Educators have a professional, ethical obligation to determine, through the systematic gathering and analysis of evidence, whether pedagogical interventions improved student learning and development in the ways for which the program was intended" (p. 386).

Best Practices

Although in the previous section we shared some best practices from the literature on specific advising initiatives, the focus of this section will be on sharing overall best practices from three researchers: Kuh (2008), Light (2003), and Cuseo (n.d.1). Kuh (2008) used survey data from the National Survey on Student Engagement (NSSE) to extrapolate five principles related to academic advising from schools with better-than-predicted graduation rates and NSSE scores based on entering student demographics and institutional characteristics (see Chapter Six for further details on these institutions, known as DEEP schools). First, schools need to adopt a "talent-development philosophy" meaning "advisors, faculty members and others subscribe to the belief that students can learn anything the institution teaches, provided the right conditions are established, including optimal portions of challenge and support" (Kuh, 2008, p. 76). Advisors play an important role in this talent-development philosophy; Kuh (2008) states that advisors need to believe passionately in the potential of their students to succeed, know the learning styles and demographics of the students they serve, and have high, but attainable, standards for students, and do everything within their power to help students achieve those standards.

Kuh's second principle (2008) is that, given today's diverse student bodies, advising needs to be a "tag team activity." This goes back to Habley's (1992) concept of advisors as the "hub of the wheel" where advisors refer students as appropriate to campus resources and help other campus units meet the needs of the students they serve. Kuh's third principle (2008) is that advisors need to work to help students be prepared for the inevitable roadblocks and disappointments they will face in pursuit of their educations. Helping students understand and navigate the culture of individual institutions is vital.

The fourth principle involves reminding advisors that each interaction they have with students has the potential to be meaningful and to have a positive impact on students' lives (Kuh, 2008). One way that advisors can accomplish this is to encourage students to become involved in cocurricular activities to enhance the learning they are acquiring inside the classroom. Finally, Kuh (2008) encourages advisors to adopt an "improvement-oriented ethos." In other words, advisors have the opportunity to serve as positive role models in terms of always striving to become better at their jobs and serving their students.

Light (2003) bases his recommendations for improving advising on a qualitative study he conducted involving interviews with 1,600 undergraduate students about their perceptions of their undergraduate experience. He found "Good advising may be the single most underestimated characteristic of a successful college experience" (Light, 2003, para. 1). Similar to Kuh's advice (2008), Light (2003) encourages advisors to persuade students to become involved in out-of-class opportunities and to be proactive about building relationships with a variety of constituents. Second, Light (2003) advocates that advisors help students select classes wisely by having them select at least one seminar-size course each semester, particularly during their freshmen and sophomore years. Also, he recommends helping students avoid the "get the requirements out of the way" approach to class selection.

Finally, Cuseo (n.d.1), after examining the literature on advising and the impact it can have on retention, shared seven principles for improving the quality of academic advising. Those principles are:

1. Providing significant incentives and rewards for advisors
2. Institutional commitment to orienting, training, and developing advising talent
3. Regular assessment and evaluation of advising services
4. Ensuring manageable advisor loads that maximize contact time with students
5. Creating incentives for students to meet with advisors
6. Ensuring the most effective advisors work with first-year students
7. Including advising effectiveness in the criteria for selection of new faculty members

Promising New Models for Innovation in Academic Advising

Now that we have shared some of the best practices in academic advising, we will showcase some advising-related programs that are living out many of these best practices. The programs we will highlight include the use of Appreciative Advising at the Student Academic Services Office at the University of North Carolina at Greensboro (UNCG) and the integration of advising with first-year seminar courses at Wheaton College.

UNCG

The Student Academic Services Office at UNCG has infused Appreciative Advising throughout the advising, teaching, and learning services it offers for first-year students, students on probation and/or readmitted to the institution, and for internal transfer pre-nursing majors. In addition, they use the six phases of Appreciative Advising to create and teach a course, SAS 100, for students on probation (Bloom, Hutson, & He, 2008). The assessment results have been impressive to date. For example, retention rates for students on probation after taking SAS 100 increased 18% after they infused Appreciative Advising principles into the course (Bloom et al., 2008). For students who have been readmitted to the institution, UNCG instated a rule that they must sign a contract agreeing to meet with an Appreciative Advisor several times during the semester—this was based on a pilot study which found that 90% of students who signed a contract to meet with an Appreciative Advisor were eligible to continue their studies after their first semester back, as compared to only 33% for control group participants (Bloom et al., 2008, p. 121).

Wheaton College

Wheaton College was selected as one of the DEEP schools by Kuh (2008) due to the school's better-than-expected performance on the National Survey on Student Engagement (NSSE). Wheaton takes a "tag team" approach to advising by having a core group of faculty and mentors assigned to first-year students, including a faculty member, administrators, librarian, and two preceptors (junior- or senior-level students). Students are assigned to the faculty member who teaches their First-Year Seminar (FYS) as their official academic advisor for the first year of college at Wheaton. These faculty members undergo extensive orientation and training to ensure their competence to serve as advisors. One of the upper-level student preceptors lives in the residence halls with students and helps them access academic support services as well as become involved in extra-curricular activities. All members of the team meet regularly with students and with each other to provide students a "freshman family" (Kuh, 2008, p. 77).

Conclusion

Academic advising has long been an important component of American higher education. This rich tradition of helping students make the most of their undergraduate experiences has been shown to have at least an indirect effect on student retention, although there is scanty empirical research to link academic advising directly to increased retention rates. There is certainly a need to improve the quality of academic advising and to better quantify the direct and/or indirect impact that high-quality advising has on student retention and other student-focused outcomes. This chapter provided an overview from the literature of some specific advising-related initiatives that have been shown to have varying levels of effectiveness. We also summarized some of the field's specific and overall best practices being utilized to enhance the quality of advising services on college campuses, as well as innovative programs at specific institutions that embody these best practices.

15

FIRST-YEAR TRANSITION PROGRAMS

The fourth and final student success area really encompasses a set of interventions that we categorize as first-year transition programs. The conceptual basis for first-year transition programming and a foundational perspective in Tinto's writings (1993) is found in the work of Van Gennep (1960). Van Gennep identified three stages of passage that take place when an individual moves from one community (social network) to another. Although Van Gennep's rites of passage are applicable to all students entering college, in the case of traditional college students, that passage is from family, hometown, and high school to college. The first stage in Van Gennep's passages is separation from at least some, if not many, of the values, norms, and behaviors that characterized past communities. Indeed, many a parent has puzzled over, rued, or decried the changes in behavior and attitude that often accompany the stage of separation. Tinto (1993) refers to the second stage transition, as a "a period of passage between the old and the new, before the full adoption of new norms and patterns of behavior and after the onset of separation from old ones" (p. 97). The final stage involves the acceptance of new norms, values, and behavioral patterns and the integration of the student into college society. In the case of first-year students, the acceptance of new norms, values, and behavioral patterns is individually nuanced and may be characterized as an adaptation or integration rather than an adoption of new norms, values, and behaviors. Nevertheless, Van Gennep's rites of passage illustrate the concept that transition programs can have a significant impact on student success. The speed at which and the degree to which students adapt to and incorporate new norms and behavioral patterns, while falling short of being termed the rites of passage, are strong determinants of student success.

There is little doubt that campus efforts focused on student transition are both popular and highly valued. In the fourth *What Works in Student Retention* survey Habley, McClanahan, Valiga, and Burkum (2010) studied the prevalence and institutional ratings of 94 retention practices broken into 12 program clusters. One of the clusters, identified as first-year transition programs, included seven practices. Table 15.1 includes the institutional respondent mean ratings on each of the seven transition

Table 15.1 Ratings and Incidence Rates for First-Year Transition Programs by Institutional Type.

Intervention	Four-Year Public	Four-Year Private	Community College
Summer orientation	3.61–93%	3.66–67%	3.33–73%
Extended freshman orientation (non-credit)	3.57–33%	3.47–34%	3.51–12%
Extended freshman orientation (credit)	3.82–24%	3.73–23%	3.69–28%
Freshman seminar/university 101 (non-credit)	3.38–9%	3.44–10%	3.38–7%
Freshman seminar/university 101 (credit)	3.74–76%	3.67–58%	3.68–52%
Living/learning communities (residential)	3.67–62%	3.38–36%	3.14–5%
Learning communities (non-residential)	3.56–44%	3.45–15%	3.22–36%
Freshman interest groups (FIGs)	3.50–27%	3.42–9%	2.89–3%
Integration of academic advising with first-year transition program	3.80–60%	3.87–51%	3.87–36%

programs as well as two additional transition-related interventions (Freshman Interest Groups and integration of advising with transition program). A rating of 1 indicates that the respondent felt the transition intervention made little or no contribution to retention and a rating of 5 indicates the intervention was a major contributor to retention. The percentage that appears in each cell of Table 15.1 is the incidence rate, the percentage of institutional respondents reporting that the transition program is in place on their campus.

It is clear that respondents believe that freshman seminar/university 101 for credit and a credit-bearing extended orientation are highly valued contributors to retention of first-year students. In addition, the integration of academic advising with first-year transition programs stands out in the mean ratings in all three institutional types.

In an additional section of the WWISR study (Habley et al., 2010), respondents were asked to identify from among the 94 retention practices the three interventions that they believed made the greatest contribution to retention. Table 15.2 includes the percentage of respondents who identified specific transition programs among the top three of 94 retention interventions.

Data from the WWISR survey provide significant support for the selection of first-year transition programs as one of the top four interventions supporting student success. Yet, as we began

Table 15.2 Transition Programs Identified Among Top Three Interventions ≥ 10% of Respondents.

Intervention	Four-Year Public	Four-Year Private	Community College
Summer orientation	11%	12%	10%
Freshman seminar/university 101 (credit)	24%	20%	10%
Learning communities (non-residential)		14%	

to organize this chapter, we were faced with a number of challenges. The first challenge was to differentiate first-year transition programs from other terms which are related: first-year experience or first year of college. A strong case is made for the integration of transition programs and services into what Barefoot et al. (2005) and Upcraft, Gardner, and Barefoot (2005) refer to as the first-year experience or the first year of college. Clearly, all aspects of campus life contribute to an effective transition to college life and build a firm foundation for student success. Although attention must be paid to the totality of experiences that take place in the first year of college, we have chosen to examine what we believe to be the most critical constituent components of those experiences: advising, assessment/course placement, developmental education/learning assistance, and first-year transition programs.

The second challenge we faced was to provide a framework for categorizing and explaining transition programs. Today's transition programs are complex and comprehensive, intended to bring about successful assimilation into campus life and leading to student satisfaction, retention, and ultimately persistence to degree. In fact, even the term *orientation*, while still in wide use, has become but one of a number of terms that describe programs under our broader umbrella heading of first-year transition programs. In addition to the term *orientation*, other terms that focus on first-year transition include, but are not limited to, *extended orientation, freshman seminar, university 101, living/learning communities, freshman interest groups (FIGS)*, and *learning communities*. Our response to this challenge was to categorically define transition programs using the terms *orientation, learning communities*, and *first-year seminars*—and we deliberately chose to organize this chapter under these categories. We fully realize that the programs we have identified have malleable definitions. What some campus administrators call an extended orientation, others call a first-year seminar, while still others use the term *university 101.* Our definition of orientation is an event that is time constrained and typically precedes the beginning of classes. A learning community is a set of two or more classes that are linked or clustered during an academic term, often around an interdisciplinary theme, and enroll a common cohort of students. Finally, we define the first-year seminar as a course for new undergraduate students designed to enhance their academic and social integration into college.

The first two challenges were exercises in defining the scaffold upon which the chapter is built—delimiting the focus and integrating the concepts and constructs into a manageable and explicable framework. The third challenge is to capture the permutations and combinations in format, content, and delivery that exist within the orientation, learning communities, and first-year seminars. This is no small task. There have been volumes written on models, implementation strategies, and logistics for each of these topics as well as multiple research studies that underscore the importance of transition programs in student success. Because recapitulating all that is known about these programs would be a gargantuan undertaking, the remaining sections of this chapter focus on framing program scope and variety, delineating the delivery models, and summarizing the literature on content and effectiveness of each of the programs. The chapter will close with observations on the implementation of a first-year transition program that melds institutional characteristics and culture with student needs.

Orientation Programs

The orientation of students to college life is a long-standing tradition. In the year 1888 the first official orientation program for new students was held at Boston University. (National Orientation Directors Association [NODA], 2008). By 1925, more than 25 colleges across the nation had developed orientation programs and a network of orientation staffers began to emerge (NODA, p. 4). Early writings on the role and function of orientation programs are simplistic but telling. Mueller (1961) suggested that orientation was primarily a public relations endeavor. She wrote, "First impressions are indelible. The success of many programs depends on a handful of people, a dozen words, a smile, a handshake" (p. 223). Mueller went on to say that "orientation is basically the faculty's show culminating in an all-important half hour with an academic advisor." Shaffer (1970) suggested that orientation was "developed out of the problems caused by the increasing heterogeneity of student populations" (Section 7, p. 121). Grier (1954) referred to orientation as "a formal program usually referred to as freshman days or orientation week immediately preceding the beginning of classes" (p. 50). As late as the 1990s, orientation was seen as a one-way communication from institution to students. Sandeen (1996) defined orientation as "the process of helping students learn the history, traditions, educational programs, academic requirements, and student life of the institution" (p. 437).

As we stated earlier, the term *orientation program* refers to activities that are time constrained and typically precede the beginning of classes. Smith and Robbins (1993) differentiate orientation programs as often shorter and more narrowly focused than programs such as first-year seminars or learning communities. Those programs, discussed later in this chapter, occur during an academic term/terms, may offer credit, and vary in format, duration, and depth.

Prior to the 1980s there were few variations in campus orientation programs. Orientation was an event. The primary difference was not generally in program content but rather in length and timing of the program. Many colleges with a regional or statewide recruiting range often offered a two- or three-day on-campus residential summer orientation program. Other colleges provided freshman days or freshman week before classes began in the fall. Though many campuses employed these more traditional orientation models, Mullendore and Banahan (2005) observed that multiple influences brought about changes in both the content and the administration of orientation programs. Among those influences were increases in academic focus, technological advances, increased involvement of parents and other family members, and the increasing diversity of students. On these last two influences, Mullendore and Banahan suggest orientation programs should be "designed to meet the needs of first-year, transfer, nontraditional, and graduate students, as well as parents and family members" (p. 393).

Despite these influences, the definition, the goals, and the program components of orientation have remained remarkably consistent over time. Mullendore and Banahan (2005) based their definition of orientation on the work of several predecessors (Perigo & Upcraft, 1989; Dannells & Kuh, 1977; Upcraft & Farnsworth, 1984). They define orientation as "a collaborative institutional effort to enhance students success by assisting students and their families in the transition to a new college environment. Orientation programs generally provide information and guidance regarding academic programs, administrative processes, campus services, facilities, and cocurricular programs" (p. 393). Perigo and Upcraft (1989) identify four major goals of orientation that are as valid today as they were in 1989. Those goals are: to help new students succeed academically, to assist students in their adjustment to and involvement with the college, to assist parents and other family members to understand the collegiate experience, and to provide the college with an opportunity to get to know incoming students. The foundation of successful orientation programs continues to rely on the balance and blend of the following activities: helping students understand their responsibilities; providing students with information about policies, programs, procedures, and requirements; informing students about the availability of services and programs; assisting students to become familiar with the campus and the community; and providing structured opportunities for students to interact with faculty, staff, and current students (Mullendore & Banahan, 2005, pp. 398–399).

Transition Is a Process

Regardless of consistency over time of the definition, goals, and program components of orientation programming, there have been fundamental changes in the manner in which colleges now assist students in making a successful transition to college. Mullendore and Banahan (2005) hint at some of those changes when commenting that "(t)he initial components of the orientation process are frequently offered during the summer or immediately prior to the beginning of the term" (p. 392). The number of campuses that have implemented first-year seminars, extended orientation programs, and learning communities testifies to the fact that transition is not complete at the conclusion of the orientation program. So, although solid orientation programs are important components of adjustment to campus life, they are only the first step in the transition process.

That recognition has resulted in a surge of longer-term transition programming over the last three decades. There are multiple justifications for this surge. First, Van Gennep (1960) suggests that shifting from one set of values and norms, to different norms and values is a process, not an event. Though many of the more traditional orientation programs have a beginning and an end, current approaches to support student transition occur over time. Whether through a first-year seminar, an extended orientation program, or a learning community, college leaders recognize that transition is not an event. Students do not make a successful transition to college life simply because they have attended a traditional orientation program. In addition, individuals who administer traditional orientation programs understand the fact that representatives of virtually every program, service, and activity on campus vie for a coveted position on the finite and time-constrained orientation agenda. The result of capitulation to such requests is an orientation program that is broad and shallow—as described earlier, a mile wide and an inch deep. Extended first-year transition programs provide the opportunity for depth and breadth in areas that are critical to student success. Finally, extended transition programming involves the timing of events and activities that take place in a typical first year. There is a tendency in traditional orientation to engage in "just in case" information giving. Students may be bombarded with pieces of information that they may or may not need at a later date. For example, "Just in case you have a room-mate concern we will tell you about the room change policy," or "Just in case you want to change your major, we will tell you about the change of major form, who needs to sign it, and where it needs to be turned in." Though these issues may become important to some students at some time during the first year, it is not likely that students will recall this information at some later date when either of these situations arise. The topics covered in many extended transition programs are often scheduled "just in time" to coincide with issues that arise throughout the term. (for example, first exam, midterm grades, course withdrawal dates, preregistration).

On a final note on the value of extended transition programming, it is an all-too-familiar scenario that traditional orientation programs may result in a philosophical and programmatic (and often unstated) conflict on program purposes. Is the orientation program the capstone of the recruiting process or is it the beginning of the transition process leading to retention? As more and more students shop colleges and financial aid packages, many admissions personnel believe that the orientation program has a dramatic effect on who enrolls and who does not enroll. And indeed it does. If the purpose of the orientation is to clinch the decision to enroll as opposed to provide a realistic introduction to academic life, the components of the program would differ markedly. Such friction does not exist when the orientation program is step one in the transition process.

Step two occurs when matriculated students enroll in first-year seminars or participate in learning communities. Learning communities and first-year seminars are described in detail in the following sections of this chapter. Because extended orientation programs cited in the WWISR study are often permutations and combinations of traditional orientation, learning communities, or first-year seminars, they are not addressed as a separate program category in this chapter.

Learning Communities

Learning communities are viewed by respondents to the 2010 *What Works in Student Retention* survey as making a major contribution to retention efforts. This section reviews the multiple applications of various learning community models.

Definition

Learning communities bring together small groups of college students who take two or more courses together (Price, 2005). Laufgraben (2005) suggests that there are numerous interpretations of the term *learning communities* in higher education. A learning community may take many forms. It may be classroom-based, curriculum based, residentially based, online, and/or faculty-based. The most common application of learning communities relating to first-year student success is the curricular learning community defined by Gabelnick, MacGregor, Matthews, and Smith (1990) as:

> Any one of a variety of curricular structures that link together several existing courses—or restructure the material entirely—so that students have opportunities for deeper understanding and integration of the material they are learning, and more interaction with one another and their teachers as fellow participants in the learning enterprise. (p. 19)

Models

A learning community in higher education is a group of individuals who share common interests, emotions, values, and beliefs and are actively engaged in learning together and from each other. Though most educators would agree with this definition, there is considerable discussion on the variety of curricular models that characterize learning communities. The Washington Center for Improving the Quality of Undergraduate Education (2010, http://www.evergreen.edu/washcenter/lcfaq .htm) states that there are three basic type of learning community structures, while B. M. Smith (1993) identified five models. Both Price (2005) and Laufgraben (2005) identify four primary learning community models. Each of those models is described below. Acknowledging that there are differences in nomenclature rather than substance, we will elaborate on the four models described by Laufgraben.

The first model, relatively straightforward, is the paired course model, in which small groups of students (usually 20–30) are enrolled together in a block of two courses. The courses share a curricular relationship and/or make logical skill area connections. For example, a small group of business majors may be co-enrolled in microeconomics and calculus for business. Among the nuances in the paired course model are shared class meetings, field trips, or service learning/com munity service. In some cases, one of the paired classes might be the first-year seminar. In a few instances, the learning community clusters four or five courses together but the learning community model is generally applied to only two of the courses.

The second learning community model is large course cohort model, which is often deployed in lecture-based introductory courses with high enrollments. Two forms of the large course model exist. The first is the Freshman Interest Group (FIG). Gabelnick et al. (1990) identify FIGs as the simplest learning community model in terms of organization and cost.

Although faculty generally play no role in FIGs, these learning communities typically include a smaller writing course and a weekly seminar often led by peer tutors or advisors who, in many cases, had previously participated in a FIG. This model often serves as an extended orientation expanding on consideration of transition issues faced by first-year students. The second large-course cohort model, the federated learning community, engages faculty members as master learners who enroll in the course and facilitate a weekly seminar that integrates the course around a common theme. In most cases, the master learner (faculty member) has no additional teaching responsibilities (Laufgraben, 2005).

The third model, team-taught learning communities, are also called coordinated studies. Team-taught learning communities include two or more courses organized around an interdisciplinary theme identified by faculty members. Price (2005) suggests that team-taught learning communities provide the most comprehensive approach because faculty members collaborate in the development of curriculum. Enrollment in these learning communities can be fairly large because they almost always include small-group discussions. Themes may focus on liberal arts topics, the development of academic skills in related disciplines, or preparation for professions.

The final learning community cited by Laufgraben (2005) and Price (2005) is the residential learning community. Based on the notion that learning also takes place outside the classroom, the primary goal of a residential learning community is the integration of students' living arrangements and academic environments. Price (2005) suggests that the curriculum of the residential learning community often parallels the paired course, the large course, or team-taught learning community models, with the major distinction being that the residential model provides opportunities for extracurricular interactions between students and faculty. A review of several college websites also provides evidence that residential learning communities may also be organized as FIGs, providing discipline-related, lifestyle-related, and interest-related affinity groupings. For example, the resident learning communities cited most recently on the University of Iowa website include: arts, business and entrepreneurship, leadership academic, dance marathon, education, global village, health sciences, healthy living networks, honors house, Iowa writers, journalism and mass communications, law studies and legal careers, men in engineering, political engagement, spectrum house, sustainability, women in science and engineering, and finally, explore, dream, discover, experience (University of Iowa, 2011).

The four learning communities described above constitute the majority of those in use across the nation, but Laufgraben (2005) also reports on learning communities for special populations of students. Among those listed by Laufgraben are students in historically difficult courses, those with unique college transition or academic needs, and students with specific career objectives.

Features and Effectiveness

Although Table 15.1 indicates that learning communities are both highly rated and most prominent in four-year public colleges, with 62% reporting residential learning communities and 44% reporting non-residential learning communities, they are not nearly as prominent in four-year private colleges and are least prominent in community colleges.

Even with this popularity, given that there are at least four learning communities models (each with permutations of its own), it is difficult to know which features of learning communities are most effective. And, surprisingly, there is little research on the common components of learning communities. The annual report of the National Survey of Student Engagement (NSSE, 2007) provides a glimpse of the elements included in the learning community experience.

As reported by students enrolled in learning communities, those elements are:

- Course or discussion group integrates learning across learning community classes (64%)
- Related to academic major (54%)
- Require out of class activities (46%)
- Learning community classes are reserved for program participants (44%)
- Class assignments frequently integrate material across courses (42%)
- Undergraduate peer advisor helps teach/coordinate (42%)
- Majority of classes taken as part of the learning community (33%)
- Residential requirement (18%) (p. 14)

In spite of wide variations in the models and the elements of learning communities, there has been significant research of learning community impact on desired student outcomes of higher education. In his literature review, Rocconi (2011) cited more than forty studies which supported a variety of positive contributions made by learning communities. Findings of those studies indicate that participation in learning communities was linked to transition to college, college grades, desired learning outcomes, satisfaction with college, and persistence and graduation. Additional learning community outcomes include student-faculty interactions, interaction with peers, time spent on academics and course involvement, higher-order thinking and problem-solving skills, writing ability, and perceptions of supportive campus environments. With the volume of evidence supporting the positive impact of learning communities, it is obvious why WWISR respondents believe that learning communities make a major contribution to student retention. Without diminishing these reported findings, Rocconi's study concurred with conclusions reached by several others that all retention interventions generally, and learning communities specifically, are indirectly—not directly—related to educational gains. Nevertheless, the indirect effects achieved through student engagement in a learning community contribute to student satisfaction, an important precursor to student success.

First-Year Seminar

Background

While many trace the birth of the first-year seminar movement to the early 1970s when the University of South Carolina introduced its University 101 course, in reality first-year seminar courses have been offered for more than 120 years. The first purported freshman seminar was delivered at Lee College in 1882, and Reed College was the first to offer academic credit for the seminar in 1911 (University of South Carolina, 2011). By 1948, a survey of freshman orientation tactics (Gordon, 1989) indicated that 43% of campuses offered a required orientation course. And, as one of the authors of this book recalls, a one-credit course in "personal adjustment" was required of all new students at his community college in the mid-1960s. Even with this long history of first-year seminar classes, the University of South Carolina's National Resource Center for the First-Year Experience and Students in Transition (NRC) has been primarily responsible for developing, promoting, and researching the freshman seminar over the last four decades.

Definition

Because of the wide variety of structures and formats, a succinct definition of the first-year seminar is difficult to craft. Hunter and Linder (2005) indicate that the first-year seminar "is centered on and concerned with the individual needs of entering students, as well as the expectations of the particular institution" (p. 275). But in spite of the various structures and formats, first-years seminars share a common function. They are small, discussion-based courses, the purpose of which is to assist students in their academic and social development. In many respects the function of the first-year seminar is similar to that of other first-year transition programs: to provide "a period of passage between the old and the new, before the full adoption of new norms and patterns of behavior and after the onset of separation from old ones" (Tinto, 1993, p. 97).

Types of First-Year Seminars

Hunter and Linder (2005) suggested that most first-year seminars fit into one of five categories. The first of these is the extended orientation course which Hunter and Linder reported was in place at 62% of the responding campuses. These courses, some offering credit, are taught by faculty, campus administrators, or student affairs staff. The primary focus of the course is on student survival and success techniques.

Academic seminars with either uniform content or content developed by individual faculty members constitute the second type of first-year seminar. Seminars with uniform content could be elective or required and may or may not be part of the general education requirement. Seminars on various topics are often based on the disciplines or personal interests of faculty members. Hunter and Linder (2005) point out that "seminar topics can vary from section to section and most likely cover a wide variety of disciplines and social issues" (p. 280).

Hunter and Linder (2005) identified three additional types of seminars offered: professional, discipline-linked, and study skills–based. The professional or discipline-related seminars focused on preparing students for study of the professional areas such as law and medicine or disciplines such as fine arts, agriculture, or science fields. Study skills seminars are intended for students with marginal academic skills and generally include note taking, reading, thinking, and calculating skills. The basic models reported by Hunter and Linder have not changed much in the decade since 2000, but between 2003 and 2009 there have been shifts in the percentage of institutions offering each of the seminar types. Table 15.3 is based on the 2003 (National Resource Center for the First-Year Experience and Students in Transition, 2005) and the 2009 Surveys of First-Year Seminars (National Resource Center for the First-Year Experience and Students in Transition, 2011) and reports on those percentages.

As an indication of the complexity of formats for first-year seminars, it is interesting to note that the hybrid seminar, not included among the response options in 2003, now accounts for 15.3% of the deployed seminar types. Additional information on seminar types based on the 2009 survey includes:

- 14.1% of institutions require the seminar for academically underprepared students.
- 21.3% had designated special seminar sections for underprepared students.
- 24.4% had designated special seminar sections for honors students

Table 15.3 Percentage of First-Year Seminar Types.

Seminar Type	2003 % Offering	2009 % Offering
Extended orientation	65.2	41.1
Academic seminar with uniform content	27.4	16.1
Academic seminar on various topics	24.3	15.4
Hybrid	N/A	15.3
Basic study skills	20.0	4.9
Professional or discipline-linked	14.2	3.7
Other	8.2	3.5

Features and Effectiveness

Over the past decade, seminar objectives have remained relatively constant, with the primary objective reported over the last four National Surveys of First-Year Seminars as the development of academic skills. On the 2009 survey (National Resource Center for the First-Year Experience and Students in Transition, 2011), academic skill development was cited as a major objective by 54.6% of the responding institutions. Additional objectives most reported in the 2009 survey were developing a connection with the institution (50.2%), and providing an orientation to various campus resources and services (47.6%).

Although there have been some shifts in nomenclature, the topics covered in first-year seminars also remained relatively stable over the past decade. Beginning with the 2003 survey, the three topics reported most often are academic support/study skills, introduction to campus resources, and academic planning/advising. It is interesting to note that two of those topics (advising and academic support) surface as two of the most critical intervention areas cited in the most recent WWISR study (Habley et al., 2010) and are topics that are discussed separately in Chapters Thirteen and Fourteen of this book.

Additional data reported in the 2009 National Survey of First-Year Seminars (National Resource Center for the First-Year Experience and Students in Transition, 2011) show significant variations in seminar length and credit. While 67.8% report a full semester seminar, 12.6% report one-half semester, 5.9% report one-quarter, and 3.9% report a full year as the length of the seminar. Credit generated was most often applied to general education requirement (53.1%) while 39.8% awarded elective credit for the seminar and 9.4% of institutions awarded credit in the major. Finally, more than 80% of the respondents reported that the seminar was letter-graded.

Table 15.1 indicates not only the popularity of the first-year seminar but also the fact that respondents believe the seminars make a very important contribution to retention. In fact, when WWISR (Habley et al., 2010) respondents were asked to identify the three retention practices from among 94 interventions that made the greatest contribution to retention, only three of the interventions were cited by 10% or more of respondents across all three institutional types. Those interventions were tutoring, early warning system, and freshman seminar/university 101 for credit. Nearly one-quarter (24%) of four-year public college respondents identified the freshman seminar among the top three. And 20% of the respondents from four-year private colleges and 10% from community colleges listed the freshman seminar among the top three retention interventions. In addition, 73.7% of respondents to the 2009 National Survey of First-Year Seminars (National Resource Center for the First-Year Experience and Students in Transition, 2011) indicated that persistence to the sophomore year was one of the three most important first-year seminar outcomes. Nearly three-quarters (73.7%) of the respondents attributed increased persistence to the first-year seminar. The other two outcomes most often cited by respondents were satisfaction with faculty at 70.9% and satisfaction with the institution (65.3%). When survey respondents, in an open-ended format, were asked to provide general reactions to the first-year seminar, the comments most often cited were related to persistence/retention. It is interesting to note that, like learning communities, much of the research suggests that the impact of first-year seminars on student persistence is indirect in nature. Although it is defensible to suggest that there is a relationship between first-year seminar participation, student satisfaction, and persistence, it is not appropriate to claim causality. That is, positive outcomes such as level of satisfaction with the institution have an indirect effect on retention. Even authors of the 2009 National Survey of First-Year Seminars (National Resource Center for the First-Year Experience and Students in Transition, 2011) suggest that the outcomes identified by survey respondents are not conclusive. That is, retention is not caused by the first-year seminar. Potts and Schultz (2008) suggest that retention is positively affected by a sense of belonging when students interact with each other, with the institution, and with faculty. They cite previous research that concludes that retention is a by-product of early academic performance, attitudes toward higher education, goal and institutional commitment, social and academic interaction, residence life experiences, faculty and staff interaction with the student, or the student's sense of community.

Framework for Implementation

Overwhelming positive public opinion (when coupled with the clear, but indirect effects on student success) makes it essential for campus leaders to include first-year transition programs as a critical component of student success. In the three preceding chapters we provided an overview of additional interventions that are critical to student success. Each of those functions could be clearly defined, featured activities that could be described and outcomes that could be measured. As we explored first-year transition programs, we concluded that first-year transition is an umbrella term for a complex and wide variety of practices and approaches. We also concluded that first-year transition is a process, not an event. The terms *orientation*, *learning communities*, and *first-year seminars* connote different meanings to different individuals, yet the terms are so broadly conceived that they have become generic in nature. The program type, models employed, students who participate, timing and length of delivery, credit offered, college personnel who deliver, intended outcomes, format, content, and assessment make it virtually impossible to identify a useful overview of best practices. As a result, we have not singled out specific institutional first-year transition programs because we believe the key to successful practice comes not from the adoption of programs that have been successfully implemented at other campuses.

It does not reside in a cookie-cutter orientation program, a prefabricated learning community, or a textbook first-year seminar. Rather, a successful first-year transition derives from the integration of student needs with institutional characteristics and culture. The result of that integration is a first-year transition program that is institutionally unique. With that understanding, we offer the following framework to guide the planning of first-year transition programs.

Identify Student Needs

Successful transition programs focus on the needs of students and although most campuses have access to data on student characteristics, many can be characterized as data rich and information poor. That is, much of the data necessary to understand the needs of students has already been captured, but it has not been studied and synthesized. Two fundamental questions must be answered: Who are our students? What are their needs? To answer, planners should review student data in the following areas:

- **Demographics:** including, but not limited to, sex, race/ethnicity, age, size of high school, parental level of education, socioeconomic status
- **Academic performance:** including, but not limited to, admission test scores, high school rank and grade point average, placement test scores
- **Academic/career plans:** including, but not limited to, choice of major, level of highest degree aspiration, career interests assessment
- **Psychosocial variables:** including, but not limited to, academic goals, achievement, motivation, self-concept, social involvement, interest patterns
- **Self-reported needs:** including, but not limited to, expressed need for instructional support (writing, math, reading, study

skills, and so on) and expressed need for noninstructional support (choice of major, disability support, personal counseling, cocurricular involvement)

- **Student opinions and attitudes:** including a broad-based assessment of student opinions and attitudes on instructional and noninstructional programs, services, and policies

Even though data in many of these categories are already collected through the admission, orientation, and course placement processes on the campus, it will probably be necessary for the planning team to recommend the use of additional sources to complete the data set and to bring these data elements together to provide a comprehensive picture of student needs.

Review Institutional Characteristics

Of equal importance in the development of a successful first-year transition programs are institutional characteristics. The following characteristics are among those that should be considered in developing a first-year transition program.

- **Locus of control:** public, private, proprietary
- **Highest degree offered:** associate, baccalaureate, graduate
- **Nature of program offerings/program mix:** liberal arts, professional, vocational
- **Selectivity:** open, liberal, traditional, selective, highly selective
- **Institutional setting:** rural, suburban, urban
- **Enrollment:** under 1,500, 1,500–5,000, 5,001–10,000, 10,000–20,000, >20,000
- **Living arrangements:** commuter, residential

Examine Institutional Culture

Although we will devote an entire chapter to creating a student success culture on campus, it is important to note here that an understanding of student needs and institutional characteristics is critical to the design of first-year transition programs; it is the positive attitudes of all campus constituencies and their commitment to student success that will ultimately determine the effectiveness of any program targeting student success. Kuh, Kinzie, Schuh, and Whitt (2005) offer six observations on campuses that created a student success culture.

- "Living" mission and a "lived" educational philosophy;
- Unshakeable focus on student learning;
- Clear pathways to student success;
- Environments adapted for educational enrichment;
- Improvement-oriented campus culture; and
- Shared responsibility for educational quality and student success.

The integration of student needs with institutional characteristics and culture may be more of an art than it is a science. It is a science because it requires campus administrators to understand the variety and complexity of transition programs available; it is an art because it requires creative program adaptations at the nexus of student and institutional factors. First-year transition programs are the foundation upon which student success is built.

Section 5

MAKING STUDENT SUCCESS A PRIORITY

16

EXPANDING THE RETENTION FRAMEWORK: IMPLICATIONS FOR PUBLIC AND INSTITUTIONAL POLICY

In the previous section we underscored the importance of specific institutional interventions that support student success: assessment/course placement, developmental education, academic advising, and first-year transition programs. Though these interventions are critical to student success, they are based on a retention definition delimited solely as an institutional outcome. If more students are to meet their educational goals, student success must include an expanded framework that is not limited to a single institution.

Limitations of the Retention Framework

In Chapter One, we challenged two assumptions confounding the existing retention framework. First, although it is convenient to assume that retention is both linear and temporal, those assumptions are the rules that have become the exceptions. And the existing definition rests on the belief that all students who enter higher education intend to earn a degree or a certificate. These assumptions have driven policy and programming decisions in colleges and have served inappropriately as proxies for effectiveness of colleges and universities.

Yet the stark reality of the retention and persistence-to-degree data is that despite the considerable energy that the higher education community has expended in understanding retention and degree completion, such understanding has not resulted in a concomitant improvement in student success in college. The community can document the personal and societal benefits that accrue from a college degree. The community can identify the student, institutional, and environmental factors contributing to retention. The higher education community can also pinpoint institutional interventions that contribute to retention. Yet, in spite of all that is known, there has been little change in retention and degree completion rates in more than four decades. Nearly one-third of all first-year students do not return for a second year, fewer than half of all students who earn bachelor's degrees do so within five years of high school graduation, and approximately 40% of all students who enter higher education in a given fall will not earn a degree anywhere at any time in their life. With the additional factors of multiple ways that students can earn college credit and the phenomena of student swirling and increased time to degree, it is not likely that the future holds a great deal of promise for major advancement in retention or degree completion based on the existing retention framework.

In addition to the faulty linear and temporal assumptions, the existing retention framework has three major limitations. The first limitation is that institutions are held accountable for retention and degree-completion outcomes over which they have some influence but very little control. Because student success is fraught with complexities, policymakers and resource allocators rely on accountability measures that sink to the lowest common denominators. How many students matriculate? How many students are retained? How many students graduate? And how long did it take them to earn their degrees?

The second limitation is that the traditional retention framework fails to take into account the significant variety of institutional types that constitute the American higher education system. Theoretically, all students who have a high school diploma or have completed the GED have access to postsecondary education. Because this is the case, first-to-second-year retention and degree completion rates vary greatly based on mission, selectivity, and the academic ability of students who enroll. Once again, accountability measures undergirding the traditional retention framework fail to take into account this institutional diversity.

The third major limitation is that institutions compare themselves to and compete with other institutions. Students are a renewable yet finite commodity. Thus, institutional success is predicated on how well a college attracts and keeps students. Those who matriculate elsewhere or students who leave the college represent loss but evince little concern for their future success as students. The traditional retention framework creates three basic comparisons and concomitant mindsets. The first is "we are better than average," which provides little stimulus to change. The second mindset is "we are about average," which may or may not stimulate change. And the third, "we are below average," should stimulate change. Though comparisons to peer group institutions may be useful as broad indicators, such comparisons do little to create a road map that leads to continuous improvement.

Static retention and degree completion rates may lead to the conclusion that institutionally based retention interventions do not yield a return on investment because they have little impact on student success. To the contrary, level rates may be an indicator of success for the very same reasons that the retention framework is flawed. That is, more students are stopping out, transferring, or swirling. And it is well documented that many students lack the requisite academic skills to be successful in college.

Expanding the Traditional Retention Framework

Though institutional retention efforts must continue, the time has come to extend the current retention framework to incorporate an expanded framework for defining the concept of student success. For far too long, the issue of retention and degree completion has been characterized by the assertion that success is determined by the number of students who enter, are retained, and earn degrees at a specific institution. If the focus is on student success, that perspective changes dramatically. That perspective acknowledges that student success, whether at the institution of first enrollment or at another institution, is a critical consideration. The extended framework, in addition to degree completion, would define success as the achievement of student-identified educational goals.

Habley and Schuh (2007b) expanded the traditional retention framework to include this broader definition of student success. A modified version of that framework appears in Table 16.1. The framework for student success in no way diminishes the importance of institutional efforts to retain and graduate students. Rather, it suggests that students who are not retained or do not graduate from one institution may achieve their goals at other institutions. They are neither personal nor institutional failures. The framework presents the argument that institutional and educational policymakers have a far greater responsibility to assist students in making successful transitions from their institutions to other educational experiences.

The extended student success framework suggests that those who make policy at the public and institutional levels must not only intensify on-campus efforts to retain students but also examine traditional definitions of student success, review policies that hinder student transitions, and explore systemic and systematic approaches to ensuring student success. The drive for accountability in higher education has led to the default position that institutional effectiveness can be measured by institutional retention and degree-completion rates. Though knowledge of such rates is informative, we suggest that this is both an unrealistic metric and a dramatic oversimplification of a very complex process. Unfortunately, these quantitative retention and degree-completion data are being used as proxies

Table 16.1 The Expanded Retention Framework.

Dimension	Retention Framework	Expanded Retention Framework
Goal	Degree or certificate at institution of first enrollment	Student defined
Where		Any college
Path to Goal	Linear	Nonlinear, discontinuous
Time to Goal	With all due speed	At student's pace
Institutional Questions	How can we best serve?	How can we best serve?
	Why did she leave?	Where is she going?
		How can we help her get there?
Student Role	Primary life role	May be one of several important life roles
Important Transitions	Into this institution	Into this institution
	Through this institution	Transition to another institution
	Graduation from this institution	Goal achievement at any institution
Relationship to Other Education Providers	Competitive	Transparent
	Opaque	Collaborative
	Discreet	Systematic
	Unsystematic	
Measure of Effectiveness	Institutional retention rate	Student success—goal achievement rate
	Institutional degree completion rate	

for quality, shaping policy decisions as well as the allocation of resources. In many senses, institutions are judged on a production model, which simply measures the output against the input, ignoring the complexities of throughput. Although institutions should strive to offer programs and services that enhance retention and degree completion, the need for an increasingly skilled workforce and the pressures of the global economy require educators and policy makers to look further than the parochial, institutionally constrained definition of retention. After all, when students succeed, institutions succeed and society benefits.

In the following sections of this chapter, we focus on the application of the expanded retention framework to public policy and institutional practice. Public policy provides direction for higher education and in the public sector defines the measures of accountability and controls the allocation of scarce resources. It is our opinion that those who determine public policy (state agencies, legislatures, coordinating and governing boards) have chosen to hold institutions accountable for outcomes that are expedient but misguided: retention and persistence to degree. We also believe that although public policy does not direct the activity of private independent colleges, it plays a major role in shaping how those colleges define and measure student success. We also contend that institutional policies must be revisited. We close the chapter with a call for voluntary institutional collaboration by suggesting that the issue of student success is far too important to be left to the cumbersome and expedient decisions of those who determine public policy.

Public Policy

To this point we have focused our attention on the institutional level, identifying retention interventions that contribute to student success. Although institutional interventions are key elements in those efforts, public policy also plays a major role in shaping the interaction between and among institutions and in promoting seamless movement of students between colleges. Following are several recommendations for enhancing that seamless movement.

Build Integrated Educational Systems

Policymakers in 40 states (Educational Commission of the States [ECS], 2008) have come to the realization that dramatic demographic shifts and the lack of alignment of the constituent parts of the educational system require a critical reexamination of how education is delivered. The result of this realization is the establishment of statewide efforts, variously identified as K–16, P–16, or P–20 initiatives. Although all levels of education are included in these initiatives, ECS suggests that education beyond high school is a "multi-layered nonsystem . . . having difficulty working together and largely disconnected from the K–12 system whose success is so vital to its own efforts" (Van de Water & Rainwater, 2001, p. 5).

Though these initiatives vary widely from state to state, state higher education executive officers suggest that efforts to align the educational system include five essential components: early outreach, curriculum and assessment systems, high-quality teaching, student financial assistance, and data and accountability systems (Lingenfelter, 2003). Just as we have offered a seamless and expanded definition of college student success, we also advocate for P–20 systems in which each level of education prepares students for an effective transition to and success at the next educational level.

Redefine Student Success

We have advocated for policymakers to expand the simplistic, linear, and time-constrained measures of the existing definition of retention. Simply stated, the current measures of institutional success are the percentage of students who enroll, the percentage that stay, and the percentage who subsequently earn a certificate or a degree. In many ways, the current approach to student success parallels a manufacturing production model. That is, the system has resource inputs (students), processes (college experiences), and outputs (degree completion). In the case of student success, however, the assumptions supporting the manufacturing model are flawed. First, not every student enrolls in a specific college with the intent of earning a degree at that college. Though many students enroll intending to earn a degree, others enroll with the plan to transfer or to upgrade employability skills. Still others enroll because intervening life experiences either require or provide the opportunity for additional education. Finally, some students simply want to explore higher education possibilities or take courses for personal enrichment. Under current measures of retention and degree completion, students whose educational goals do not result in a certificate or a degree achieve their worthwhile educational goals only to be counted as dropouts. Their stories are personal success stories but by current measures, institutional failures. Institutions that serve a significant number of these students generally do not fare very well when retention and degree completion are the metrics to which they are held accountable.

In addition, not every student who enters with the intent of completing a degree completes that degree according to a traditional timetable. Some students earn degrees on a part-time basis while meeting obligations of the workplace or family. Others do not enroll continuously. That is, they stop out of college for a variety of reasons, either planned or unplanned. They are on a different time line and in a different personal trajectory. When institutions are asked to report retention statistics, students who are not currently enrolled are also counted as dropouts. Such students are pursuing their goals on a time line of their own making. Institutions that serve a significant number of these students generally do not fare very well when retention and degree completion are the metrics by which they are held accountable.

The parallels between the current retention and degree completion approach and the manufacturing model are striking. In the manufacturing model, input resources are treated through a standardized, efficient, and timely process—the end result of which meets precise product specifications. When student success is defined as retention and persistence to degree then colleges and universities are responsible for processing students through a predetermined, sequential, efficient, and timely process that results in the ultimate measure of success, certificate, or degree attainment.

The problem with the focus on retention and persistence to degree is that students are human capital not raw material. Goals, expectations, and attitudes are shaped and reshaped by the college experience. To expect that all students aspire to a degree, that all students have identified and are committed to a specific academic program, that all students have the motivation, finances, and life contexts that enable them to pursue their educational goals in a timely fashion, is sheer folly. Yet, the operant definition of student success for public policy is retention and degree attainment.

In Chapter One, we challenged readers to think about how things might be done differently if we put retention and degree completion in the background and focused our attention on a more comprehensive definition of student success. Accomplishing this requires the identification of multiple positive student outcomes—outcomes that may vary from institution to institution and from individual to individual. Many of these definitions reside in student answers to five major questions upon entry into college (and subsequently at various intervals during their enrollment).

1. What is the most important reason you are attending college this term?

   Learn skills to get a new job

   Learn skills to advance in job

   Take classes that apply to a degree or certificate

   Satisfy general education requirements

   Improve basic skills in English, reading, or mathematics

   Take courses for personal interest

2. Will you be attending full-time or part-time?

3. What is your current educational goal?

> Classes only (no certificate or degree at this time)
>
> One- or two-year certificate or diploma
>
> Two-year college degree
>
> Four-year college degree
>
> Graduate degree
>
> Not sure

4. Have you decided on a program of study? If yes, which program?

5. Do you plan to reach achieve your educational goal here or at another educational institution?

The combination of answers to this set of questions provides pertinent information to assist in the identification of student goals. In addition, it is important to note that not all of the goals exist within the traditional parameters of retention and degree achievement.

Measure and Reward Student Success

There are many possible examples in which students are successful, but by the traditional measures of retention and persistence to degree, institutions are not. What we are advocating for is that institutional accountability metrics should be predicated on individual student success. This may appear to be a very difficult task, but we believe it is not. It requires identifying individual goals as students enter college, monitoring progress toward (or redefining) those goals, and finally measuring goal achievement. Institutional success is measured by the number (or percentage) of students who achieve their defined (or redefined) goals not solely by the number (percentage) of students who are retained and persist to degree. Collecting such information may even provide evidence of value added for students whose initial goals for education are exceeded. For example, a student who enrolls to take courses of personal interest may end up earning a certificate or a degree.

We are not suggesting that the metrics of retention and persistence to degree be abandoned. They are an important component of student success. We do believe, however, that such accountability metrics must be more narrowly applied: only to degree-seeking students, because student success comes in many forms and because many of the factors of attrition are not controlled by the college. Finally, we believe that institutions should be measured on improvement rather than by comparison to mean retention and degree-completion rates of similar institutions. Current retention comparisons yield institutions that are above the mean, those that are at the mean, and those who fall below the mean. If all institutions improve in retention and degree completion, the mean moves up and there will still be institutions below the mean. Such comparisons are uninformative and counterproductive at best and demoralizing and deleterious at worst.

Policymakers should reengineer the standard accountability metrics to focus on the percentage of students who enter higher education at *any* institution, the percentage of students who are retained in higher education at *any* institution, and the percentage of students who complete degrees or achieve their goals at *any* institution. While a number of formulae for measuring student success have been suggested, one formula provides for broad applicability at institutional, system, state, and even federal levels. It accounts for multiple institutions of enrollment and variable attendance patterns. This formula considers the ratio of first-time, full-time, degree-seeking students divided into the number of graduates six years later (three years later at a two-year college). As an example, a four-year institution with a first-time, full-time degree-seeking enrollment of 1,000 that graduates 800 students six years later would have a student-success ratio of .8. The ratio reflects not only the retention and degree-completion rates of students who entered the institution six years earlier, but it also takes into account those individuals who transferred into the institution as well as those who may have stopped out of the institution for a period of time. Although this formula is not a panacea, it acknowledges that fact that achieving a degree is far less likely to be a linear and temporal process. In addition, this formula provides a clearer and fairer metric than current retention and degree completion rates.

Minimize the Complexity of the Transfer Process

One of the major premises of the expanded student success framework is that fewer and fewer students enroll, progress, and achieve their educational goals at one institution within a defined time period. Because that is the case, seamless movement from one institution to another has become a far more critical factor now than it has been in the past. Yet, student transfer from one institution to another is fraught with complexity and confusion. Students are caught between the program requirements and academic policies of the institution from which they are transferring and those of the institution to which they are transferring. Institutional autonomy, curricular complexity, faculty prerogative, and just plain resistance to change often stand in the way of interinstitutional cooperative and collaborative efforts. In this section, we discuss three collaborations that policy makers should promote. Those are common course numbering, course applicability systems, and articulation agreements. The discussion of these areas which follows provides several examples of cooperation and collaboration.

Common Course Numbering System. A common course numbering system across colleges and universities would greatly assist student transitions from institution to institution. There are several examples of statewide common course number systems. Florida's Statewide Course Numbering System (http://scns.fldoe.org/scns/public/pb_index.jsp), created in the 1960s, and is an important component in Florida's K–20 seamless system of articulation. The system provides a database of postsecondary courses at public vocational-technical centers, community colleges, universities, and participating nonpublic institutions. The Texas Common Course Numbering System (http://www.tccns.org) is a voluntary, cooperative effort among community colleges and universities. It provides a shared, uniform set of course designations for students and their advisors to use in determining both course equivalency and degree applicability of transfer credit on a statewide basis. And, as reported in the *Arizona Republic* (2010), a law passed by the state legislature requires Arizona's three universities and 21 community colleges to develop a common course-numbering system.

Although implementation of common course numbering systems has the potential to enhance student transition between and among institutions, most current systems fall short of the mark because they are incomplete. Some systems exclude important sectors of postsecondary education (for example, private, technical, or proprietary colleges) while other systems are voluntary. There are also institutional barriers to common course numbering, not the least of which is faculty resistance. Some of that resistance is based in the general notion that such a system usurps the faculty's autonomy over the curriculum. Still other faculty resistance comes when discussions of alignment of learning outcomes under a specific course number reach an impasse. Finally, there is resistance from individuals responsible for the logistical changes (for example, catalogs, transcripts, course descriptions, class scheduling, and degree audits) that accompany a common course numbering system.

Course Applicability Systems. Students' decisions to transfer are often predicated on the availability of courses and the acceptance and application of credits earned at other institutions. Yet, at many institutions decisions about the applicability of prior credit takes place immediately before or, in some cases, after a student has enrolled. The result is that some students enroll in courses which replicate content taken at other institutions or, in a worst-case scenario, discover that requirements for additional coursework will extend the length of time to program completion. We are calling for a broad-based course applicability system that enables prospective students to search institutions to ascertain the availability of courses and the applicability to academic programs of credits they have earned at other institutions.

Currently, many states have developed course applicability systems for in-state institutions. Although Arizona may soon implement a common course numbering system, the state is currently utilizing an exemplary statewide course applicability system, AZTransfer (http://www.aztransfer.com/). This online tool was designed for use by students transferring within Arizona's public institutions of higher education—community colleges, tribal colleges, and state universities—and by the advisors and faculty who assist them. The site is user-friendly but it does not include private colleges. A similar system exists in Indiana's Transfer IN.net (http://www.transferin.net/College-Students/CTL .aspx) which is in the process of including private colleges which voluntarily participate. Some state course applicability systems include only those institutions which opt to participate.

An interstate course applicability collaboration, U-Select (https://www.transfer.org/uselect/) is a 19-state, web-based transfer information system that provides students and advisors with fast and accurate course and transfer equivalency information. A student can obtain program information, course descriptions and equivalencies, and information on admissions and financial aid through U-Select. Although this site shows promise, participation is voluntary and, in some states, only a few institutions participate.

Articulation Agreements. More often than not, an articulation agreement is primarily an understanding that delineates the application of credits between or among institutions. Some articulation agreements are arranged between two or more institutions, whereas others involve a statewide policy on the transfer of courses between and among public two-year and four-year colleges. Still another example of an articulation agreement was implemented by the League for Innovation in the Community College (2001). Member schools in the league partnered with eight four-year colleges to facilitate the transfer of students among partner colleges.

Though it is clear that the applicability of credit is a primary issue in successful student transition, institutions should also consider broadening institutional connections to ensure successful student transitions. As an example, the 2 Plus 2 program (http://www.uiowa.edu/2plus2/how_plan_works/index.html) is an agreement between the University of Iowa and three community colleges: Kirkwood, Eastern Iowa, and Iowa Western. The program features:

- Guaranteed early registration for the first semester at the University of Iowa
- Contact with admission counselors and academic advisors
- A university ID card, e-mail account, and electronic access to student records
- Use of the career center
- Use of the university library
- Student-priced discounts on tickets to university events

Our search for collaborative practices simplifying college-to-college transition leads us to conclude that significant efforts are under way in each of these areas. We applaud these efforts while at the same time call for greater levels of institutional, system, and state collaboration to facilitate the ease of transfer. We note that these examples are not complete: some are voluntary and some exclude institutional types. Our biggest concern, however, is the entanglement of multiple levels of collaborations/agreements involving institutions, consortiums, higher education systems, and states. There are agreements between two institutions and others between one institution and many institutions. There are agreements between two-year and four-year colleges within a state. And, there are collaborations involving several states, but not all. The current patchwork of agreements is fraught with gaps. Some colleges participate in multiple agreements while other colleges participate in no agreements. The result of all these efforts is a complex and unsystematic web of relationships that serves institutional purposes while, at the same time, disserves student transitions. In reality, this is a nonsystem of loosely coupled agreements that assist students who transfer between the institutions involved, but add a layer of complexity for students who fall outside the agreements. Unless policymakers focus attention on expanding, streamlining, and simplifying common course numbering, course applicability, and articulation agreements, students will continue to fall through the transition cracks and student success will be minimized.

Establish a Student Postsecondary Education Clearinghouse

Although redefining and measuring student success and such efforts as common course numbering, articulation agreements, course applicability systems, and P–20 approaches show great promise for increasing student success, those efforts are situational. That is, they apply only to some institutions, only in some situations, or only in some jurisdictions. The efforts are also fragmented in that each approach is useful but provides only a single piece of the student success puzzle. What is lacking is the integration of these approaches into a coherent national system (clearinghouse) that facilitates student transitions and, in turn, enhances student success. The clearinghouse would feature two components: a centralized course applicability repository and a system of retrievable student portfolios. Input data would be provided by the institution and by individual students. At the core of the clearinghouse would be an extensive course-equivalency database. Although development of the course-equivalency database could be a complex and long-term undertaking, initial equivalency tables could be constructed from existing articulation agreements and course applicability systems. Participating institutions would provide the clearinghouse with information on articulation agreements and on course applicability data from college, system, intra- and interstate partnerships.

The clearinghouse would also be a repository for student-specific data elements. Data elements might include, but need not be limited to, assessment data (admission test scores, placement test scores, advanced placement, and CLEP), dual enrollment credits, college transcripts, degree audit, and other biographic, demographic, psychosocial, and career development information that supports the transition process. Individual student input data would be identified by and supplied with the permission of the student and would be stored in a transportable, student-owned, and student-controlled portfolio supporting seamless transition from institution to institution.

The student portfolio would serve two critical functions. First, it would provide a secure, official, and accessible record of a student's cumulative postsecondary history. The portfolio could be requested by the student or, at the student's request, be sent directly to an institution as part of the transition process. The inclusion of the course equivalency database in the clearinghouse would provide additional functionality. No matter how many transcripts were included in the portfolio, the student could query the course applicability tables to see how credit from multiple institutions would apply to academic programs at institution to which the portfolio is sent.

The postsecondary education clearinghouse would also benefit institutions in two major ways. First, the clearinghouse would eliminate much (but not all) of the work associated with transfer-credit evaluation. As the system grows, more and more course equivalencies would be articulated. The second major benefit of the clearinghouse would be the availability of timely, complete, and accurate information during academic advising and registration, thus leading to a smoother transition in support of student success.

Institutional Practices

In the previous section of the book, we focused on four major intervention areas that support retention and persistence to degree within the institution. In addition, we have provided recommendations for public policy. In this section of the chapter we will review practices that extend the retention framework. These practices include actively seeking collaborative relationships, expanding the development of programs and services, and measuring student success.

Collaborative Relationships

In the public policy section of this chapter we identify the need for high-level collaboration in the areas of course applicability, common course numbering, and articulation agreements. Though implementation of these areas on a national level may take years to establish, institutional leaders should initiate discussion and implementation of cooperative agreements with other institutions, across multi-institution systems, and when possible within states and across states. Such discussions should begin with institutions that are in close proximity as well as those institutions which share a common affiliation. In addition to providing greater clarity to the transfer of courses, institutions may also collaborate in other ways, including shared faculty or staff, shared space, shared access to student events, and shared use of library materials.

Because academic preparation of entering college students resides in the K–12 system, college administrators should take the lead in promoting collaboration and initiating dialogue with elementary, middle school, and high school teachers on the disconnect between what students are taught and how they are taught and the level of preparation necessary to be successful in college. In its recent National Curriculum Survey, ACT (2009c) reported that 91% of high school teachers felt students in their subject area were prepared for college. In that same survey, only 26% of college faculty felt that students were prepared in their subject areas. In addition, 71% of high school teachers reported that their state's standards prepare students "well" or "very well" for college, whereas only 28% of college instructors felt that state standards led to adequate preparation for college. Both high school teachers and college instructors felt strongly about curriculum depth while suggesting that state standards focused on breadth. Finally, both high school teachers and college instructors believe that less emphasis should be placed on skills such as financial, health, and media literacy than on skills directly related to the content areas of English, mathematics, reading, or science. Advocates suggest that high school academic standards and expectations should be a mile deep and an inch wide (depth in core academic skill areas) rather than a mile wide and an inch deep (breadth across multiple content areas). If these differences are to be bridged, college personnel must take the lead by reaching out to K–12 teachers to close the gaps between what is taught in high school classes and what is necessary to succeed in college. The results of these dialogues will be improved high school instruction, better prepared students, and ultimately, increased college success rates.

Redesign Teacher Preparation Programs

Because teacher quality and effectiveness in K–12 education is pivotal to academic readiness for college, institutions must undertake a critical review of teacher preparation programs. Levine (2006b) reported that 62% of teachers surveyed believed that they were not prepared to cope with the realities of today's classrooms. Levine goes on to suggest that teacher education programs as they currently exist are increasingly irrelevant in meeting the needs of today's educational system. And, as a further indicator of the need for revision in approaches to teacher education, the policy implications summary from a recent ACT National Curriculum Study (2009c) indicates that one of its primary findings was that high school learning standards are not sufficiently aligned with postsecondary expectations. The report goes on to state that:

> Compared to high school teachers, college instructors continue to rate fewer content and skills as being of higher importance, and more skills as being of little or no importance, in the courses they teach and too many of the skills rated as important by high school teachers are not the fundamentals of each discipline that college instructors insist their students must have mastered by the time they enter credit-bearing college courses. (p. 8)

Course Placement Practices

Course placement practices are thoroughly discussed in Chapter Twelve, but the importance of an effective course placement program cannot be underestimated. At a minimum, course placement involves assessing students' academic skills and providing them with instruction that is appropriate to their skills.

In Chapter Seven we detailed the current crisis in student academic preparation for college, suggesting that only about one-quarter of high school graduates were fully prepared for college success in English, reading, mathematics, and science. These basic skills gaps can be effectively addressed only through accurate assessment for course placement which guides development education and other forms of learning support. Failure to assess and place students in courses commensurate with their basic skills is a recipe for failure.

Provide Transition Advising Services for Departing Students

Over the past several decades there has been significant attention paid to advising and counseling services provided to students prior to and during enrollment. There is evidence that community colleges provide support for students transferring to four-year degree granting institutions. Yet, there is little evidence that four-year colleges provide the same care and nurturance to students who intend to, or eventually will, pursue their educational goals at another institution. As we reported earlier, many students attend multiple institutions before earning a degree and it is not uncommon for students to be enrolled at more than one institution at a time. Though it is not possible to anticipate all student departures, success in the new institution will be greatly enhanced if transition advising and counseling services are provided. Students who receive assistance in making a graceful transition out of one institution into another are far more likely to ultimately succeed in reaching their educational goals. An added benefit accrues to institutions which assist departing students. Even though students will not be retained or persist to graduation, they will be far more likely to speak positively about the institution than those students who are left to their own devices in making the transition to another college.

Institutional Policies and Requirements

Many institutional policies and requirements have been instituted to ensure the academic integrity of a degree. Yet, they may also have the unintended consequence of disserving students transitioning into, within, or out of the institution. Most of these policies involve the application for credit for students in transition. Below are just a few examples of common policies that deserve institutional examination.

- Applicability of transferred courses to general education, major, minor, or elective requirements
- Number of transferred credit hours to general education, major, minor, or elective requirements
- Number of credit hours earned in residence
- Number of host institution credit hours earned during the final terms of enrollment
- Treatment of credits converted from a quarter system to a semester system (or vice versa)
- Treatment of credits earned at other institutions while a student is on academic suspension from the host institution
- Differential interpretation of upper-division and lower-division courses
- Acceptance of credits that do not apply to a degree
- Transfer of courses the student took pass-fail or in which the student did not earn a grade of C or higher
- Credit for developmental coursework
- Credit for prior learning
- Credit taken at a proprietary college or at a technical college

Though the examples above apply primarily to transfer students, there are also a number of policies within a given institution that have the potential to thwart progress of continuing students. Among those are:

- Academic progress policies that allow students to continue enrollment long past a realistic opportunity for recovering good standing
- General education requirements that are prescribed by major

- Academic programs with minimum entry thresholds
- Academic programs that exclude students for failure to meet prescribed expectations
- Policies on repeating courses and calculation of grade point average
- Requiring students to declare a major (within a prescribed time period)
- Disincentives for students who have earned the requisite number of hours to graduate but have not declared a program of study or filed an application for graduation
- Expectations created through a degree guarantee program
- Academic appeal process
- Class and course withdrawal policies (and relationship to financial aid)

Our inclusion of these policies is not intended as a criticism of them, nor is it an exhaustive compilation of institutional policies that can have an impact on student success. Rather, it provides a stimulus to review institutional policies from the perspective of student success.

Measuring Student Success

In the absence of a comprehensive definition of student success, institutions will continue to be held accountable and funded on the basis of the politically expedient and all-too-simplistic definition of retention: the percentage of students who are retained and the percentage of students who earn a certificate or a degree. Earlier in this chapter we built a case for the development of public policy based on the expanded definition of student success. Although we believe public policy should be driven by the expanded definition and concomitant accountability measures must be based on that definition, we are also realists. Shifts in public policy will most likely be controversial, hard-fought, and time-consuming. It is clear that if the expanded retention framework is to become reality, then institutions individually or collectively must tell their stories—not anecdotally, but through a consistent and shared definition of student success supported by accurate and comprehensive data gathering. We recommend that institutions study criteria and actively participate in one of the two voluntary groups described below.

Voluntary System of Accountability (VSA). VSA is an initiative by public four-year universities to supply consistent, accessible, and comparable information on the undergraduate student experience. The VSA is cosponsored by the Association of Public and Land-Grant Universities (APLU) and the Association of State Colleges and Universities (AASCU). Institutional data are collected in three areas: consumer information, student experiences and perceptions, and student learning outcomes. The VSA provides a uniform methodology for calculating student success and progress. Data are reported for participating colleges at College Portraits of Undergraduate Education (http://www.collegeportraits.org/). Statistics reported for first-time full-time students and for first-time transfer students are the percentage of students who graduated from the institution, those who were still enrolled at the institution, or those who graduated from another institution. These percentages are reported for four years and six years after initial enrollment.

Voluntary Framework of Accountability (VFA). The VFA a national system of community college accountability developed by the American Association of Community Colleges (AACC, n.d.) and funded through the Lumina Foundation and the Bill and Melinda Gates Foundation. Success measures and reporting cohorts below are posted on the VFA website: http://www.aacc.nche.edu/Resources/aaccprograms/vfa/Pages/default.aspx)

I. College Readiness Measures:
- Percentage of students:
  - Attempting and the percentage of students completing developmental courses in math or English/reading
  - That complete all developmental education
  - That complete an initial college-level math or English/reading course

II. Progress Measures (for those completing at least 15 credits)
- Percentage of first term course success rates
- Percentage of part-time students who reach 24 credits by the end of year two
- Percentage of full-time students who reach 42 credits by the end of year two
- Percentage of students retained at the end of the first term
- Percentage of students that reach the second year who are still enrolled, transferred to another institution, and/or completed a certificate or degree
- Percentage of course success rate at the end of year two

III. Outcomes and Success Measures
- The percentage of students that:
  - Earn an associate's degree either with or without transfer
  - Earn less than associate's degree (certificate) with or without transfer
  - Transfer to a four-year institution without earning a degree or certificate
  - Transfer to another community college
  - Are still enrolled six years later
  - Left campus in good academic standing (30+ credits; 2.0 GPA) without earning a degree (certificate) or left institution (not in good academic standing)

Participation in the VSA or the VFA provides institutions with common definitions and common metrics that provide a comprehensive picture of their contribution to student success.

Conclusion

We believe that those who make public policy will in time develop measures of accountability that recognize that student success and institutional quality are determined by many more measures than retention and persistence to degree. But we also believe that student success is far too important to wait. We call upon institutions to continue to pursue voluntary collaborations that will define and measure the multiple dimensions of student success. In doing so, institutions will drive public policy rather that react to it and retreat from it. In addition, we call upon higher educators to review institutional practices and policies, revising or eliminating those practices that impede student success.

17

CREATING A STUDENT SUCCESS CULTURE

The purpose of this chapter is to provide a framework for taking the knowledge acquired throughout this book and applying it at your institution. In other words, now that we have showcased a number of perspectives on what it takes to create a culture where all students can be successful, discussed the components of student success, and identified specific student success practices, how can this information can be effectively utilized to create a student success culture on your campus? After all, becoming informed about student success means nothing if institutional representatives are not able to convert this information into action. There is no cookie-cutter recipe for creating change on college campuses. Each institution's culture is unique and distinct. Describing one institution's methodology for improving student success or changing the institution's culture does not mean the exact same methodology will bear similar results at any other institution.

As discussed in Chapter Six, institutional culture plays a crucial role in the success or failure of any new student success–related initiative. Chapter Six highlighted best practices and general principles from the literature on how to improve student persistence on all types of college campuses (Kinzie & Kuh, 2004; Kramer & Associates, 2007; Kuh, Kinzie, Schuh, & Whitt, 2005; Hurtado, Milem, Clayton-Pedersen, & Allen, 2008). However, as Habley posits, a corollary of Hacken's Law is "The belief that understanding alone will stir an organization to action is one of mankind's greatest illusions" (Habley, 1996).

Thus, this chapter is not going to be a regurgitation of the best practices and principles on how to change an institution's culture to focus more on student success. Instead, we will make the case for why higher education institutions need to adopt a new grass roots approach to creating a culture that values student success. We will then provide a positive and proven organizational development approach that can be utilized to implement sustainable change on your campus.

A Typical Institutional Approach to Student Success

Consider how one midsize public institution has chosen to handle student success. As is typical at many institutions that are trying to increase student success, a retention committee, cochaired by a mid-level student affairs administrator and a faculty member, leads a team of 25 student affairs professional staff members and one or two faculty members. It is unclear to the members of the committee to whom the committee reports—some say it is to the Provost's Office, but others think that it reports to the Office of the Vice President for Student Affairs. Given that faculty representation is scarce on the committee, most of the attendees at meetings are lower- to mid-level student affairs administrators. The student affairs professional that cochairs the meeting has appointed subgroups to explore issues such as retention best practices at other peer institutions while another is charged with analyzing student data. The meetings are spent with the subgroups discussing their charges and next steps. But nobody seems to know where the results of the committee will be shared. Year after year, the committee makes no new progress despite the best intentions of the committee to increase student retention rates. Frustrated by the committee's lack of progress and the increasing pressure on the institution to do a better job of retaining and graduating students, the committee is temporarily disbanded while the upper administration struggles to find a more effective way to increase retention rates. This scenario is not atypical of the dead-ends that retention committees are running into all across the country.

Why a New Approach to Implementing Student Success Initiatives Is Needed

Part of the issue in this scenario is the institution's focus on student retention. If simply knowing which initiatives have been proven to increase student retention rates at other institutions, our nation would not be faced with our current reality: more than four out of ten students that enter higher education will not complete a bachelor's degree within six years (National Center for Educational Statistics, 2010b). Across the United States, institutions desperately want their students to be successful and are spending millions of dollars to increase their student retention rates.

As we have done throughout the book, our emphasis shifts the focus from a student retention focus to a student success paradigm. Why are so many of our institutional retention efforts failing? Tinto (2005) points to the failure of student retention initiatives to gain broad institution-wide support as one factor:

> It is one thing to establish a program; it is another to integrate it into the fabric of institutional life . . . The truth of the matter is that while many institutions tout the importance of increasing student retention, not enough take student retention seriously. (p. 6)

As Tinto (2005) has said, "What is not to be done is doing more of the same" (p. 5). Thus, our shift to creating a campus culture that values and actively promotes student success is a refreshing and needed shift in focus from the outdated and ineffective emphasis on simply retaining students. As mentioned in the preface, the student success paradigm is built on helping students achieve their educational goals, regardless of whether that means that students enroll in multiple higher education institutions to accomplish those goals or complete them in a prescribed amount of time. The emphasis switches from what the institution can do to retain the students at the institution to a fully student-centered approach that seeks to meet the unique needs and goals of individual students.

Appreciative Inquiry: A Different Approach to Change

Albert Einstein once said, "We can't solve problems by using the same kind of thinking we used when we created them." Earlier we made the case for shifting the focus from student retention to student success, and in this section of the chapter we will make a case for making the shift of viewing student success as a "problem" issue to one that views student success as an opportunity to bring the campus community together to focus on helping students achieve their educational goals. The mindset of student success = a problem is a mindset that has proven ineffective and detrimental. As the Einstein quote alludes, a new type of thinking is needed to change institutional culture to focus more on student success.

We suggest that instead of looking at student success as a problem, we help the campus community reframe student success into an opportunity. It is an opportunity to bring the campus together in a shared community-building cause that allows everyone on campus to celebrate its strengths and successes in enhancing student success, and to create a new, ideal vision of what student success will look like on that particular campus. In addition, we will be presenting a framework for translating this shared vision into reality by providing a mechanism for engaging members of the college community to contribute to making this vision a reality. We need look no further than the organizational development literature for a tried-and-true approach to creating positive change that can indeed make this scenario a reality.

The organizational development theory of Appreciative Inquiry was created in 1979 by David Cooperrider at Case Western Reserve University. At the time, Cooperrider was conducting research interviews in a hospital when he realized the questions that he was asking of his study participants influenced the types of responses he received. He quickly discovered when he asked positive, open-ended questions that respondents shared their stories and had more energy and enthusiasm than when he asked negative, closed questions. From this experience, he developed a four-phase theory he named Appreciative Inquiry:

> Appreciative Inquiry is a bold shift in the way we think about and approach organization change. The ultimate paradox of Appreciative Inquiry is that it does not aim to change anything. It aims to uncover and bring forth existing strengths, hopes, and dreams: to identify and amplify the positive core of the organization. In so doing, it transforms people and organizations. With Appreciative Inquiry, the focus of attention is on positive potential—the best of what has been, what is, and what might be. It is a process of positive change. (Whitney & Trosten-Bloom, 2003, p. 15)

Appreciative Inquiry (AI) has proven to be a powerful approach for creating positive change in businesses, nonprofit organizations, and educational institutions. It has improved the profitability of businesses and the organizational effectiveness of nonprofits and educational institutions. Why is AI an effective approach to change? The answer plays itself out in a number of ways. First, AI recognizes organizations are not composed of robots; rather, they are composed of people. People value opportunities to participate, share their stories with others, learn and grow, and have a role in shaping the future of organizations (Whitney & Trosten-Bloom, 2003). "Appreciative Inquiry works because it liberates power. It unleashes both individual and organizational power. It brings out the best of people, encourages them to see and support the best of others, and generates unprecedented cooperation and innovation" (Whitney & Trosten-Bloom, 2003, p. 19). AI allows people to build relationships, have their voices heard, be positive, choose how they will participate in the change effort, and then feel supported for their efforts (Whitney & Trosten-Bloom, 2003). In short, Appreciative Inquiry provides a platform for people to become positively engaged in the change process.

The benefits of AI extend far beyond individual participants. Organizations benefit because substantive change is accelerated and it involves a timely way of bringing organizational members together to create visions, make decisions, and make commitments for action (Whitney & Trosten-Bloom, 2003). The reason AI is an appropriate approach to creating change in higher education settings is higher education institutions are complex organizations with multiple layers, silos, and members. AI has proven to be most effective in creating comprehensive change in complex organizations dealing with complicated issues:

> By comprehensive change we mean change in orientation—strategic shifts in the relationship of the enterprise with its environment changes in the way the work of the organization is done, and/or changes in how the organization approaches problems of leadership, performance, conflict, power, and equity. (Watkins & Mohr, 2001, p. 22)

There is no doubt that campus constituents may be wary of any effort to promote change. We have all seen "flavor of the day" approaches (such as TQM) utilized in higher education settings that have completely flopped, leaving many members of the campus community somewhat jaded or even hostile about any mention of a "new approach" to change. Yet the beauty and impact of AI is in its simplicity and its emphasis on the involvement of all members of the campus community in not just carrying out a plan for change, but also in the creation of the plan. Instead of being a top-down exercise where upper-level administrators dictate the future of the institution, AI is a bottom-up approach where new and creative ideas emerge from members of the campus community. A cocreated vision and plan for successfully executing that vision are the outcomes of the AI approach.

Appreciative Inquiry has the power to change the culture of the institution by changing the dialogue that occurs at the proverbial "watercooler." The economic pressures that higher education institutions face impact the people that work there. Employees want their institutions and students to be successful and want to play a part in that success. Until this point there has not been a proven way for engaging employees in this process. Watkins and More (2001) write, "There is a geometrically increasing demand for people in organizations to shift direction, make more effective use of new technologies, and respond to crises in shorter and shorter time frames with fewer and fewer resources" (p. 24). AI provides a new and empowering approach to change.

Appreciative Inquiry Summit

There are at least eight ways of engaging participants using the organizational development theory of Appreciative Inquiry (Whitney & Trosten-Bloom, 2003). The two types of engagement that are most appropriate for higher education institutions are Whole-System 4-D Dialogue and the Appreciative Inquiry Summit. The Whole-System 4-D Dialogue is typically used over a longer period of time (often two months to a year) and is done at multiple sites. This approach uses the 4-Ds of Appreciative Inquiry—Discover, Dream, Design, and Deliver—to frame appreciative interviews.

For the purposes of this chapter, however, we will be focusing on an Appreciative Inquiry (AI) Summit because it can be used to jump-start change initiatives in two to four days and can be used with groups of 50 to over 2,000 (Whitney & Trosten-Bloom, 2003). The AI Summit provides an opportunity for all constituent groups to have their voices heard within the 4-D framework, but it also adds in a Define phase prior to delving into the subsequent four phases (Discover, Dream, Design, and Deliver).

Overview of the AI Summit Phases

The Define phase involves putting together an appropriate committee to determine what the topic of the AI summit will be. In this case, the obvious topic would be student success. Next, the Discover phase involves allowing summit participants to discuss the best of what is already happening within the organization as it relates to the topic of the summit. The Dream phase gives summit attendees an opportunity to share their own personal vision of what the organization can accomplish in the future. Once a common vision for the group has been identified, the Design phase involves group members devising a plan for making that dream a reality. Finally, in the Deliver phase, assignments are made based on participant interests to carry out the work that needs to be done to accomplish the shared vision of the organization.

Although space considerations preclude us from going into a great deal of detail about each of the five phases as they relate to retention efforts, we will provide enough of an overview of each phase to help the reader understand the basic premises of each phase. For those who would like to learn more about the specific details of conducting a successful Appreciative Inquiry summit, there are numerous books that can serve as good resources (Ludema, Whitney, Mohr, & Griffin, 2003; Watkins & Mohr, 2001; Whitney & Trosten-Bloom, 2003).

Define Phase. The Define phase is the first step in the Appreciative Inquiry summit and it involves figuring out what the focus of the summit will be. However, before defining the focus of the summit, it is important to establish a leader and a campuswide student success committee to guide the AI summit as well as subsequent student-focused efforts. Habley and McClanahan (2004) point to the importance of designating a high-level campus official who has the title and clout to guide student success initiatives. Appointing a well-qualified and respected leader will be one of the most important keys for ensuring student success initiatives that emerge out of the Appreciative Inquiry summit become a reality. It is our opinion that if institutions want to fully engage faculty in the process, the person in charge of the student success initiatives should report directly to the Provost/Vice President for Academic Affairs and have a title that highlights this reporting line (for example, Associate Provost).

Once the leader of campus success initiatives has been designated, the next step is for that leader to appoint a campuswide student success planning team. Habley & McClanahan's recommendation (2004) that a "broad-based campus planning team should engage in the study of student needs" (p. 21) for campus retention initiatives also rings true for the proposed student success team. The planning team must have a blend of faculty members, academic administrators, student affairs administrators, staff, and students. The blend will be different for each institution, but our advice is to make sure that faculty members are equally, if not overly, represented in the mix.

This planning team will serve as the guiding team for the AI summit and the leader of the group should "make sure there is a powerful group guiding the change—one with leadership skills, bias for action, credibility, communications ability, authority, and analytical skills" (Kotter, 2007, para. 2). The job of the AI summit planning team is to

> design, orchestrate, and carry out the entire process from start to finish. They are the ones who link appreciative inquiry to the organization's core issue or opportunity, and who ensure that the AI Summit is tailored to meet the needs and culture of the organization. (Ludema et al., 2003, p. 29)

According to Whitney & Trosten-Bloom (2003), the job description for the team leading the AI Summit should be broad. Their duties include deciding on a topic for the summit, identifying the desired outcomes of the summit, building awareness of the initiative and the summit, and communicating before, during, and after the summit with members of the campus community. After the summit, this team will work hard to keep the working task groups that emerge out of the summit coordinated, scheduled, and on task.

In an AI summit focused on student success, the planning team needs to conduct an analysis of student characteristics (Lotkowski, Robbins, & Noeth, 2004; Habley & McClanahan, 2004) as well as programs that are already in place at the institution that promote student success.

Habley and McClanahan (2004) provide the following list of student data areas to review:

- Demographics: including, but not limited to, sex, race/ethnicity, age, size of high school, parental level of education, socioeconomic status, etc.

- Academic performance: including, but not limited to, admission test scores, high school rank and grade point average, placement test scores, etc.

- Academic plans: including, but not limited to, choice of major, level of highest degree aspiration, etc.

- Non-academic variables: including, but not limited to, academic goals, achievement motivation, self-concept, social involvement, interest patterns, etc.

- Self-reported needs: including, but not limited to, expressed need for instructional support (writing, math, reading, study skills, etc.) and expressed need for noninstructional support (choice of major, disability support, personal counseling, cocurricular involvement, etc.)

- Student opinions and attitudes: including a broad-based
  assessment of student opinions and attitudes on instructional and non-instructional programs, services, and policies (p. 22)

The planning team can utilize existing campus data sources
to begin compiling the data set for analysis. Ideally, the data collected can be broken down by student characteristics such as
race/ethnicity, first-generation, and at-risk population (Habley &
McClanahan, 2004).

The second form of analysis involves examining the current state of student success efforts already underway on campus.
One way to document student success efforts on campus is to
fill out the Prevention, Intervention, and Recovery Initiatives
Chart (Table 17.1) that was developed at Miami University's
Hamilton campus (J. E. Murray, personal communication, July 1,
2010). This chart should be distributed widely across campus so
that all student success units (colleges, departments, and student affairs subunits) have the opportunity to share how they
contribute to student success. Once all campus units have documented their initiatives, the AI summit committee can compile
the results and analyze the areas of strength and weakness in
terms of meeting the needs of students.

Defining the Topic. After the analysis of student characteristics and student-success–related programs that are already
in place has been conducted, the student success team can
now begin to determine what the topic of the AI summit will
be. Lewis, Passmore, and Cantore (2008) identified six criteria
to keep in mind as the student success team begins to determine the topic for the AI Summit: keep the topic open enough
that there is room for new issues to evolve during the process,
each member of the team needs to keep an open mind about
the topics under consideration, and the emphasis should be

Table 17.1 Prevention, Intervention, and Recovery Initiatives Chart.

	Prevention	*Intervention*	*Recovery*
Curricular	Orientation class Study skills class Choosing a major class Advising syllabus	Study skills class	Study skills class
Policies	Mandatory advising for all new students Midterm grades reported by faculty Intrusive advising and cold calls	Mandatory advising for probationary students	Fresh start Petitions for suspension, dismissal Limit credit hours for probationary students
Programs	Orientation sessions Athletic study tables	Outreach for midterm grades Outreach for students on Warning Workshops on test taking, stress management, study skills. . .	Academic Recovery Program (ARP) Workshops on test taking, stress management, study skills. . .

on outcomes and not the details of how the outcomes will be accomplished. The remaining principles include ensuring that the topic is positively phrased, gathering input from people across campus about defining the topic for the summit, and ensuring that the topic is one that will generate interest and excitement amongst campus constituents (Lewis et al., 2008). We would suggest that the committee consider basing their topic on student success. One way to frame the topic is to use one or more of the three conditions for students to be successful in college that we laid out in the preface to this book: how to assist students in learning, educate students about developing behaviors and personal characteristics that contribute to persistence (for example, motivation, commitment, engagement, and self-regulation), or assist students in identifying and committing to an appropriate plan of study.

Clearly, the definition of the topic is one of the most important steps in the AI summit process. "Appreciative Inquiry leads us to define the summit task as an affirmative call to action. Effective AI Summit tasks are actionable and engaging and command the attention of the whole organization" (Ludema et al., 2003, p. 30). This focus on identifying a positive topic (for example, increase the number of students who have developed a clear plan for achieving their educational goals by 50%) versus a negative topic (for example, decrease student dropout rate between first and second year) is important because "human systems move in the direction of what they study, the choice of what to study—what to focus organizational attention on—is fateful" (Whitney & Trosten-Bloom, 2003, p. 7). The main premise of Appreciative Inquiry is positive in nature—celebrating the best of what has been as well as the best of what the organization can become. If the topic selected is stated in terms of a problem rather than an opportunity, the entire AI summit process will not be successful.

Once the topic for the AI summit is identified, the planning team is then charged with identifying who will participate in the summit. When selecting summit participants, the ideal is to have all campus constituents attend a two-to-four-day summit. Ideally, these constituents include faculty, administrators, student affairs professionals, facilities staff, the president, and the provost. It is plausible to accomplish this goal at smaller public and private institutions, but larger institutions may not have the space to accommodate everyone in one facility. Those institutions then must decide whether they will offer multiple summits, use a different AI engagement methodology, or ensure that a significant number of people from each constituent group are selected to represent their coworkers at the summit. Again, the ideal is to have all employees attend the entire summit (or one of a series of summits offered on the same topic).

The planning team is also charged with designing the format for the AI summit. This can be done by the team by itself using the AI summit books and/or internet resources, or institutions may decide to hire an AI consultant to coach the planning team from the definition of the topic phase through the delivery phase. This latter option may be the most efficient for colleges and universities. To create the agenda for the summit, the retention team, with or without the assistance of an AI consultant, will likely need to schedule one to two full days together to plan the event in such a way that it meets the needs and culture of the particular campus, but also uses the four phases of AI to guide their work (Ludema et al., 2003).

Additional principles for conducting an effective AI summit include securing a location that is healthy and allows all summit participants to be in the room at the same time, comprehensive planning of the summit, ensuring that the focus stays positive throughout the summit and that the facilitators' role is minimal (Ludema et al., 2003).

Discover Phase. The Discover phase marks the end of the preparation phase by the AI planning team and the beginning of the actual AI summit where the participants have gathered. Once everyone at the summit has been greeted by the president, the leader of the planning team, or another high-ranking university official, typically provides an overview of AI and the four phases. Afterwards, the Discover phase begins and it involves getting participants talking about the best of "what is" currently happening in the organization and the best of "what has been" in terms of the history of the organization as it relates to the topic of the summit (Lewis, Passmore, & Cantore, 2008; Watkins & Mohr, 2001; Whitney & Trosten-Bloom, 2003).

Lewis et al. (2008) have identified six key elements for successful implementation of the Discover phase: agreeing that the topic selected by the planning team is appropriate, using the Discover questions that the planning team has identified, engaging people in one-on-one conversations where they ask each other the Discover questions, collecting the stories that emerge from participant responses to the Discover questions, mapping the larger groups' answers, and identifying key enduring factors that "have sustained the organization over time" (p. 50).

Examples of pertinent Discover questions that participants can ask each other about retention-related issues include:

1. Tell me about a time when you had a positive impact on a student.
2. Tell me about a time when you were really proud to be associated with this institution.
3. When our institution is at its best, why does it attract students to the institution?
4. When our institution is at its best, how does it ensure that students are successful?
5. Give me an example of what makes this institution great or unique.

Participants are typically given time to ask and answer these questions with a partner. Subsequently, each pair groups with four or five other pairs to share their stories. Those small groups then advance what they feel are the key stories that best represent what was discussed in the pairs. Then members of the planning team compile the results, identify themes that emerge, and share this information broadly with the entire campus community.

Dream. The Dream phase is all about determining the collective hopes and dreams of the assembled summit attendees. "The dream phase involves challenging the status quo by envisioning a preferred future" (Watkins & Mohr, 2001, p. 44).

The key to the Dream phase is to encourage participants to dream big, without regard to money, time, or the "realities" of the organization's current status.

There are five steps to conducting a successful Dream phase. The first is to have the pairs in the Discover phase transition to asking questions that are about their preferred future vision of the institution in relation to the identified topic of the AI summit. Sample Dream questions that may relate to a student success-focused summit topic include: It is five years from now and the *New York Times* is showcasing our institution as one where every student is thriving both inside and outside the classroom. What aspects of our campus are highlighted in the article? How does the campus look different? How did the changes come about? What are the specific things that helped make this happen? What is the most exciting part of this dream to you?

Lewis et al.'s next Dream phase steps (2008) include having the pairs share their Dream discussions with their small group. The small groups share their findings with the larger group. After participants build a "dream map" that covers the larger groups' compiled dreams, they then head into the Design phase.

Design. Once the summit participants agree on a shared vision of what they want the future of the organization to look like in relation to the topic of the summit, the Design phase is focused on cocreating a plan to make the dream a reality.

> The design phase is concerned with making decisions about the high-level actions which need to be taken to support the delivery of the dream. This involves moving to agree to a common future dream and the actions to support this. (Lewis et al., 2008, p. 58)

The steps in the Design phase involve shifting the conversation from the Dream phase to discussions about what needs to be accomplished. Typically the large group works together "to identify what groups in the organization are needed to bring the dream to life" (Lewis et al., 2008, p. 50). The summit planning team can lead discussions about what the key themes and initiatives need to be and then give summit participants an opportunity to join small groups based on alignment of their interests with the key themes and initiatives. These theme-based small groups then create project statements that focus on what the theme-based groups all agree to accomplish (Lewis et al., 2008).

Findings from this book as well as other student success-related resources can be used to help the theme-based groups identify initiatives that have proven to help students be successful.

The Design phase also involves the small theme-based groups establishing "realistic short-term and long-term retention, progress, and completion goals" (Habley & McClanahan, 2004, p. 24). Each theme-based group needs to ensure there are enough "low-hanging fruit" goals that can be accomplished without too much difficulty (although not too easily) in order to gain momentum for the initiative and to give members of the theme-based group as well as other campus constituents confidence these new student success–focused goals are obtainable (Habley & McClanahan, 2004).

Longer-term goals can be more difficult for the theme-based groups to establish. These goals should be reviewed by the planning team to make sure these goals are realistic and consistent with other institutional initiatives.

Deliver Phase. The Deliver phase, also known as the Destiny phase, is focused on making the plan that was cocreated during the Design phase a reality by putting the plan into motion. The Deliver phase "focuses specifically on personal and organizational commitments and paths forward" (Whitney & Trosten-Bloom, 2003, p. 9). Action is the name of the game in this phase and action is an attainable outcome, partly because of all the positive experiences that summit participants have had throughout the first three phases of the journey. They have had the opportunity to share their stories and dreams with their coworkers and they have been able to talk to others who are interested in initiatives they are passionate about. The positive momentum that has been built up to this point will be crucial in giving participants the motivation to become involved in the work needed to make the group's dream a reality. One great aspect of AI is people feel connected to the plan because they have ownership in creating the plan and thus are motivated to execute the plan in the Deliver phase.

Lewis et al. (2008) offer steps to making the Deliver phase a success, including transitioning the conversations in the theme-based groups from setting goals to actually doing the work needed to meet the goals. The groups come up with an action plan containing clear next steps. Within the groups people commit to the roles they are willing to take on. At this point, the groups transition from theme-based groups to action groups.

It is important for the newly formed action groups to be informed that they will likely encounter setbacks and resistance (Habley & McClanahan, 2004). The old saying that change is hard is indeed a truism. In general, people do not embrace change, even when it benefits them. So, the action groups need to be reminded of this upfront and throughout the process by the planning team. As the action groups encounter the inevitable surprises and setbacks, they must be willing to learn from their mistakes and make mid-course adjustments.

The final step in a successful Deliver phase at a summit is to celebrate the accomplishments of the group over the course of the summit (Lewis et al., 2008). Participants should be thanked for their time and participation in summit activities and reminded that this is only the first step in the journey of increasing student success on campus.

Conclusion

This chapter focused on providing a new framework for creating a campus environment that values student success and the unique culture of each campus. By looking at student success as an opportunity instead of a problem and by using the organizational development theory of Appreciative Inquiry, institutions can revolutionize their approach to establishing a campus culture focused on student success. Appreciative Inquiry utilizes one of the oldest approaches to creating a new culture by engaging campus constituents in dialogue about the best of what has been, what is, and what might be. Einstein once said, "Any intelligent fool can make things bigger, more complex, and more violent. It takes a touch of genius—and a lot of courage—to move in the opposite direction." Appreciative Inquiry is the simple solution to creating a unified culture that values student success.

18

LEADING THE CAMPUS TO STUDENT SUCCESS

It is very unlikely that you will have read this book from cover to cover. But even if you have read only a few of the chapters, it is probable that you have arrived at this chapter feeling at least somewhat discouraged about the potential for enhancing student success on your campus. Although high school grades have improved and graduation rates have increased, students in the educational pipeline appear to be no better prepared for college than their predecessors, and changing demographics indicate that those population cohorts least likely to be prepared for, enroll in, and succeed at college are increasing dramatically. Interventions touted to improve retention and persistence to degree have changed little over the last four decades while retention and persistence to degree rates have changed even less. Colleges expend significant resources to compete for what amounts to a continuous flow of qualified first-year students. Tweaking an oft-heard aphorism, "The more things stay the same, the more they stay the same." Or, stated another way, "Insanity is doing the same thing over and over again and expecting a different outcome" (multiple attributions). We have provided the reader with book sections on the importance and impact of student success, a new definition of student success, the conditions necessary for student success, and the dominant practices leading to student success. These perspectives, for the most part, have been macro in nature: focusing on the nation or on institutional categories. Chapters Sixteen and Seventeen bring the issue of student success closer to home by providing recommendations for policymakers and for building an institutional culture of student success.

This final chapter zeroes in on the micro level. It is about you and the role you play in the process of improving student success on your campus. Regardless of your role in the formal structure of your campus or the power and authority vested in your position, you can become a leader who challenges the status quo, and advocates for programs and services that increase the likelihood of student success. The basis for this chapter is an article appearing in *Liberal Education*, a publication of the Association of American Colleges. It was written by George Klemp (1988), who at the time served as president of a consulting firm specializing in human resources management. The concepts are based on his study of behaviors which differentiated exemplary performers from average performers. One of the major conclusions he reached was "that the amount of formal knowledge one acquires about a content area is generally unrelated to superior performance." (p. 37). This finding is particularly difficult for academics to comprehend, for in the intellectual community, content-specific knowledge is the coin of the realm. Knowledge is king!

But knowledge is not enough. Klemp's assertion is consistent with Habley's corollary (1996) to Hacken's law, which we introduced in the previous chapter: the belief that understanding alone will stir an organization to action is one of mankind's greatest illusions. In much the same way that data alone is not useful until it is used to answer a question or applied to a decision, knowledge may inform but, does not, in and of itself, lead to action. Klemp discovered that the difference between exemplary performers and average performers had much more to do with *how they used* what they knew and understood than it did with *what* they knew and understood. He identified a set of three capabilities that form the scaffold for the rest of this chapter which we believe can guide the way you think about student success. Those capabilities are cognitive skills, interpersonal abilities, and intrapersonal factors.

Cognitive Skills

The first set of capabilities identified by Klemp is cognitive skills. He suggests that content-specific knowledge usually atrophies in a relatively short period of time and he speculates on the enduring qualities of the knowledge acquisition. He suggests that cognitive skills have three enduring qualities: evaluative thinking, conceptualization, and systematic thinking. Taken together, Klemp designates these three capabilities as "human knowing." Each of these three qualities is described below.

Evaluative Thinking

Evaluative thinking is the capacity to think in a disciplined way. An evaluative thinker is one who can separate the pertinent and relevant information from that which is irrelevant. It is the ability to diagnose, to recognize gaps and discrepancies, and to piece together a description of the situation in much the same way as a doctor makes a diagnosis or a salesperson sizes up the customer. Evaluative thinking focuses on the question, Where are we? It is not, however, a matter of intuition or hunch. In Chapter Ten we underscored the importance of collecting and analyzing information on student demographics, academic performance, academic plans, opinions, needs, attitudes, and psychosocial characteristics. Of equal importance is understanding the characteristics that differentiate students who stay from students who leave.

Evaluative thinking requires establishing a definition of student success, collecting reliable baseline data, and tracking existing success rates. This may seem like a relatively elementary activity. Yet, as we pointed out in Chapter One, defining retention is one of the most vexing problems facing retention researchers. Using an approach that focuses on the number of students who entered and comparing it to the number of students who continue to enroll is, by all definitions, a gross and uninformative methodology. Continuous tracking of students is an essential element in the evaluative process. Although it is true that the majority of student departures occur between the beginning of the first year and the beginning of the second year, significant attrition does occur after students enter the second year. And it is also true that many campuses have deployed a front-loading strategy that commits significant resources to first-to-second-year retention interventions only to experience no concomitant increase in degree completion rates. Certainly students must survive to the second year in order to complete a degree. But first-to-second-year survival is simply the first benchmark in a continuous process that leads to degree completion. The second benchmark is progression rate. Progression is defined as the percentage of first-time, full-time students who are retained for a second year *and* have achieved academic standing as second year (sophomore) students. Students who are retained but fail to make reasonable progress in academic standing are far more likely to drop out during the second and subsequent years. The final benchmark is degree completion rate. The evaluative thinker realizes that if a campus is to improve on these three benchmarks, it is necessary that retention interventions be sustained throughout a student's enrollment and that those interventions are systematically applied to all facets of the student experience.

Conceptualization

Conceptualization involves the ability to discern and synthesize new patterns from information where no patterns existed before. It is the ability to define and articulate what the organization might become. Conceptualization is seeing the big picture, defining the vision, and setting goals. Conceptualization focuses on two questions. Where do we want to be? How will we benchmark our progress? Success or failure in the achievement in retention, progression, and degree completion often rests on the establishment of realistic short-term and long-term goals. Goals that are set too high often result in frustrated faculty and staff and dwindling commitment to improve student success rates. Although the conventional wisdom suggests that about one-third of all first-year students fail to return for a second year, establishing that figure as an institutional goal is sheer folly. Such a goal is as inappropriate to an open-admission community college as it is to a highly selective private college. As a result, the goals for retention, progression, and degree completion must focus on incremental improvements in the institution's current baselines in those areas. As we described in Chapter Five, small but realistic goals for improved retention can have a significant effect on the institution's fiscal situation.

Where possible, the overall institutional goal should be supported by disaggregated target goals for selected programs and for selected student groups. For example, within an overall institutional goal to improve first-to-second-year retention, the planning team might establish subgoals for at-risk students, undecided students, or for students who participate in supplemental instructional programs. Or, as the result of the implementation of a particular program strategy, a target goal could be established for students who participate in that program strategy, with success rates compared with those of students who did not participate in the program.

A corollary to setting realistic goals is to allow ample time for interventions to have an impact on student retention. It is unreasonable to assume that a new or enhanced retention strategy will be flawlessly implemented in its first incarnation. And it is equally unreasonable to assume that a retention intervention will meet or exceed its retention goal in the first year of implementation. Program adjustments will most assuredly need to be undertaken. Because of these factors, patience is counseled. Goals for first-to-second-year retention and progression are not likely to be achieved for at least two years or, in some cases, longer. And, the impact on degree completion may not be fully realized for five to seven years.

Figure 18.1 Considerations in the Change Process

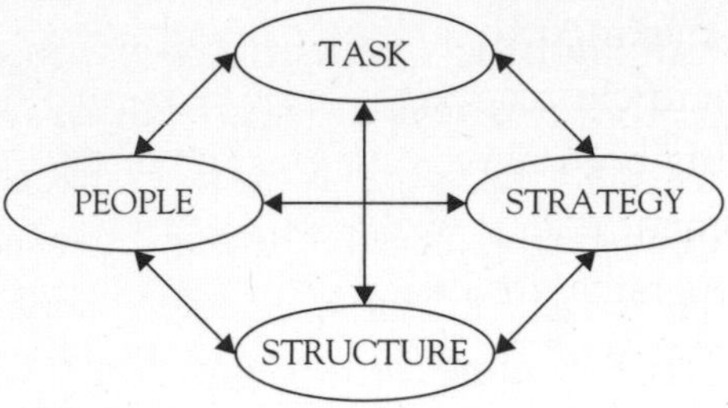

Systematic Thinking

The third cognitive capability cited by Klemp is systematic thinking. Systematic thinking involves understanding the people involved in implementation, the structures in which those people work, and identifying appropriate strategies to accomplish the task(s) at hand. Figure 18.1 depicts the relationships between and among those factors.

Systematic thinking involves the orchestration of people, tasks, structures, and strategies. It involves the ability to organize and plan work in an orderly sequence; to identify efficient and effective pathways to goal achievement. It focuses on the question, How will we get there? If the process of evaluative thinking and creative conceptualization have been thoroughly addressed, it is likely to result in the identification of groups of students or retention interventions that should be targeted in the retention effort. The history of WWISR surveys reported in Chapter Eleven provides a consistent and compelling case in support of four retention interventions that, in the opinion of survey respondents, make a difference in student success. Yet, it is important to note that virtually *none* of practices with the highest incidence rates cited in the surveys are among those cited as having the greatest impact on retention. This phenomenon suggests that few gains in student retention are the result of conducting business as usual—doing what everyone else is doing. Finally, survey results strongly suggest that campus efforts should focus on high-impact, value-added retention interventions. Of the retention interventions included in the surveys, strategies cited by respondents as making the greatest contribution to retention fall into the four main clusters described in chapters which appear in Section 4 of this book: first-year transition programs, academic advising, assessment/course placement, and learning support.

Because programs in each of these four categories exist to some degree at every college, it is essential to focus on the assessment of the degree to which these interventions address identified student needs. In some situations this assessment will lead to recommendations for minor changes in the definition and delivery of these interventions. But in other cases, significant program changes or realignments may be indicated. One of the primary reasons for a broad-based retention planning team is to provide support for some of the more significant program changes or realignment that may be needed.

Two caveats are in order. The first is that successful interventions at one institution may not necessarily yield the same results at another institution. Far too often, campuses intent on fixing the retention problem scurry to adopt solutions that are in place at other campuses only to discover that the interventions yielded no significant improvement in student success rates. Effective retention interventions must be adapted to integrate student needs with institutional capabilities. An advising center at an open admission community college would be organized differently than at a public liberal arts college. First-year seminars, as we pointed out in Chapter Fourteen, vary in content, scope, and delivery. The first-year seminar would take on far different characteristics at a traditional admission four-year public college than it would at a private, highly-selective, four-year college. The issue here is adaptation rather than adoption. Interventions cannot be blindly adopted. They must be carefully adapted.

The second caveat is that institutions desperate to improve student success should avoid the shotgun approach—that is, implementing multiple interventions in the hopes that one or more of the interventions will enhance student success. Such an approach is counterproductive for two reasons. First, it dilutes both fiscal and human resources. And second, such an approach makes it far more difficult to assess the impact of interventions on student success. The WWISR studies (Habley & McClanahan, 2004; Habley, McClanahan, Valiga, & Burkum, 2010) provide some assistance by identifying the practices that respondents believe have the greatest impact on retention. It is interesting to note that only 10 interventions were consistently identified as having the greatest impact on retention (see Chapter Eleven).

The three cognitive capabilities identified by Klemp form the scaffold of human knowing as they are applied to effective planning for student success. If these capabilities are attended to in the planning process three critical questions will be answered: Where are we? Where do we want to be? How will we get there?

Interpersonal Abilities

Evaluative thinking, conceptualization, and systematic thinking are essential to the process of improving student success. But in and of themselves these cognitive skills will not bring about improvement in student success rates. Requisite to success is the second set of capabilities. These capabilities, identified by Klemp as "human being" are interpersonal skills: the impressions we make, how we say things, and the messages we communicate by what we say and, more importantly, by what we do. The three interpersonal skills identified by Klemp are described below.

Sensitivity

As the saying goes, if the only tool you have is a hammer, every problem looks like a nail (multiple attributions). Many a great idea has failed miserably because the communicator of the idea failed to take into account the needs, expectations, strengths, and concerns of the individuals to whom the idea was being communicated. Some people resist new ideas simply because they do not want to change, whereas others resist new ideas because they have anxieties about status, power, influence, and threat to established routines. New ideas affect individuals differently.

Influence Skill

Getting things done is not simply a matter of having the right and good idea, because nothing gets done in an organization by one person. An idea is a passive nonentity until it is shared with and supported by others. Because this is the case, the ability to persuade others that the idea is both good and right, an absolute necessity. Klemp (1988) states:

> On one level, one's influence skills reflect one's ability to convince others through logically arguing the correctness of an idea; at a more subtle level however, effective influence comes from one's ability to understand the needs, expectations, and hidden agendas of others so that what is said falls on favorable ears. (p. 39)

More often than not, individuals assess new ideas from the personal perspective of "What's in it for me?" Influence requires crafting an argument that exhibits sensitivity to the needs and expectations of the individual one is trying to influence.

The ability to influence others, then, is more of an art than it is a science. Because individuals have differential needs and expectations, framing the idea in a manner which is sensitive to these differences is a critical factor in achieving broad-based support. In fact, the skillful influencer must not only be able to discern the needs and expectations of individuals, but must also adapt the persuasive techniques to maximize the likelihood of a positive response. A hammer will not work when a scalpel is needed.

Finally, influence is not a one-way street. In the course of influencing others, we often learn new information which can improve the idea. It is also possible that the process of influencing others may yield barriers, some surmountable and some not. As a result, the ability to influence others should be a give and take which is characterized by negotiation and compromise. The result of negotiation is likely to improve the idea and gain support it.

Using Informal Process

Many of the most important people on campus are not necessarily those who have formal power and authority. Although support from those in positions of authority is essential, that support is not enough. Particularly on a college campus, it is the opinion leaders—those who have important information, those who serve as resources, and those who can support an idea—who are most instrumental in acceptance and adoption. Because this is the case, informal process requires talking with people, building close working relationships, making yourself known to others, and knowing who to call upon to make things happen.

Building relationships with others to gain support for the adoption of new ideas requires networking and boundary spanning. Networking involves engaging individuals with whom a person regularly interacts to support an idea or set of activities. Networks are intended to extend the concept of teamwork beyond the immediate peer group to other groups or units with related functions. A boundary spanner is an individual who links ideas across the traditional and formal organizational structure by reaching out to individuals in organizational units that have either a direct or an indirect impact on an idea.

Using informal process not only relies heavily on influence skills, but also on the identification of the positions individuals are likely to take when encountering a new idea. Assume for a few moments that there are four descriptors that characterize an individual's reaction to a new idea: activist, collaborator, cynic, and skeptic. These four descriptors are depicted in Figure 18.2.

Figure 18.2 Attitudes Toward Change

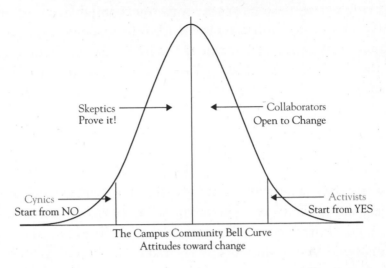

Skeptics
Prove it!

Collaborators
Open to Change

Cynics
Start from NO

Activists
Start from YES

The Campus Community Bell Curve
Attitudes toward change

Although roles occupied by campus personnel rarely fit a normal distribution, Figure 18.2 serves as an illustration of the distribution of the four roles. An activist is an individual who generally embraces new ideas, sometimes without conducting a critical review of the idea. An activist is an individual who thrives on change for change's sake. A collaborator is an individual who embraces new ideas, but only after some thoughtful consideration. A cynic is an individual who generally rejects new ideas without engaging in discussion or consideration. A cynic can always be counted on for a negative response to a new idea. Finally, the skeptic is an individual who is willing to learn, but has yet to be persuaded. The skeptic, characterized by some as a devil's advocate, is one who raises critical issues and engages in argumentation, not necessarily to oppose an idea, but simply to make people discuss and consider the idea more thoroughly. Activists will support change but may need some reining in. Collaborators need no persuasion. No amount of persuading, urging, or cajoling is likely to change the cynic. We firmly believe that the majority of effort and energy should be spent influencing the skeptics. If one is successful in using an informal process to persuade the skeptics, a critical mass in support of the new program idea is far more likely to occur.

The interpersonal abilities of sensitivity, influence, and the use of informal process articulated by Klemp as "human being" are essential to the adoption of retention interventions. Without interpersonal abilities, a good idea will be no more than a good idea.

Intrapersonal Factors

The final component of Kemp's trio of individual success characteristics is intrapersonal factors, a set of qualities that operate at a deep level within the self. Klemp's notion of intrapersonal factors deviates slightly from a more traditional definition of intrapersonal intelligence as our cognitive ability to understand and sense our "self." Intrapersonal intelligence allows us to tap into our being—who we are, what feelings we have, and why we are this way. Although intrapersonal intelligence is a broad construct, Klemp zeroes in on just three intrapersonal traits of the successful performer: confidence, initiative, and persistence. He labels these three factors as "human doing."

Confidence

Klemp (1988) defines confidence as "the ability to stand up for one's own beliefs when one knows one is right, to be able to express one's differences with others freely and openly, and to confront challenges and problems directly" (p. 40). Confidence supports risk taking, compelling people to try things they have not tried before because they have feared failure. Confidence is a natural outcome that occurs at the confluence of cognitive skills and interpersonal abilities. It evolves from a thorough assessment of the current state of affairs, a clear vision of the desired outcome(s), and an organized plan for achieving the outcome(s). And it is the product of persuasion, sensitivity to others, and the skillful use of informal process. Perhaps James Neil Hollingworth (aka Ambrose Hollingworth Redmoon or Ambrose Redmoon) said it best: "Confidence is not the absence of fear, but rather the judgment that something is more important than the fear" (Redmoon, 1991).

Initiative

When it comes to getting things done, people can be divided into three groups: those who make things happen, those who watch what happens, and those who wonder what happened. Those who make things happen, people with initiative, are often called self-starters or action-oriented. Initiators are confident in their cognitive skills and competent in their interpersonal skills. They are not content sitting on the sidelines. They act independently and with decisiveness. Klemp suggests that a major obstacle in every organization comes from people who lack a sense of urgency about a new idea and need to be motivated by others. They sit back, waiting for someone else to take the lead. He believes that initiative is difficult to teach others because it is rooted in the intrapersonal quality of motivation: what pushes or pulls an individual to start, direct, sustain, and finally end an activity. Chinese philosopher Lao Tzu (as quoted in Chan, 1963) suggested that "A journey of a thousand miles begins with a single step." Taking the initiative means taking the first step.

Persistence

Klemp believes that the final intrapersonal characteristic, persistence, may be the most important one. He cites the old adage "If at first you don't succeed, try, try again." Quotations on the importance of persistence abound, but one we like is often attributed to Thomas A. Edison: "Many of life's failures are people who did not realize how close they were to success when they gave up." A persister is one who moves forward without quitting in the face of defeat and despite poor odds for success. Is that not the behavior we seek to engender in our students?

Conclusion

It is clear that defining retention, attrition, and persistence and the constructs related to student success is fraught with pitfalls and complexity. We have projected that with the changing demographics and lackluster academic performance of current students, the issue of college success will likely move from critical to urgent to dire within the next few decades. We have chronicled campus efforts and cited best practices to improve college success rates. Finally, we have documented the notion that success rates are stagnant and globally noncompetitive.

We would not have written this book if we did not believe that this picture could change. And we believe that change will result from three things. First, the retention paradigm should be expanded to focus on student success. We believe that student success will be enhanced when institutions cooperate and collaborate in an open and seamless system that focuses on student goal achievement. In addition, we believe that there needs to be a greater balance in the allocation of human and fiscal resources utilized to attract students and those utilized to retain students. That balance suggests that the institution should enroll all the students it is capable of serving and should serve all the students that it is capable of enrolling. Finally, we believe that each member of the college community can make a difference in the lives of students. We believe that you can make a difference! We trust that if you apply your human knowing, your human being, and your human doing, you will make that difference.

Appendix A

WHAT WORKS IN STUDENT RETENTION, 2004 SURVEY

SECTION A

1. Is there an individual designated to coordinate retention activities on your campus?

   Yes ☐   (Go to item 2.)

   No ☐   (Skip to item 3.)

2. What is this individual's title?

   _____

   _____

   _____

   _____

   _____

3. Have you established a goal for the **retention of students** from the **first to second year?**

   Yes ☐   (Go to item 4.)

   No ☐   (Skip to item 6.)

4. Based on your current **first-to-second-year** retention rate, what percentage increase have you established as your **retention goal?**

   _____ %

5. In how many years do you intend to reach this **retention goal?**

   _____ # of year(s)

6. Have you established a goal for **student degree completion** at your institution?

   Yes ☐   (Go to item 7.)

   No ☐   (Skip to Section B.)

7. Assuming a 6-year timeframe for 4-year institutions and a 3-year timeframe for 2-year institutions, what percentage increase have you established as your **student degree completion goal?**

   _____ %

8. In how many years do you intend to reach this **student degree completion goal?**

   _____ # of year(s)

SECTION B: INSTITUTIONAL ISSUES, CHARACTERISTICS, AND SERVICES

To what degree is each of the following **institutional** issues, characteristics, or services a factor contributing to attrition on your campus?

Major Factor Contributing to Attrition					Issues, Characteristics, and Services
Moderate Factor Contributing to Attrition					
Not a Factor Contributing to Attrition					
5	4	3	2	1	
☐	☐	☐	☐	☐	1. student employment opportunities
☐	☐	☐	☐	☐	2. extracurricular programs
☐	☐	☐	☐	☐	3. curriculum issues
☐	☐	☐	☐	☐	4. quality of teaching
☐	☐	☐	☐	☐	5. academic advising
☐	☐	☐	☐	☐	6. amount of financial aid available to students

Major Factor Contributing to Attrition					Issues, Characteristics, and Services
Moderate Factor Contributing to Attrition					
Not a Factor Contributing to Attrition					
5	4	3	2	1	
☐	☐	☐	☐	☐	7. financial aid services
☐	☐	☐	☐	☐	8. admissions practices/requirements
☐	☐	☐	☐	☐	9. student-institution "fit"
☐	☐	☐	☐	☐	10. personal counseling services
☐	☐	☐	☐	☐	11. career exploration services
☐	☐	☐	☐	☐	12. student involvement in campus life

☐ ☐ ☐ ☐ ☐ 13. attitude of faculty toward students

☐ ☐ ☐ ☐ ☐ 14. attitude of staff toward students

☐ ☐ ☐ ☐ ☐ 15. academic support services (learning centers, similar resources)

☐ ☐ ☐ ☐ ☐ 16. rules and regulations governing student behavior

☐ ☐ ☐ ☐ ☐ 17. residence halls

☐ ☐ ☐ ☐ ☐ 18. other on-campus housing

☐ ☐ ☐ ☐ ☐ 19. personal contact between students and faculty

☐ ☐ ☐ ☐ ☐ 20. cultural environment

☐ ☐ ☐ ☐ ☐ 21. social environment

☐ ☐ ☐ ☐ ☐ 22. intellectual stimulation or challenge

☐ ☐ ☐ ☐ ☐ 23. student engagement in classroom (active learning)

☐ ☐ ☐ ☐ ☐ 24. the number and variety of courses offered

SECTION C: STUDENT CHARACTERISTICS

To what degree do each of the **student characteristics** below contribute to **attrition** on your campus?

Major Contribution to Attrition					Student Characteristics
Moderate Contribution to Attrition					
No Contribution to Attrition					
5	4	3	2	1	
☐	☐	☐	☐	☐	1. inadequate preparation for college-level work
☐	☐	☐	☐	☐	2. lack of educational aspirations and goals
☐	☐	☐	☐	☐	3. first generation to attend college
☐	☐	☐	☐	☐	4. commuting/living off-campus
☐	☐	☐	☐	☐	5. socio-economic disadvantage
☐	☐	☐	☐	☐	6. indecision about major
☐	☐	☐	☐	☐	7. indecision about career goal
☐	☐	☐	☐	☐	8. inadequate financial resources
☐	☐	☐	☐	☐	9. weak commitment to earning a degree
☐	☐	☐	☐	☐	10. lack of motivation to succeed

Major Contribution to Attrition					Student Characteristics
Moderate Contribution to Attrition					
No Contribution to Attrition					
5	4	3	2	1	
☐	☐	☐	☐	☐	11. physical health problems
☐	☐	☐	☐	☐	12. mental or emotional health problems
☐	☐	☐	☐	☐	13. lack of support from significant others (e.g., spouse, parents, peers)
☐	☐	☐	☐	☐	14. too many family demands
☐	☐	☐	☐	☐	15. too many job demands
☐	☐	☐	☐	☐	16. poor social integration (peer group interaction, extracurricular activities)
☐	☐	☐	☐	☐	17. poor academic integration
☐	☐	☐	☐	☐	18. distance from permanent home
☐	☐	☐	☐	☐	19. poor study skills
☐	☐	☐	☐	☐	20. inadequate personal coping skills

SECTION D: ON-CAMPUS PRACTICES

Listed below is a series of programs, services, curricular offerings, and interventions that **may make a contribution to retention on your campus.** First indicate if the feature is or is not offered on your campus. Then, if a feature is offered, indicate the degree to which you think it contributes to retention on your campus.

Programs, Services, Curricular Offerings, Interventions	Offered at Your Institution? No	Offered at Your Institution? Yes (If yes, how much of a contribution to campus retention?)	Major Contribution to Retention 5	Moderate Contribution to Retention 4 3	No Contribution to Retention 2 1

First-Year Programs

1. pre-enrollment orientation
2. extended freshman orientation (non-credit)
3. extended freshman orientation (credit)
4. freshman seminar/university 101 (non-credit)
5. freshman seminar/university 101 (credit)

Academic Advising Programs

6. advising interventions with selected student populations

(continued)

(continued)

| | Offered at Your Institution? | | Major Contribution to Retention | Moderate Contribution to Retention | No Contribution to Retention |
Programs, Services, Curricular Offerings, Interventions	No	Yes (If yes, how much of a contribution to campus retention?)	5 4	3 2	1
7. advisor training	☐	☐ →	☐ ☐	☐ ☐	☐
8. increased advising staff	☐	☐ →	☐ ☐	☐ ☐	☐
9. integration of advising with first-year transition programs	☐	☐ →	☐ ☐	☐ ☐	☐
10. academic advising centers	☐	☐ →	☐ ☐	☐ ☐	☐
11. centers that combine advisement and counseling with career planning and placement	☐	☐ →	☐ ☐	☐ ☐	☐
12. advisor manual/handbook	☐	☐ →	☐ ☐	☐ ☐	☐
13. application of technology to advising	☐	☐ →	☐ ☐	☐ ☐	☐
Assessment Advising Programs					
14. classroom assessment	☐	☐ →	☐ ☐	☐ ☐	☐
15. course placement testing (mandated)	☐	☐ →	☐ ☐	☐ ☐	☐

16. course placement testing (recommended) □ ↑ □ □ □ □ □

17. outcomes assessment □ ↑ □ □ □ □ □

18. diagnostic academic skills test(s) □ ↑ □ □ □ □ □

19. learning styles inventory(ies) □ ↑ □ □ □ □ □

20. motivation assessment(s) □ ↑ □ □ □ □ □

21. values inventory(ies) □ ↑ □ □ □ □ □

22. interest inventory(ies) □ ↑ □ □ □ □ □

23. vocational aptitude test(s) □ ↑ □ □ □ □ □

24. personality test(s) □ ↑ □ □ □ □ □

Career Planning and Placement Programs

25. career development workshops or courses □ ↑ □ □ □ □ □

26. internships □ ↑ □ □ □ □ □

27. cooperative education □ ↑ □ □ □ □ □

28. individual career counseling services □ ↑ □ □ □ □ □

29. computer-assisted career guidance □ ↑ □ □ □ □ □

30. job shadowing □ ↑ □ □ □ □ □

(continued)

(continued)

Programs, Services, Curricular Offerings, Intervention

	Offered at Your Institution?		Major Contribution to Retention / Moderate Contribution to Retention / No Contribution to Retention				
	No	Yes (If yes, how much of a contribution to campus retention?)	5	4	3	2	1

Learning Assistance/Academic Support/Intervention Programs

	No	Yes →	5	4	3	2	1
31. learning communities	☐	☐ →	☐	☐	☐	☐	☐
32. supplemental instruction	☐	☐ →	☐	☐	☐	☐	☐
33. summer bridge program	☐	☐ →	☐	☐	☐	☐	☐
34. remedial/developmental coursework (required)	☐	☐ →	☐	☐	☐	☐	☐
35. remedial/developmental coursework (recommended)	☐	☐ →	☐	☐	☐	☐	☐
36. comprehensive learning assistance center/lab	☐	☐ →	☐	☐	☐	☐	☐
37. mathematics center/lab	☐	☐ →	☐	☐	☐	☐	☐
38. writing center/lab	☐	☐ →	☐	☐	☐	☐	☐
39. reading center/lab	☐	☐ →	☐	☐	☐	☐	☐
40. foreign language center/lab	☐	☐ →	☐	☐	☐	☐	☐
41. tutoring program	☐	☐ →	☐	☐	☐	☐	☐

42. study skills course, program, or center

43. early warning system

44. mid term progress reports

45. performance contracts for students in academic difficulty

46. degree guarantee program

47. organized student study groups

48. service learning program

Mentoring Programs

49. peer mentoring

50. faculty mentoring

51. staff mentoring

52. community member mentoring

Faculty Development Programs

53. teaching techniques

54. assessing student performance

(continued)

(continued)

Programs, Services, Curricular Offerings, Intervention	Offered at Your Institution? No	Yes (If yes, how much of a contribution to campus retention?)	Major Contribution to Retention 5	Moderate Contribution to Retention 4	3	2	No Contribution to Retention 1
55. instructional use of technology	☐	☐ →	☐	☐	☐	☐	☐
56. writing across the curriculum	☐	☐ →	☐	☐	☐	☐	☐
57. interdisciplinary courses	☐	☐ →	☐	☐	☐	☐	☐
58. enhanced/modified faculty reward system	☐	☐ →	☐	☐	☐	☐	☐
Parent Programs							
59. parent newsletter	☐	☐ →	☐	☐	☐	☐	☐
60. parent orientation	☐	☐ →	☐	☐	☐	☐	☐
61. advisory group	☐	☐ →	☐	☐	☐	☐	☐
Campus Programs							
62. freshman interest groups (FIGs)	☐	☐ →	☐	☐	☐	☐	☐
63. diversity information/training	☐	☐ →	☐	☐	☐	☐	☐

64. residence hall programs

65. fraternities/sororities

66. recreation/intramurals

67. academic clubs

68. cultural activities program

69. leadership development

Programs for Sub-populations

70. adult students

71. commuter students

72. gay/lesbian/bisexual/transgender students

73. women

74. racial/ethnic minorities

75. honor students

Additional Activities

76. time management course/program

(continued)

(continued)

Programs, Services, Curricular Offerings, Intervention	Offered at Your Institution? No	Yes (If yes, how much of a contribution to campus retention?)	Major Contribution to Retention / Moderate Contribution to Retention / No Contribution to Retention				
			5	4	3	2	1
77. health and wellness course/program	☐	☐ →	☐	☐	☐	☐	☐
78. personal coping skills course/program	☐	☐ →	☐	☐	☐	☐	☐
79. social skills course/program	☐	☐ →	☐	☐	☐	☐	☐
80. required on-campus housing for freshmen	☐	☐ →	☐	☐	☐	☐	☐
81. library orientation, workshop, and/or course	☐	☐ →	☐	☐	☐	☐	☐
82. motivation and goal setting workshop/program	☐	☐ →	☐	☐	☐	☐	☐

Other Programs/Offerings – Please specify.

83. _____ ☐ ☐ ☐ ☐ ☐

84. _____ ☐ ☐ ☐ ☐ ☐

SECTION E

From the preceding 84 items (Section D, beginning on page 2),
write the **item number and text** for the 1-3 items that have the
greatest impact on retention on your campus.

Item # _____ Text _____

Item # _____ Text _____

Item # _____ Text _____

SECTION F

Indicate if any of the ACT programs listed below are used
on your campus to enhance your retention efforts?

☐   ACT Assessment   ☐   ASSET

☐   COMPASS/ESL   ☐   CAAP

☐   DISCOVER   ☐   Evaluation Survey/
                                   Services (ESS)

SECTION G

Please provide the following information.

Name _____

Job Title _____

Mailing Address _____

_____

_____

Phone _____

Email _____

We will prepare a monograph reporting results of this survey and highlighting exemplary retention programs. Would you agree to a brief followup survey or phone call should we identify your retention program as one that we may include/reference in this publication?

Yes ☐   **No** ☐

Thank you!
Please return your completed survey in the enclosed envelope. (ACT, Inc., 65;
500 ACT Drive; Iowa City, IA 52243)

Appendix B

WHAT WORKS IN STUDENT RETENTION?

Fourth National Survey

This study reiterates ACT's ongoing commitment to help colleges and universities better understand the impact of campus practices on college student retention and persistence to degree attainment. Throughout the last three decades, ACT has conducted a number of research studies relevant to college student success. Postsecondary educators use the results from these research efforts to enhance the quality of programs leading to student success. These projects include, among others, the following:

- Three National Surveys on Retention: *What Works in Student Retention?*
- Six National Surveys on Academic Advising Practices
- Annual Report on National Retention and Persistence to Degree Rates

Your participation in this effort, the 4th National Survey on Retention, will make a significant contribution to a better understanding of retention practices.

> Directions: Please complete each set of items on this survey, and then return your completed survey in the envelope provided or mail it to: ACT, Inc.; Survey Research Services 47; PO Box 168; Iowa City, IA 52243.

SECTION 1: BACKGROUND INFORMATION

1. Is there a person on your campus who is responsible for the coordination of retention programs?
   - ☐ Yes
   - ☐ No (Skip to Question 3.)

2. What title <u>most closely approximates</u> that of the individual? (Check only one.)
   - ☐ Chief Executive/President
   - ☐ Provost
   - ☐ Associate/Assistant Provost
   - ☐ Chief Academic Affairs Officer/Campus Dean
   - ☐ Associate/Assistant Academics Affairs Officer
   - ☐ Chief Student Affairs Officer
   - ☐ Associate/Assistant Student Affairs Officer
   - ☐ Chief Enrollment Management Officer
   - ☐ Associate/Assistant Enrollment Management Officer
   - ☐ Director
   - ☐ Associate/Assistant Director
   - ☐ Coordinator
   - ☐ Specialist

3. Approximately what percentage of your undergraduate credit hours is offered through online instruction?
   _____ %

   - ☐ Don't know/Unavailable

4. Check all of the transfer-enhancement programs below in which your institution participates.

   A. Common Course number system
   - ☐ With selected college(s)
   - ☐ With selected group or consortium of colleges
   - ☐ Systemwide
   - ☐ Statewide
   - ☐ None of the above

   B. Articulation agreements
   - ☐ With selected college(s)
   - ☐ With selected group or consortium of colleges
   - ☐ Systemwide
   - ☐ Statewide
   - ☐ None of the above

   C. A course applicability system (any system that informs students on the applicability of credits earned at other institutions)
   - ☐ With selected group or consortium of colleges
   - ☐ Systemwide
   - ☐ Statewide
   - ☐ Multi-state
   - ☐ None of the above

SECTION II: RETENTION AND DEGREE-COMPLETION RATES

1. What is your institution's *current* **first-year to second-year retention rate** (for first-time, full-time students)?

   _____

   % (percent retained)
   ☐   Don't know/Unavailable

2. Does your institution have a specific **goal** for its **first-year to second-year retention rate?**

   ☐   No (Skip to Question 3.)

   ☐   Don't know/Unavailable (Skip to Question 3.)

   ☐   Yes ⟶ If yes: The goal for the student retention rate (% of students who will be retained – <u>not</u> percent increase) and the schedule for achieving that goal are:

   a. _____
      % (percent retained goal)

   b. Timeframe for achieving that goal

   ☐   No specific timeframe
   ☐   One year
   ☐   Two years
   ☐   Three years
   ☐   Four years
   ☐   Five years
   ☐   More than five years

3. Assuming a 6-year timeframe for four-year institutions and a 3-year timeframe for two-year institutions, what is your institution's *current* **student degree-completion rate?**

   _____

   % (percent retained goal)
   ☐   Don't know/Unavailable

4. Does your institution have a **specific goal** for its **student degree-completion** rate (6-year graduation timeframe for four-year institutions or 3-year graduation timeframe for two-year institutions)?

   ☐   No (Skip to Section III.)

   ☐   Don't know/Unavailable (Skip to Section III.)

   ☐   Yes ⟶ If yes: The goal for the student degree completion rate (% of students who complete degrees – <u>not</u> percent increase) and the schedule for achieving that goal are:

   a. _____% (degree-completion rate goal)

   b. Timeframe for achieving that goal

   ☐   No specific timeframe
   ☐   One year
   ☐   Two years
   ☐   Three years
   ☐   Four years
   ☐   Five years
   ☐   More than five years

SECTION III: FACTORS AFFECTING STUDENT ATTRITION AT YOUR SCHOOL

This section contains a list of student and institutional characteristics or factors that can affect attrition. **To what degree does each factor affect attrition at your school?**

Major Effect on attrition at your school
Moderate Effect on attrition at your school
Little or No Effect on attrition at your school

5 4 3 2 1

☐ ☐ ☐ ☐ ☐	1.	student employment opportunities
☐ ☐ ☐ ☐ ☐	2.	level of student preparation for college-level work
☐ ☐ ☐ ☐ ☐	3.	relevancy of curricula
☐ ☐ ☐ ☐ ☐	4.	student access to needed courses in the appropriate sequence
☐ ☐ ☐ ☐ ☐	5.	student first-generation status
☐ ☐ ☐ ☐ ☐	6.	accuracy of information provided by academic advisors
☐ ☐ ☐ ☐ ☐	7.	availability of academic advisors

Major Effect on attrition at your school
Moderate Effect on attrition at your school
Little or No Effect on attrition at your school

5 4 3 2 1

☐ ☐ ☐ ☐ ☐	8.	level of academic advisors' concern for students
☐ ☐ ☐ ☐ ☐	9.	student low socio-economic status
☐ ☐ ☐ ☐ ☐	10.	amount of financial aid available to students
☐ ☐ ☐ ☐ ☐	11.	student access to financial aid advising
☐ ☐ ☐ ☐ ☐	12.	ratio of loans to other forms of financial aid
☐ ☐ ☐ ☐ ☐	13.	level of student commitment to earning a degree
☐ ☐ ☐ ☐ ☐	14.	student-institution "fit"

- [ ] [ ] [ ] [ ] 15. level of certainty about career goals
- [ ] [ ] [ ] [ ] 16. extracurricular programs
- [ ] [ ] [ ] [ ] 17. student educational aspirations and goals
- [ ] [ ] [ ] [ ] 18. community/living off-campus
- [ ] [ ] [ ] [ ] 19. level of certainty about educational major
- [ ] [ ] [ ] [ ] 20. adequacy of personal financial resources
- [ ] [ ] [ ] [ ] 21. level of student motivation to succeed
- [ ] [ ] [ ] [ ] 22. student physical health issues
- [ ] [ ] [ ] [ ] 23. adequate academic/learning support services
- [ ] [ ] [ ] [ ] 24. level of emotional support from family, friends, and significant others
- [ ] [ ] [ ] [ ] 25. residence hall facilities
- [ ] [ ] [ ] [ ] 26. programs to support students' transition to residence hall living
- [ ] [ ] [ ] [ ] 27. level of job demands on students
- [ ] [ ] [ ] [ ] 28. quality of interaction between faculty and students

- [ ] [ ] [ ] [ ] 29. consistency of instructional quality
- [ ] [ ] [ ] [ ] 30. out-of-class interaction between students and faculty
- [ ] [ ] [ ] [ ] 31. student study skills
- [ ] [ ] [ ] [ ] 32. student engagement opportunities in the classroom (active learning)
- [ ] [ ] [ ] [ ] 33. quality of interaction between staff and students
- [ ] [ ] [ ] [ ] 34. student mental or emotional health issues
- [ ] [ ] [ ] [ ] 35. rules and regulations governing student behavior
- [ ] [ ] [ ] [ ] 36. student family responsibilities
- [ ] [ ] [ ] [ ] 37. campus safety and security
- [ ] [ ] [ ] [ ] 38. student peer group interaction
- [ ] [ ] [ ] [ ] 39. cultural activities
- [ ] [ ] [ ] [ ] 40. distance from students' permanent homes
- [ ] [ ] [ ] [ ] 41. level of intellectual stimulation or challenge for students
- [ ] [ ] [ ] [ ] 42. student personal coping skills

SECTION IV: ON-CAMPUS RETENTION PRACTICES

Listed below is a series of programs, services, curricular offerings, and interventions that may make a contribution to retention on your campus.

First indicate if the practice is or is not offered at your school.

Then, if a practice is offered, indicate the degree to which you think it contributes to retention at your school.

	Offered at Your Institution?		Major Contribution to retention
	No	Yes (Then what degree of contribution to campus retention?)	Moderate Contribution to retention
			Little or No Contribution to retention
Programs, Services, Curricular Offerings, Interventions			5 4 3 2 1

First-Year Transition

1. summer orientation

2. extended freshman orientation (non-credit)

3. extended freshman orientation (credit)

4. freshman seminar/university 101 (non-credit)

5. freshman seminar/university 101 (credit)

6. living/learning communities (residential)

7. learning communities (non-residential)

8. parent/family orientation

Academic Advising

9. training for faculty academic advisors

10. training for non-faculty academic advisors

11. advising interventions with selected student populations

12. increased number of academic advisors

13. integration of advising with first-year transition programs

14. academic advising center

15. center(s) that integrates academic advising with career/life planning

16. assessment of faculty academic advisors

17. assessment of non-faculty academic advisors

18. application of technology to advising

19. recognition/rewards for faculty academic advisors

20. recognition/rewards for non-faculty academic advisors

21. specified student learning outcomes (syllabus) for advising

22. online advising system

23. campus-wide assessment/ audit of advising

(continued)

417

(continued)

Programs, Services, Curricular Offerings, Interventions	Offered at Your Institution? No	Yes (Then what degree of contribution to campus retention?)	Major Contribution to retention 5	4	Moderate Contribution to retention 3	2	Little or No Contribution to retention 1
Assessment							
24. mandated placement of students in courses based on test scores	☐	☐ →	☐	☐	☐	☐	☐
25. recommended placement of students in courses based on test scores	☐	☐ →	☐	☐	☐	☐	☐
26. diagnostic academic skills assessment	☐	☐ →	☐	☐	☐	☐	☐
27. outcomes assessment	☐	☐ →	☐	☐	☐	☐	☐
28. learning styles assessment	☐	☐ →	☐	☐	☐	☐	☐
29. values assessment	☐	☐ →	☐	☐	☐	☐	☐
30. interest assessment	☐	☐ →	☐	☐	☐	☐	☐
31. vocational aptitude assessment	☐	☐ →	☐	☐	☐	☐	☐
32. personality assessment	☐	☐ →	☐	☐	☐	☐	☐
Career Planning and Placement							
33. career exploration workshops or courses	☐	☐ →	☐	☐	☐	☐	☐

34. internships ☐ ☐ ↑ ☐☐☐☐

35. cooperative education ☐ ☐ ↑ ☐☐☐☐

36. individual career counseling ☐ ↑ ☐☐☐☐

37. computer-assisted career guidance ☐ ↑ ☐☐☐☐

38. job shadowing ☐ ↑ ☐☐☐☐

Learning Assistance/Academic Support

39. supplemental instruction ☐ ↑ ☐☐☐☐

40. summer bridge program ☐ ↑ ☐☐☐☐

41. remedial/developmental coursework (required) ☐ ↑ ☐☐☐☐

42. remedial/developmental coursework (recommended) ☐ ↑ ☐☐☐☐

43. comprehensive learning assistance center/lab ☐ ↑ ☐☐☐☐

44. mathematics center/lab ☐ ↑ ☐☐☐☐

45. writing center/lab ☐ ↑ ☐☐☐☐

46. reading center/lab ☐ ↑ ☐☐☐☐

47. foreign language center/lab ☐ ↑ ☐☐☐☐

48. tutoring ☐ ↑ ☐☐☐☐

49. study skills course, program, or center ☐ ↑ ☐☐☐☐

50. early warning system ☐ ↑ ☐☐☐☐

51. mid-term progress reports ☐ ↑ ☐☐☐☐

52. performance contracts for students in academic difficulty ☐ ↑ ☐☐☐☐

(continued)

419

(continued)

Programs, Services, Curricular Offerings, Interventions	Offered at Your Institution? No	Yes (Then what degree of contribution to campus retention?)	5	4	3	2	1
			Major Contribution to retention		Moderate Contribution to retention		Little or No Contribution to retention
53. organized student study groups	☐	☐	☐	☐	☐	☐	☐
54. service learning program	☐	☐	☐	☐	☐	☐	☐
55. ESL program	☐	☐	☐	☐	☐	☐	☐
56. online learning support	☐	☐	☐	☐	☐	☐	☐
57. library orientation, workshop, and/or course	☐	☐	☐	☐	☐	☐	☐
Mentoring							
58. peer mentoring	☐	☐	☐	☐	☐	☐	☐
59. faculty mentoring	☐	☐	☐	☐	☐	☐	☐
60. staff mentoring	☐	☐	☐	☐	☐	☐	☐
61. community member mentoring	☐	☐	☐	☐	☐	☐	☐
Faculty Development							
62. instructional (teaching) techniques	☐	☐	☐	☐	☐	☐	☐
63. assessing student performance	☐	☐	☐	☐	☐	☐	☐

64. faculty use of technology in teaching

65. faculty use of technology in communicating with students

66. writing across the curriculum

67. interdisciplinary courses

68. enhanced/modified faculty reward system

Financial Aid

69. pre-enrollment financial aid advising

70. workshops in money management

71. short-term loans

Co-curricular Services/Programs for Specific Student Sub-populations

72. adult students

73. commuter students

74. ESL students

75. female students

76. first-generation students

77. gay/lesbian/bisexual/transgender students

78. honor students

(continued)

(continued)

Programs, Services, Curricular Offerings, Interventions

Offered at Your Institution?

No / Yes (Then what degree of contribution to campus retention?)

- Major Contribution to retention
  - Moderate Contribution to retention
    - Little or No Contribution to retention

	No	Yes	5	4	3	2	1
79. international students	☐	☐ →	☐	☐	☐	☐	☐
80. racial/ethnic minority students	☐	☐ →	☐	☐	☐	☐	☐
81. veterans	☐	☐ →	☐	☐	☐	☐	☐
82. other (specify.) _____	→						

Other Activities/Programs

	No	Yes	5	4	3	2	1
83. degree guarantee program	☐	☐ →	☐	☐	☐	☐	☐
84. freshman interest groups (FIGs)	☐	☐ →	☐	☐	☐	☐	☐
85. college-sponsored social activities	☐	☐ →	☐	☐	☐	☐	☐
86. diversity information/training	☐	☐ →	☐	☐	☐	☐	☐
87. student leadership development	☐	☐ →	☐	☐	☐	☐	☐

88. time management course/program ☐ ☐ ☐☐☐☐☐

89. health and wellness course/program ☐ ☐ ☐☐☐☐☐

90. personal coping skills course/programs ☐ ☐ ☐☐☐☐☐

91. motivation and goal setting workshop/program ☐ ☐ ☐☐☐☐☐

92. residence hall programs

93. fraternities/sororities ☐ ☐ ☐☐☐☐☐

94. required on-campus housing for freshman ☐ ☐ ☐☐☐☐☐

Other Programs, Services, Curricular Offerings, Interventions that contribute to retention at your school (Please specify.)

95. _____ ☐ ☐☐☐☐☐

96. _____ ☐ ☐☐☐☐☐

SECTION V

From the 96 items in Section IV (beginning on page 3), write the item number and text for the 1 to 3 items among the 96 that have the greatest positive impact on retention at your school.

Item # _____ Text _____

Item # _____ Text _____

Item # _____ Text _____

SECTION VI

We will prepare a report containing the results of the survey. Would you agree to a brief follow-up survey or phone call should we identify your retention program for inclusion?

Yes ☐
No ☐

If yes, please provide the following information.
Name _____
Job Title _____
Mailing Address _____
_____
_____
Phone _____
Email _____

SECTION VII: COMMENTS

If you would like to share information or comments that would enlighten our understanding of retention problems and/or solutions at your school, please write them in the space below.

References

Achieving the Dream (n.d.). College implementation strategy overview. Chapel Hill, NC: MDC. Retrieved from http://www.achieving thedream.org/CAMPUSSTRATEGIES/STRATEGIES ATACHIEVINGTHEDREAMCOLLEGES/implementationstrategy overview.tp#developmentaleducation

ACT. (1995). *Technical manual: Revised unisex edition of the ACT Interest Inventory (UNIACT)*. Iowa City: Author.

ACT. (2005). *Crisis at the core*. Iowa City: Author.

ACT. (2006). *COMPASS reference manual*. Iowa City: Author.

ACT. (2007). The ACT technical manual. Retrieved from http://www.act.org/research/researchers/techmanuals.html

ACT. (2008). *Student Readiness Inventory SRI user's guide*. Iowa City: Author.

ACT. (2009a). *The ACT Interest Inventory technical manual*. Retrieved from http://www.act.org/research/researchers/techmanuals.html

ACT. (2009b) *Focusing on the essentials for college and career readiness: policy implications of the ACT national curriculum survey results 2009*. Iowa City: Author.

ACT. (2009c). *National curriculum survey*. Iowa City: Author.

ACT. (2010a). *ACT profile report—national*. Iowa City: Author.

ACT. (2010b). *The ACT technical manual*. Iowa City: ACT.

ACT. (2010c). *Minding the gaps*. Iowa City: Author

ACT. (2010d). Retention and persistence to degree tables. Retrieved from http://www.act.org/research/policymakers/reports/graduation.html

ACT. (2010e). *What are ACT's college readiness benchmarks?* Iowa City: Author.

Adelman, C. (1999). *Answers in the tool box: Academic intensity, attendance patterns, and bachelor's degree attainment* (Research Report No. PLLI-1999–8021). Retrieved from ERIC (ED431363).

Adelman, C. (2004). *Principal indicators of student academic histories in postsecondary education, 1972–2000*. Washington, DC: U.S. Department of Education, Institute of Educational Sciences.

Allen, D. (1999). Desire to finish college: An empirical link between motivation and persistence. *Research in Higher Education, 40*, 461–485.

Allen, W. R. (1985). Black student, white campus: Structural, interpersonal, and psychological correlates of success. *Journal of Negro Education*, 5, 134–147.

Allen, J., & Robbins, S. (2008). Prediction of college major persistence based on vocational interests and first-year academic performance. *Research in Higher Education, 49*(1), 62–79.

Allen, J., & Robbins. S. (2010). Effects of interest-major congruence, motivation, and academic performance on timely degree attainment. *Journal of Counseling Psychology, 57*(1), 23–35.

Allen, J., Robbins, S., Casillas, A., & Oh, I.-S. (2008). Why college students stay: Using academic performance, motivation, and social engagement constructs to predict third-year college retention and transfer. *Research in Higher Education. 49*(7), 647–664.

American Association of Community Colleges (AACC). (n.d.). Voluntary framework of accountability. Retrieved September 15, 2011 from http://www.aacc.nche.edu/Resources/aaccprograms/vfa/Pages/default.aspx

American Association of State Colleges and Universities. (2005). *Student success in state colleges and universities*. Washington, DC: Author.

American Counseling Association (ACA) & the Association for Assessment in Counseling. (1987). *Responsibilities of users of standardized tests: RUST statement revised*. Alexandria, VA.

Appleby, D. C. (2008). Advising as teaching and learning. In V. N. Gordon, W. R. Habley, & T. J. Grites (Eds.), *Academic advising: A comprehensive handbook* (2nd ed., pp. 85–102). San Francisco: Jossey-Bass.

Arendale, D. R. (2004). Pathways of persistence: A review of postsecondary peer cooperative learning programs. In I. M. Duranczyk, J. L. Higbee, & D. B. Lundell (Eds.), *Best Practices for access and retention in higher education (pp. 27–40)*. Minneapolis: Center for Research on Developmental Education and Urban Literacy, General College, University of Minnesota.

Arendale, D. R. (2005). Terms of endearment: Words that help define and guide developmental education. *Journal of College Reading and Learning, 35*(2), 66–82.

Arendale, D. R., et al. (2007). A glossary of developmental education and learning assistance terms. *Journal of College Reading and Learning, 38*(1), 10–34.

Arizona Republic (2010). New law requires common course number system for Arizona colleges. Retrieved September 18, 2011 from http://www.azcentral.com/community/phoenix/articles/2010/08/08/20100808college-course-numbers-new-law.html

Ashbaugh, J. A., Levin, C., & Zaccaria, L. (1973). Persistence and the disadvantaged college student. *Journal of Educational Research, 67*(2), 64–66.

Ashburn, E. (2006, October 27). Living Laboratories. *Chronicle of Higher Education.* Retrieved from http://chronicle.com

Astin, A. W. (1975). *Preventing students from dropping out.* San Francisco: Jossey-Bass.

Astin, A. W. (1984). Student involvement: A developmental theory for higher education. *Journal of College Student Personnel.* 25(4), 297–308.

Astin, A. W. (1993). *What matters in college?* San Francisco: Jossey-Bass.

Astin, A. W. (1999). Student involvement: A developmental theory for higher education. *Journal of College Student Development, 40*(5), 587–98.

Astin, A. W., & Oseguera, L. (2005). College and institutional influences of degree attainment. In A. Seidman (Ed.), *College student retention: Formula for student success.* Westport, CT: Praeger Publishers.

Attewell, P., Lavin, D., Domina, T., & Levey, T. (2006). New evidence on college remediation. *Journal of Higher Education, 77*(5), 886–924.

Bahr, P. R. (2010). Making sense of disparities in mathematics remediation: What is the role of student retention? *Journal of College Student Retention, 12*(1), 25–49.

Barefoot, B. O., Gardner, J. N., Cutright, M., Morris, L. V., Schroeder, C. C., Schwartz, S. W., Siegel, M. J., & Swing, R. L. (2005). *Achieving and sustaining institutional excellence for the first year of college.* San Francisco: Jossey-Bass.

Baskin, T. W., Slaten, C. D., Sorenson, C., Glover-Russell, J., & Merson, D. N. (2010). Does youth psychotherapy improve academically related outcomes? *Journal of Counseling Psychology, 57,* 290–296.

Baum, S., & Payea, K. (2005a). *Education pays, 2004: The benefits of higher education for individuals and society.* New York: College Board.

Baum, S. & Payea, K. (2005b). *Education pays update: A supplement to the education pays 2004.* New York: College Board.

Beal, P. E., & Noel, L. (1980). *What works in student retention: The report of a joint project of the American College Testing Program and the National Center for Higher Education Management Systems.* Iowa City: ACT.

Bean, J. P. (1980). Dropouts and turnover: The synthesis and test of a causal model of student attrition. *Research in Higher Education, 12*(2), 155–187.

Bean, J. P. (1985). Interaction effects based on class level in an explanatory model of college student dropout syndrome. *American Educational Research Journal, 22*(1), 35–65.

Bean, J., & Eaton, S. B. (2002). The psychology underlying successful retention practices. *Journal of College Student Retention, 3*(1), 73–89.

Bean, J. P. (1990). Using retention research in enrollment management. In D. Hossler, J. P. Bean and Associates (Eds.), *The strategic management of college enrollments* (170–185). San Francisco: Jossey-Bass.

Beck, & Davidson. (2001). Establishing an early warning system: Predicting low grades in college students from survey of academic orientations scores. *Research in Higher Education, 42*(6), 709–723.

Becker, G. S. (1964). *Human capital.* New York: National Bureau of Economic Research.

Beil, C., & Shope, J. H. (1990). *No exit: Predicting student persistence.* Paper presented at the Annual Forum of the Association of Institutional Research, Louisville, KY. Retrieved from http://eric.ed.gov/PDFS/ED321669.pdf

Berger, J. B., & Braxton, J. M. (1998). Revising Tinto's interactionalist theory of student departure through theory elaboration: Examining the role of organizational attributes in the persistence process. *Research in Higher Education, 39,* 103–119.

Berger, J. B., & Milem, J. F. (1999). The role of student involvement and perceptions of integration in a causal model of student persistence. *Research in Higher Education, 40,* 641–664.

Berkner, L., He, S., & Cataldi, E. F. (2002). *Descriptive summary of 1995–96 beginning postsecondary students: Six years later* (NCES 2003–151). Washington, DC: National Center for Education Statistics.

Bettinger, E. P., & Long, B. T. (2008). Addressing the needs of underprepared students in higher education: Does college remediation work? *The Journal of Human Resources, 44*(3), 736–771.

Biswas, R. (2007). Accelerating remedial math education: How institutional innovation and state policy interact. Retrieved from: http://www.achievingthedream.org/_pdfs/_publicpolicy/remedialmath.pdf

Blaich, C. F., & Wise, K. S. (2011). *From gathering to using assessment results: Lessons from the Wabash National Study* (NILOA Occasional Paper No. 8). Urbana: University for Illinois and Indiana University, National Institute for Learning Outcomes Assessment.

Bloom, D. E., Hartley, M., & Rosovsky, H. (2006). Beyond private gain: The public benefits of higher education. *International Handbook of Higher Education, 18*(1), 293–308.

Bloom, J. L., Hutson, B. L., & He. Y. (2008). *The appreciative advising revolution.* Champaign, IL: Stipes.

Bloom, J. L, & Martin, N. A. (2002). Incorporating appreciative inquiry into academic advising. *The Mentor, 4*(3). Retrieved from http://www.psu.edu/dus/mentor.

Boylan, H. R., & Saxon, D. P. (2005). *What works in remediation: Lessons from 30 years of research.* Boone, NC: National Center for Developmental Education. Retrieved from http://inpathways.net/Boylan—What%20Works.pdf

Braxton, J. M. (Ed.). (2000). *Reworking the student departure puzzle: New theory and research on college student retention*. Nashville: Vanderbilt University Press.

Braxton, J. M., & Brier, E. (1989). Melding organizational and interactional theories of student attrition: A path analytic study. *Review of Higher Education, 13*, 47–61.

Braxton, J. M., Hirschy, A. S., & McClendon, S. A. (2004). *Understanding and reducing college student departure*. No. 3. ASHE-ERIC Higher Education Research Report Series. San Francisco: Jossey-Bass.

Braxton, J. M., & Mundy, M. E. (2002). Powerful institutional levers to reduce college student departure. *Journal of College Student Retention, 3*(1), 91–118.

Breneman, D. W., & Haarlow, W. N. (1998, July). Remedial education: Costs and consequences. *Remediation in higher education*. Symposium conducted by the Thomas B. Fordham Foundation, *2*(9), 1–57. Retrieved from http://eric.ed.gov/PDFS/ED422770.pdf

Brown, T. (2008). Critical concepts in advisor training and development. In V. N. Gordon, W. R. Habley, & T. J. Grites (Eds.), *Academic advising: A comprehensive handbook* (2nd ed., pp. 309–322). San Francisco: Jossey-Bass.

Brown, L. L., & Robinson Kurpius, S. E. (1997). Psychosocial factors influencing academic persistence of American Indian college students. *Journal of College Student Development, 38*, 3–12.

Brown, S. D., Ryan Krane, N. E., Brecheisen, J., Castelino, P., Budisin, I., Miller, M., & Edens, L. (2003). Critical ingredients of career choice interventions: More analyses and new hypotheses. *Journal of Vocational Behavior, 62*, 411–428.

Calcagno, J. C., & Long, B. T. (2008). *The impact of postsecondary remediation using a regression discontinuity approach: Addressing endogenous sorting and noncompliance* (Working Paper No. W14194). Washington, DC: National Bureau of Economic Research. Retrieved from http://www.nber.org/papers/w14194

Camara, W. J., & Echternacht, G. (2000). *The SAT I and high school grades: Utility in predicting success in college*. New York: College Board.

Carnevale, A. P., Smith, N., & Strohl, J. (2010). *Help wanted: Projections of jobs and education requirements through 2018*. Washington, DC: Georgetown University, Center on Education and the Workforce.

Chan, W. (1963). *Way of Lao-Tzu*. Library of Liberal Arts. Upper Saddle River, NJ: Prentice Hall.

Chemers, M. M., Hu, L., & Garcia, B. F. (2001). Academic self-efficacy and first year college student performance and adjustment. *Journal of Educational Psychology, 93*, 55–64.

Chickering, A. W. (1994). Empowering lifelong self-development. *NACADA Journal, 14*(2), 50–53.

Chickering, A. W., & Gamson, Z. F. (Eds.). (1987). Seven principles for good practice in undergraduate education. *AAHE Bulletin: March:* 3–7

Christman, P. (2005, October). Narrative advising: A hands on approach to effective change. Presented at the national conference of the National Academic Advising Association, Las Vegas.

Clark, E. C., & Kalionzes, J. (2008). Advising students of color and international students. In V. N. Gordon, W. R. Habley, & T. J. Grites (Eds.), *Academic advising: A comprehensive handbook* (2nd ed., pp. 204–225). San Francisco: Jossey-Bass.

CNN. (2008, August 13). Minorities expected to be majority in 2050. Retrieved from http://www.cnn.com/2008/US/08/13/census.minorities/index.html

Cohn, J. (1988). *Statistical power analysis for the behavioral sciences.* Hillsdale, NJ: Erlbaum.

Cohen, P. A., Kulik, J. A., & Kulik, C. C. (1982). Educational outcomes of tutoring: A meta-analysis of findings. *American Educational Research Journal, 19*(2), 237–248, doi 10.3102/00028312019002237.

College Board. (2009). *Total group profile report.* New York: Author.

College Board. (2010a). AP exam scores. Retrieved from http://professionals.collegeboard.com/higher-ed/placement/ap/exam/grades

College Board. (2010b). *AP exam volume (2000–2010).* Retrieved from http://professionals.collegeboard.com/profdownload/Exam-Volume-Change-2010.pdf

Cook, S. (1999). A chronology of academic advising in America. *The Mentor, 1*(2). Retrieved from http://www.psu.edu/dus/mentor

Cooperrider, D. L., & Srivastva, S. (1987). Appreciative inquiry in organizational life. *Research in Organizational Change and Development, 1*(1), 129–169.

Cooperrider, D. L. (1990) *Positive image, positive action:* The affirmative basis of organizing. In S. Srivastva & D.L. Cooperrider (Eds.), *Appreciate management and leadership: the power of positive thought and action in organizations* (pp. 91–125). San Francisco: Jossey-Bass.

Cope, R. G., & Hannah, W. (1975). *Revolving college doors: The causes and consequences of dropping out, stopping out, and transferring.* New York: Wiley.

Council of Chief State School Officers & the National Governors Association Center for Best Practices. (2010). *Introduction to the common core state standards.* Washington, DC: Author.

Covington, M. V. (2000). Goal theory, motivation, and school achievement: An integrative review. *Annual Review of Psychology, 51,* 171–200.

Cowart, S. C. (1987). *What works in student retention in state colleges and universities.* Iowa City: ACT.

Crookston, B. B. (1972). A developmental view of academic advising as teaching. *Journal of College Student Personnel, 13,* 12–17.

Cuseo. J. (2008). Assessing advisor effectiveness. In V. N. Gordon, W. R. Habley, & T. J. Grites (Eds.), *Academic advising: A comprehensive handbook* (2nd ed., pp. 369–385). San Francisco: Jossey-Bass.

Cuseo, J. (n.d.1). Academic advisement and student retention: Empirical connections and systemic interventions. Retrieved from http://www.uwc.edu/administration/academic-affairs/esfy/cuseo/

Cuseo, J. (n.d.2). "Red flags": Behavioral indicators of potential student attrition. Retrieved from http://www.uwc.edu/administration/academic-affairs/esfy/cuseo/.

Dannells, M., & Kuh, G. D. (1977). Orientation. In W.T. Packwood (Ed.), *College Student Personnel Services.* Springfield, IL: Thomas.

Daugherty, T. K., & Lane, E. J. (1999). A longitudinal study of academic and social predictors of college attrition. *Social Behavior and Personality, 27,* 355–362.

Davidson, W. B., Beck, H. P., & Silver, N. C. (1999). Development and validation of scores on a measure of academic orientations in college students. *Educational and Psychological Measurement, 59*(4), 678–693.

Davis, K. J. (2003). Advisor training and development workshops. In *Advisor training: Exemplary practices in the development of advisor* (pp. 13–16) [Monograph No. 9]. Manhattan, KS: National Academic Advising Association.

Dawis, R. V., Fruehling, R. T., Oldham, N. B., & Laird, D. A. (1989). *Psychology: Human relations and work adjustment.* New York: Gregg Division, McGraw-Hill.

Dawis, R., & Lofquist, L. (1984). *A psychological theory of work adjustment: An individual differences model and its application.* Minneapolis: University of Minnesota Press.

Department of Housing and Urban Development. (n.d.). FY 2010 income limits. Retrieved from http://www.huduser.org/portal/datasets/il/il10/index.html

Donnay, D. A., Morris, M. L., Schaubhut, N. A., & Thompson, R. C. (2005). *Strong Interest Inventory Manual.* Mountain View, CA: CPP.

Doty, C. S. (2003). Supplemental Instruction: National data summary, 1998–2003. Retrieved from http://www.umkc.edu/cad/si/si-docs/National%20Supplemental%20Instruction%20Report%2098–03.pdf

Drake, J. K. (2008). Recognition and reward for academic advising in theory and in practice. In V. N. Gordon, W. R. Habley, & T. J. Grites (Eds.), *Academic advising: A comprehensive handbook* (2nd ed., pp. 396–412). San Francisco: Jossey-Bass.

Durkheim, E. (1951). *Suicide: A study in sociology.* New York: The Free Press.

Eccles, J. S., & Wigfield, A. (2002). Motivational beliefs, values, and goals. *Annual Review of Psychology, 53*, 109–132.

Educational Commission of the States. (2008). State P-16 and P-20 Council Considerations. Retrieved from http://www.ecs.org/clearinghouse/79/87/7987.pdf

Education Trust. (2010). College results online. Retrieved from http://www.collegeresults.org/default.htm

Educational Policy Institute. (n.d.). Retention Calculator. Retrieved from http://www.educationalpolicy.org/calculator

Elkins, S. A., Braxton, J. M., & James, G. W. (2000). Tinto's separation stage and its influence on first-semester college student persistence. *Research in Higher Education, 41*(2), 251–268.

Elliott, K. M., & Healy, M. A. (2001). Key factors influencing student satisfaction related to recruitment and retention. *Journal of Marketing for Higher Education, 10*(4), 1–11. doi: 10.1300/J050v10n04_01

EPE Research Center. (2008). *Lowest to highest graduation rates in the nation's 50 largest school districts: Class of 2005.*

Ethington, C. A., & Smart, J. C. (1986). Persistence to graduate education. *Research in Higher Education, 24*, 287–303.

Evans, J. H., & Burck, H. D. (1992). The effects of career education interventions on academic achievement: A meta-analysis. *Journal of Counseling and Development, 71*, 63–68.

Financial Aid Facts. (2011). Retrieved from http://www.finaidfacts.org/.

Frank, R. H. (2001). Higher education: The ultimate winner-take-all market? In M. E. Devlin, & J. W. Meyerson (Eds.), *Forum futures: Exploring the future of higher education, 2000 papers* (pp. 3–12). San Francisco: Jossey-Bass

Frost, S. H. (2000). Historical and philosophical foundations for academic advising. In V. N. Gordon, W. R. Habley, et al. (Eds.), *Academic advising: A comprehensive handbook* (2nd ed., pp. 3–17). San Francisco: Jossey-Bass.

Fuertes, J. N., & Sedlacek, W. E. (1995). Using noncognitive variables to predict the grades and retention of Hispanic students. *College Student Affairs Journal, 14*(2), 30–36.

Gabelnick, F., MacGregor, J., Matthews, R. S., & Smith B. L. (1990). Learning communities: Creating connections among students, faculty, and disciplines. *New Directions for Teaching and Learning, 41.* San Francisco: Jossey-Bass.

Gattis, K. W. (2003). What supplemental instruction tells us about effective tutor training. In Susan Deese-Roberts (ed.), *Tutor training handbook* (pp. 45–54). Auburn, CA: College Reading & Learning Association.

Gillispie, B. (2003). History of academic advising. Retrieved from: http://www.nacada.ksu.edu/Clearinghouse/

Glenn, D. (2010, February 7). How students can improve by studying them-selves. *Chronicle of Higher Education*. Retrieved from http://chronicle.com/

Gloria, A. M., Kurpius, S.E.R., Hamilton, K. D., & Wilson, M. S. (1999). African American students' persistence at a predominantly white university: Influence of social support, university comfort, and self-beliefs. *Journal of College Student Development, 40*, 257–268.

Golfin, P., Jordan, W., Hull, D., & Ruffin, M. (2005). *Strengthening mathematics skills at the postsecondary level: Literature review and analysis*. Washington, DC: U.S. Department of Education.

Gonzalez, J. (2010, April 20). Melinda Gates pledges $110-million to help 2-year colleges improve remedial education. *Chronicle of Higher Education*. Retrieved from http://chronicle.com

Gordon, V. N. (1989). Origins and purposes of the freshman seminar. In M. L. Upcraft, J. N. Gardner, & Associates (Eds.), *The freshman year experience: helping students survive and succeed in college* (pp. 183–197). San Francisco: Jossey-Bass.

Gordon, V. N. (2006). *Career advising: an academic advisor's guide*. San Francisco: Jossey-Bass.

Greene, J., & Foster, G. (2003). *Public high school graduation and college readiness rates in the United States* (Education Working Paper No. 3). New York: Manhattan Institute, Center for Civic Information.

Grier, D. J. (1954). The new student arrives at college. In Lloyd-Jones, E. and Smith, M.R. (Eds.), *Student personnel work as deeper teaching*. New York: Harper & Brothers.

Grosset, J. M. (1991). Patterns of integration, commitment, and student characteristics and retention among younger and older students. *Research in Higher Education, 32*, 159–178.

Grossman, M. (2006). Education and non-market outcomes. In E. Hanushek & F. Welch (Eds.), *Handbook of the economics of education* (pp. 347–408). Amsterdam, Netherlands: Elsevier.

Grubb, W. N. (2001). *From black box to Pandora's box: Evaluating remedial/developmental education* (CCRC Brief 11). New York: Columbia University, Teachers College, Community College Research Center.

Guthrie, J. W. (Ed.). (2002). *Encyclopedia of education* (Vol. 1). Macmillan Reference Library.

Habley, W. R. (1981). Academic advising: Critical link in student retention. *NASPA Journal, 28*(4), 45–50.

Habley, W. R. (1983). Organizational structures for academic advising: Models and implications. *Journal of College Student Personnel, 24*(6), 535–540.

Habley, W. R. (1992, July). Key concepts in academic advising. Presentation at the ACT Summer Institute on Academic Advising, Iowa City.

Habley, W. R. (1996). *Initiating and implementing change on campus.* Presentation at AAHE Faculty Roles and Rewards Conference, New Orleans.

Habley, W. R. (2004a). Advisor load. Retrieved from: http://nacada.ksu.edu/Clearinghouse/AdvisingIssues/advisorload.htm

Habley, W. R. (Ed.). (2004b). *The status of academic advising: Findings from the ACT Sixth National Survey* [Monograph No. 10]. Manhattan, KS: National Academic Advising Association.

Habley, W. R., & McClanahan, R. (2004). *What works in student retention.* Iowa City: ACT.

Habley, W. R., McClanahan, R., Valiga, M., & Burkum, K. (2010). *What works in student retention.* Iowa City: ACT.

Habley, W. R., & Schuh, J. H. (2007a). Intervening to retain students. In G. Kramer (Ed.), *Fostering student success in the campus community* (pp. 343–368). San Francisco: Jossey-Bass.

Habley, W. R., & Schuh, J. H. (2007b). Intervening for student success. In G. Kramer (Ed.), *Fostering student success in the campus community.* San Francisco: Jossey-Bass.

Hagedorn, L. S. (2005). How to define retention: A new look at an old problem. In A. Seidman (Ed.). *College student retention: Formula for student success* (pp. 89–106). Greenwich, CT: Praeger.

Hagen, P. L. (1994). Academic advising as dialectic. *NACADA Journal, 14*(2), 85–88.

Hagen, P. L., & Jordan, P. (2008). Theoretical foundations of academic advising. In V. N. Gordon, W. R. Habley, & T. J. Grites (Eds.), *Academic advising: A comprehensive handbook* (2nd ed., pp. 17–35). San Francisco: Jossey-Bass.

Harding, B. (2008). Students with specific advising needs. In V. N. Gordon, W. R. Habley, & T. J. Grites (Eds.), *Academic advising: A comprehensive handbook* (2nd ed., pp. 189–203). San Francisco: Jossey-Bass.

Haycock, K. (2006, March 10). Student readiness: The challenges for colleges. *Chronicle of Higher Education.* Retrieved from http://chronicle.com

Heckman, J. J., & LaFontaine, P. A. (2007). *The American high school graduation rate: Trends and levels.* IZA DP No. 3216, Forschungsinstitut zur Zukunft der Arbeit.

Hemwall, M. K. & Trachte, K. (1999). Learning at the core: Toward a new understanding of academic advising. *NACADA Journal, 19*(1), 5–11.

Hemwall, M. K. & Trachte, K. (2003). Learning at the core: Theory and practice of academic advising in small colleges and universities. In M. K. Hemwall and K. Trachte (Eds.), *Advising learning: Academic advising from the perspective of small colleges and universities* (pp. 5–11) [Monograph No. 8]. Manhattan, KS: National Academic Advising Association.

Hemwall, M. K. & Trachte, K. (2005). Academic advising as learning: 10 organizing principles. *NACADA Journal, 25*(2), 74–83.

Hilbe, J. M. (2009). *Logistic regression models*. Boca Raton, FL: Chapman & Hall/CRC Press.

Hill, K., Hoffman, D., & Rex, T. R. (2005, October). *The value of higher education: Individual and societal benefits*. Tempe: Arizona State University, Seidman Research Institute, W.P. Carey School of Business. Retrieved from http://wpcarey.asu.edu/seid/upload/Value%20Full%20Report_final_october%202005a.pdf

Holland, J. L. (1997). *Making vocational choices* (3rd ed.). Odessa, FL: Psychological Assessment Resources.

Horn, L. J. (1998). *Stopouts or stayouts? Undergraduates who leave college in their first year: Statistical analysis report*. Washington, DC: U.S. Department of Education, National Center for Educational Statistics.

Hosmer, D. W., & Lemeshow, S. (2000). *Applied logistic regression* (2nd ed.). New York: Wiley.

Hossler, D., Bean, J. P., & Associates. (1990). *The strategic management of college enrollments*. San Francisco: Jossey-Bass.

Hsieh, P., Sullivan, J, & Guerra, N. (2007). A closer look at college students: Self-efficacy and goal orientation. *Journal of Advanced Academics, 19*, 454–476.

Hunter, J. E., & Schmidt, F. L. (2004). *Methods of meta-analysis: Correcting error and bias in research findings*. Thousand Oaks, CA: Sage.

Hunter, M. S., & Linder, C. W. (2005). First-year seminars. In M. L. Upcraft, J. N. Gardner, & B. O. Barefoot (Eds.), *Challenging and supporting the first-year student: A handbook for improving the first year of college*. San Francisco: Jossey-Bass.

Hurtado, S., Milem, J. F., Clayton-Pedersen, A. R., and Allen, W. R. (1998). Enhancing campus climates for racial/ethnic diversity: Educational policy and practice. The Review of Higher Education, 21(3), 279–302.

Huy, L., Casillas, A., Robbins, S., & Langley, R. (2005). Motivational and skills, social, and self-management predictors of college outcomes: Constructing the Student Readiness Inventory. *Educational and Psychological Measurement, 65*(3), 482–508.

Iffert, R. E. (1957). *Retention and withdrawal of college students* (U.S. Department of Health, Education, and Welfare Bulletin No. 1). Washington, DC: U.S. Government Printing Office.

The Institute for Higher Education Policy. (1998, March). *Reaping the benefits: Defining the public and private value of going to college*. Washington, DC: The Institute for Higher Education Policy.

Iowa Department of Education. (2010). *Annual condition of education report*. Des Moines: Author.

Jackson, D. N. (1984). *Personality research form manual*. Port Huron, MI: Research Psychologists Press.

Jacobson, E. (2006). Higher placement standards increase course success but reduce program completions. *The Journal of General Education, 55*, 138–159.

Jobs for the Future, & Delta Cost Project. (2009). Calculating cost-return for investments in student success. Retrieved from: http://www.deltacost project.org/resources/pdf/ISS_cost_return_report.pdf

Joint Committee on Testing Practices. (2002). *Code of fair testing practices in education*. Washington, DC: American Psychological Association.

Jones-White, D. R., Radcliffe, P. M., Huesman, R. L., & Kellogg, J. P. (2009). Redefining student success: Applying different multinomial regression techniques for the study of student graduation across institutions of higher education. *Research in Higher Education, 51*(2), 154–174.

Joshi, R. M. (2009) *International business*. New York: Oxford University Press.

Keniston, K. (1966). The faces in the lecture room. In Morison, R. S. (Ed.), *The contemporary university: USA*. Boston: Beacon Press.

Kezar, A. (2007). Creating and sustaining a campus ethos encouraging student engagement. *About Campus, (11)*6, 13–18. doi: 10.1002/abc.190

Killough, A. C. (2009, April 21). Obama administration joins effort to fix remedial education. *Chronicle of Higher Education*. Retrieved from http://chronicle.com

King, M. C. (2008). Organization of academic advising services. In V. N. Gordon, W. R. Habley, & T. J. Grites (Eds.), *Academic advising: A comprehensive handbook* (2nd ed., pp. 242–252). San Francisco: Jossey-Bass.

King, N. S. (2008) Advising delivery: Group strategies. In V. N. Gordon, W. R. Habley, & T. J. Grites (Eds.), *Academic advising: A comprehensive handbook* (2nd ed., pp. 279–291). San Francisco: Jossey-Bass.

Kinzie, J. & Kuh, G. D. (2004). Going DEEP: Learning from campuses that share responsibility for student success. *About Campus, 9*(5), 2–8. doi: 10.1002/abc.105

Klemp, G. O. (1988, May-June) The meaning of success: A view from outside the academy. *Liberal Education.* 74, 37–41.

Kotter, J. (2007). The 8-step process of successful change. Retrieved from http://www.ouricebergismelting.com/html/8step.html

Kozeracki, C. A. (2002). ERIC review: Issues in developmental education. *Community College Review, 29*(4), 83–100.

Kramer, G. L., & Associates (Eds.). (2007). *Fostering student success in the campus community*. San Francisco: Jossey-Bass.

Kramer, G. L., & Childs, M. W. (Eds.). (1996). Transforming academic advising through the use of information technology. [Monograph No. 4.] Manhattan, KS: National Academic Advising Association, Kansas State University (ERIC Document Reproduction Service No. ED 412 813).

Krosteng, M. V. (1992). Predicting persistence from the student adaptation to college questionnaire: Early warning or siren song? *Research in Higher Education, 33,* 99–111.

Kuh, G. D. (2001). Assessing what really matters to student learning: Inside the National Survey of Student Engagement. *Change, 33*(3), 10–17, 66.

Kuh, G. D. (2007, June 15). How to help students achieve. *Chronicle of Higher Education.* Retrieved from http://chronicle.com

Kuh, G. D. (2008). Advising for student success. In V. N. Gordon, W. R. Habley, & T. J. Grites (Eds.), *Academic advising: A comprehensive handbook* (2nd ed., pp. 68–84). San Francisco: Jossey-Bass.

Kuh, G. D., Kinzie, J., Buckley, J. A. Bridges, B. K., & Hayek J. C. (2006, November). What matters to student success: A review of the literature commissioned report for the National Symposium on Postsecondary Student Success: Spearheading a dialog on student success. Paper presented at the National Symposium on Postsecondary Student Success: Spearheading a Dialog on Student Success, Washington, DC.

Kuh, G. D., Kinzie, J., Schuh, J. H., & Whitt, E. J. (2005). *Student success in college: Creating conditions that matter.* San Francisco: Jossey-Bass.

Kuh, G. D., & Love, P. G. (2000). A cultural perspective on student departure. In J. M. Braxton (Ed.), *Reworking the student departure puzzle: New theory and research on college student retention.* Nashville: Vanderbilt University Press.

Kuh, G. D., & Whitt, E. J. (1988). The invisible tapestry: Culture in American colleges and universities. (ASHE-ERIC Higher Education Report No. 1).Washington, DC: George Washington University.

Kuhtmann, M. (2005). Socratic self-examination and its application to academic advising. *NACADA Journal, 25*(2), 37–48.

Lapan, R. T., Gysbers, N. C., & Sun, Y. (1997). The impact of more fully implemented guidance programs on the school experiences of high school students: A statewide evaluation study. *Journal of Counseling and Development, 75,* 292–302.

Laufgraben, J. L., (2005). Learning Communities. In M. L. Upcraft, J. N. Gardner, & B. O. Barefoot (Eds.), *Challenging and supporting the first-year student: A handbook for improving the first year of college.* San Francisco: Jossey-Bass.

League for Innovation in the Community College (2001). League for Innovation announces articulation agreements. Retrieved from http://www.league.org/league/about/press/articulation_agreements.htm

Lenning, O. T. (1978). *An optimistic alternative: Keeping enrollment up.* Paper presented at the annual convention of the American Association for Higher Education, Chicago.

Lenning, O. T., Sauer, K., & Beal, P. E. (1980). *Student retention strategies.* AAHE-ERIC/ Higher Education Research Report No. 8.

Leonard, M. J. (2008). Advising delivery: Using technology. In V. N. Gordon, W. R. Habley, & T. J. Grites (Eds.), *Academic advising: A comprehensive handbook* (2nd ed., pp. 292–306). San Francisco: Jossey-Bass.

Lerner, J. B., & Brand, B. (2006). *The college ladder: Linking secondary and postsecondary education for success for all students*. Washington, DC: American Youth Policy Forum.

Leuwerke, W. C., Robbins, S. B., Sawyer, R., & Hovland, M. (2004). Predicting engineering major status from mathematics achievement and interest congruence. *Journal of Career Assessment, 12*(2), 135–149.

Levine, A. (2001). Higher education as a mature industry. In P. Altbach, P. Gumport, & D. B. Johnstone (Eds.), *In defense of American higher education* (pp. 39–58). Baltimore, MD: The Johns Hopkins University Press.

Levine, A. (2006a). Educating school teachers. Retrieved from http://www.edschools.org/pdf/Educating_Teachers_Report.pdf

Levine, A. (2006b) A higher bar for future teachers. Retrieved from http://www.boston.com/news/education/higher/articles/2006/10/31/a_higher_bar_for_future_teachers/

Lewis, S., Passmore, J., & Cantore, S. (2008). *Appreciative inquiry for change management: Using AI to facilitate organizational development*. Philadelphia: Kogan Page.

Light, R. J. (2003). Enhancing students' college experience with specific advising suggestions. *Academic Advising Today, 26*(2). Retrieved from http://www.nacada.ksu.edu

Lingenfelter, P. E. (2003). Educational accountability: Setting standards, improving performance. *Change, 35*(2), 18–23.

Lloyd-Jones, E., & Smith, M. R. (Eds.). (1954). *Student personnel work as deeper teaching*. New York: Harper & Brothers.

Lofquist, L. H., & Dawis R. V. (1991). *Essentials of Person-Environment-Correspondence Counseling*. Minneapolis: University of Minnesota Press.

Lotkowski, V. A., Robbins, S. B., & Noeth, R. J. (2004). The role of academic and non-academic factors in improving college retention. Iowa City: ACT Policy Report. Retrieved from http://www.act.org/research/policy/index.html

Lowenstein, M. (2000, April 14). Academic advising and the "logic" of the curriculum. *The Mentor, 2*(2). Retrieved from http://www.psu.edu/dus/mentor

Lowenstein, M. (2005). If advising is teaching, what do advisors teach? *NACADA Journal, 25*(2), 65–73.

Ludema, J. D., Whitney, D., Mohr, B. J., & Griffin, T. J. (2003). *The appreciative inquiry summit: A practitioner's guide for leading large-group change*. San Francisco: Berrett-Koehler.

Martorell, P., & McFarlin, I. (2007, September). Help or hindrance? The effects of college remediation on academic and labor market outcomes. Retrieved from http://zxtm01-ti-1.utdallas.edu/research/tsp-erc/pdf/wp_mcfarlin_2007_help_or_hindrance.pdf

Mauer, M. (1994). *Americans behind bars: The international use of incarceration, 1992–93*. Washington, DC: The Sentencing Project.

Mause, K. (2009). Education and the excessive-signaling hypothesis. *American Journal of Economics and Sociology*. 68(5), 1107–1133.

Maxwell, M. (1990). Does tutoring help? A look at the literature. *Review of Research in Developmental Education, 7*(4), 1–5. Retrieved from http://eric.ed.gov/PDFS/ED326287.pdf

McCabe, R. H. (2000). *No one to waste*. Washington, DC: Community Press.

McCabe, R. H., & Day, P. R., Jr. (Eds.). (1998). Developmental education: A twenty-first century imperative. Mission Viejo, CA: League for Innovation in the Community College. Retrieved from http://eric.ed.gov/PDFS/ED421176.pdf

McCalla-Wriggins, B. (2009). Integrating career and academic advising: Mastering the challenge. Retrieved from: http://www.nacada.ksu.edu/Clearinghouse/M02/Career-Advising.htm

McDivitt, P. J., & Gibson, D. (2004). Guidelines for selecting appropriate tests. In J. Wall & G. Walz (Eds.), *Measuring up: Assessment issues for teachers, counselors, and administrators*. Greensboro, NC: ERIC Counseling and Student Services Clearinghouse and the National Board for Certified Counselors.

McGillin, V. A. (2010). Foreword. In P. L. Hagen, T. L. Kuhn, & G. M. Padak (Eds.). *Scholarly inquiry into academic advising* (pp. 5–9) [Monograph No. 20]. Manhattan, KS: National Academic Advising Association.

McGrath, M., & Braunstein, A. (1997). The prediction of freshman attrition: An examination of the importance of certain demographic, academic, financial, and social factors. *College Student Journal, 31*, 396–408.

McMahon, W. W. (2009). *Higher learning, greater good: The private and social benefits of higher education*. Baltimore, MD: Johns Hopkins University Press.

Melander, E. R. (2005). Advising as educating: A framework for organizing advising. *NACADA Journal, 25*(2), 84–91.

Merisotis, J. P., & Phipps, R. A. (2000, Fall). Remedial education in colleges and universities: What's really going on? *The Review of Higher Education, 24*(1), 67–85.

Merriam-Webster. (2002). Webster's Third New International Dictionary, Unabridged. Retrieved from http://unabridged.merriam-webster.com.

Metzner, B. S. (1989). Perceived quality of academic advising: the effect on freshman attrition. *American Educational Research Journal, 26*(3), 422–442.

Michael, R. (1982). Measuring non-monetary benefits of education. In W. W. McMahon and T. Geske (Eds.), *Financing education: Overcoming inefficiency and inequity*. Urbana: University of Illinois Press.

Mohr, J., Eiche, K., & Sedlacek, W. (1998). So close, yet so far: Predictors of attrition on college seniors. *Journal of College Student Development, 39*, 343–354.

Mollison, A, (2006). Surviving a midlife crisis: Advanced placement turns fifty. *Education Next, 6*(1), 34–9.

Mortenson, T. (2010) Measuring U.S. education performance and progress against the OECD competition, 1995 to 2007. *Postsecondary Education Opportunity, 216*.

Mueller, K. H. (1961). *Student personnel work in higher education*. Boston: Houghton Mifflin.

Mullendore, R. H., & Banahan, L. A. (2005). Designing orientation programs. In M. L. Upcraft, J. N. Gardner, & B. O. Barefoot (Eds.), *Challenging and supporting the first-year student: A handbook for improving the first year of college*. San Francisco: Jossey-Bass.

National Academic Advising Association [NACADA]. (2006). NACADA concept of academic advising. Retrieved from http://www.nacada.ksu.edu/clearinghouse/advisingissues/concept-advising.htm

National Academic Advising Association [NACADA]. (2007). NACADA Career Advising Survey. Retrieved from https://online.ksu.edu/Survey/PublicReport?offeringId=61917

National Assessment of Educational Progress. (2006). The nation's report card: Science 2005. Retrieved from http://nationsreportcard.gov/science_2005/

National Assessment of Educational Progress. (2008a). 2008 long term trend: Reading overall results. Retrieved from http://nationsreportcard.gov/ltt_2008/ltt0003.asp

National Assessment of Educational Progress. (2008b). 2008 long term trend: Mathematics overall results. Retrieved from http://nationsreportcard.gov/ltt_2008/ltt0002.asp

National Assessment of Educational Progress. (2008c). The nation's report card: Writing 2007. Retrieved from http://nationsreportcard.gov/writing_2007/

National Center for Educational Statistics. (2001). Community college transfer rates to 4-year institutions. Retrieved from http://nces.ed.gov/pubsearch/pubsinfo.asp?pubid=2001197

National Center for Educational Statistics. (2002). Descriptive summary of 1995–96: Beginning postsecondary students: Six years later. Retrieved from http://nces.ed.gov/pubsearch/pubsinfo.asp?pubid=2003151

National Center for Education Statistics. (2003). *Digest of education statistics 2002* (NCES 2003–160). Washington, DC: U.S. Department of Education, Office of Educational Research and Improvement.

National Center for Education Statistics. (2005). Dual enrollment of high school students at postsecondary institutions: *2002–03* (NCES 2005–008). Retrieved from http://nces.ed.gov/surveys/peqis/publications/2005008/2a.asp

National Center for Education Statistics. (2009a). Digest of education statistics, 2008 (NCES 2009–020). Retrieved from http://nces.ed.gov/fastfacts/display.asp?id=98

National Center for Educational Statistics. (2009b). Digest of educational statistics 2009. Table 334: Average undergraduate tuition and fees and room and board rates charged for full-time students in degree-granting institutions, by type and control of institution: 1963–64 through 2008–09. Retrieved from http://nces.ed.gov/programs/digest/d09/tables/dt09_334.asp?referrer=list

National Center for Educational Statistics. (2009c). Distance education at degree-granting postsecondary institutions: 2006–07 (Report No. 2009044). Retrieved from http://nces.ed.gov/pubsearch/pubsinfo.asp?pubid=2009044

National Center for Educational Statistics. (2009d). Percentage of first-year undergraduate students who took remedial education courses, by selected characteristics: 2003–04 and 2007–08. Retrieved from http://nces.ed.gov/programs/digest/d10/tables/dt10_241.asp

National Center for Educational Statistics. (2010a). The condition of education 2010 in brief (NCES 2010–029). Retrieved from http://nces.ed.gov/pubsearch/pubsinfo.asp?pubid=2010029

National Center for Education Statistics (2010b). *Fast facts*. Retrieved from http://nces.ed.gov/fastfacts/display.asp?id=40

National Center for Educational Statistics. (2010c). Postsecondary institutions and price of attendance in the United States: Fall 2009, degrees and other awards conferred: 2008–09, and 12-month enrollment: 2008–09 (Report No. 2010161). Retrieved from http://nces.ed.gov/pubsearch/pubsinfo.asp?pubid=2010161

National Center for Education Statistics. (2010d). Web table—*Profile of undergraduate students: Trends from selected years, 1995–95 to 2007–08*. Washington, DC: U.S. Department of Education. Retrieved from http://nces.ed.gov/pubsearch/pubsinfo.asp?pubid=2010220

National Orientation Directors Association. (2008). *Member handbook*. Minneapolis: University of Minnesota.

National Resource Center for the First-Year Experience and Students in Transition. (2005). *The 2003 national survey of first-year seminar programs*. Columbia: The University of South Carolina.

National Resource Center for the First-Year Experience and Students in Transition. (2011). *The 2009 national survey of first-year seminars*. Columbia: The University of South Carolina.

National Survey of Student Engagement. (2007). *Experiences that matter: Enhancing student learning and success.* Bloomington: Indiana University, Center for Postsecondary Research.

Neumann, G., Olitsky, N., & Robbins, S. (2009). Job congruence, academic achievement, and earnings. *Labour Economics, 16,* 503–509.

Noble, J., & Camara, W. J. (2004). Issues in college admissions testing. In J. Wall & G. Walz (Eds.), *Measuring up: Assessment issues for teachers, counselors, and administrators.* Greensboro, NC: ERIC Counseling and Student Services Clearinghouse and the National Board for Certified Counselors.

Noble, J., & Radunzel, J. (2007). *College readiness = college success beyond the first year.* Paper presented at the Annual Forum of the Association for Institutional Research in Kansas City, MO.

Noble, J., & Sawyer, R. L. (2004). Is high school GPA better than admissions test scores for predicting academic success in college? *College and University, 79, 4,* 17–22.

Noble, J. P., Schiel, J. L., & Sawyer, R. L. (2004). Assessment and college course placement. In J. Wall & G. Walz (Eds.), *Measuring up: Assessment issues for teachers, counselors, and administrators.* Greensboro, NC: ERIC Counseling and Student Services Clearinghouse and the National Board for Certified Counselors.

Noel, L. (Ed.). (1978). *Reducing the dropout rate* (New Directions in Student Services Series). San Francisco: Jossey-Bass.

Noel, L., Levitz, R., Saluri, D., & Associates. (1986). *Increasing student retention.* San Francisco: Jossey-Bass.

Noel-Levitz. (n.d.). Return on investment estimator. Retrieved from https://www.noellevitz.com/NR/rdonlyres/4077497B-1367-4AF8-A451-6E1243675033/0/ReturnonInvestmentEstimator.pdf

Noel-Levitz. (2009). Cost of recruiting report: Comparative benchmarks for two-year and four-year institutions. Retrieved from www.noellevitz.com/BenchmarkReports

Noeth, R. J., & Wimberley, G. L. (2002). *Creating seamless educational transitions for urban African American and Hispanic students.* Iowa City: ACT.

Nord, C., Roey, S., Perkins, R., Lyons, M., Lemanski, N., Brown, J., & Schuknecht, J. (2011). *The nation's report card: America's high school graduates* (NCES 2011–462). U.S. Department of Education, National Center for Education Statistics. Washington, DC: U.S. Government Printing Office.

O'Banion, T. (1972). An academic advising model. *Junior College Journal, 42*(6), 62–69.

O'Brien, C. (1997, August). *Now what? Life after college for recent graduates.* Washington, DC: The Institute for Higher Education Policy and the Education Resources Institute.

Ogden, P., Thompson, D., Russell, A., & Simons, C. (2003). Supplemental Instruction: Short- and long-term impact. *Journal of Developmental Education, 26*(3), 2–8.

O'Hear, M., & MacDonald, R. (1995). A critical review of research in developmental education, Part I. *Journal of Developmental Education, 19*(2), 2–6.

Oliver, M. L., Rodriguez, C. J., & Mickelson, R. A. (1985). Brown and black in white: The social adjustment and academic performance of Chicano and black students in a predominantly white university. *Urban Review, 17*(1), 3–23.

Oliver, L. W., & Spokane, A. R. (1988). Career-intervention outcome: What contributes to client gain? *Journal of Counseling Psychology, 35,* 447–462.

Osher, L. W., Ward, J. L., Tross, S. A., & Flanagan, W. (1995). *The College Adjustment Inventory* [Technical report]. Atlanta: Georgia Institute of Technology.

Organization of Economic Cooperation and Development (OECD). (2009). What students know and can do: Student performance in reading, mathematics, and science. *Executive Summary: Programme for International Student Assessment.* Retrieved from http://www.oecd.org/dataoecd/54/12/46643496.pdf

Osipow, S. (1990). Convergence in theories of career choice and development; Review and prospect. *Journal of Vocational Behavior, 36,* 122–131.

Pantages, T. J., & Creedon, C. F. (1978). Studies of college attrition: 1950—1975. *Review of Educational Research, 48,* 49–101.

Pardee, C. F. (2000). Organizational models for academic advising. In V. N. Gordon, W. R. Habley, et al. (Eds.), *Academic advising: A comprehensive handbook* (pp. 192–209). San Francisco: Jossey-Bass.

Pascarella, E. (1985). College environmental influences on learning and cognitive development: A critical review and synthesis. In J. Smart (Ed.), *Higher education: Handbook of theory and research* (Vol. 1). New York: Agathon.

Pascarella, E. T., & Chapman, D. (1983). A multi-institutional, path analytic validation of Tinto's model of college withdrawal. *American Educational Research Journal, 20,* 87–102.

Pascarella, E. T., & Terenzini, P. T. (1977). Patterns of student–faculty informal interaction beyond the classroom and voluntary freshman attrition. *Journal of Higher Education, 48,* 540–552.

Pascarella, E. T., & Terenzini, P. T. (1991). *How college affects students: Findings and insights from twenty years of research.* San Francisco: Jossey-Bass.

Pascarella, E. T., & Terenzini, P. T. (2005). *How college affects students, volume 2, a third decade of research.* San Francisco: Jossey-Bass.

Pascarella, E. T., Terenzini, P. T., & Wolfe, L. M. (1986). Orientation to college and freshman year persistence/withdrawal decisions. *Journal of Higher Education, 57*(2), 155–175.

Passel, J. S., & Cohn, D. (2008). *U.S. population projections: 2005–2050.* Washington, DC: Pew Research Center.

Patton, L. D., Morelon, C., Whitehead, D., & Hossler, D. (2006). Campus-based retention initiatives: Does the emperor have clothes? *New Directions for Institutional Research, 130,* 9–24.

Paunonen, S. V., & Ashton, M. C. (2001). Big five predictors of academic achievement. *Journal of Research in Personality, 35,* 78–90.

Pavel, D. M., & Padilla, R. V. (1993). American Indian and Alaska native postsecondary departure: An example of assessing a mainstream model using national longitudinal data. *Journal of American Indian Education, 32,* 1–23.

Payne, E. M., & Lyman, B. G. (1996). Issues affecting the definition of developmental education. In. J. L. Higbee, & P. L. Dwinell (Eds.), *Defining developmental education: Theory, research, & pedagogy* (pp. 11–20). Carol Stream, IL: National Association for Developmental Education.

Perigo, D. J., & Upcraft, M. L. (1989). Orientation programs. In M. L. Upcraft, J. N. Gardner, & Associates (Eds.), *The freshman year experience: Helping students survive and succeed in college.* San Francisco: Jossey-Bass.

Perkhounkova, Y., Noble, J. P., & Sawyer, R. (2005). *Modeling the effectiveness of developmental instruction* (ACT Research Report: 2005–2). Iowa City: ACT.

Pervin, L. A., Reik, L. E., & Dalrymple, W. (1966). The dropout in conflict with society. In L. A. Pervin, L. E. Reik, & W. Dalrymple. (Eds), *The college dropout and the utilization of talent.* Princeton, NJ: Princeton University Press.

Peterson, M., Wagner, J. A., & Lamb, C. W. (2001). The role of advising in non-returning students' perceptions of their university. *Journal of Marketing for Higher Education, 10*(3), 45–59. doi: 10.1300/J050v10n03_03.

Pike, G. R., & Kuh, G. D. (2005). A typology of student engagement for American colleges and universities. *Research in Higher Education, 46*(2), 185–206.

Pike, G. R., Schroeder, C. C., & Berry, T. R. (1997). Enhancing the educational impact of residence halls: The relationship between residential learning communities and first-year college experience and persistence. *Journal of College Student Development, 38,* 609–621.

Pine, J. (2001). *Wit and wisdom of the American presidents.* Mineola, NY: Dover.

Porchea, S., Allen, J., Robbins, S., & Phelps, R. (2010). Predictors of long-term enrollment and degree outcomes for community college students:

Integrating academic, psychosocial, socio-demographic, and situational factors. *Journal of Higher Education, 81*(6), 750–778.

Porter, S. R., & Umbach, P. D. (2006). College major choice: An analysis of person-environment fit. *Research in Higher Education, 47,* 429–449.

Potts, G., & Schultz, B. (2008). The freshman seminar and academic success of at-risk students. *College Student Journal, 2*(2-B).

Prediger, D. J. (1995). Assessment in career counseling (ERIC Digest Report No. EDO-CG-95-18). Retrieved from http://eric.ed.gov/

Price, D. V. (2005). *Learning communities and student success in postsecondary education.* New York: MDRC (formerly Manpower Demonstration Research Corporation).

Price, J. L., & Mueller, C. W. (1981). A causal model of turnover for nurses. *Academy of Management Journal, 24,* 543–565.

Pryor, J. H., Hurtado, S. DeAngelo, L., Blake, L. P., & Tran, S. (2009). *The American freshman: National norms fall 2009.* Los Angeles: Cooperative Institutional Research Program, Higher Education Research Institute, University of California.

Pryor, J. H., Hurtado, S., Saenz, V. B., Santos, J. L., & Korn, W. S. (2007). *The American freshman: Forty year trends.* Los Angeles: Cooperative Institutional Research Program, Higher Education Research Institute, University of California.

Quotations of Abraham Lincoln. (2003). Bedford, MA: Applewood Books.

Rainsford, G. N. (1972). *Congress and higher education in the nineteenth century.* Knoxville: University of Tennessee Press.

Rawlins, W. K., & Rawlins, S. P. (2005). Academic advising as friendship. *NACADA Journal, 25*(2), 10–19.

Redmoon, A. (1991, Fall). No peaceful warriors! *Gnosis: A Journal of Western Inner Traditions.*

Robbins, S., Allen, J., Casillas, A., Peterson, C. H., & Le, H. (2006). Unraveling the differential effects of motivational and skills, social, and self-management measures from traditional predictors of college outcomes. *Journal of Educational Psychology, 98*(3), 589–616.

Robbins, S., Lauver, K., Le, H., Davis, D., Langley, R., & Carlstrom, A. (2004). Do psychosocial and study skill factors predict college outcomes? A meta-analysis. *Psychological Bulletin, 130*(2), 261–288.

Robbins, S., Oh, I., Button, C., & Le, H. (2009). *The effects of college interventions on psychosocial mediators and academic and persistence outcomes: An integrated meta-analysis.* Manuscript submitted for publication.

Robinson, D. R., Schofield, J. W., & Steers-Wentzell, K. L. (2005). Peer and cross-age tutoring in math: Outcomes and their design implications. *Educational Psychology Review, 17*(4), 327–362, doi: 10.1007/s10648-005-8137-2

Rocconi, L. M. (2011). The impact of learning communities on first year students' growth and development in college. *Research in Higher Education, 52*, 178–193.

Roscoe, R. D., & Chi, M. T. H. (2007). Understanding tutor learning: Knowledge-building and knowledge-telling in peer tutors' explanations and questions. *Review of Educational Research, 77*(4), 534–574, doi: 10.3102/00346543073099920

Rosenbaum, J. E., Redline, J. & Stephan, J. L. (2007). Community college: The unfinished revolution. *Issues in Science and Technology, 23*(4), 49–56.

Roueche, J. E., & Roueche, S. D. (1999). *High stakes, high performance: Making remedial education work.* Washington, DC: American Association of Community Colleges.

Ryan, N. E. (1999). *Career counseling and career choice goal attainment: A meta-analytically derived model for career counseling practice* (Unpublished doctoral dissertation). Loyola University, Chicago.

Ryland, E. B., Riordan, R. J., & Brack, G. (1994). Selected characteristics of high-risk students and their enrollment persistence. *Journal of College Student Development, 35*, 54–58.

Ryu, M. (2010). *Minorities in higher education.* Washington, DC: American Council on Education.

St. John, E. P., Cabrera, A. F., Nora, A., & Asker, E. H. (2000). Economic influences on persistence reconsidered: How can finance research inform the reconceptualization of persistence models? In J. M. Braxton (Ed.), *Reworking the student departure puzzle* (pp. 29–47). Nashville, TN: Vanderbilt University Press.

Sandeen, A. (1996). Organization, functions, and standards of practice. In S. R. Komives & D. B. Woodward (Eds.), *Student services: A handbook for the profession* (3rd ed.). San Francisco: Jossey-Bass.

Sawyer R., & Schiel, J. (2000). *Posttesting students to assess the effectiveness of remedial instruction in college* (ACT Research Report: 2000–7). Iowa City: ACT.

Schein, E. H. (2004). *Organizational culture and leadership* (3rd ed.). San Francisco: Jossey-Bass.

Schmidt, P. (2007). High-school students aim higher without learning more, federal students find. *The Chronicle for Higher Education, 53*(27), A32.

Schmidt, P. (2008, 4 July). 3 new studies question the value of remedial college courses. *Chronicle of Higher Education, 54*(43), A18. Retrieved from http://chronicle.com

Schreiner, L. A., & Anderson, E. (2005). Strengths-based advising: A new lens for higher education. *NACADA Journal, 25*(2), 20–29.

Schuh, J. H. (2005). Finances and retention: Trends and potential implications. In A. Seidman (Ed.), *College student retention: Formula for student success* (pp. 89–106). Greenwich, CT: Praeger.

Seidman, A. (1991). The evaluation of a pre/post admissions/counseling process at a suburban community college: Impact on student satisfaction with the faculty and the institution, retention, and academic performance. *College and University*, 66(4), 223–232.

Seidman, A. (Ed.). (2005a). *College student retention: Formula for student success*. Westport, CT: Praeger.

Seidman, A. (2005b). Where we go from here: A retention formula for student success. In A. Seidman (Ed.), *College student retention: Formula for student success*. Westport, CT: Praeger Publishers.

Self, C. (2008). Advising delivery: Professional advisors, counselors, and other staff. In V. N. Gordon, W. R. Habley, & T. J. Grites (Eds.), *Academic advising: A comprehensive handbook* (2nd ed., pp. 267–278). San Francisco: Jossey-Bass.

Senko, C., Hulleman, C. S., & Harackiewicz, J. M. (2011). Achievement goal theory at the crossroads: Old controversies, current challenges, and new directions. *Educational Psychologist*, 46, 26–47.

Shaffer, R. H. (1970). Orientation of new students. In A. Knowles. (Ed.), *Handbook of college and university administration*. New York: McGraw-Hill.

Silvia, P. J. (2006). *Exploring the psychology of interest*. New York: Oxford University Press.

Simons, H. D., & Van Rheenen, D. (2000). Noncognitive predictors of student athletes' academic performance. *Journal of College Reading and Learning*, 30, 167–181.

Smith, B. M. (1993). The effect of quality of effort on persistence among traditional-aged community college students. *Community College Journal of Research and Practice*, 17, 103–122.

Smith, B. L. (1993). Creating learning communities. *Liberal Education*. 70(4), 32–39.

Smith, L., & Robbins, S. (1993). Enhancement programs for entering majority and minority freshmen. *Journal of Counseling and Development*, 71, 510–514.

Solberg, V. S., Gusavac, N., Hamann, T., Felch, J., Johnson, J., Lamborn, S., & Torres, J. (1998). The adaptive success identity plan (ASIP): A career intervention for college students. *Career Development Quarterly*, 47, 48–95.

Spady, W. G. (1970). Dropouts from higher education: An interdisciplinary review and synthesis. *Interchange*, 1(1), 64–85.

Spady, W. G. (1971). Dropouts from higher education: Toward an empirical model. *Interchange*, 2(3), 38–62.

Spradlin, T. E., Burroughs, N. A., Rutkowski, D. J., Lang, J. R., & Hardesty, J. W. (2010). College persistence and completion strategies: opportunities for scaling up. *Education Policy Brief*, 8(4), 1–16.

Steele, G. E., Kennedy, G. J., & Gordon, V. N. (1993). The retention of major changers: A longitudinal study. *Journal of College Student Development 34*, 58–62.

Stern, G. (1970). *People in context: Measuring person–environment congruence in education and industry.* New York: Wiley-Interscience.

Stillwell, R. (2010). *Public school graduates and dropouts from the common core of data: School year 2007–08* (NCES 2010–341). Washington, DC: National Center for Education Statistics, Institute of Education Sciences, U.S. Department of Education.

Stoecker, J., Pascarella, E. T., & Wolfe, L. M. (1988). Persistence in higher education: A 9-year test of a theoretical model. *Journal of College Student Development, 29*, 196–209.

Strong American Schools. (2008). Diploma to nowhere. Washington, DC: Author. Retrieved from http://www.deltacostproject.org/resources/pdf/DiplomaToNowhere.pdf

Suen, H. (1983). Alienation and attrition of black college students on a predominantly white campus. *Journal of College Student Personnel, 24*, 117–121.

Summerskill, J. (1962). Dropouts from college. In N. Sanford (Ed.), *The American college.* New York: Wiley.

Terenzini, P. T. (1996, February). First generation college students: Characteristics, experiences, and cognitive development. *Research in Higher Education, 37*(1), 1–22.

Tierney, W. G. (1988, January-February). Organizational culture in higher education: Defining the essentials. *The Journal of Higher Education, 59*(1), 2–21.

Tinto, V. (1975). Dropout from higher education: A theoretical synthesis of recent research. *Review of Educational Research, 45*(1), 89–125.

Tinto, V. (1987). *Leaving college: Rethinking the causes and cures of student attrition.* Chicago: The University of Chicago Press.

Tinto, V. (1988). Stages of student departure: Reflections on the longitudinal character of student leaving. *Journal of Higher Education, 59*(4), 438–455.

Tinto, V. (1993). *Leaving college: Rethinking the causes and cures of student attrition.* Chicago: University of Chicago Press.

Tinto, V. (2005, July 27–30). Student retention: What next? Presentation at the National Conference on Student Recruitment, Marketing, and Retention in Washington, DC.

Tobolowsky, B. F., & Associates (2008). *2006 National Survey of First-Year Seminars: Continuing innovations in the collegiate curriculum* (Monograph No. 51). Columbia: University of South Carolina, National Resource Center for the First-Year Experience and Students in Transition.

Topping, K. J. (1996). The effectiveness of peer tutoring in further and higher education: A typology and review of the literature. *Higher Education, 32*(3), 321–345.

Trabant, T. D. (2006). Advising syllabus 101. Retrieved from: http://www.nacada.ksu.edu/Clearinghouse/AdvisingIssues/syllabus101.htm

Tracey, T. J. (2002). Development of interests and competency beliefs: A 1-year longitudinal study of fifth-to eighth-grade student using the ICA-R and structural equation modeling. *Journal of Counseling Psychology, 49,* 148–163.

Tracey, T. J., & Robbins, S. B. (2006). The interest-major congruence and college success relation: A longitudinal study. *Journal of Vocational Behavior, 69,* 64–89.

Tracey, T. J., & Sedlacek, W. E. (1984). Noncognitive variables in predicting academic success by race. *Measurement and Evaluation in Guidance, 16,* 171–178.

Trippi, J., & Cheatham, H. E. (1991). Counseling effects on African American college student graduation. *Journal of College Student Development, 32,* 342–349.

Tross, S. A., Harper, J. P., Osher, L. W., & Kneidinger, L. M. (2000). Not just the usual cast of characteristics: Using personality to predict college performance and retention. *Journal of College Student Development, 41,* 323–334.

Troxel, W. G. (2008). Assessing the effectiveness of the advising program. In V. N. Gordon, W. R. Habley, & T. J. Grites (Eds.), *Academic advising: A comprehensive handbook* (2nd ed., pp. 386–395). San Francisco: Jossey-Bass.

University of Iowa. 2 plus 2 plan. Retrieved from http://www.uiowa.edu/2plus2/how_plan_works/index.html

University of Iowa. (2011). Living learning communities. Retrieved from http://www.uiowa.edu/admissions/undergrad/housing/learning-comm.htm.

University of Missouri at Kansas City, The International Center for Supplemental Instruction. (2010). Supplemental instruction overview. Retrieved from http://www.umkc.edu/cad/si/overview.shtml

University of South Carolina. (2011). History of first year seminar and university 101 program. Retrieved from http://sc.edu/univ101/aboutus/history.html

Upcraft, M. L., & Farnsworth, W. M. (1984). Orientation programs and activities. In M. L. Upcraft (Ed.), *Orienting students to college* (pp. 27–38). San Francisco: Jossey-Bass.

Upcraft, M. L., Gardner, J. N., & Barefoot, B. O. (2005). *Challenging and supporting the first-year student: a handbook for improving the first year of college.* San Francisco: Jossey-Bass.

U.S. Bureau of the Census. (2010). Money income of householders: 1967–2008. Retrieved from http://www.census.gov/compendia/statab/2011/tables/ 11s0689.xls

U.S. Bureau of Labor Statistics. (2010a). College enrollment and work activity of 2009 high school graduates. Retrieved from http://www.bls.gov/news.release/hsgec.nr0.htm

U.S. Bureau of Labor Statistics. (2010b). Employment projections: education pays. Retrieved from http://www.bls.gov/emp/ep_chart_001.htm

U.S. Bureau of Labor Statistics. (2011a, May 4). Education pays. Retrieved from http://www.bls.gov/emp/ep_chart_001.htm

U.S. Bureau of Labor Statistics. (2011b, May 6). Employment status of the civilian population 25 years and over by educational attainment. Retrieved from http://www.bls.gov/news.release/empsit.t04.htm

U.S. Census Bureau. (2010a). America's families and living arrangements. Retrieved from http://www.census.gov/population/www/socdemo/hh-fam/cps2010.html

U.S. Census Bureau. (2010b). Annual estimates of the population of metropolitan and metropolitan statistical areas: April 1, 2000 to July 1, 2009 (CSV). Retrieved from http://www.census.gov/popest/metro/files/2009/CBSA-EST2009–alldata.csv.

U.S. Census Bureau. (2010c). Statistical Abstract of the United States: 2010 (PPL-148; earlier PPL and P-20 reports; and data published on the Internet). Retrieved from http://www.census.gov/population/www/socdemo/school.html

U.S. Census Bureau, Population Division. (1996). Population Projections for States by Age, Sex, Race, and Hispanic Origin: 1995 to 2025 (PPL-47, Preferred Series, PPL-47). Retrieved from http://www.census.gov/population/www/projections/ppl47.html

U-Select. Retrieved from https://www.transfer.org/uselect/

Van Gennep, A. (1960). *The rites of passage*. Chicago: The University of Chicago.

Van Iddekinge, C. H., Putka, D. J., & Campbell, J. P. (2011). Reconsidering vocational interests for personnel selection: The validity of an interest-based selection test in relation to job knowledge, job performance, and continuance intentions. *Journal of Applied Psychology*, 96, 13–33.

Van de Water, G., & Rainwater, T. (2001). *What is P-16 education? A primer for legislators—a practical introduction to the concept, language and policy issues of an integrated system of public education*. Denver: Education Commission of the States.

Visher, M. G., Bhandari, R., & Medrich, E. (2004). High school career exploration programs: Do they work? *Phi Delta Kappan*, 86, 135–138.

Wall, J. E., & Walz, G. R. (Eds.). (2004). *Measuring up: Assessment issues for teachers, counselors and administrators*. Greensboro, NC: ERIC Counseling and Student Services Clearinghouse and the National Board of Certified Counselors (NBCC).

Washington Center for Improving the Quality of Undergraduate Education. (2010). *Learning Communities National Resource Center Directory*. Retrieved from http://www.evergreen.edu/washcenter/Directory_search.asp

Washington State Board for Community and Technical Colleges [WSBCTC]. (2005). *I-BEST: A program integrating adult basic education and workforce training* (Research Report N. 05–2). Olympia, WA: Washington State Board for Community and Technical Colleges.

Wasley, P. (2007, February 9). A secret support network. *Chronicle of Higher Education*. Retrieved from http://chronicle.com

Watkins, B. T. (1983, May 4). The cost of recruiting is on the rise, survey finds. *The Chronicle of Higher Education*, p. 7.

Watkins, J. M., & Mohr, B. J. (2001). *Appreciative inquiry: Change at the speed of imagination*. San Francisco: Jossey-Bass/Pfeiffer.

Western Interstate Commission for Higher Education (WICHE). (2008). Knocking at the college door: Projections of high school graduates by state and race/ethnicity, 1999–2022 (ED500532). Retrieved from http://www.eric.ed.gov/ERICWebPortal/detail?accno=ED500532

Whiston, S. C., Brecheisen, B. K., & Stephens, J. (2003). Does treatment modality affect career counseling effectiveness? *Journal of Vocational Behavior, 62*, 390–410.

Whiston, S. C., Sexton, T. L., & Lasoff, D. L. (1998). Career-intervention outcome: A replication and extension of Oliver and Spokane (1988). *Journal of Counseling Psychology, 45*, 150–165.

White, C. L. (1988). Ethnic identity and academic performance among black and white college students: An interactionist approach. *Urban Education, 23*, 219–240.

Whitney, D. R. (1989). Educational admissions and placement. In R. L. Linn (Ed.), *Educational measurement* (3rd ed., 515–526). New York: American Council on Education and Macmillan.

Whitney, D., & Trosten-Bloom, A. (2003). *The power of appreciative inquiry: A practical guide to positive change*. San Francisco: Berrett-Koehler.

Williamson, D., & Creamer, D. (1988). Student attrition in 2- and 4-year colleges: Application of a theoretical model. *Journal of College Student Development, 29*, 210–217.

Williamson, E. G. (1961). *Student personnel services in colleges and universities*. New York: McGraw-Hill.

Wimberly, G. L. III (2000). Links between social capital and educational attainment among African American adolescents. *Dissertation Abstracts International, 61*(03), 1172. (UMI No. 9965178).

Winston, G. C. (2004). Differentiation among U.S. colleges and universities. *Review of Industrial Organization, 24*(4), 331–354.

Winston, R. B., Ender, S. C., Miller, T. K. (1982). Academic advising as student development. *New Directions for Student Services, 1982* (17), 3–8. doi: 10.1002/ss.37119821703

Woodring, P. (1968). *The higher learning in America: A reassessment.* New York: McGraw-Hill.

Woodruff, D. J., & Ziomek, R. L. (2004). *High school grade inflation from 1991 to 2003* (ACT Research Reports 2004–4). Iowa City: ACT.

World Economic Forum. (2010). *Global Competitiveness Report 2009–2010.* Retrieved from http://www3.weforum.org/docs/WEF_Global CompetitivenessReport_2010-11.pdf

Young, B. C., & Sowa, C. J. (1992). Predictors of academic success for black student athletes. *Journal of College Student Development, 33*, 318–324.

Young, R. B., Backer, R., & Rogers, G. (1989). The impact of early advising and scheduling on freshman success. *Journal of College Student Development, 30*, 309–312.

Zirkel, P. A. (2007). Grade inflation: High schools' skeleton in the closet. *Education Week, 26*(29), 40.

Name Index

A

Adelman, C., 5, 190, 230
Allen, D., 142
Allen, J., 147, 149, 150, 168, 170, 172, 182, 184, 187, 188, 189, 197, 209, 248
Allen, W. R., 104, 109, 143, 363
Anderson, E., 288
Appleby, D. C., 303
Arendale, D. R., 255, 256, 268, 269, 275, 281
Ashburn, E., 270
Asker, E. H., 25
Askin, T. W., 166
Astin, A. W., 4, 5, 6, 11, 12, 22, 23, 25, 32, 33
Attewell, P., 259

B

Backer, R., 291
Bahr, P. R., 190
Banahan, L. A., 317, 318
Barefoot, B. O., 314
Baum, S., 67, 71
Beal, P. E., 8, 38, 117, 214
Bean, J. P., 6, 7, 12, 22, 23, 24, 39, 139
Beck, H. P., 272
Becker, G. S., 25
Beil, C., 291
Berger, J. B., 24
Berkner, L., 5, 14
Bettinger, E. P., 266
Bhandari, R., 165
Biswas, R., 189
Blaich, C. F., 184

Blake, L. P., 119
Bloom, J. L., 64, 65, 66, 72, 288, 308
Boylan, H. R., 261, 267, 268, 271
Brack, G., 14–24
Brand, B., 120
Braunstein, A., 143
Braxton, J. M., 19, 21, 24, 27
Brecheisen, B. K., 164
Breneman, D. W., 255
Bridges, B. K., 19, 95
Brown, S. D., 163, 164
Brown, T., 294, 295
Buckley, J. A., 19, 95
Burck, H. D., 165
Burkum, K., 38, 87, 117, 217, 236, 262, 283, 390
Burroughs, N. A., 19
Button, C., 191, 197

C

Cabrera, A. F., 25
Calcagno, J. C., 262, 265, 266, 281
Camara, W. J., 247
Campbell, J. P., 170
Cantore, S., 373, 376
Carlstrom, A., 140
Carnevale, A. P., 58
Casillas, A., 147, 150, 182, 187
Cataldi, E. F., 5, 14
Chan, W., 395
Cheatham, H. E., 291
Chemers, M. M., 142
Chi, M. T. H., 271
Chickering, A. W., 12, 33, 34, 35, 286
Childs, M. W., 301

Christman, P., 288
Clark, E. C., 296
Clayton-Pedersen, A. R., 104,
    109, 363
Cohen, J., 144
Cohen, P. A., 271
Cohn, D., 48
Cook, S., 284, 285
Cooperrider, D., 367
Cope, R. G., 6, 229, 230
Covington, M. V., 139
Cowart, S. C., 117, 214, 225
Creamer, D., 143
Creedon, C. F., 37
Crookston, B. B., 285
Cuseo, J., 272, 273, 276, 291, 301,
    305, 307

D

Dalrymple, W., 6
Dannells, M., 317
Daugherty, T. K., 142
Davidson, W. B., 272
Davis, D., 140
Davis, K. J., 295
Dawis, R. V., 166, 179, 183
Day, P. R., Jr., 257
DeAngelo, L., 119
Domina, T., 259
Donnay, D. A., 167
Doty, C. S., 269
Drake, J. K., 302, 303
Durkheim, E., 20, 21

E

Eaton, S. B., 22
Eccles, J. S., 139
Echternacht, G., 247
Edison, T. A., 395–396
Eiche, K., 142
Einstein, A., 366, 381
Elkins, S. A., 21
Elliott, K. M., 291
Ender, S. C., 286
Ethington, C. A., 142, 143
Evans, J. H., 165

F

Farnsworth, W. M., 317
Foster, G., 278
Frank, R. H., 82, 83
Frost, S. H., 283, 284
Fruehling, R. T., 183
Fuertes, J. N., 143

G

Gabelnick, F., 320, 321
Gamson, Z. F., 12, 33, 34, 35
Garcia, B. F., 142
Gardner, J., 223–224
Gardner, J. N., 314
Gates, M., 256, 257
Gattis, K. W., 271
Gibson, D., 239, 249
Gillispie, B., 283
Glenn, D., 280, 281
Gloria, A. M., 142
Glover-Russell, J., 166
Golfin, P., 190
Gonzalez, J., 255, 257, 278
Gordon, V. N., 291, 298, 325
Greene, J., 278
Grier, D. J., 316
Griffin, T. J., 370
Grosset, J. M., 142
Grossman, M., 74
Grubb, W. N., 262
Guerra, N., 261
Guthrie, J. W., 4, 5, 6
Gysbers, N. C., 165

H

Haarlow, W. N., 255
Habley, W. R., 14, 29, 38, 74, 87, 91,
    92, 117, 118, 136, 214, 217, 232, 236,
    262, 264, 267, 269, 270, 271, 273,
    275, 276, 277, 283, 289, 290, 292,
    294, 295, 297, 298, 300, 301, 304,
    306, 313, 328, 340, 371, 372, 373,
    379, 380, 390
Hagedorn, L. S., 3, 9, 15
Hagen, P. L., 288
Hamilton, K. D., 1424

Hannah, W., 6, 229, 230
Harackiewicz, J. M., 261
Hardesty, J. W., 19
Harding, B., 296
Hartley, M., 64, 65, 66, 72
Haycock, K., 258, 260
Hayek, J. C., 19, 95
He, S., 5, 14
He, Y., 288, 308
Healy, M. A., 291
Heckman, J. J., 49
Hemwall, M. K., 287, 288
Hill, K., 67
Hirschy, A. S., 27
Hoffman, D., 67
Holland, J. L., 166, 167, 168, 179, 183, 248
Horn, L. J., 6
Hossler, D., 7, 39, 95
Hovland, M., 248
Hsieh, P., 261
Hu, L., 142
Huesman, R. L., 14
Hull, D., 190
Hulleman, C. S., 261
Hunter, J. E., 138, 198
Hunter, M. S., 325, 326, 327
Hurtado, S., 104, 109, 110, 116, 119, 363
Hutson, B. L., 288, 308
Huy, L., 147

I

Iffert, R. E., 6

J

Jacobson, E., 190
James, G. W., 21
Jones-White, D. R., 14
Jordan, P., 288
Jordan, W., 190
Joshi, R. M., 58

K

Kalionzes, J., 296
Kellogg, J. P., 14
Keniston, K., 6
Kennedy, G. J., 291

Kezar, A., 106, 107, 108
Killough, A. C., 255, 256, 259, 278, 279
King, M. C., 289, 290
King, N. S., 300
Kinzie, J., 14, 19, 36, 95, 105, 107, 108, 110, 333, 363
Klemp, G., 384, 385, 388, 390, 391, 394, 395
Korn, W. A., 119
Kotter, J., 371
Kozeracki, C. A., 256, 257, 258, 267, 268, 271
Kramer, G. L., 14, 104, 107, 108, 113, 114, 115, 301, 363
Kuh, G., 12, 14, 19, 24, 25, 36, 95, 102, 103, 105, 107, 110, 111, 112, 116, 264, 291, 292, 300, 305, 306, 308, 309, 317, 333, 363
Kuhtmann, M., 288
Kulik, C. C., 271
Kulik, J. A., 271
Kurpius, S.E.R., 142

L

LaFontaine, P. A., 49
Laird, D. A., 183
Lamb, C. W., 291
Lane, E. J., 1424
Lang, J. R., 19
Langley, R., 140, 147
Lao Tzu, 395
Lapan, R. T., 165
Lasoff, D. L., 163
Laufgraben, P. F., 320, 321, 322, 323
Lauver, K., 140
Lavin, D., 259
Le, H., 140, 150, 191, 197
Lenning, O. T., 4, 5, 6, 7, 8
Leonard, M. J., 301
Lerner, J. B., 120
Leuwerke, W. C., 248
Levey, T., 259
Levine, A., 94, 135, 356
Levitz, R., 8, 81, 88
Lewis, S., 373, 374, 376, 378, 379, 380
Light, R. J., 305, 306

Lincoln, A., 64
Linder, C. W., 325, 326, 327
Lingenfelter, P. E., 343
Lloyd-Jones, E., 8
Lofquist, L., 166, 183
Long, B. T., 262, 265, 266, 281
Lotkowski, V. A., 372
Love, P. G., 25
Lowenstein, M., 288
Ludema, J. D., 370, 371, 375, 376
Lyman, B. G., 256

M

MacDonald, R., 262
MacGregor, J., 320
Martin, N. A., 288
Martorell, P., 265, 266
Matthews, R. S., 320
Mauer, M., 71
Mause, K., 82
Maxwell, M., 271
McCabe, R. H., 253, 257
McCalla-Wriggins, B., 300
McClanahan, R., 38, 87, 117, 118, 214,
    217, 236, 262, 283, 371, 372, 373,
    379, 380, 390
McClendon, S. A., 27
McDivitt, P. J., 239, 249
McFarlin, I., 265, 266
McGillin, V. A., 290
McGrath, M., 143
McMahon, W., 65, 67, 68, 69, 71, 72, 73,
    74, 75, 76, 77
Medrich, E., 165
Melander, E. R., 288
Merisotis, J. P., 255, 259, 262
Merson, D. N., 166
Metzner, B. S., 291
Michael, R., 75
Mickelson, R. A., 143
Milem, J. F., 104, 109, 363
Miller, T. K., 286
Minter, J., 81
Mohr, B. J., 368, 369, 370, 377
Mohr, J., 142
Mollison, A., 123
Morelon, C., 95

Morris, M. L., 167
Mortenson, T., 59
Mueller, C. W., 23, 316
Mueller, K. H., 8
Mullendore, R. H., 317, 318
Mundy, M. E., 21
Murray, J. E., 373

N

Neumann, G., 172, 183
Noble, J. P., 52, 54, 131, 246, 247
Noel, L., 38, 81, 88, 117, 214
Noeth, R. J., 163, 372
Nora, A., 25
Nord, C., 118, 119

O

Obama, B., 255, 256
O'Banion, T., 285, 286, 287
O'Brien, C., 71
Ogden, P., 269
Oh, I.-S., 182, 187, 191, 197
O'Hear, M., 262
Oldham, N. B., 183
Olitsky, N., 172, 183
Oliver, L. W., 163
Oliver, M. L., 143
Oseguera, L., 32, 33
Osipow, S., 161, 166

P

Pantages, T. J., 37
Pardee, C. F., 289
Pascarella, E. T., 19, 21, 28, 74, 75, 76,
    138, 142, 143, 273, 275, 291
Passel, J. S., 48
Passmore, J., 373, 376
Patton, L. D., 95
Payea, K., 67, 71
Payne, E. M., 256
Perigo, D. J., 317
Perkhounkova, Y., 246
Pervin, L. A., 6
Petersen, C. H., 150
Peterson, M., 291
Phelps, R., 149, 189, 209

Phipps, R. A., 255, 259, 262
Pike, G. R., 24
Pine, J., 63
Porchea, S., 149, 189, 209
Porter, S. R., 172
Potts, G., 330
Prediger, D. J., 168
Price, D. V., 320, 321, 322
Price, J. L., 23
Pryor, J. H., 119
Putka, D. J., 170

R

Radcliffe, P. M., 14
Radunzel, J., 52, 54, 131
Rainwater, T., 343
Redden, 279
Redline, J., 261
Reik, L. E., 6
Rex, T. R., 67
Riordan, R. J., 142
Robbins, S., 140, 144, 147, 149, 150,
    168, 170, 172, 182, 183, 184, 187,
    188, 189, 191, 195, 197, 198, 199,
    200, 201, 204, 208, 209, 248, 316
Robbins, S. B., 172, 183, 248, 372
Robinson, D. R., 270, 271
Rocconi, L. M., 324
Rodriguez, C. J., 143
Rogers, G., 291
Roscoe, R. D., 271
Rosenbaum, J. E., 261
Rosovsky, H., 64, 65, 66, 72
Roueche, J. E., 239
Roueche, S. D., 239
Ruffin, M., 190
Russell, A., 269
Rutkowski, D. J., 19
Ryan, N. E., 163
Ryland, E. B., 142
Ryu, M., 231, 232

S

Saenz, V. B., 119
Saluri, D., 8
Sandeen, A., 316
Santos, J. L., 119

Sauer, K., 8
Sawyer, R., 246, 247, 248
Saxon, D. P., 261, 267, 268, 271
Schaubhut, N. A., 167
Schein, E. H., 102, 103, 104
Schiel, J., 246
Schmidt, F. L., 138, 198
Schmidt, P., 120, 255,
    265, 266
Schofield, J. W., 270
Schreiner, L. A., 288
Schuh, J. H., 14, 74, 88, 90, 91, 110,
    333, 340, 363
Schultz, B., 330
Sedlacek, W. E., 142, 143
Seidman, A., 14, 19, 29, 291
Self, C., 290
Senko, C., 261
Sexton, T. L., 163
Shaffer, R. H., 316
Shope, J. H., 291
Silver, N. C., 272
Silvia, P. J., 163
Simons, C., 269
Simons, H. D., 142
Slaten, C. D., 166
Smart, J. C., 142, 143
Smith, B. L., 291, 320
Smith, B. M., 321
Smith, L., 316
Smith, M. R., 8
Smith, N., 58
Solberg, V. S., 142
Sorenson, C., 166
Sowa, C. J., 143
Spady, W. G., 20
Spokane, A. R., 163
Spradlin, T. E., 19
St. John, E. P., 25
Steele, G. E., 291
Steers-Wentzell, K. L., 270
Stephan, J. L., 261
Stephens, J., 164
Stocker, J., 143
Strohl, J., 58
Suen, H., 142
Sullivan, J., 261

Summerskill, J., 6
Sun, Y., 165

T

Terenzini, P. T., 19, 21, 74, 75, 76, 138, 142, 273, 275, 291
Thompson, D., 269
Thompson, R. C., 167
Tinto, V., 11, 20, 21, 36, 37, 39, 139, 147, 311, 326, 365
Tobolowsky, B. F., 174
Topping, K. J., 270
Trabant, T. D., 303
Tracey, T. J., 163, 172, 183
Trachte, K., 287, 288
Tran, S., 119
Trippi, J., 291
Trosten-Bloom, A., 367, 368, 369, 370, 372, 375, 376, 379
Troxel, W. G., 305

U

Umbach, P. D., 172
Upcraft, M. L., 314, 317

V

Valiga, M., 38, 87, 117, 217, 236, 262, 283, 390
Van de Water, G., 343
Van Gennep, A., 21, 311, 318
Van Iddekinge, C. H., 170
Van Rheenen, D., 142
Visher, M. G., 165

W

Wagner, J. A., 291
Wasley, P., 272
Watkins, B. T., 81, 370
Watkins, J. M., 368, 369, 376, 377
Whiston, S. C., 163, 164
White, C. L., 143
Whitehead, D., 95
Whitney, D. R., 236, 367, 368, 369, 370, 372, 375, 379
Whitt, E. J., 14, 36, 102, 103, 108, 110, 333, 363
Wigfield, A., 139
Williamson, D., 143
Williamson, E. G., 8
Wilson, M. S., 142
Wimberley, G. L., 163, 184
Winston, G. C., 82
Winston, R. B., 286
Wise, K. S., 184
Wolfe, L. M., 21, 143
Woodring, P., 6
Woodruff, D. J., 119

Y

Young, B. C., 143
Young, R. B., 291

Z

Zimmerman, B. J., 280
Ziomek, R. L., 119
Zirkel, P. A., 119

Subject Index

Page references followed by *fig* indicate an illustrated figure; followed by *t* indicate a table.

A

Academic advising: defining, 285–287; history of, 283–285; link between retention and, 290–292; major advising theories on, 287–289; organizational delivery models of, 289–290; providing services for departing students, 357; *WWISR Survey* (2010) findings on, 292. *See also* Faculty; Students

Academic advising centers: increasing number of, 297–298; integrated with career planning, 298, 300

Academic Advising Clearinghouse (NACADA), 304

Academic advising models: University of North Carolina at Greensboro (UNCG), 307–308; Wheaton College, 308–309

Academic advising practices: academic advising center, 293*t*, 297–298; academic advising center integrated with career planning, 298, 300; advising interventions with selected student populations, 293*t*, 296–297; advising syllabus—specifying student learning outcomes, 299*t*, 303–304; application of technology to advising, 299*t*, 301–302; assessment of faculty and non-faculty advisors, 299*t*, 300–301; campuswide assessment of advising, 299*t*, 304–305; increased number of advisors, 293*t*, 297; integration of advising with first-year programs, 299*t*,

300; Kuh, Light, and Cuseo's research on best, 305–307; online advising system, 299*t*, 304; overview of, 292, 294; recognition/rewards for faculty and non-faculty advisors, 299*t*, 302–303; training for faculty and non-faculty advisors, 293*t*, 294–296

Academic boredom/academic stimulation, 29*fig*, 30–31

Academic discipline factor, 159

Academic performance: academic skills assessment based on high school, 246–247; evidentiary based approach to institutional interventions, 197–208; expected and hypothesized paths to outcomes, 185*fig*; indirect effects of traditional predictors of, 187; results path model of, 186*fig*; success in college developmental courses, 189–197; testing Pyramid for Success results for, 184–189

Academic preparation: ACT on low percentage of, 235; advanced placement courses on the rise, 122–124; assessment of, 124–128; attrition due to lack of, 117–118; dual enrollment rise, 120–122; impact on college success, 130–133*t*; percentage of students achieving at least 2.5 GPA, 131*t*–132; percentage of students making reasonable progress by performance level, 132*t*; percentage of students persisting to degree by performance level, 133*t*; percentage of students retained from year-to-year performance level, 132t; rising high school grades indicator of, 118–120; what can be done to improve, 133–136; WWISR (2010) respondents on attrition due to poor, 235–236. *See also* Pyramid for Success

Academic Readiness: how to address variations in, 196–197; as pillar of student success, 196fig; student effort ratings on, 192–197

Academic-related skills, 143t

Academic self-efficacy, 142t

Academic skills assessment: establishing cutoff scores for, 244–246; high school academic performance used for, 246–247; test selection for, 239–244

Academic underpreparedness: college success impacted by, 128–130; role of educators in, 134

Accelerated Learning Groups (ALGs), 268

Accountability: how faulty assumption regarding student behaviors impact, 14–18; increasing pressures for higher education, 94–95; VFA (voluntary framework of accountability), 360–362; VSA (voluntary system of accountability), 360

ACCUPLACER scores, 249

Achieving the Dream, 267, 268

ACT: ACT Career Planning Program of, 164; on causality for attrition focus on student characteristics, 7; College Readiness Assessments (EXPLORE, PLAN, and the ACT), 124, 127, 128t, 129t–130t; on community college students graduation, 54; degree-completion rates (1983-2011) collected by, 230; on information supporting course placement decisions, 239; Institutional Data Questionnaire (IDQ) of, 229; on low percentage of academically prepared students, 235; National Curriculum Survey by, 135–136, 355, 356; on prerequisite skills required for student success, 189; *Retention and Persistence to Degree Tables* by, 56; *Sixth Survey of Academic*

Advising report by, 294, 297; statistics on student departure, 6; statistics on student graduation rates, 15. *See also What Works in Student Retention* (WWISR) [ACT]

ACT College/High School Reports, 173

ACT scores: as academic success predictor, 147, 149; career fit tied to interests measured by, 170–173fig; as course placement factor, 249; as demographic data, 113; HS-tested graduates, 124, 127, 128t, 129t–130t, 131; meta-analysis results: predictors of GPA, 145–146t; meta-analysis results: predictors of retention, 144–145t; Pyramid for Success consideration of, 185; sample SRI-college profiles using, 150t–153t; study on GPA being more accurate predictor than, 247. *See also* SAT scores

Active learning instruction, 34

Advanced Placement (AP) program, 122–124

African Americans. *See* Black non-Hispanics

Age differences of student (2009), 45

Alaskan Natives. *See* American Indians/ Alaskan Natives

America Diploma Project, 259

American Association of Community Colleges (AACC), 257, 360

American Association of State Colleges and Universities (AASCU), 38, 215, 221

American Council on Education (ACE), 231

American Counseling Association, 240

The American Freshman: Forty Year Trends (Pryor, Hurtado, Saenz, Santos, & Korn), 119

American Indians/Alaskan Natives: Averaged Freshman Graduation Rates (FGR), 50t–52; percentage moving through college, 52–54; projected change in high school graduates, 49t; projected population percentage change (1995-2025), 47t–48

Appreciative Advising, 288–289, 307, 308

Appreciative Inquiry (AI): advising delivery framework using, 288–289; Appreciative Inquiry Summit approach to, 369–380; as approach to change, 366–369; origins and early development of, 367–368; Whole-System 4-D Dialogue approach to, 369

Appreciative Inquiry (AI) Summit: Define phase of, 370–373; defining the topic, 373–376; Deliver phase of, 379–380; description of, 369–370; Design phase of, 378–379; Discover phase of, 376–377; Dream phase of, 377–378

Arizona Republic (newspaper), 349

Arizona's AZTransfer, 350

Articulation agreements, 350–352

Artifacts, 103

Asian/Pacific Islanders: Averaged Freshman Graduation Rates (FGR), 50t–52; participation/completion of college by, 56t–57; percentage moving through college, 52–54; projected change in high school graduates, 49t; projected population percentage change (1995-2025), 47t–48

Association of American Colleges, 384

Association of Public and Land-Grant Universities (APLU), 360

Association of State Colleges and Universities (ASSCU), 360

Attitudes toward change, 393fig

Attrition: costs of, 84–90; definition of, 9; lack of academic preparation cause of, 117–118; minority student rates of, 231–234; negative connotations of, 13; Survey of Academic Orientations on indicators of, 272; Tinto's theory of, 247–248; WWISR (2010) respondents on lack of academic preparation cause of, 235–236; the WWISR reports on institutional characteristics contributing to, 218–221. *See also* Dropout students; Retention

Attrition costs: additional types of, 90; financial aid as, 88–89; instructional staff and related, 89; lost tuition/fees, 84–87; recruitment costs and, 88t

Averaged Freshman Graduation Rates (FGR), 49–50t

AZTransfer (Arizona), 350

B

Beal-Noel study (1980), 38

Bean's Model of Student Departure, 23–24

Beliefs/values, 103

Bill and Melinda Gates Foundation, 255, 360

Bisexual students, 296

Black non-Hispanics: Averaged Freshman Graduation Rates (FGR), 50t–52; participation/completion of college by, 56t–57; percentage moving through college, 52–54; projected change in high school graduates, 49t; projected population percentage change (1995-2025), 47t–48; Pyramid for Success on academic achievement of, 187, 188; WWISR study findings on attrition and retention of, 231–234

Boston University, 315

Brief therapy counseling theory, 288

C

California Department of Education and State Board of Education, 259

California State system, 259–260

Career Center Resources by Stage, 177fig–178fig

Career Decision Making Model, 176fig

Career development: fit-based enhancements for institutions, 172–179; Habley's Retention Model on student success and, 29fig, 30; person-environment fit as foundation of, 166–172; structured career exploration and planning, 161–166. *See also* Pyramid for Success

Career fit-based enhancements: Career Center Resources by Stage, 177fig–178fig; Career Decision Making Model, 176fig; career guidance and coaching, 175–179; curriculum-based enhancements as part of first-year experience, 174–175; examining student measured and expressed interests, 172–174; risk indices, 173–174*fig*

Career guidance/coaching, 175–179

Career person-environment fit: benefits of a, 170, 172; how to measure a, 168–170; institutional enhancements for, 172–179; overview of the, 166–168; percentage of students attaining postsecondary degree using, 171*fig*; percentage of students persisting in current major using, 171*fig*; review of, 183; World-of-Work Map used for, 168, 169*fig*, 173, 188

Carnegie Commission on Higher Education, 284

Case Western Reserve University, 367

Change leadership: Albert Einstein on, 366, 381; Appreciative Inquiry (AI) approach to, 366–380; attitudes toward change by, 393*fig*; cognitive skills required for, 385–390; considerations in the change process for, 388*fig*; interpersonal abilities required for, 390–394; intrapersonal factors required for, 394–396; lessons learned from history of *WWISR Surveys*, 388–390

The Chronicle of Higher Education, 265

City Tech program (New York City), 277, 280–281

Civic life, 72. *See also* Democracy

Code of Fair Testing Practices in Education (2002), 239

Cognitive skills: conceptualization, 386–387; consideration in the change process, 388*fig*; description of, 385; evaluative thinking, 385–386; systematic thinking, 388–390

College attendance patterns, 44

College Board, 66, 123

College Board's Advanced Placement (AP) program, 122–124

College development courses: best practices of, 191*fig*; description and functions of, 189–190; goals, best practices, and assessments used during, 190–192; student effort ratings, 192–197; three pillars of success for, 196*fig*

College Portraits of Undergraduate Education, 360

College Readiness Assessments (EXPLORE, PLAN, and the ACT), 124, 127, 128*t*, 129*t*–130*t*

College Student Retention: Formula for Student Success (Seidman), 14

Columbia University's Community College Research Center, 189

Commitment to college factor, 159

Communicating high expectations, 35

Community College Research Center (Columbia University), 189

Community colleges. *See* Two-year colleges

COMPASS scores, 192–193*t*, 195, 249

Completion. *See* Graduation

Concept of Academic Advising (NACADA), 286–287

Conceptualization, 386–387

Concern for students, 29*fig*, 31

Condition of Education (NCES), 55

Confidence, 394–395

Consumer decision making, 75

Consumer Price Index, 82

Contextual influences, 143*t*

Cooperative instruction, 34

Council for the Advancement of Standards (CAS), 285, 304

Course placement: additional considerations for, 247–248; assessment of academic skills for, 239–248; benefits of an effective program for, 237–238; defining, 236–237; recommended institutional practices for, 356–357; sources of information supporting decisions for, 238–239

Course placement models: Decision Zone Placement Model, 252*fig*; Multiple Conditions Placement Model, 250*fig*; Multiple Considerations Placement Model, 250–251*fig*; overview of the four basic, 248–249; Test Only Placement Model, 249*fig*

Courses: AP courses, 123; CLEP or International Baccalaureate credit for, 237; collaborative institutional

relationships related to, 354–355; college development, 189–197; dual enrollment credit for, 120–122, 237; improving course applicability systems, 349–350; library orientation, workshop, or, 262, 274t, 277; recommended common course numbering system for, 348–349; remedial, 262, 263t, 264–268; University 101 (University of South Carolina), 325
Cultural perspectives, 25–26
Culture: artifacts of, 103; basic underlying assumptions of, 103–104; espoused beliefs and values of, 103. *See also* Institutional culture; Student success culture
Curriculum-based career fit enhancements, 174–175

D
Data-Ideas, 188
Decision Zone Placement Model, 252*fig*
DEEP (Documenting Effective Educational Practice) Project: description of, 36; institutional culture and student engagement findings of, 104–107; student success findings by, 110–113; Wheaton College's academic advising model, 308–309
Define phase (Appreciative Inquiry Summit), 370–373
Degree completion rates, 228–231
Deliver phase (Appreciative Inquiry Summit), 379–380
Delta Project, 97
Democracy, 73. *See also* Civic life
Demographics: college-bound population, 48–49t; completing college, 54–57; of the educational pipeline, 46–57; graduation at two- and four-year colleges, 54–57; impact of educational attainment, 57–61; moving through college, 52–54; moving toward college, 49–52; student characteristics, 43, 44–46
Departure: Bean's Model of Student Departure on, 23–24; cultural beliefs related to, 25–26; how engagement prevents, 12; how institutional integration prevents, 11; how institutional involvement prevents, 11; terms related to description of, 6; theoretical perspectives on, 20–39
Design phase (Appreciative Inquiry Summit), 378–379
Development courses. *See* College development courses
Developmental education: defining, 256–257; issues to consider in, 257–262; research on remedial coursework and, 256–257; WWISR (2010) findings on, 262–273
Developmental education initiatives: description of, 255; Early Warning Systems, 262, 263t, 271–273; used at four-year and two-year colleges, 263t; Learning Assistance Practices, 273–277; remedial coursework, 262, 263t, 264–268; Supplemental Instruction (SI), 262, 263t, 268–270; tutoring programs, 262, 263t, 270–271; WWISR Survey (2010) on, 262–277
Developmental education issues: debate on whether higher education should offer developmental education, 258; debate over responsibility for developmental program demands, 258–260; use of diagnostic tests and assessment, 260–261; lack of depth in literature on development education, 261–262
Developmental education models: City Tech program (New York City), 277, 280–281; El Paso Community College and UTEP, 277, 278–279; I-BEST program (Washington), 277, 279–280
Diagnostic tests/assessment, 260–261
Digest of Educational Statistics (NCES), 55
Discontinued students, 6
Discover phase (Appreciative Inquiry Summit), 376–377
Diversity: enhancing campus climates for, 109–110; higher education benefit to, 72. *See also* Race/ethnic student demographics

Dream phase (Appreciative Inquiry Summit), 377–378

Dropout students: institutional involvement for prevention of, 11; negative connotations of, 13; stopout versus, 5; student departure by, 6; Survey of Academic Orientations on indicators of, 272; WWISR studies findings on dropout-prone characteristics, 222t. *See also* Attrition

Dual Advising Model, 290

Dual enrollment programs, 120–122

Durkheim's suicide model, 21

E

Early Assessment Program (California), 259–260

Early Warning Systems, 262, 263t, 271–273

Eastern Iowa College, 351

Economic perspectives, 25

Education Amendments (1972), 64

Education at a Glance report (2009), 59

Education Trust, 230

Educational attainment demographics: description of impact of, 57–59; OECD/Mortenson data and global competitiveness index, 60–61; secondary school enrollment rates, 59; tertiary type A (bachelor's degree) and tertiary type-B attainment rates, 60; tertiary type-A (bachelor's degree) enrollment rates, 60; upper secondary (high school) graduation rates, 59–60

Educational Commission of the States (ECS), 342, 343

Educational persistence model, 139t–140

Educational Policy Institute (EPI), 87

Effort × Abilities = Reward ratio, Habley's Retention Model on student success and, 29fig, 31–32

El Paso Community College (Texas), 277, 278–279

Emerging Scholars Program (ESP), 268

Employment: as higher education benefit, 70; higher salaries benefits of higher education for, 69–70

Engagement. *See* Student engagement

English as a Second Language (ESL) programs, 262, 274t, 277

Environmental awareness, 73

ESL programs, 262, 274t, 277

Espoused beliefs/values, 103

Evaluative thinking, 385–386

EXPLORE program, 124, 127, 128t, 129t–130t

F

Faculty: academic advising training for, 294–296; assessment of academic advising by, 300–301; instruction that encourages contact between students and, 34; recognition/rewards for advisors among, 302–303; redesigning teacher preparation programs for, 355–356. *See also* Academic advising

Family background statistics, 45

Family size, 76

Feedback component of instruction, 34

Financial Aid Facts, 89

Financial issues: costs related to financial aid, 88–89; Habley's Retention Model on student success and, 29fig, 32; recruitment costs, 80–84, 88t; student statistics (2009) on, 45; student success factor of financial support, 143t; tuition/fees, 81, 84–87t, 91t

First-Year Experience (FYE): association of risk level and academic service use of retention and GPA during, 207t, 208; college intervention strategies for, 198t–199; curriculum-based enhancements as part of, 174–175; integration of advising with, 299t, 300; meta-analytic study findings on limited academic influence of programs, 201–203

First-year seminar: background information on, 325; definition of, 325–326; features and effectiveness of, 328–330; types of, 326–327t

First-year transition program implementation: examining institutional culture for, 333; identifying student needs for, 331–332; issues to consider for, 330–331; reviewing institutional characteristics for, 332

First-year transition programs: challenges of, 314–315; first-year (or freshman) seminar, 312t, 325–330; framework for implementation, 330–333; identified by respondents as effective intervention, 313t; learning communities, 312t, 320–325; orientation, 312t, 315–320; origins and early development of, 311–312; ratings and incidence rates by institutional type, 312t

Florida's Statewide Course Numbering System, 348–349

Fostering Student Success in the Campus Environment (Kramer & Associates), 14, 107–109

Four-year colleges: demographics of students moving through, 53, 54; hierarchical linear regression models GPAs at, 155t; hierarchical logistic regression models predicting retention at, 157t; race/minority degree completion rates at, 54–57; summary of retention rates (1983-2011) of, 229t; WWISR study findings on attrition/retention of minority students at, 231–234, 233t; WWISR Survey (2010) on learning initiatives used at, 263t. *See also* Institutions; Two-year colleges

Freshman Interest Groups (FIGs), 312t, 314, 321–322, 323

G

Gates Foundation, 255, 360

Gay students, 296

GED completion, 17, 338

Gender differences: in high school grades, 119; Pyramid for Success consideration of, 185; student statistics (2009) on, 45

General self-concept, 142t–143t

G.I. Bill, 284

GLBT students statistics (2009), 46

GPA: association of risk level and academic service use of retention

and first-year, 207t, 208; general motivational measures predictive of, 159; hierarchical linear regression models predicting four-year institution, 155t; hierarchical linear regression models predicting two-year institutions, 156t; meta-analysis of psychosocial constructs predicting, 145–146t; percentage of students achieving at least 2.5, 131t–132; Pyramid for Success consideration of, 185; study on ACT scores being less accurate predictor than, 247. *See also* HSGPA predictor factor

Graduation: Averaged Freshman Graduation Rates (FGR), 49–50t; data on retention and degree completion rates of, 228–231; demographics of students achieving, 54–57; description and statistics on, 9–10; faulty assumption regarding student goal of, 14–17; NCES on current rates of, 365; race/minority at two- and four-year colleges, 54–57; testing Pyramid for Success results for timely, 184–189

Guidelines for Academic Advising (CAS), 304

H

Habley & McClanahan study (2004), 38

Habley's Retention Model, 29fig–32

Hacken's Law, 363, 384

Hanover College (Indiana), 272

Health concerns, Habley's Retention Model on student success and, 29fig, 32

Health/life expectancy, 74

High expectations, 35

High schools. *See* Secondary schools

Higher Education: Standards and Guidelines for Academic Advising (NACADA), 286

Higher Education Act (1965), 64

Higher education benefits: history of, 63–65; private economic, 69–71; private social, 74–76; public economic, 65–68; public social, 71–73

Higher Education Research Institute (HERI), 23

Higher Learning, Greater Good: The Private and Social Benefits of Higher Education (McMahon), 65

Hispanics: participation/completion of college by, 56*t*–57; percentage moving through college, 52–54; projected change in high school graduates, 49*t*; projected population percentage change (1995-2025), 47*t*–48; WWISR study findings on attrition and retention of, 231–234

Hobbies/leisure activities, 76

HSGPA predictor factor, 149, 187. *See also* GPA

I

I-BEST program (Washington), 277, 279–280

Indiana's Transfer IN.net, 350

Industrial Revolution, 162

Influence skill, 391–392

Informal process of change, 392–394

Initiative (characteristic of), 395

The Institute for Higher Education Policy, 63, 64, 65, 66, 67, 68, 70, 71, 72

Institution size, 143*t*

Institutional characteristics: the WWISR reports (1980, 1987) on attrition/retention contribution by, 218–220; the WWISR reports (2004) on attrition/retention contribution by, 220; the WWISR reports (2010) on attrition/retention contribution by, 220–221

Institutional culture: DEEP Study findings on, 104–107; defining, 102; "Enhancing Campus Climates for Racial/Ethnic Diversity" findings on, 109–110; *Fostering Student Success in the Campus Community* findings on, 107–109; framework of, 104; levels of, 102–104; strategies for fostering student success, 110–116. *See also* Culture; Student success culture

Institutional Data Questionnaire (IDQ), 229

Institutional factors: institutional conditions tied to retention, 33–36; institutional interventions contributing to retention, 37–39; research focus on student attrition due to, 7

Institutional interventions. *See* Retention interventions

Institutional retention practices: collaborative relationships, 354–355; course placement practices, 356–357; institutional policies and requirements, 357–359; measuring student success, 359–362; provide transition advising services for departing students, 357; redesign teacher preparation programs, 355–356

Institutional selectivity, 143*t*

Institutions: career fit-based enhancements for, 172–179; causality for attrition focus on students instead of, 7, 33–39; conditions contributing to retention, 33–36; economic impact of higher education, 68; fit-based enhancements for, 172–179; how student behaviors are used to measure success of, 17–18; leading the campus to student success, 383–396; minimizing the complexity of transfer between, 348–352; practices to facilitate retention framework, 354–362; ratings and incidence rates of orientation programs by type of, 312*t*; research on enrollment patterns at, 14–16; summary of retention rates (1983-2011) by type of, 229*t*; terms associated with, 7–10; terms related to interactions between students and, 10–12. *See also* Four-year colleges; Retention interventions; Two-year colleges

Instructional Effectiveness: guidelines for, 34–36; as pillar of student success, 196*fig*

Instructional guidelines: DEEP project, 36; promoting student learning,

34–35; Tinto's principles and application to retention, 36

Integrated educational systems, 342–343

Integrated theoretical perspectives, 26–29

Integration: description and benefits of, 11; reflecting on definition and meaning of, 13–14; Tinto's model focused on, 21

Interest-major: career fit-based enhancement of examining student's, 172–174; career fit tied to, 170–173fig; UNIACT career interest inventory on, 172

International Center for Supplemental Instruction (UMKC), 269

Interpersonal abilities: attitudes toward change, 393fig; description of, 390; influence skill, 391–392; using informal process, 392–394; sensitivity, 390–391

Intrapersonal factors: confidence, 394–395; description of, 394; initiative, 395; persistence, 395–396

Investing in Student Success Cost-Return Calculator (ISS Calculator), 97

Involvement: description and benefits of, 11; psychosocial factor of social, 142t; reflecting on definition and meaning of, 13–14

Iowa Department of Education, 121

Iowa Western College, 351

Iowa's Postsecondary Educational Opportunity program, 121

IPEDS Graduation Rates survey, 9–10

IPEDS (Integrated Postsecondary Education Data System): graduation data collected by, 9; IPEDS Graduation Rates survey, 9–10; retention as defined by, 10

Irrelevance/relevance, Habley's Retention Model on student success and, 29fig, 30

ISS Calculator, 97

J

Jobs for the Future, 97

John Hopkins Career Center, 177–178, 179

John Hopkins faculty advising system, 284

Joint Committee on Testing Practices, 239

K

K-12 schools. See Secondary schools

K-16 initiatives, 343

Kenyon College, 284

Kirkwood College (Iowa), 351

Knowledge: lack of relationship between superior performance and, 384; as not being enough to create student success, 384

L

Leadership. See Student success leadership

League for Innovation in the Community College, 351

Learning: active, 34; instruction guidelines that promote, 34–35; respecting diverse talents and ways of, 35; time on task impact on, 35. See also Student success

Learning Assistance Practices: description of, 273; ESL programs, 262, 274t, 277; learning labs, 274t, 275; library orientation, workshop, or course, 262, 274t, 277; midterm progress reports, 274t, 275–276; online student learning, 262, 274t, 277; organized study groups, 274t, 276; performance contracts, 274t, 276; service-learning programs, 262, 274t, 276; study skills course, program, or center, 274t, 275; summer bridge programs, 273, 274t, 275

Learning communities: definition of, 320; features and effectiveness of, 323–325; models of, 321–323; WWISR Survey (2010) on retention impact by, 320

Learning labs, 274t, 275

Leaving College: The Causes and Cures of Student Attrition (Tinto), 13

Lee College, 325

Legislation: Education Amendments (1972), 64; Higher Education Act (1965), 64; Morril Act (1862), 64; National Defense Act, 64

Leisure activities/hobbies, 76

Lesbian students, 296

LGBT (lesbian, gay, bisexual, and transgender) students, 296

Liberal Education (publication), 384

Library orientation, workshop, or course, 262, 274t, 277

Life expectancy, 74

Lifelong learning skills, 76

Lumina Foundation, 97, 360

M

Marital status statistics, 45

Midterm progress reports, 274t, 275–276

Minorities in Higher Education (Ryu), 231

Model of Student Departure, 23–24

Morril Act (1862), 64

Motivation: indirect effects of traditional predictors and, 187; Student Academic Behavior and Motivation pillar of success, 192–196; theoretical perspectives on, 139t–140

Motivation theory, 289

Multiple Conditions Placement Model, 250fig

Multiple Considerations Placement Model, 250–251fig

N

NAEP Pipeline: math scores (1986-2008), 126t; reading scores (1984-2008), 125t; science scores (1996-2005), 127t; writing scores (1998-2007), 126t

National Academic Advising Association (NACADA), 285, 286, 298

National Assessment of Educational Progress (NAEP), 120, 124, 125, 126, 127

National Center for Educational Statistics (NCES): Averaged Freshman Graduation Rates (FGR), 49–50t; *Condition of Education* by, 55; on current graduation rates, 365; *Digest of Educational Statistics* by, 55; on dual enrollment by high school students, 121; on lack of academic preparation of enrolled students, 253; NAEP administered by the, 124; online or hybrid course enrollments report (2006-07) by, 94; part-time students, 4; reporting on AP courses, 123; student characteristics (2009), 44–46; transfer students, 5; tuition and fees increase report by, 81

National Center for Higher Education Management Systems (NCHEMS), 38, 214

National Curriculum Survey (ACT), 135–136, 355, 356

National Defense Act, 64

National Institutes of Health, 67

National Orientation Directors Association (NODA), 315

National Resource Center for the First-Year Experience and Students in Transition, 325, 327, 328, 329

National Science Foundation, 67

National Student Clearinghouse, 153

National Survey of First-Year Seminars, 328, 329

National Survey of Student Engagement (NSSE), 104–105, 291, 292, 305, 308, 323

New York Times, 378

Noel-Levitz Return on Investment Estimator, 96–97

Non-faculty advisors: assessment of academic advising by, 300–301; recognition/rewards for, 302–303; training of, 294–296

Nonpersistence, 6

Northern Arizona University (NAU): association of risk level and academic service use on retention and first-year GPA, 207fig, 208; description of the, 204; initiative outcome findings at, 206–208; institution-wide retention initiative using informatics at, 204–206; key findings and recommendations for, 208; resource and services utilization at, 207t; tracking student retention outcomes (2008), 206t

O

Online student learning, 262, 274t, 277
Organization for Economic Cooperation and Development (OECD), 59, 124, 125, 126
Organizational perspectives, 23–24
Orientation programs, ratings and incidence rates by institution type, 312t

P

P-16 initiatives, 343
P-20 initiatives, 343, 352
Pacific Islanders. See Asian/Pacific Islanders
Peer-Led Team Learning (PLTL), 268
People-Things, 188
Perceived social support, 142t
Performance contracts, 274t, 276
Persistence, 395–396
Persistence to degree: description and statistics on, 9–10; negative connotations of, 13; theoretical perspectives on, 20–39
Person-Environment (PE) fit models, 166–179, 183
Personal status benefits, 75–76
Personal student problems, 29fig, 32. See also Psychosocial characteristics
Physical energy notion, 25
PLAN program, 124, 127, 128t, 129t–130t
Positive psychology constructs, 288–289
Postsecondary education clearinghouse, 352–354
Preventing Students from Dropping Out (Astin), 11, 13
Prevention, Intervention, and Recovery Initiatives Chart, 373, 374t

Programme for International Student Assessment (PISA), 124, 125, 126, 127
Psychological energy notion, 25
Psychological perspectives, 22–23
Psychosocial characteristics: ACT/SAT and/or HSGPA scores indicators of, 149–150, 151fig–153fig; categorizing psychosocial factors (PSFs), 199t–200; as course placement consideration, 247–248; description and overview of, 137–138; differential effects of psychosocial and traditional predictors of college success, 154–160; Student Academic Behavior and Motivation, 192–197; Student Readiness Inventory (SRI) assessment of, 147–149, 150t, 199t–200. See also Personal student problems; Student behaviors
Psychosocial constructs: description of, 138–139; from educational persistence model, 139t–140; meta-analysis results: predictors of retention, 145t; meta-analysis to understand individual, 144–146; from motivational theory perspectives, 139t–140; of study skill factor and representative measures, 141t–143t
Public policy recommendations: build integrated educational systems, 342–343; establish student postsecondary education clearinghouse, 352–354; measure and reward student success, 346–348; minimize the complexity of transfer process, 348–352; redefining student success, 343–346
Pyramid for Success: academic performance and timely degree attainment for testing, 184–189; illustrated diagram of, 182fig; implications for institutional interventions, 197–208; overview of the, 181–184; as robust organizer for creating student success interventions, 209. See also Academic preparation; Career development; Psychosocial characteristics

Q

Quality of life, 75

Quotations of Abraham Lincoln (2003), 64

R

Race/ethnic student demographics: Averaged Freshman Graduation Rates (FGR), 49–50t; completing college, 54–57; graduation at two- and four-year colleges, 54–57; moving through college, 52–54; participation/completion of college, 56t–57; predicted by the year 2050, 43; shifting and diversifying population of, 47t–48; statistics (2009), 44. *See also* Diversity

Racial/ethnic differences: in attrition and retention, 231–234; enhancing campus climates for diversity of, 109–110; in high school grades, 119; Pyramid for Success consideration of, 187, 188; student demographics, 49–57

Reciprocity, 34

Recruitment: admissions funnel delineating, 79; contrasting retention and, 90–95; costs of, 80–84; ROI (return on investment) in, 92–93

Recruitment costs: direct, 80–82; factors impacting, 88t; indirect, 82–84; to recruit undergraduate student (1983-2009), 81t; tuition and fees (1983-2010), 81, 84–87t, 91t

Reducing the Dropout Rate (Noel), 13

Reed College, 325

Remedial coursework: negative connotation of, 256; research on developmental education and, 257; *WWISR Survey* (2010) recommendations on, 262, 263t, 264–268. *See also* Developmental education

Responsibilities of Users of Standardized Tests (1987), 240

Retention: absence of clear definition and measures of, 91–92; contrasting recruitment and, 90–93; as defined by IPEDS, 10; definitions of, 7–8; difficulty of defining process of, 79–80;

faulty assumptions regarding, 14–17; hierarchical logistic regression models predicting four-year institutions, 157t; hierarchical logistic regression models predicting two-year institutions, 158t; institutional conditions contributing to, 33–36; IPEDS system to collect data on, 9; lack of consensus on how to measure, 8–9; link between academic advising and, 290–292; meta-analysis of psychosocial constructs predicting, 145t; minority student rates of, 231–234; negative connotations of, 13; research on factors leading to, 12; shift from pejorative to affirmative terminology of, 12–13; student characteristics contributing to, 32–33; summary of retention rates by institutional type (1983-2011), 229t; tuition/fees impacted by improved rates of, 87t; 2007 retention in 2008 results of institutional interventions, 206t. *See also* Attrition

Retention and Persistence to Degree Tables (ACT), 56

Retention framework: expanding the traditional, 339–342; institutional practices role in, 354–362; limitations of the, 337–339; public policy recommendations to facilitate, 342–354

Retention institutional practices: collaborative relationships, 354–355; course placement practices, 356–357; institutional policies and requirements, 357–359; measuring student success, 359–362; Prevention, Intervention, and Recovery Initiatives Chart on, 373, 374t; provide transition advising services for departing students, 357; redesign teacher preparation programs, 355–356

Retention interventions: academic advising, 283–309; association of risk level and academic service use of retention and first-year GPA, 207t; categorizing types of, 198t; comparing recruitment and, 93–95; contributing to retention, 37–39; developmental education initiatives, 255–281; evidentiary based approach to, 197–208; First-Year Experience (FYE), 174–175, 198t–203, 207t, 208, 299t, 300; first-year transition programs, 311–333; fit-based enhancements, 172–179; minority student respondents identifying effective, 233t; need for evidence of student success and, 95–98; need for new approach to implementing, 365–366; one-on-one meetings in student affairs, 205t; research and evaluation informing best practices for, 203–208; resource and services utilization of, 207t; 2007 retention in 2008 results of, 206t. *See also* Institutions; Student success; *What Works in Student Retention* (WWISR) [ACT]

Return on Investment Estimator, 96–97

Risk indices, 173–174*fig*

S

SAT scores: as academic success predictor, 147, 149; as course placement factor, 249; entering class admission test pipeline to college (2006-2010), 128t; meta-analysis results: predictors of GPA, 145–146t; meta-analysis results: predictors of retention, 144–145t. *See also* ACT scores

Secondary schools: academic skills assessment based on academic performance during, 246–247; Advanced Placement (AP) programs of, 122–124; debate over developmental program responsibility of, 258–260; dual enrollment programs participation by, 120–122; enrollment rates, 59; graduation rates, 59–60; rising level of grades from, 118–120

Seidman's retention formula, 29

Self-concept, 142t–143t

Self-Contained model, 290

Sensitivity, 390–391

Service-learning programs, 262, 274t, 276

SES (socioeconomic status), 185

Sixth Survey of Academic Advising report (Habley), 294, 297

Smaller families, 76

Social capital, 183–184

Social involvement, 142t

Sociological perspectives, 20–22

Socratic Advising, 288

Staff-related attrition costs, 89

Statement of Core Values (NACADA), 286

Stayouts, 6

Stopout students, 5

Strategic Intervention Model for Developmental Math Education, 194t, 195

Strong American Schools, 255

Structured career exploration/planning: description of, 161–162; effective interventions for, 163–164; example of outcomes at different life stages, 165fig; how it may impact academic outcomes, 165–166; importance and benefits of, 162–163; possible outcomes of, 164–166

Structured Learning Assistance (SLA), 268

Student Academic Behavior and Motivation: how to address variations in, 196–197; as pillar of success, 196; student effort ratings on importance of, 192–196

Student Academic Services Office (UNCG), 307

Student behaviors: engagement, 12; faulty assumptions regarding, 14–18; graduation/completion/persistence to degree, 9–10; institutional integration, 11; institutional involvement, 11; institutional success tied to, 17–18; interactions between student and institution, 10–12; progression, 10; reflections on definitions and constructs of, 12–14; retention, 7–9, 10, 12–13, 20–39; student who leave but may persist elsewhere, 4–6; students who leave, 6–7, 13, 20–39; students who persist, 4, 13, 20–39; swirling pattern of, 5–6. *See also* Psychosocial characteristics

Student characteristics: Bean's Model of Student Departure using, 23–24; contributing to retention, 32–33; demographics of, 43, 44–46; past research focus on attrition due to, 7; psychosocial, 137–160, 199t–200, 247–248

Student effort ratings: combining COMPASS scores and, 192–193t, 195; description of, 192; implications and recommendations related to, 194–197; mean math gain scores, 194t; moderation of behavior on outcomes of, 193–194

Student engagement: DEEP Project findings on institutional culture and, 104–107; description and benefits of, 12; institutional culture to enhance, 101–116; reflecting on definition of, 13–14; theoretical perspectives on retention and, 20–39

Student enrollment: research findings on patterns of, 14–16; student behaviors impacting, 4–14

Student motivation: indirect effects of traditional predictors and, 187; motivation theory on, 289; Student Academic Behavior and Motivation pillar of success, 192–196; theoretical perspectives on, 139t–140

Student postsecondary education clearinghouse, 352–354

Student Readiness Inventory (SRI): as career fit enhancement, 175; categorizing interventions related to, 199t; definitions and sample items by student control factor, 148t; description of, 147, 149, 199; how to predict academic success using, 149–150; sample SRI-college profiles, 150t–153t

Student study groups, 262

Student success: advising syllabus specifying learning outcomes and, 303–304; examining perspectives on, 3; faulty assumptions regarding, 14–18; fresh

ideas for, 112–113; leading the campus to, 383–396; minimizing the complexity of transfer process for, 348–352; need for new approach to implementing initiatives for, 365–366; public policy recommendation for redefining, 343–346; sleeper principles for, 111–112; strategies for fostering culture for, 110–116; terms associated with behaviors related to, 4–14; theoretical perspectives of, 20–39; three pillars of, 196*fig*; tried-and-true guiding principles for, 111. *See also* Learning; Retention interventions

Student success components: academic preparation, 117–136, 235–236; career development, 29*fig*, 30, 161–179; institutional culture, 101–116; psychosocial characteristics, 137–160, 199t–200, 247–248; Pyramid for Success, 182–209

Student success constructs: conceptualization, 386–387; confidence, 394–395; evaluative thinking, 385–386; influence skill, 391–392; using informal process, 392–394; initiative, 395; persistence, 395–396; sensitivity, 390–391; systematic thinking, 388–390

Student success culture: using Appreciative Inquiry to develop, 366–380; importance to success or failure of any new initiative, 363; Prevention, Intervention, and Recovery Initiatives Chart to promote, 373, 374t; typical institutional approach to, 364–365. *See also* Culture; Institutional culture

Student Success in College (Kuh, Kinzie, Schuh, & Whitt), 14, 110

Student success leadership: cognitive skills required for, 385–390; interpersonal abilities required for, 390–394; intrapersonal factors required for, 394–396; issues to consider for, 383–384

Student success measures: expanding the retention framework using rewards and, 346–348; issues to consider for, 359–360; VFA (voluntary framework of accountability), 360–362; VSA (voluntary system of accountability), 360

Students: academic preparation of, 117–136, 235–236; causality for attrition focus on characteristics of, 7, 32–33; developing reciprocity and cooperation among, 34; dropout, 5–6, 11, 13, 222t, 272; institutional factors tied to behaviors of, 17–18, 33–39; instruction that encourages contact between faculty and, 34; LGBT (lesbian, gay, bisexual, and transgender), 296; stopout, 5; transfer, 4–6, 348–352, 357. See also Academic advising

Students with disabilities: advising interventions for, 296–297; student statistics (2009) on, 46

Study skills course, program, or center, 274t, 275

Suicide model (Durkheim), 21

Summer bridge programs, 273, 274t, 275

Supplemental Instruction (SI), 262, 263t, 268–270

Supplementary Advising Model, 290

Survey of Academic Orientations, 272

Swirling attendance pattern, 5–6

Systematic thinking, 388–390

T

Teacher preparation programs, 355–356

Technology: applied to academic advising, 299t, 301–302; higher education benefit related to use of, 72–73

Tertiary type-A (bachelor's degree): attainment rates, 60; enrollment rates, 60

Test Only Placement Model, 249fig

Texas Common Course Numbering System, 349

Theoretical perspectives: cultural, 25–26; economic, 25; Habley's Retention Model, 29fig–32; on institutional conditions contributing to retention, 33–36; on institutional interventions

contributing to retention, 37–39; integrated, 26–29; organizational, 23–24; psychological, 22–23; Seidman's retention formula, 29; sociological, 20–22; on student characteristics contributing to retention, 32–33

Theories: definition of, 26–27; motivation, 289; student success explanations through integrated, 26–29; Tinto's theory of attrition, 247–248; Work Adjustment, 183

Theory of Work Adjustment, 183

Tidewater Community College (Virginia), 269

Time on task, 35

Timely degree attainment. See Graduation

Tinto's theory of attrition, 247–248

Total Intake Advising Model, 290

Transfer process: articulation agreements to minimize complexity of, 350–352; common course numbering system to minimize complexity of, 348–349; course applicability system to minimize complexity of, 349–350

Transfer students: minimizing complexity of process for, 348–352; providing transition advising services for, 357; statistics on number of, 5; success of, 4–6

Transgender students, 296

Tuition/fees: attrition costs of lost, 84–87; improvement in retention rates on, 87t; increasing rates (1983-2010) of, 91t; NCES report on increased, 81

Tutoring programs, 262, 263t, 270–271

Two-year colleges: advising centers integrated with career planning at, 298, 300; demographics of students moving through, 53–54; hierarchical linear regression models predicting GPA at, 156t; hierarchical logistic regression models predicting retention at, 158t; Pyramid for Success applied to students of, 186; race/minority degree completion rates at, 54–57; summary of retention rates (1983-2011) of,

229t; WWISR study findings on attrition/retention of minority students at, 231–234, 233t; *WWISR Survey* (2010) on learning initiatives used at, 263t. *See also* Four-year colleges; Institutions
2 Plus 2 program, 351

U

U-Select, 350
Underachievers, 6
UNIACT career interest inventory, 172
United States: demographics of college-bound in the, 48–49t; educational attainment demographics in the, 57–61; higher education public and private benefits for the, 63–76; impact of educational attainment in the, 57–61; shifting and diversifying population of the, 47t–48
University 101 course (University of South Carolina), 325
University of California, Los Angeles, 23
University of Iowa, 323, 351
University of Missouri at Kansas City (UMKC), 268–269
University of North Carolina at Greensboro (UNCG), 307, 307–308
University of South Carolina: National Resource Center for the First-Year Experience and Students in Transition (NRC), 325, 327, 328, 329; University 101 course of, 325
University of Texas at El Paso (UTEP), 277, 278–279
U.S. Bureaus of Labor Statistics (BLS), 50, 57–58, 69
U.S. Census Bureau, 47, 82
U.S. Department of Education, 125

V

Values/beliefs, 103
Video-Based Supplemental Instruction (VSI), 268
Voluntary framework of accountability (VFA), 360–362
Voluntary system of accountability (VSA), 360

W

Walmart, 97
Washington Center for Improving the Quality of Undergraduate Education, 321
Western Interstate Commission for Higher Education (WICHE), 49
What Works in Student Retention (Beal & Noel) [1980]: ACT-NCHEMS joint project of, 214–215; on influence of institutional characteristics, 218–220; on influence of student characteristics, 221–222t; overview of, 214–215; on retention and degree completion rates, 228–231
What Works in Student Retention (Cowart) [1987]: ACT-AASCU joint project of, 215; on influence of institutional characteristics contributing, 218–220; on influence of student characteristics, 221–222t; overview of, 215; on retention and degree completion rates, 228–231
What Works in Student Retention (Habley & McClanahan) [2004]: on influence of institutional characteristics, 220; on influence of student characteristics, 221–224; on one of top three effective interventions/practices cited by respondents, 228t; overview of the, 215–216; on retention and degree completion rates, 228–231
What Works in Student Retention (Habley, McClanahan, Valiga, & Burkum) [2010]: on Early Warning Systems, 262, 263t, 271–273; on effectiveness of learning communities, 320, 324; findings on academic advising, 292; findings on developmental education, 262–273; on five select learning initiatives from, 263t; on influence of institutional characteristics, 220–221; on influence of student characteristics, 222t–224; on one of top three effective interventions/practices cited by respondents, 228t, 328–329; overview of the, 217–218; on remaining thirteen learning assistance

initiatives, 273–277; reporting on minority study attrition and retention, 232–234; on required and recommended remedial college courses, 262, 263t, 264–268; Respondents identifying poor academic preparation as cause of attrition in, 235–236; on retention and degree completion rates, 228–231; on Supplemental Instruction (SI), 262, 263t, 268–270; survey respondents of, 218t; on top four learning assistance initiatives, 262, 264; on transition program effectiveness identified by respondents, 313t; on tutoring programs, 262, 263t, 270–271

What Works in Student Retention (WWISR) [ACT]: comparing findings of all four studies, 218–228; on findings about retention program administration, 92; on learning support program effectiveness, 138; lessons learned from history of, 388–390; on low academic achievement as primary cause of dropout behavior, 117; on mean retention goal for four-year public colleges (2010), 87; on minority student attrition and retention, 231–234; overview of the four surveys conducted for, 38, 213–218; retention and degree completion rates findings in, 228–231; survey response rates of the four surveys, 214. *See also* ACT; Retention interventions

Wheaton College, 307, 308–309

White non-Hispanics: Averaged Freshman Graduation Rates (FGR), 50t–52; participation/completion of college by, 56t–57; percentage moving through college, 52–54; projected change in high school graduates, 49t; projected population percentage change (1995-2025), 47t–48

Whole-System 4-D Dialogue, 369

Wilbur Wright College, 191–192

Workforce: educational attainment demographics impact on the, 57–61; higher education private benefits for the, 69–71; higher education public benefits for the, 67–68

World Economic Forum, 61

World-of-Work Map, 168, 169fig, 173, 188